Dictionary of
KEY
WORDS

關鍵字詞典

● Mary Edwards

Macmillan

© Copyright Mary Edwards 1985

All rights reserved. No reproduction, copy or transmission
of this publication may be made without written permission.
No paragraph of this publication may be reproduced, copied
or transmitted save with written permission or in accordance
with the provisions of the Copyright Act 1956 (as amended).
Any person who does any unauthorised act in relation to
this publication may be liable to criminal prosecution and
civil claims for damages.

First published 1985

Published by Macmillan Publishers Ltd
London and Basingstoke
*Associated companies and representatives in Accra,
Auckland, Delhi, Dublin, Gaborone, Hamburg, Harare,
Hong Kong, Kuala Lumpur, Lagos, Manzini, Melbourne,
Mexico City, Nairobi, New York, Singapore, Tokyo*

British Library Cataloguing in Publication Data
Edwards, Mary
Dictionary of key words.
1. English language — Dictionaries
I. Title
423   PE1628

ISBN 0-333-38879-8

This is an authorized Taiwan edition
published under special agreement with
the proprietor for sale in Taiwan only.

Published by Bookman Books, Ltd.
5, LANE 62, ROOSEVELT RD. SEC. 4, TAIPEI,
TAIWAN 10764

有著作權　◇　不准翻印
臺內著字第　　　　號

定價：100 元

出版者／書　林　出　版　有　限　公　司
發行人／蘇　　　正　　　隆
門市部／臺北市羅斯福路四段62巷5號
電　話／392-4715・392-8617
郵　撥／0114570-4　書林書店
新聞局登記局版臺業字第一八三一號
中華民國七十八年一月出版

Contents

Preface   v

Key Words   1

Index of Related Words   207

Preface

At the Intermediate level, learners of English usually know a lot of words but they cannot use them all confidently or follow conversations in idiomatic English even when the words seem familiar. Also, learners may know the main structures of English but sometimes need to check a point of grammar. This book is intended to provide help with these problems.

It is a dictionary in the sense that it offers an alphabetical list of words with their meanings, but its main purpose is to concentrate on the key words which cause most difficulty for Intermediate learners and to provide examples of normal use and simple explanations of structures.

The words chosen are the ones which learners most often say they know but cannot use. The reasons for difficulty with any particular word might be that
— it means something different from a similar word in the student's own language
— it is used in various idioms
— it forms part of two or more grammatical structures
— it belongs to a family of words with overlapping meanings and patterns of use.

This book is clearly not a substitute for detailed dictionaries and grammar books. It is a handy reference book of useful examples and explanations of 'everyday' English, based on the experience of many students and several teachers in different parts of the world.

How to use this book

You can look up a word by simply looking for it in its alphabetical order as a headword. But remember, it may appear as one form of a headword (eg **said** is a form of **say**) or as a related word listed under the headword (eg under **sense** you will find senseless, sensible, sensitive, sensuous, sensual, sensation and sensational). Related words are not always in alphabetical order but in the order a good teacher might consider is the most useful one, to help students to understand the relationships between them. An alphabetical index of related words is given on pages 207-216.

On the next page is an extract from the text, showing how word classes, forms, structures, alternatives, idioms etc are shown.

headword — **forget** /fə'get/ — phonetics
word class — *verb* irregular, **forgot, forgotten** — information about form
first meaning — Ⓐ (=remember) ●'What's her name?' 'I **forget**'.
+ *-ing* (= something done but lost to memory) ●I shall never **forget** [meet**ing**] her, though. — opposite of or contrasting with
structure — (+ *to* + *infinitive*) (= didn't remember in time) ●I brought the tomatoes but I **forgot** to bring the salt. ●Did you **forget** to ask the price? — optional words
second meaning — Ⓑ (= ignore) ●Don't **forget** me when you're rich! — example
sequence of examples — ❖ *in idioms* ●'I'm sorry I broke that glass.' 'Oh, **forget** it.' (Never mind, it doesn't matter.) ●I quite **forgot myself** and used some very bad language. (lost my self-control).

forgive
verb irregular, **forgave, forgiven** — other forms of verb: past simple, past participle
overlapping meanings — (= say or feel no longer angry, willing to accept someone/something with imperfections) ●I was unkind last night; please **forgive** me if you can. ●God will **forgive** you your sins if you are sorry.
+ *person object/possessive adjective*
+ *-ing* ●I cannot **forgive** him/his **calling me a liar**. — alternatives

related word — **forgiving**
adjective (= lenient, able to forgive) — meaning
●She has a sweet, **forgiving** nature.

forgiveness
noun (= act of forgiving, mercy)
●If you accidentally step on someone's foot, say you are sorry but don't beg for **forgiveness**!

❖ *in idioms* ●It's best to **forgive and forget**. (not be bitter) ●**Forgive me, but** what you say is not true. (Pardon my saying so — a formal version of *excuse me*, usually said before contradicting someone, or being necessarily rude) — paraphrase

Abbreviations
AmE   American English   BrE   British English   CEG   *Current English Grammar*

vi

Only helpful information is given. For example, the past simple and past participle of regular verbs are not shown because they are formed by adding *-ed* to the infinitive. Where it seems helpful, extra information is given about
— differences between British and American usage
  eg **get** AmE **got, gotten**
— pronunciation (IPA phonetics based on Gimson's 14th edition of Daniel Jones' *English Pronouncing Dictionary*)
— formality level
  eg informal, literary
— most frequently used word order
  eg **never** mid-position
— likely sources of confusion
  eg **little** . . . *small* refers only to size; **little** often suggests an attitude to smallness. ●Poor **little** boy! He's lost.

Where a word has clearly distinct meanings, they are labelled A, B etc
  eg **about**
  A (= here and there)
  B (= a little more or a little less than, approximately)
Closely related or overlapping meanings are separated by commas (as in B above).

Examples are given for every word printed in bold type, in normal use. They often illustrate the alternative meanings or structures better than an explanation. The difference between **lend** and **borrow** becomes clear from the example and the paraphrase which follows it in brackets:
●Please can I borrow your pen for a minute? (Will you lend it to me?)
Each example is preceded by the symbol ● and each series of idiomatic uses, including compounds and collocations, is marked by a symbol ❖.

Where brief information and examples may not be enough, readers are given cross-references to other words, and particularly to articles about problems of grammar, such as **auxiliary verbs, reported speech** or **semi-colon.** These entries on grammar and punctuation are shown on tint. Together they form a short revision course on the main points of English grammar, but further information on difficult points can be found in detailed grammar books, such as *Current English Grammar* by Sylvia Chalker (Macmillan 1985), referred to in this book as CEG with the number of the first relevant section on a difficulty. Other recommended sources of grammatical information are, in order of complexity (simplest first):

A Practical English Grammar A J Thomson and A V Martinet (OUP)
A Communicative Grammar of English G Leech and J Svartvik (Longman)
A University Grammar of English R Quirk and S Greenbaum (Longman)

Recommended dictionaries (also in order of complexity/length):
Macmillan Student's Dictionary
Webster's New Students'. Dictionary
Longman Dictionary of Contemporary English
Oxford Advanced Learner's Dictionary   MARY EDWARDS

Key Words

A

a, an
article indefinite (determiner) used only with singular, countable nouns. Use **an** before words beginning with vowel sounds (*a, e, i, o, u*) or mute (silent) *h*. ●**an** egg ●**an** hour ●**A** car arrived and the driver got out. ●I'd like **a** glass of milk. (not *a milk) ●**a** dozen ●**a** hundred ●**a** million ●What **an** attractive girl! ●It's quite **a** large organisation.
preposition ●four times **a** day ●$3 **a** metre
See also **few, rather a, such a, the,** ARTICLES.

able
adjective predicative, used with verb *to be* to supply missing parts of *can*. Usually *be able* + *to* + *infinitive*. ●He will be **able** to finish it tomorrow. ●She has been **able** to read since she was four years old. ●I am not **able** to move. (I cannot move.)

unable
adjective (= not able) ●He was **unable** to say. (He couldn't say.)

enable
verb (= make able, make possible) + *object* + *to* + *infinitive*
●The money **enabled** him to buy food.

ability
noun (= power, skill) ●She has great musical **ability**.

disability
noun (= handicap, disadvantage) ●Deafness can be a severe **disability**.

disabled
adjective/noun past participle ●**Disabled** people/The **disabled** need friendly help.
For more details see CEG 6.3.

about
preposition (= concerning) ●Are you sure **about** the arrival time? ●He was talking **about** his childhood.
adverb
A (= here and there) Don't rush **about**; sit down. ●Leaves floated **about** on the water.
B of degree (= a little more or a little less than, approximately) ●Give me **about** a kilo. ●He left at **about** midday.
❖ *in idioms* ●What/How **about** a drink? (Would you like one?) ●What/How **about** going home now? (Do you agree?) ●I know all **about** you; your sister told me. ●You should not **play about**. (waste time) ●With a map, he can **find his way about**. (go to places without asking for help) ●Is the manager **about**? (somewhere near) ●He **orders** me **about**. (treats me like a servant) ●The change was **brought about** democratically. (made to happen) ●We were **about to** leave when the message came. (We were on the point of leaving.) used to express 'future in the past' ●I'm **not about to** waste money on you. (I refuse to . . .) informal
See also **around**.

above /əˈbʌv/
preposition (= higher than, over, ≠ below) ●We flew in the sunlight **above** the clouds. ●Your marks in the exam are **above** average. ●**Above** all, hold on to your passport. (Most important)
adverb (= higher on a page, earlier in a text) ●The figures [given] **above** show this.

abroad
See **broad**.

accident
noun (= unfortunate event, causing damage) ●His foot was injured in a road **accident**.

accidental
adjective (= unplanned) ●All **accidental** damage must be paid for.

accidentally
adverb (= by accident, unintentionally, ≠ purposely) ●He **accidentally** stepped on the cat.
❖ *idiom* ●We met **by accident** in the street. (chance, not planned)

accommodate
verb (= have room for) ●The hotel can **accommodate** 60 guests.

3

according to

accommodating
adjective (= helpful, adaptable) •The manager was very **accommodating** and changed the room arrangements.

accommodation
noun non-countable (= place to live) •They were all looking for comfortable **accommodation**.

according to
prepositional phrase •**According to** his teacher, he is a fool. (That's what his teacher says, but his teacher may be wrong.) not *according to me. Say 'in my opinion'. •Everything went **according to** plan. (as planned) •**According to** the records, you have not paid this bill. (I rely on the records, not my own memory; this is not personal) •**According to** the evidence, that is true.

account
noun
A (= story, explanation) •He gave a long **account** of the battle.
B (= record of money, fund) •There's no money in my savings **account**. •Please put it on my **account**. (debit it — send the bill later)

account for
verb •Please **account for** the loss of $150. (answer for, explain) •Can you **account for** his strange remark?

accountant
noun •The **accountant** keeps all financial records in order.
❖ *in idioms* •You must **take his age into account**. (consider his age) •**By all accounts**, he is very clever. (Everyone says so.) •The meeting started late **on account of** the bus strike. (because of) •**On no account** touch the red button. (Don't touch it for any reason.) •She is in business **on her own account**. (independently)

accuse
verb +*person object*+*of*+*noun* (= charge someone with doing wrong) •Nobody **accused** him of murder.

accused
adjective/noun •The **accused** (men) were questioned today.

ache /eɪk/
noun (= continuous pain) •I have a nasty **headache**; I can't work. •There's an **ache** in the back of my neck.
verb (= to have or suffer continuous pain) •Ice cream makes my teeth **ache**. •My feet **ached** from walking all day.
❖ *in compounds* •head-**ache** •stomach-**ache** •ear-**ache** •tooth-**ache** •heart-**ache** (worry, misery)
❖ *in idioms* •I was **aching to** tell you the secret. (I wanted to tell you very much.) •He told me about all his **aches and pains**. (minor ailments)

across
See **cross**.

act
verb
A (= behave, do things) •He **acts** like a little child. •Think before you **act**.
B (= play a part, do duty, represent) •She **acted** the Queen in a film. •Will you **act** as interpreter, please? •His lawyer **acted** for him; he did not appear in court himself.
noun
A (= deed) •It was a brave **act**, to rescue a drowning man.
B (= part of a play) •We left after the first **act**.

action
noun
A (= what is done, the way something works) •The **action** of the heart is like a pump. •**Actions** speak louder than words.
B (= operation) •You must see that machine in **action**. •The lift is out of **action**. (broken, not working)

activity
noun •Her **activities** include gardening and photography.

inactivity
noun non-countable (= doing nothing) •**Inactivity** is bad for your health.

active
adjective
A (=working, energetic) •At 75, he was still **active**.
B (in grammar ≠ passive) •**Active** verbs are more direct than passive ones.
See also PASSIVE.

actual
adjective (=real, factual) •The **actual** words were quoted.

actually
adverb frequently a sentence adverb
A (=in spite of what you probably think) •**Actually,** he is an expert mechanic.
B (=really, precisely) •I didn't **actually** see it but I know it happened.
C (=as a matter of fact, starting a conversation) •**Actually,** I remember Sophie well.

adjectives
1 Adjectives tell us more about nouns or complete the meaning of certain verbs such as *be, seem, appear, look, sound, feel, taste, smell*. Most adjectives can be used in both ways and in two positions, attributive or predicative.
ATTRIBUTIVE POSITION before a noun •a **large** house •a **serious** question •the **unhappy** child •**strange** people •**old** men
PREDICATIVE POSITION after a verb, as complement, when the adjective is really describing the subject of the sentence •The house is **large**. •She looks **serious**. •Is the child **unhappy**? •They seem **strange**. •When the room got **dark**, I went **cold** with fear and though I became **hungry**, I sat **quiet** and **still**.
2 Adjectives are sometimes used as nouns •He drove a **convertible** (car) and wore **casuals** (casual clothes). •Feed the **poor**. •Help the **unemployed**. •The **dead** are buried here. •The **greatest** is/are . . .
   Nouns are constantly used as adjectives •**sugar**-bowl •**bus** stop •**murder** weapon •**newspaper** man •**fruit**-seller •**street**-seller •**bathroom** light •**light** bulb
3 Several adjectives used together are usually in the following order: 1 size, shape, age; 2 colour; 3 origin; 4 materials; 5 purpose (eg •a **huge old brown Spanish leather travelling** bag) The order of adjectives can only be learned properly by listening because there are so many variations.
4 Adjectives which cause problems (because they can be used only in certain ways or positions or have various meanings in different positions) are listed in this book with examples.
5 Several words can be used as both adjectives and adverbs •**late** •**loud** •**high** Also note these adjectives which look like adverbs •**friendly** •**lovely** •**lively** •**lonely** •**cowardly** •**deadly**
See also **cheap, clean, close, dead, direct, easy, fast, fine, flat, free, hard, high, just, late, loud, low, pretty, quick, right, slow, straight, sure, tight, well, wide, wrong,** COMPARISON, DEMONSTRATIVE, PHRASE (adjectival), POSSESSIVE, RELATIVE (adjectival clause).
For details see CEG 8.

admire
verb transitive (=have a good opinion of, respect — no suggestion of surprise) •I admire his paintings but not his politics.

admirer
noun (=follower, supporter) •She is a pretty girl with many **admirers**.

admiration
noun •I was filled with **admiration** for his courage.

admirable
adjective (=fine, excellent) •The aims of this charity are **admirable**; I hope they can be achieved.

admit
verb
A (=confess) + *that* •I admit I made a mistake.

adverbs

B (=allow to enter) •This ticket **admits** one person only.
admission
noun
A (=confession) •It was an **admission** of guilt.
B (=cost of entry, permission to enter) •**Admission: $2** •No **admission** without a pass.
admittance
noun (=right to enter) •Private, no **admittance**.

adverbs
1 Adverbs tell us more about verbs, adjectives, other adverbs, and whole sentences (sentence adverbs, disjuncts).
ABOUT VERBS •I am sure they will play **well here tomorrow**. (How? Where? When?) •He arrived **there unexpectedly today**. (Where? How? When?)
ABOUT ADJECTIVES AND ADVERBS •He was **very** tired and **rather** hungry so he ate **quite** early and slept **extremely** soundly.
ABOUT WHOLE SENTENCES
•**Fortunately**, no harm was done.
•**However**, I don't believe him.
•Sophie will marry him, **nevertheless**.
2 Adverbs can go in three positions:
(a) *end position* (final, at the end of the clause) •He left the room **sadly**.
(b) *mid-position* (before the verb or part of the verb) •He **sadly** left the room. •He was **sadly** leaving the room.
(c) *initial position* (at the beginning) •**Sadly**, he left the room. (This is ambiguous; it may mean he was sad or that his leaving was a pity)
3 Most adverbs can go in both end and mid-position but initial position is used mainly by sentence adverbs and adverbs of time and frequency. •**Immediately**, everything changed. •**Once**, I lived in Canada. •**Surprisingly**, he died.

In general, *time* adverbs go in end or initial position, not in the middle •**Tomorrow** it will be all right./It will be all right **tomorrow**. *Place* adverbs (often phrases) are often at the end but stay close to verbs like *come, go, arrive* etc. •Yesterday he sat quietly **at the back**. •Go **home** quickly now.
   The order of adverbs cannot be learnt by rules, however. It is partly a matter of style and convention. Adverbs which cause problems because they can be used in different ways or in different positions are listed in this book with examples.
4 There are words which can be used as both adverbs and adjectives. •He came **early**, on the **early** train. Several adverbs do not end in -*ly*, or have different meanings with or without the -*ly* ending. •He works **hard**./He **hardly** works at all. •Come **quick[ly]** •Go **straight** home.
See also CAUSE, CONDITION, MANNER, PHRASE (adverbial), PLACE, PURPOSE, TIME.
For more details see CEG 9.

advise
verb (=counsel, suggest what is to be done)
+*person object* + *to* + *infinitive*
•I **advise** you to go by air.
+*object* [-*ing*] •I **advise** flying, not driving.
+*that* + *object* + *should* •I **advise** that you should not travel by road.
+*on, what, where etc* •Please **advise** me on travelling. Can you **advise** me where to stay, what to take and how to arrange it?
advice
noun non-countable •I followed his good **advice** and found work quickly. •Here is a piece of **advice**: consult your bank manager first.
adviser/advisor
noun •His medical **adviser** told him to rest.

advisable, inadvisable
adjective •It is not **advisable** to leave your door unlocked, in fact it's quite **inadvisable**.

affect
verb
A (= cause a change) •The amount of water **affects** the plant's growth rate.
B (= produce feelings of love, sadness) •She was **affected** by his pathetic story.

affection
noun non-countable (= gentle love) •I have always had an **affection** for her.

affectionate
adjective (= loving) •Her **affectionate** mother believed her.

affectionately
adverb used to sign personal letters •Yours **affectionately**, Sophie.
See also **effect**.

afford
verb (= have enough money, time etc for) usually with *can, could*, mainly in negatives and questions.
•Can we **afford** a taxi? (Have we got enough money to pay for it?)
•I can't **afford** to stop working.
•If he can **afford** cigars, he must be rich.

afraid
adjective predicative
A (= frightened) •The dog was **afraid**. (not *an afraid dog but a frightened dog)
afraid + of •Are you **afraid** of ghosts? •I'm **afraid** of getting lost. (that I might get lost)
afraid + to •I was **afraid** to open the door. (because the dog would bite me)
B (= sorry) used for polite regret
•I'm **afraid** he's not here now.
•I can't help you, I'm **afraid**.
•'Has he gone?' 'I'm **afraid** so.' (sorry, yes) •'Can you tell me?' 'I'm **afraid** not.' (sorry, no) •I'm very much **afraid** that I'm too late.

after
preposition (= following, later than) •Tuesday comes **after** Monday.
•He will arrive just **after** me.

•**After** taking my name and address, he asked me a lot of questions.
conjunction •**After** you'd left, the party was boring.
adverb not used in formal English.
•They had a drink and went home **after**.

afterwards
adverb in correct English not in mid-position *he went afterwards home. •They went home **afterwards**. •**Afterwards**, we can go to a cinema.

❖ *in idioms* •He's right **after all**. (in spite of everything) •**After all**, he is only a child. (You must remember that) •Who will **look after** the children when she goes to prison? (take care of) •I think **he's after her**. (trying to attract her)
•The baby **takes after** his father; he's always smiling. (resembles).

again
adverb (= once more, another time) •Please will you say that **again**?
•I never saw him **again**.

❖ *in idioms* •They asked me **again and again**. (many times) •She visits me **now and again** (sometimes) •But **then, again**, it is not easy for him. (another point to consider)

against
preposition (= opposite to, next to, ≠ for) •Are you for or **against** the proposal? •I'm **against** spending so much money. •He's swimming **against** the current. (in the opposite direction) •He was leaning **against** the door when it opened and he fell over. (on) •The red curtain looks good **against** the white wall. (next to, in contrast with) •I agreed **against** my will. (I didn't want to)

ago
adverb end position only (= past, gone by) •They came here a year **ago**. •How long **ago** was that party? •It was long **ago**; it was before I met you.
NB 1 Not used with perfect aspect — not *He has come a year ago.
2 In reported speech, **ago** is often

7

agree

changed to *before*. •'I saw her three days **ago**.' He said he had seen her three days before.
3 **Ago** is never used with *since*. Not *It is three days ago since he saw her, but •It is three days since he saw her. Or, •He saw her three days **ago**.
See also **before, for, since**.

agree
verb
+ *with* + *object* •He **agrees** with me. He **agrees** with my idea. (He thinks the same as I do.)
+ *to* + *object* •He has **agreed** to my plan. (It is accepted) •Has he **agreed** to everything? Has everything been **agreed**?
+ *that*, + *on*, + *about* •He **agrees** that it is too expensive. We **agree** on/about the problem of expense. (We share that opinion.)
+ *to* + *-ing/to* + *infinitive* •He **agreed** to pay[ing] half. [He said he would pay half.]
In a discussion •I **agree**. (You're right)
I'm afraid I don't **agree**. (You're wrong)
disagree
verb intransitive •I **disagree** (with you). (You're wrong)
agreement
noun •We are in **agreement**. (We agree) •Can they ever reach **agreement** about the control of nuclear weapons? •We had an **agreement** (contract).
disagreement
noun •They had a little **disagreement**. (quarrel)
agreeable
adjective
A (= pleasant) •We had a very **agreeable** dinner.
B (= ready to agree) •He was **agreeable** to that suggestion.
disagreeable
adjective (= unpleasant) •Smoking is a **disagreeable** habit.

ahead
adverb end position only (= in front, in the future) •I'll go **ahead** and buy the tickets. (both meanings

possible). •We must plan **ahead**.
•I see trouble **ahead**. •She is **ahead** of you in her school-work.
❖ *in idioms* •'Can I borrow this pen?' 'Yes, go **ahead**.' (do it, help yourself) •He is certain to **get ahead** if he works hard. (succeed)

alike
See **like**.

alive
See **live**.

all
adjective (determiner/pre-determiner) used with non-countable and plural countable nouns •**all** these milk bottles •**all** this milk
If used with singular countable nouns **all** means *the whole of* •**all** of the cake •**All** sorts of people waited **all** day. **All** of them/They **all** wanted to see him.
adverb
A (= completely) •I was **all** covered in mud.
B (= much, so much) •If I work overtime, I earn **all** the more.
pronoun (= everybody, everything) •**All** are welcome.
❖ *in idioms* •We found **all but** two. (all except two, only two were not found) •**That's all**. (There is no more, the end) •Is this milk **all right**? (good, OK) •'Will you help me?' '**All right**.' (Yes, OK) •She ate everything, bones **and all**. (including the bones) •I met my grandmother, **of all people**, in the disco. (a surprising meeting) •The score was 3 **all**. (3 – 3) •**All the same** I don't like it. (Even so, nevertheless) •I knew he was the thief **all along**. (all the time) •There were 150 **all told**. (in all, counting them all.) It's **all over**. (finished) •**All in all**, we enjoyed it. (on the whole) •He's **not all** that clever. (not so very clever) — informal •There's no money, **none at all**. (absolutely none) •I don't like this music **at all**, do you? (in any way) •The children aren't **at all** tired. •'Are they tired?' 'Not at all.' (absolutely not) •'I'm sorry to

8

be a nuisance.' '**Not at all.**' (That's all right — a reply to apology) ●**For all** his money, he's an unhappy man. (In spite of his money) ●It happened **all at once.** (suddenly) ●They worked **all together.** (not separately, co-operatively) ●She was **all ears** when I told her the story. (listening very carefully). ●You must decide now **once and for all.** (finally) ●I'm **all for** enjoying life. (in favour of).
NB 'Not all the babies are boys.' = 'Some are girls'. But 'None of the babies are boys.' = 'All are girls.' 'All babies *are* beautiful' = 'Every baby *is* beautiful.'
See also **altogether, always, some.** For more details see CEG 3.3.

allow /əˈlaʊ/
verb
A (= permit, let) ●Smoking is not **allowed.** (You must not smoke)
+ *person object* + *to* + *infinitive* ●Will you **allow** me to ask a question?
+ *-ing* ●He doesn't **allow** talking in class.
B (= provide for) ●He **allows** his son $500 a month. ●**Allowing** [time] for delays, we need three weeks.

allowance
noun (= money etc for special purpose) ●He has a big travel **allowance.**
idiom ●We must **make allowances for** his age. (be tolerant, take it into consideration)

allowable
adjective (= permissible) ●In this game, second attempts are not **allowable.**
See also **must, permit.**

almost
adverb of degree, usually mid-position (= nearly, very nearly, practically, ≠ exactly, quite) ●**Almost** all the food was eaten. ●She **almost** always forgets my name. ●I've **almost** reached the end. ●She **almost** didn't catch the bus. ●Sophie **almost** never visits me nowadays. (hardly ever) ●**Almost** nothing has been built. (hardly anything, hardly any houses) ●He is **almost** a year old.

alone
adverb/adjective predicative
A (= without company) ●My mother is **alone.** Not *an alone mother ●Are you all **alone?**
B (= without help) ●He built the house alone.
C (= only) ●God **alone** understands it.
❖ *in idioms* ●**Leave me alone/Let me alone!** (Don't touch me, don't interfere with me.) ●He can't speak properly, **let alone** sing a song. (even less, not to mention)
See also **lonely, only.**

along
adverb added to verbs of movement (= on, in the same direction) ●We hurried **along**, but they walked **along** slowly.
preposition ●They walked **along** the river bank. ●I saw him **along** here. (in this area, street etc)
❖ *in idioms* ●How are you **getting along?** (Tell me about your progress.) ●**Bring** your sister **along.** (with you) ●I **go along with** that. (I agree) — informal ●**All along**, I knew he was lying. (all the time)

already
adverb mid or end position (= by now, sooner than expected, ≠ not yet) ●He has **already** paid.
NB 1 Not used with past time expressions. Not *He has already paid yesterday.
2 Often used in questions which really express surprise. ●Is it **already** dry? (It's dry. That was quick!)
3 In British English not used with past simple. Say 'I've **already** spent £100.' American English allows. 'I **already** spent $50.'

all ready
●They are **all ready.** ●(All of them are ready, or they are completely ready)
See also **just, still, yet.**

also
adverb usually refers to predicate,

alternate

not subject (= as well, too, besides)
• Jane **also** speaks French (as well as German) • We play in the evenings and **also** on Sundays. • She is not only an excellent pianist but **also** a wonderful singer. • Vegetables are easy to grow. **Also,** they are very good for you.
See also **as well, besides, too.**

alternate
adjective /ɔːlˈtɜːnət/
(= happening by turns) • He works on **alternate** days. (Monday, Wednesday, Friday)

alternative
adjective (= that may be used instead) • We went by the **alternative route.** (the other possible one)

alternate
verb /ˈɔːltəneɪt/ (= follow by turns) • Day **alternates** with night. • Her mood **alternated** between sadness and happiness.

alternative
noun (= other choice) • There's no **alternative;** we must pay. • The **alternative** to prison was death.

alternately
adverb • The squares on a chess board are arranged **alternately,** black and white.

alternatively
adverb • We can wait for the bus. **Alternatively,** we can get a taxi.

although /ɔːlˈðəʊ/
conjunction subordinate, introduces concession clauses (= in spite of the fact that) • **Although** it is difficult, we shall do it. (We'll do it in spite of the difficulty. or It's difficult but we'll do it.) • He helped me **although** he didn't know me. (He didn't know me. Nevertheless, he helped . . . .)

though
conjunction slightly less formal and can be preceded by *even,* an intensifier: • Even **though** it's difficult, we'll do it. • **Though** he didn't know me, he helped me.
adverb in final or mid-position
• He didn't know me. He helped me, **though.** • The real difficulty, **though,** is the date of delivery.
See also **as if** (for **as though**), **even, in spite of,** CONCESSION.

altogether
adverb
A (= completely) • He is a fool but not **altogether** bad.
B (= on the whole) • There were some problems, but **altogether,** it worked very well.

always
adverb frequency, mid-position
(= at all times) • I **always** stay in bed late on Sundays. • He has **always** lived in that house.
• **Always** fasten your seat belt. Used with a progressive verb it implies frequent unexpected or irritating acts: • They are **always** digging up this bit of the road.
• You're **always** forgetting to pay.

among/amongst /əˈmʌŋ/ /əˈmʌŋst/
preposition (= in the middle of a number or a mass) • I saw many Disney films, 'Fantasia' **amongst** others. • The thief was hidden **among** the crowd. • **Among** his admirers is the princess. • Fighting was common **among** the prisoners.
See also **between.**

amount
noun + *of,* used with non-countable nouns (= quantity)
• There's a large **amount** of coffee in Brazil.
verb + *to* • It **amounts** to very little. (It's not much when you add it up.)
See also **number** (for countable nouns) and QUANTITY.

and
conjunction co-ordinating • milk **and** sugar • milk, sugar **and** tea • talking **and** laughing • talking, laughing **and** singing • He plays **and** sings. • He plays, she sings **and** I sell the tickets.
Instead of a *to* infinitive: • Try **and** come soon. (Try to come soon.)
• We must wait **and** see. (wait until we see) • Hurry up **and** open it. (Open it quickly.) • Go **and** post this letter (Go out to) or in AmE, 'Go post it . . .'

angry
  adjective (= in a bad temper)
  + *with* + *person* ●Please don't be **angry** with me!
  + *about* + *a thing, an action*
  ●'What's he **angry** about?' 'Losing his watch.'
  anger
  noun ●He spoke in **anger**. (angrily)
  verb transitive ●It **angered** me to hear him say that. (It made me angry)

another
  adjective determiner, always one word (= one more, different).
  ●Have **another** drink? ●This is **another** kind.
  pronoun (= an extra, different one) ●Have **another** ●I don't like it; bring me **another**.
  one another
  pronoun (= each other) ●They love **one another**. (mutual feelings)
  See also **else, other**.

answer /ˈɑːnsə*/
  noun (= reply, solution) ●What **answer** did you get to your letter? ●We can't find the **answer** to that question.
  verb (= reply to) ●He **answered** me at once. ●He **answered** my question at once. Not *to me and not *to my question. ●Please **answer** the phone.
❖ *in idiom* ●I will **answer** for their safety. (guarantee they are safe)

ante-
  prefix (= before, ≠ post-) ●**ante**date ●**ante**room

anti-
  prefix (= against, being opposite to, ≠ pro) **anti**septic, **anti**social

anxious [**for, about**]
  adjective
  A (= worried) ●Her mother was getting **anxious** about her because it was late and she hadn't come.
  B (= eager) ●Everyone is **anxious** for a peaceful agreement.
  + *to* + *infinitive* ●I am **anxious** to discuss it with him.
  + *for* + *object* + *to* + *infinitive*
  ●He was **anxious** for us to understand his point of view.

anxiety
  noun
  A ([= cause of] fear, worry) ●The long delay added to our **anxieties**.
  B (= eagerness) ●His **anxiety** to help is almost embarrassing.

any
  adjective determiner
  1 with non-countable and plural nouns in negative or almost negative expressions and in questions. ●There isn't **any** bread here. (There's no bread, there is none.) ●I've got hardly **any** butter, but there's some cheese. (There isn't much butter). ●Did you buy **any** biscuits? (The answer may be *yes* or *no*. With *some* the expected answer is *yes*.) ●If there's **any** beer, pour it out. (I do not know if we have any or not)
  2 emphatic **any** (all sorts, it doesn't matter which) ●**Any** cheese makes me ill. ●He will drink **any**thing.
  ●You can come here at **any** time ... well, **any** day but Friday.
  ●You must pay for **any** glasses that are broken.
  pronoun ●'Where are the glasses?' 'I haven't got **any**.' ●Have you washed **any**?
  Before a determiner, use *of*
  ●Are **any** of your friends here?
  ●I haven't met **any** of the students yet.
  adverb (= to any degree) ●Are you feeling **any** better? (at all better)
  ●We'll buy it if it's **any** good. (But if it's no good, we won't.) ●It isn't **any** use crying. (It would be more useful to do something.)
❖ *in compounds* ●Is **any**body/**any**one at home? (Is the house occupied?)
  ●There isn't **any**thing here. (nothing here) ●**Any**thing will do for supper. (It doesn't matter what we eat) ●**Any**where she goes, he goes too. (No matter where)
  ●**Any**how, it makes no difference. (Whatever happens) ●**Any**how, what about your problem? (changing the subject) ●She hates me but I love her **any**way. (in any case) informal

apart

NB Do not confuse with separate words: **any one, any way,** where **any** is stressed: •There are several possibilities, **any one** of which would be all right. •Can I help you in **any way?**

❖ *in idioms* He is **anything but** sensible. (not sensible at all) •Is he **anything like** your father? (at all similar to) •Are we **anywhere near** solving the problem? (almost) •**At any rate,** we are safe. (Even if we are uncomfortable.) •**In any case,** don't worry. (Whatever happens) See also **no, none, some.**

apart
adverb
A (= separate, ≠ together) •They kept her **apart** from the others. •They are married but living **apart.**
B (= as well as) •**Apart** from the expense, it would be inconvenient.
C (= aside, not counting) •Joking **apart,** what is your job, really?
adjective (= different, independent) predicative only, not *an apart city. •The two cities are far **apart.**

appear
verb
A intransitive (= come into view) •The moon **appeared** from behind the cloud.
B + *complement* (= seem) •He **appeared** [to be] sensible, but he was really mad. •There **appears** to be a mistake.

disappear
verb (= go out of sight) •Then it **disappeared** behind the clouds.

appearance
noun (= coming into sight) •His sudden **appearance** gave us a fright. •Her **appearance** had changed. (She looked different)
in idioms •Although they are poor now, they try to **keep up appearances.** (look as grand as before) •**To all appearances.** it is perfect. (but the perfection is superficial)

apparent
adjective (= clear, easy to see) •The explanation was soon **apparent.**

apparently
adverb often a sentence adverb •**Apparently,** they intend to discuss it. (It seems that, I am told) See also **seem.**

apostrophe [']
punctuation mark used to show 1 possession and 2 letters omitted
1 possession
(a) •John's book (the book belonging to John) •The woman's remarks (what she said) •today's paper (the one published today) •a pound's worth of petrol (the amount you get for £1)
(b) 's is also used for plurals which do not end in *s* •the children's toys •women's work but use s' for regular plurals •girls' school •babies' clothes
NB When the possessor is not a person, it is usual to use *of* instead •the sides *of* the box •the keys *of* the typewriter or, even more often, use one noun as an adjective •*typewriter* keys •*bathroom* light •*summer* holidays
2 letters omitted in short forms of verbs, in informal writing •I don't •he doesn't •they're here •I'll go • she isn't •he'd see •you're right •I can't
For more details see CEG 2.23.

are
verb part of verb *to be,* present tense after *you* (both singular and plural) we and *they.* •Who **are** you? (What's your name?) •How **are** you? (Tell me about your health.) •Where **are** you from? (What nationality are you? or where is your home?) •You **are** to stay here. (You must stay here). Frequently shortened to *you're, we're* and *they're.* In the negative *aren't,* also used in the first person in negative questions: •I'm a fool, **aren't** I? Not *I aren't. See also **be.**

argue
verb intransitive (= use reason to support a case, discuss, quarrel)

+ *with* + *person* + *about* + *thing*
●He **argued** with the taxi-driver about the fare. ●Never **argue** about the law with a lawyer.
+ *that* ●He **argued** that we should pay because we had suggested getting a taxi.
+ *for*, + *against* ●He **argued** for the traditional system and against changing anything.
argument
noun (= logical process) ●His **argument** was sound; he had proved the point. ●They were having an **argument** about nothing.

around
adverb
A (= about, on all sides) ●Can I just look **around**?
B (= near, in the area) ●My glasses are somewhere **around**.
preposition (= same as **round**) ●It was **around** midnight. ●They sat **around** the fire talking. ●Travelling **around** the country, he met some interesting people.
❖ *idiom* ●He's **been around**. (has a lot of experience of life)
See also **about, round**.

arrange
verb (= put in order, organise) ●She **arranged** the flowers in a vase. ●I've **arranged** the papers in alphabetical order.
+ *for* ●Please **arrange** for dinner to be served earlier than usual.
+ *to* ●We **arranged** to meet them at eight o'clock.
arrangement
noun ●She made all the **arrangements**. (organised everything) ●Dinner is served in the hotel but you make your own **arrangements** for lunch. ●Perhaps we can come to an **arrangement** with the manager. (make an informal agreement)

arrive
verb intransitive (= come) Not * + *to* ●The visitors have **arrived**. ●She won't **arrive** home till Friday.
+ *at* ●We **arrived** at the station/at the theatre at midnight/at once (specific places and times)

+ *in* ●They will **arrive** in England/in the mountains/in summer/in time/in a bad mood. (generalised, areas or periods of time)
arrival
noun ●The **arrival** of the plane has been delayed.

articles
1 **a/an** *indefinite article* (used with singular countable nouns only)
●**a** bottle (not a particular one)
2 **the** *definite article* (used with countable nouns, singular and plural) ●**the** bottle ●**the** bottles (and non-countable nouns) ●**the** milk (always referring to particular, known items)
3 no article (used with plural or non-countable nouns when the reference is general) ●bottles ●milk
●I'd like **a** cup of coffee and some cake. (not yet visible and definite)
●I don't like **the** coffee; it's too weak. (this particular coffee) ●I don't like coffee or cake. (any coffee, cake in general)
NB 1 When we mention something for the first time we normally use **a/an** (or *some* with uncountable nouns and plurals) but when we mention it a second time we use **the**. ●He wore **a** uniform. **The** jacket was bright red and he had **a** sword, too. **The** blade shone. **The** uniform was splendid.
2 There are some expressions with no article where you would expect one ●to/at/from school ●to/at/from university ●to/in/into/out of prison/hospital/bed ●to/at/from work ●to/at sea ●at home ●away from home ●for/at/to breakfast/dinner/supper ●at night ●on foot ●go to sleep ●by car/bus/train/bicycle/air/tube/boat (etc)
3 Singular countable nouns always have an article ●**a** mistake ●**the** mistake (not *mistake). People's jobs also have articles ●She is **a** dentist. (not *She is dentist.) Things spoken of as 'things in

13

as

general' usually have no article
• Children are never quiet. For them, quietness is just not natural.
4 (a) Articles come before adjectives • **a** big fat hen • **the** nice old man (b) but **the** comes after *all* and *both* • Dry all **the** glasses. • both **the** girls (c) **a** comes after *rather, quite, such* and *what* • rather **a** long way • quite **a** big box • such **a** lovely view • What **a** night!
See also **a, an, some, the**.
For more details see CEG 3.4.

as

conjunction subordinate
A (=when, while) • **As** he was eating his breakfast, he heard the door bell ring. • **As** people get older, they lose some hair.
B (=because) • **As** I didn't know the way, I asked a man. • **As** he was obviously ill, we called the doctor.
C (=in the same way as) • He worked carefully, **as** an expert works.
preposition (=in the role of) • **As** a doctor, he can say what medicine she needs. (Because he is a doctor). • I speak now **as** a friend, not **as** a teacher.

❖ *in idioms* • Address **as above**. (higher up the page) • **As before**, the engine failed. (For the second time) • **As I said before**, it's mine. (I repeat) • **As I was saying** . . . (getting the conversation back to where you want it) • We can all do **as we like**. (what we want) • Put an M or an F, **as the case may be**. (according to the sex in each case) • **As usual** the bus was late. (No surprise) • **As a rule**, I don't drink tea. (Usually) • I hope he tells us; **as it is**, we don't know what's happening. (in present circumstances) • Leave things **as they are**. (Don't change them) • He is, **as it were**, a father to me. (not a real one, so to speak) • Is it expensive [**as**] **compared with** others on the market? (in comparison with) • **Clever as he is**, he can't answer that question. (Though he is clever)

as if, as though
• He is walking **as if** he were ill.
• You look **as if** you need a rest. (tired) • It's not **as if** she knew me. (If she knew me, things would seem different) • It looks **as if** he will die. (He is expected to die) • He was dressed **as** [if he were] a woman. • She treated me **as** [if I were] a stranger.

as . . . as, so . . . as
(at least the same height, age, size etc) • He's nearly **as** tall **as** his father. • You must go **as** soon **as** possible. (at the earliest possible moment) • You know **as** well **as** I do. (You really know.) • She is not **so** pretty (or **as** pretty) **as** I expected.

the same as
• Her dress is exactly **the same as** mine. (identical)

so as
expresses purpose • He worked hard **so as** to pay his debts. • She hurried **so as** not to miss the bus.

such as
(=for example) • Large animals **such as** elephants are more easily seen than small ones.

❖ *in idioms* • You can borrow it **as long as** you're not careless with it. (if, provided that) • **As far as I know**, he's not here. (To the best of my knowledge) • He would [**just**] **as soon** stay **as** go. (He doesn't mind which) • Take **as much time as you need**. (Don't hurry) • Men, **as well as** women, like flowers. (Not only women) • Children like flowers, **as well**. (too) • Make enquiries **as to** the details/where he is/how it can be done. (about) • **As for** you, you're just a thief. (like *as to* but usually contemptuous.) • **As yet**, we've had no reply. (Up to now, so far) • You **might as well** call me a liar. (What you have said is the same as calling me a liar)
See also **also, like, than**.

ashamed
adjective predicative only
(=embarrassed, feeling guilt about something)
+ *of* •Don't be **ashamed** of your work; it's very good. •You should be **ashamed** of yourself, talking in that rude way. •I'm **ashamed** of you; my own child behaving so badly.
+ *to* •He was **ashamed** to tell the truth. •I'm **ashamed** to admit my mistake.

shameful
adjective (=shocking, disgraceful)
•It is **shameful** that he neglected her.

shame
noun
A (=guilt) •His **shame** prevented him from speaking.
B (=pity) •What a **shame** he wasn't here! (how sad)

ask
verb (=enquire, demand, request)
+ *a question,* + *the way,* + *the price etc* •Don't **ask** too many questions. •He **asked** the price of the old car.
+ *person object* + *question etc* •She **asked** me the way to the church.
+ *if/whether* •I shall **ask** if it is true. (I shall say 'Is it true?') •He **asked** whether I understood. (He said 'Do you understand what I mean?')
+ *how, why, where etc* •Shall I **ask** him why he's here? •He **asked** her where she had been. •**Ask** her how we get to the church.
+ *person* + *to* + *infinitive* (=demand or request) •I **asked** the children to leave the room. •She **asked** me not to tell her father. •Will you **ask** your friends to come in?
+ *for* •He only **asked** for some water. •Did you **ask** him **for** the money?
+ *person* + *to* + *meal, occasion* •I **asked** her to the party. •She **asked** me to dinner. (invited)

aspect
There are in English (a) progressive (or continuous) aspect showing 'limited duration' and (b) perfect[ive] aspect showing a relation between past and present.
PROGRESSIVE ASPECT marked by the verb **be** in various tenses + *present participle (-ing)* •He **is/was/will be** working in the morning.
PERFECT ASPECT marked by the verb **have** + *past participle (-ed)* •He **has/had/will have** worked long enough. (so now he wants/so then he wanted/will want a rest)
Both progressive and perfect aspect can be shown together •He **has/had/will have/would have** (etc) been working all night.
For more details see CEG 4.3.

at
preposition
A showing position in time or space •**at** 10.30 •**at** dinner-time •**at** Christmas •**at** the office •**at** the table •**at** the entrance •**at** a friend's (house) •**at** the top
B adding the idea of direction or intention to many verbs •He ran **at** the thief with a knife. (attacked) •He aimed the gun **at** the bird. •He shouted **at** me angrily. •He threw it **at** her, but missed.

❖ *in collocations* •I'm **surprised at** the cost, and even more **surprised at him** agreeing to pay. •He'll be **amused at** your suggestion. •'Are you **good at** maths?' 'No, I'm very **bad at** doing anything with my brain.'

❖ *in idioms* •Come here **at once**. (immediately) •He doesn't drink **at all**. (He never drinks.) •Does he work **at all**? (Does he ever work?) •'Sorry.' '**Not at all**.' (It doesn't matter.) •**At last**, the bus came. (Finally) •**At first**, I didn't believe it. (To begin with) •**At the moment** he's out of work. (Now) •It cost **at least** £100. (perhaps more) •He could **at least** send a card. (if he can't write a proper letter) •**At**

15

attributive

best, he can hope to come second. (Certainly not first) •He's not **at his best**. (in perfect health or condition) •Go through the door **one at a time**. (not all at once, all together) •He sold them **at $2 each**. •I don't know where he is **at present/at the moment**. (now)
See also **get at, look at, point at, take** [someone] **at his word, work at, in, on**.

attributive
See ADJECTIVES.

auxiliary verbs
Auxiliary verbs go with other verbs 'to help' show tense, questions and aspect. The main English auxiliary verbs are **be, have** and **do**. These can also be used as ordinary verbs. The modal auxiliary verbs **can, could, may, might, will, would, shall, should, ought** and **need** add to the verbs they are helping such ideas as possibility, probability, intention and necessity. All these verbs form questions by inversion •**Is** he there? •**May** I go? •**Will** they telephone? •**Could** he understand it? They vary in their scope and usage.
See separate entries for all these verbs.
See also ASPECT, CONDITION, CONTRACTION, FUTURE, MODALS, NEGATIVE, PASSIVE, PAST, PERFECT, PRESENT, PROGRESSIVE, TENSE.
For more details see CEG 4.

available
adjective (= able to be got, used, visited etc) •Water is **available** from the river. •When will the doctor be **available**?
unavailable
(= impossible to get, visit etc) •When fresh fruit is **unavailable**, use dried fruit.

await
See **wait**.

awake
See **wake**.

away
adverb usually placed after the verb A (= from a place) •He ran **away** and never came back.
B (= absent) •He was **away** last term.
C (= distant) •He lives 20 miles **away**.
D (= all the time) •She worked **away** till six o'clock.
E (= in a safe or correct place) •Please put the gun/food/books **away**.
F (= to an end) •The difficulty passed **away**. •The water boiled **away**.
❖ *in idioms* •I'll do it right **away**. (immediately) informal •Don't take it **away**. (remove it) •Let's do **away** with these stupid laws. (abolish them) •Keep **away** from the deep water. (Avoid it) •Go **away**! (Leave me!) •Don't give **away** my secret. (reveal) •He gave **away** all his money. (donated it to others)
See also **far** (away from), **give way, put away, throw away**.

B

back
noun
A (= part of the body) •She carried the baby on her **back**. •If you lie on your **back**, you will snore.
B (≠ front) •The price is written on the **back**. •We couldn't hear because we were at the **back**.
adjective (≠ front) •He came in by the **back** door.
adverb after verbs
A (= not forwards, in a reverse direction) •It's dangerous here; go **back**! •She looked **back** and waved goodbye.
B (= to the original position, place) •I like it here, so I've come **back**. •The cost of going there and **back** was £9. •Put everything **back** where it was before. •He went abroad but now he's **back** again. •My letters were sent **back**. (returned to me) •Cats always find their way **back** home. •He took the books **back** to the library. He took

be

back the books/He took them
back. but not *He took back them.
● The food was so bad that I
demanded my money back. ● This
music brings back old memories.
● Please pay me back the money I
lent you.
C (= in answer) ● Will you ring him
back, please? ● If I write to you, I
hope you'll write back.
verb
A (= go, drive backwards) ● He
backed the car out of the garage.
B (= support, speak for) ● If you
propose it, I'll back you up.
  backwards
adverb (= in the reverse, wrong
direction, ≠ forwards) ● Can you
say the alphabet backwards,
beginning with Z?
❖ *in compounds* ● background
● backbone ● back seat etc (often
used figuratively): ● What's his
background? (history, experience)
● You need backbone to fight him.
(courage) ● I'm not going to take a
back seat. (stay in a subordinate
role)
❖ *in idioms* ● He arranged it behind
my back. (without telling me) ● She
turned her back on me. (refused to
look at me) ● It was in the back of
my mind. (I had a vague idea
about it.) ● Put your back into your
work. (Work hard.)
See also again.
bad
adjective (≠ good) comparative:
worse, superlative: worst ● Smoking
is bad for you. ● This milk has
gone bad. (It's not fresh) ● 'Was
the weather good?' 'Not bad.'
(fairly good)
  badly
adverb
A (≠ well) comparative: worse,
superlative: worst ● The food was
badly cooked; either cold or burnt.
B (= very much) ● My hair badly
needs cutting.
bath
noun (= tub for washing yourself
in) ● There is a shower, but not a
real bath.

verb (= use the bath) ● Will you
bath before breakfast? formal —
we usually say: Are you going to
have or take a bath? ● She can bath
the baby now.
  bathroom
noun (= room with bath/
euphemism for toilet, WC, lavatory
etc) ● He wants to go to the
bathroom.
  bathe
verb (= go swimming) ● Can you
bathe in the river?
bare
adjective (= uncovered, empty)
● The floor was bare and so were
the shelves; no carpet, no books.
● We walked with bare feet on the
sand.
  barely
adverb (= scarcely, hardly) ● He has
barely enough money for food.
See also hardly.
be
verb irregular, was/were, been;
1 auxiliary; 2 as an ordinary verb
(= exist, call yourself) ● What will
you be when you grow up?
FORMS
(a) *present*
I am/I'm [not]
you, we, they are[n't]/[not]/
you're, we're, they're [not]
he, she, it is[n't]/[not]/
he's, she's, it's [not]
(b) *past*
I, he, she, it was[n't]/[not]
you, we, they were[n't]/[not]

Used as an auxiliary to make
progressive tenses ● I am working
hard. ● Are you listening? ● He was
working hard. ● Were they waiting?
● She'll be visiting her father. ● He
won't be expecting her. ● I'd be
lying in the sun if I were at home.
● Have they been helping you?
● It's being mended now.
  being /'biːɪŋ/
present participle
(a) used in all passive continuous
verbs ● The room is being cleaned.
● It was being cleaned half an hour
ago. ● Are we being told the truth?
● She isn't being asked to leave.

17

bear

•The house wasn't **being** repaired.
(b) used, like other participles, to start a sentence •**Being** inquisitive, I opened the box. (As I am inquisitive)
(c) as a noun-equivalent
+*complement* •**Being** inquisitive often causes trouble.
noun
A (=creature) •Other **beings** may live in space, besides human **beings**
B (=existence) •The committee is already in **being**.
been /biːn/ /bɪn/
past participle
(a) in *present perfect passive* •It's **been** cleaned. •Has it **been** done?
(b) in *present perfect progressive* •She's **been** cleaning it for hours. •He hasn't **been** doing anything. •What have you **been** doing?
(c) in *past perfect progressive* and *future perfect progressive* •He'd **been** helping her. •He will have **been** working for ten hours.
(d) in *past perfect passive* and *future perfect passive* •He'd **been** told. •She'll have **been** warned.
(e) as alternative *past participle* (=gone [and come back]) •'Have you **been** to Paris?' 'I've **been** once.'
❖ *in idioms* •For the time **being**, we can live here. (Temporarily) •'**How old/heavy/tall is she?**' (age, weight, height) 'She's 29./She's 150 lb./She's 1.5 metres.' •He **is to** leave. (It is arranged. He must) For more details see CEG 4.10.

bear /beə*/
verb irregular **bore, borne**
A (=carry) •The ice will not **bear** your weight.
B (=tolerate, put up with) •I can't **bear** the pain.
+*-ing* •He can't **bear** waiting in queues.
+*to* + *infinitive* •I can't **bear** to watch; I'll close my eyes.
❖ *in idioms* •That joke **doesn't bear** repea**ting**. (It is not funny the second time) •**Bear** this **in mind**. (Remember it) •The results **bore out** what I said. (confirmed,

proved) •**Bear up**, it will soon be over! (Don't be sad, cheer up)
born not **borne*
passive past participle •He was **born** in 1948. •When were you **born**?

beat
verb irregular **beat, beaten**
A (=hit with a stick) •We don't **beat** children nowadays.
B (=win a contest against) •Our team **beat** all the others. (We won.)
C (=[maintain a] rhythm) •My heart was **beating** fast.
noun •My heart-**beat** increased.

because
conjunction subordinate (=for the reason that) •'I eat potatoes **because** I like them.' 'Why?' '**Because** they taste delicious.' Possible but slightly unusual at the beginning of a sentence, where it emphasises the dependent clause:
•**Because** I had no money, I was forced to beg.
because of
preposition (=as a result of) •Did you leave **because of** me? •It was **because of** what you said.
See also **as, for,** CAUSE.

become
verb irregular **became, become** (=get [to be]) •He **became** King when he was a child. •The room is **becoming** darker. •It has **become** obvious that he is lying.
❖ *idiom* •What will **become of** the old ways? (happen to)

before
preposition (=in advance of, ≠after) •Try to be here **before** the meeting. •Everything will change **before** long. (soon) •The prisoner stood **before** the judge. (in front of)
adverb (=in advance, in the past) •Have you seen this film **before**? •When he was introduced, I realised we had met **before**. Used in reported speech, to replace *ago*: 'I worked here three years ago.'/He said he had worked there three years **before**.
conjunction subordinate, time •She

beneath

washed her hands **before** she started cooking. ●Let me talk to you **before** you go. Not *will go. ●**Before** he decides to marry her, he should look at her mother.

beg
verb (=ask for, pray for) +*for* +*object* ●The old man was **begging** for money.
+*person object* +*to* +*infinitive* ●She **begged** him to stay with her.
❖ **in idioms** ●'No, my name is not Smith.' '**I beg your pardon**.' (sorry) ●'My name's Xzygorghsk.' '**I beg your pardon?**' (Please say that again.)

begin
verb irregular **began, begun** (=start) ●When does the class **begin**? ●I'm **beginning** to feel hungry. ●It's time to **begin** the match. ●She **began** talking about her work.

beginning
noun ●Please begin at the **beginning** and explain everything. ●It was a disaster from **beginning** to end. (completely)

beginner
●You're an expert; I'm only a **beginner.**
❖ *idiom* ●**To begin with**, he's too young. Also . . . (First, one reason, etc)

behave
verb (=act, manage oneself) ●The children **behaved** well in the bus. ●I hope you'll **behave** yourself when I'm not here.

-behaved
past participle with *well* or *badly* ●She is a difficult, badly-**behaved** child.

behaviour
noun ●His **behaviour** was strange. (Why did he behave like that?)

behind
preposition (=at the back of, ≠in front of) ●The gun was hidden **behind** the curtain. ●Look out! There's someone **behind** you.
adverb (=at the back, where we were before) ●He went out but she stayed **behind** to look after the baby. ●Don't leave your parcel **behind** when you hurry away.
noun (=bottom, part of body which you sit on) informal. ●She's getting fat because she sits on her **behind** all day.
❖ *idiom* ●We're **behind time**. (late)

believe
verb
+*object* ●Do you **believe** his story?
+*that* ●He **believes** [that] the world will end next year, but nobody **believes** him. ●What he says can't be **believed**. ●'Is this true?' 'I **believe** so.' (or 'I **believe** not.')
+*in* ●I **believe** in exercise. (have faith in) ●Many people **believe** in magic.

belief
noun (=faith) ●He was a saint and he died for his **beliefs**. ●It is my **belief** that he will be remembered for a long time.

belong
verb
A (=have a proper place) ●Where does this book **belong**? (Where is its place?)
B (=be possessed by) ●It **belongs** to me. (It's mine) ●Who does that lovely car **belong** to? (Whose is it?)
C (=be a member of) ●She **belongs** to a drama club.

belongings
noun plural (=possessions) ●Don't leave your **belongings** here; they might be stolen.

below
adverb (=in a lower place, of lower rank, etc, ≠above) ●From a plane, the houses **below** look very small. ●Cheap fares are available for children aged 12 and **below**.
preposition (=in a lower place etc than) ●Her skirt came **below** the knee. ●We can't see what is **below** the surface.
See also **beneath, under**.

beneath
adverb (=in or to a lower place, ≠above) formal ●The moon looked down on the world **beneath**.
preposition
A (=below, under, at the foot of)

19

beside

●He was buried **beneath** the oak tree. ●Flowers grow **beneath** the walls.
B (= unworthy of) ●She thinks it **beneath** her to travel on an ordinary bus.

beside
preposition (= alongside, by the side of) ●My glasses are on the table **beside** my bed.

besides
preposition (= as well as, in addition to) ●There are many angry customers, **besides** me.
adverb sentence adverb (= also) ●I don't like this dress. **Besides**, it's too expensive.
See also *also, too*.

best
adjective/adverb superlative (of **good, well**, ≠ **worst**) ●He wears his **best** clothes on Sundays. ●Is this the **best** method?
pronoun (= the best one/ones) ●Take only the **best** of them.
❖ *in idioms* ●**Do your best** to find it. (Try as hard as you can) ●It wasn't pleasant but we **made the best of it**. (We didn't complain)

bet
verb irregular, **bet/betted**
A (= risk money etc on predicting future events) ●I **bet** he wins the race. ●I **bet** he doesn't. ●Will you **bet** me £5 (that he wins)? ●Do you often **bet** on horses? ●I don't often **bet**; my sister doesn't **bet** at all.
B (= be certain) ●I **bet** you are an American. ●You **bet** I am! (I certainly am) informal
noun (= an agreement to bet, the money at risk) ●The horse won the race and I won my **bet**.

better
adjective/adverb comparative (of **good, well**, ≠ **worse**) ●This cake is good but that one is **better**. ●This work is bad; can't you do **better** than this? ●He'd look **better** with his hair cut. ●Your English gets **better** and **better**. ●Try again. Yes, that's **better**. ●I hope you'll feel **better** soon. (no longer ill, not sick) ●Are you any **better** now?

had better
verb (= it would be better for) ●You'**d better** go now. (It would be better for you to go now.) ●He'**d better** not say that. (I advise him not to say that.) ●**Hadn't** you **better** shut the door? (Wouldn't it be a good idea to shut it?)
❖ *in idioms* ●He is **better off** than me. (richer) ●He **knows better than to** disobey me. (He is not silly enough to make me angry.)

between
preposition (= in the middle of, usually two) ●We passed on the road **between** here and London. ●I saw a fight **between** two dogs. ●You must choose **between** these two (or three) possibilities. But not *share between three: use *among* three or more. ●Put the tray here **between** him and me. Not *between he and I.
❖ *in idioms* ●**Between you and me/Between ourselves**, he lost the money. (Don't tell anyone else.) ●It must be black or white, nothing **in between**. (not grey)
See also *among*.

beyond
preposition (= further than) ●You can't go **beyond** the gate. ●It's **beyond** me. (I can't understand it)
adverb (= further away) They walked out of the garden into the field **beyond**.

big
adjective (= large, great)
Big is less formal than *great* and usually refers to size only. ●**Big** books are not necessarily great books. (They may not be worth reading.) ●We've made a **big** step forward. ●He gave me a great **big** kiss.

bill
noun (= account, statement of money owed) ●Could I have the **bill**, please? ●He paid the **bill** with a credit card.

bit
noun (= piece) ●Can I have a **bit** of cheese? ●There are little **bits** of

chocolate in this ice-cream. •His sculptures are made out of **bits** and pieces. (odds and ends, assorted things)
 a bit
  adverb (= rather, a little, slightly) •It's **a bit** hot; shall I open a window? •At 85, he's **a bit** too old for skiing. •Can you help me? I've got **a bit** of a problem. •'Do you mind?' 'Not **a bit**.' (not at all)

blame
 verb (= hold somebody responsible for something bad) •You mustn't **blame** (it on) him. (It's not his fault.) •Who is to **blame**? (Whose fault is it?) •'I shall complain.' 'I don't **blame** you.' (I agree: you should complain) •Can you **blame** him for being late? (You can understand why he is late, can't you?) •I'm not to **blame** for the delay. (I didn't cause it.)
 noun (= guilt) •We must all share the **blame** for this accident.

body
 noun
  A (= a person's physical being) •His **body** is weak but his mind is strong.
  B (= a dead person or animal) •The **body** was buried in the churchyard.

book
 noun (= literary work, volume) •Have you read his latest **book**?
 verb (= reserve) •I've **booked** a table in the restaurant for two at 8.30. •It's **booked** up; I can't get tickets.

bore
 verb
  A (= make a hole, usually with a drill) •They use powerful machines to **bore** for oil and water.
  B (= make [someone] tired, uninterested) •I hope you are not **bored** by these old stories?
 noun (= person who is dull, thing which is dull or unpleasant) •She can be rather a **bore** if she starts talking about her problems. •It's a **bore**, having to start again at the beginning.

boring
 adjective (≠ interesting, = dull) •We had to listen to a lot of **boring** details.

born
 See **bear**.

borrow
 verb (= take something intending to return it, ≠ lend) •He **borrowed** a lot of money from the bank to buy his car. •Please can I **borrow** your pen for a minute? (Will you lend it to me?)

both
 adjective determiner/predeterminer (= two out of two) •Please keep **both** hands on the steering wheel. •Did he hurt **both** his feet, or only one?
 pronoun •**Both** of them came when I rang the bell. •They are **both** well. •His son and his daughter have **both** passed the exam. •They **both** look beautiful. Let's buy **both**.

both ... and
 conjunction (= not only ... but also) •**Both** women **and** children work in the fields. •She **both** feared **and** hoped for the phone call. •I am **both** shocked **and** disappointed by your news.
 See also **also, each.**

bother /ˈbɒðə*/
 verb mostly in negatives and questions (= trouble, worry) •Don't **bother** him now; he's busy. •I'm sorry to **bother** you, but you're sitting on my book. •He doesn't **bother** to knock, he just walks in.
 noun (= difficulty, trouble) •We had a lot of **bother** finding our way. •Would it be a **bother** to you if I stayed the night?

bottom
 noun
  A (≠ top) •His name is at the **bottom** of the list. •The ship sank to the **bottom** of the sea.
  B (= part of body you sit on) •Don't sit on that chair; you'll get wet paint on your **bottom**.
 ❖ *in idioms* •I speak from the

21

brackets

bottom of my heart. (with sincerity, truly) ●We can't afford it and **that's the top and bottom of it.** (all there is to say) ●I shall **get to the bottom of** this mystery. (discover the facts) ●**At bottom,** he's all right. (Fundamentally, despite appearances)

brackets [( )]
punctuation mark (parentheses)
1 to enclose and separate words not required by the grammar of the sentence ●A beautiful woman (who can she be?) is coming to the door.
2 for examples ●Don't eat too many dairy foods (milk, butter and cheese).
3 to replace the commas round a non-defining relative clause if it needs emphasis ●The President (who is arriving today) has been ill.

break /breɪk/
verb irregular, **broke, broken**
A (=damage, destroy) ●Somebody has **broken** this window.
B (=separate) ●Be careful! It **breaks** easily.
C (=law, rules, promises) ●If you **break** the rules, you will be punished.
noun (=interval) ●Let's have a **break** for coffee. ●He worked without a **break** for six hours.
breakdown
●There was a **breakdown** in the peace talks and fighting started again. ●When her child died, she had a **breakdown.** (usually a nervous or mental collapse)
❖ *in compounds* ●**outbreak** (sudden eruption of war, violence, disease), ●**break**through (step forward, major development)
❖ *in idioms* ●Their marriage **broke up** after only four years. (They separated or divorced) ●Let's **break** this problem **down** and look at its parts. (analyse) ●The car **broke down** and we had to walk. (It stopped working) ●War **broke out** when the treaty was ignored. (started) ●It **broke her heart** to say

goodbye. (made her despair) ●**I'm broke.** (I have no money) slang.

breathe /briːð/
verb (=respire) ●Fish do not **breathe** as people do. ●I can hardly **breathe,** this room is so smoky. ●Can you hear the baby **breathing?**
breath /breθ/
noun (=inhalation) ●Take a deep **breath** before you go under water. ●Let's go outside for a **breath** of fresh air.
❖ *in idioms* ●We were **out of breath** when we got to the top of the hill. ●We waited for the results in great excitement, **holding our breath.**

bring /brɪŋ/
verb irregular, **brought, brought** (≠take) ●Please **bring** your books with you. ●He **brought** his friend to my party.
+*person object* +*object* ●Could you please **bring** me my glasses when you come back?
upbringing
noun (=training in the home, family) ●His mother died when he was young, so he had a difficult **upbringing.**
❖ *in idioms* ●Parents should **bring up** their children to look after their own clothes. (train) ●Don't **bring** that subject **up.** (mention) ●This figure is **brought forward** from last month's bill. (repeated this month)

broad /brɔːd/
adjective (=wide, ≠narrow) ●There are **broad** views of the countryside from the windows.
broadly
adverb often a sentence adverb (=in general terms) ●**Broadly,** we agree, but in detail there are differences between us.
abroad
(=in foreign countries) ●He lived **abroad** for many years.
broaden
verb ●Travelling is said to **broaden** the mind.
breadth
noun (=width) ●The **breadth** of the river is ten metres.
❖ *compound* ●She is **broad**-minded;

22

she does not expect everyone to agree with her views.
build /bɪld/
  verb irregular, **built, built** (=construct) ●We're **building** a new house. It is **built** of bricks.
  building
  noun ●The school is the tallest **building** in the street.
❖ *idiom* ●He's **building up** the business. (making it grow)
business /'bɪznɪs/
  noun
  A (=trade, occupation) ●He has a profitable insurance **business**.
  B (=affair, concern) ●I'm tired of the whole **business** of cooking and cleaning.
  adjective ●He's a **business** man with a **business** address and you can phone him in **business** hours. ●**Business** letters are more formal than personal ones.
  business-like
  adjective (=seriously organised) ●Let's be **business-like**; we can't play games.
❖ *in idioms* ●Are they still **in business?** (trading) ●**Keep out of other people's business.** (Don't interfere) ●He was travelling **on business.** (not for pleasure) ●I've always found it easy to **do business** with him. (negotiate, deal, trade) ●Let's **get [down] to business.** (begin the real task, job) ●I shall **mind my own business.** (not ask questions) ●He **has no business** to borrow my car. (no right)
busy /'bɪzɪ/
  adjective (=occupied, working) ●He is too **busy** to talk to you now. ●Are you **busy?** Or can you stop for a minute? ●I'm **busier** than ever; there's so much work.
  busily
  adverb (=industriously) ●She was **busily** preparing for the trip.
but
  conjunction co-ordinating (showing a contrast, opposition) ●I like him **but** I don't like her. ●I'd love to come **but** I can't. ●They're

expensive **but** worth the money.
  preposition (=except) after *everybody, all, anything, no, who, anywhere, nobody* etc. ●**All but** two were found. (Only two were lost) ●She eats **nothing but** bananas. (only bananas) ●**Everyone** knew you were here **but** me. (I was the only one who didn't know.) ●**Who but** Sophie could wear a hat like that one? (Only Sophie could) ●He lives in the **next** house **but** one. (There is one house in between.) ●'Have you finished?' '**All but.**' (nearly) ●**But for** him, I should be dead. (Without his help).
buy /baɪ/
  verb irregular, **bought, bought** /bɔːt/ (=purchase)
  ●If you **buy** things cheap[ly] and sell them dear[ly] you soon get rich.
  +*person object* +*object* ●He **bought** his wife a fur coat.
  +*object* +*for* +*person object*
  ●Did he **buy** one for me?
  noun informal (=a purchase) ●It's a good **buy**. (a bargain, good value)
by
  preposition
  A (=near) ●He lives **by** the station. ●Come and sit **by** me.
  B (=before) ●He ought to be here **by** now. ●Please get it done **by** tomorrow.
  C (=with the help of) ●It is worked out **by** computers. ●He makes money **by** selling things.
  D (in passive sentences +*agent*) ●The cat was chased **by** the dog. ●The body was found **by** the old butler. Compare: 'He was frightened **by** a noise.'
  adverb (=past) ●We watched the procession go **by**. ●Please let me get **by**.
❖ *in compounds* ●**By**-pass the town if you can. (Avoid it, go on the by-pass if there is one.) ●The **by**-roads are not as well-kept as the main roads. (secondary roads) ●One of the **by**-products of making coal-gas is coke.

call

❖ *in idioms* ●It's **made by hand.** (hand-made) ●**Three metres by two metres.** (3m × 2m) ●I was **by myself.** (alone) ●She did it **all by herself.** (without help) ●She knows the words **by heart.** (remembers them perfectly) ●I know him **by name** but not **by sight.** (I have heard of him but not met him.) ●I opened your letter **by mistake.** (in error) ●His remark **took me by surprise.** (I was not expecting him to say that.) ●The road is closed **by order of** the police. (because the police have ordered it to be closed) ●What do you **mean by** this behaviour? (Explain why you are behaving badly.) ●**By the way,** I shall be late tonight. (It isn't important, but I'll tell you. ●He is better than the others, **by far.** (He is much better. ●Who is that **book by?** (Who is the writer?)
See also **come by, drop by, get by, go (by), put by.**

C

call
verb
A (=give a name to) ●They **called** the baby Thomas. ●What's this **called?**
B (=make a visit, make contact) ●Please **call** [in] on me if you're passing my house. ●I'll **call** you when lunch is ready. ●I've been robbed; **call** the police. (phone) ●'Did anyone **call** while I was out?' 'Yes, Mr Baxter; he wants you to **call** him back.'

can /kæn/ /kən/
verb auxiliary, modal
FORMS
(a) *present* **I, you, he, she, it, we, they can['t/not]**
(b) *past conditional* (all persons) **could[n't]/[not]**
(c) no *infinitive,* no *future* form, so **be able** or **can** are used.
A (=be able) ●I hope **to be able to/I can/I shall be able** to tell you soon. ●'He **can** swim very well.' 'Can he swim to the other side?'

(in reported speech: She said he **could/was able** to swim very well and I asked if he **could/was able** to swim to the other side.) See **could** for ambiguities.
B (=may, have permission) ●**Can** I open the window, please? (May I, do you mind if I open it?) ●'You **can** borrow my bicycle if you like.' (in reported speech: She said I **could/might** borrow her bicycle.)
C (=logical possibility) ●He **can't** be her father; he's only 32. ●They **can't** have finished already.
❖ *in idioms* ●I **can't help** laughing when I think of the look on his face. (I have to laugh) ●I **can't wait to** tell you all my news. (I'm impatient)
See also **able, allow, could, may, might, must, permit,** AUXILIARY VERBS, MODALS.
For more details see CEG 6.3.

care
verb (=have feelings) mainly negatives and questions ●She doesn't **care** what happens; she is indifferent. ●Does he **care** about her? ●He wouldn't **care** if he never saw her again. ●I don't **care** what you think.
noun non-countable (=thoughtfulness, attention) ●Handle with **care.** ●I leave these documents in your **care.**

careful
adjective ●Please be **careful** with these plates; they're very precious.

careless
●He's very **careless;** always breaking things.
❖ *in idioms* ●Would you **care for** a glass of orange-juice? (an offer; Would you like . . . ?) ●She **took care of** my children while I was away. (looked after them) ●I sent it **care of** (c/o) his office because I didn't know his private address.

carry
verb (=hold, bear) Not *clothes, see **wear.** ●This suitcase is very heavy; I can't **carry** it.
❖ *in idioms* ●You must **carry out** my orders exactly. (do just what I tell

you) •After the coffee break we **carried on with** our work./**carried on** work**ing**. •I was completely **carried away** by the music. (I forgot reality.)

case
noun
A (= box, crate, container, suitcase) •Put the camera back in its **case**, please. •You can leave your **case** in Left Luggage.
B (= example, instance) •Here is a sad **case** of neglect. •**In** this **case**, the doctor decided not to operate.
❖ *in idioms* •Take an umbrella **in case** it rains. (to provide for the possibility) •**In case of fire**, break the glass. (If there is a fire) •I don't like it and **in any case** I can't afford it. (anyhow) •You think he stole it but **that's not the case**. (he didn't)

cash
noun non-countable (= money, actual coins) •He will not accept a cheque; he wants **cash**. •I have a little **cash** in my pocket.
verb (= exchange, turn into money) •Where's the bank? I must **cash** a cheque.

catch /kætʃ/
verb irregular **caught, caught** /kɔ:t/
A (= trap, hook) •We **caught** a lot of fish. •**Catching** flies is difficult.
B (= arrive in time for, not miss) •If you hurry, you'll **catch** the bus.
❖ *in idioms* •He tried to **catch me (out)** by asking me difficult questions. (prove me wrong) •He was a long way ahead; I couldn't **catch up with** him. (go fast enough to come level with him) •I **didn't quite catch** what you said. (I didn't hear; would you repeat it?) •I **caught sight of** him once in the street. (saw him for a moment)
•Try to **catch the waiter's eye**. (attract his attention) •The car **caught fire**. (started burning) •It's a good idea; I think it might **catch on**. (become popular) •You'll **catch a cold** if you go out in this rain.
•Is that disease **catching**? (infectious)

cause
Expressions of cause, purpose and result answer questions such as *Why? What caused it? What was the intention? What was the effect?*
PHRASES •**because of** the bad weather •**owing to** storms •**to** make a profit •**for** the money •**so as to** see better •**on account of** her illness •**for** writing with
participle •**Seeing** no one, I opened the door. (since/because I saw no one)
CLAUSES (subordinate clauses below printed in **bold**)
adverbial clauses •He put the light on for it was getting dark. (*for* links two main clauses) •He put the light on **because it was getting dark**. •**As it was getting dark**, he put the light on. •**Since it was getting dark**, he put the light on.
noun clauses •The reason for putting the light on was **that it was getting dark**. (noun clause, complement of *was*)
OTHER EXPRESSION OF CAUSE/ PURPOSE
in order to + *infinitive* •I came here [**in order**] **to** help you. •**To** show you what I mean, here's an example. •The towel is **to** dry your hands on, not **to** wipe the floor with.
make + *object* + *infinitive* (without *to*) •Can you **make** this tin-opener work?
get + *object* + *to* + *infinitive* •I **got** the car to start by pushing it along the road.
get + *object* + *past participle* •I must **get** the windows cleaned soon. (I can clean them myself or pay a window cleaner to do it).
have + *object* + *past participle* •She **has** the windows cleaned every month. (she pays a window cleaner to do it) •Have you **had** your hair cut? (Have you been to the hairdresser?)
See also **as, because, for, get, have, make, since,** CLAUSE, INFINITIVE. For more details see CEG 11.18.

25

certain

certain /'sɜːtən/
adjective usually predicative
(=sure) •Our team looks **certain** to win. (I think they will win.) •Our team is/are **certain** of winning. (They think they'll win.) •'Do you think so?' 'I'm **certain** of it.' •Are you **certain** of the time we arrive? •I'm not **certain** that he will come today.
uncertain
adjective (=unsure)•He felt **uncertain** what to do next.
certainly
adverb (=definitely, without doubt) •She's **certainly** pretty but is she nice? •'Will you help me?' '**Certainly**.' (Yes, of course) •'Are you paying for him?' '**Certainly** not.' (No, definitely not)
❖ **in idioms** •I don't know **for certain** which day I go. (with certainty) •Please **make certain** this is the right number. (Check)
See also **sure**.

chance
noun
A (=opportunity) •This is a good **chance** to talk to her. •You won't get another **chance** like this. •I found it by **chance** — I was looking for something else.
B (=probability) •This horse has no **chance** of winning. •The **chances** are he will be last.

change
verb
A (=alter, make an alteration) •I hope the weather **changes** soon. •Please wait while I **change** (my clothes). •Do we have to **change** trains?
B (=exchange) •If you keep the receipt, the shop will **change** the skirt. (let you choose another one instead)
noun
A countable (=alteration, difference) •The new government made many **changes**. •There's been a **change** of plan.
B non-countable (=small coins, balance paid back) •Have you got any **change**? I've got to make a phone call. •I think you've given me the wrong **change**.
❖ **in idioms** •Can I **change places with** you? (exchange seats, situations etc.) •I've **changed my mind** about marrying him. (I think differently about it now.) •Let's go this way **for a change**. (for the sake of variety)

charge
verb
A (=ask for — a price) •How much do they **charge** for this room?
B (=accuse) •He was **charged** with murder.
noun
A (=payment) •There is no **charge**. (It is free)
B (=accusation) •'He was arrested.' 'On what **charge**?'

choose /tʃuːz/
verb irregular, **chose, chosen**, (=select) •Can I **choose** the colour of the carpet? •Has he **chosen** the biggest cake? (picked) •She wants to **choose** her husband for herself. •He didn't **choose** to speak. He **chose** not to. (He remained silent.)
choice /tʃɔɪs/
noun non-countable (=selection, act of choosing) •Have you made your **choice** yet? •What **choice** does he have? (What else can he do?)
❖ **idiom** •There's **not much to choose between them**. (They are almost the same.)

---

clauses

1 Clauses contain finite verbs; phrases do not. The words in **bold** in these sentences are different types of clauses.
(a) •**The teacher will explain the problem**. (main clause; complete simple sentence)
(b) •**She will explain it** and [**she will**] **ask you questions**. (two main clauses, joined by a conjunction, forming a compound sentence)
(c) •**When you are ready**, [1] she will explain. [2] (complex sentence with [1] subordinate dependent

26

clause, adverbial, saying more about the verb *will explain* in [2] main clause)
(d) •The teacher, **who understands the problem,** will explain it. (Subordinate adjectival relative clause, saying more about the noun *teacher,* subject of the main clause)
(e) •She explains **that the two theories conflict.** (subordinate noun clause, the object of the verb *explains,* equivalent to the problem)
2 Subordinate clauses, doing the work of adverbs, adjectives and nouns, can be categorised and sub-classified in several ways but the following examples illustrate the major patterns.
adverbial
time •I'll call you **when it's ready.**
place •She found the bag **where she'd left it.**
manner •She loved her dog **as a mother loves a child.**
condition •He will take the money **if you offer it.**
concession •He refused the money, **although he needed it.**
cause •I came **because you called me.**
purpose •They hurried **so that they would be in time.**
result •They hurried, **so [that] they were in time.**
comparison •They arrived sooner **than we expected.**
adjectival (relative)
defining subject •The office **that deals with passports** is upstairs.
defining object •The form **you need** is XJ30.
non-defining subject •Sophie, **who is a silly girl,** crashed my car into a wall.
non-defining object •Mrs Brown, **whom I'd met before and spoken to,** did not recognise me.
noun
subject •**What he's going to do next** is worrying me.
object •She told him **that she didn't know.**

represented by *it* •It is a pity **that he won't take it.**
See also **it, that, which, who,** ADJECTIVES, ADVERBS, CAUSE, COMPARISON, CONCESSION, CONDITION, MANNER, NOUNS, PHRASE, PLACE, PURPOSE, RELATIVE, RESULT, SENTENCE, SUBORDINATE, TIME.

clean
adjective (≠ dirty) •Are your hands **clean?** •Cats are **cleaner** than dogs.
verb transitive (=make clean)
•I haven't **cleaned** the car for weeks. •Can I wash this suit or must I [dry] **clean** it?
cleaning
noun (=task of cleaning) •Do you do all the **cleaning** or do you have some help?
cleaner
noun
A (=person paid to clean rooms) •A **cleaner** comes twice a week.
B (=shop that cleans clothes) plural •Don't wash this. Take it to the [dry] **cleaners.**
clear
adjective (=transparent, easily understood) •We could see fish in the **clear** water. •This diagram will make the process **clear** to you.
verb (=remove unwanted things) •Please **clear** the table when you've finished eating.
❖ *in idioms* •**Clear off!** We don't want you here. (go away) informal •Recent information has **cleared up** the mystery. (explained) •She has **cleared everything up** and left. (packed her bags, tidied the room etc)
close
verb /kləʊz/ (=shut)
•Please **close** the window. •They have **closed** the road for repairs. •The bank **closes** at three o'clock.
adjective mostly predicative /kləʊz/ (=near) •His house is quite **close.** •We won the match but it was very **close.** (a close fight, not an easy win)

cloth

closely
adverb (= keeping near) ●He followed her **closely** all the way.

cloth /klɒθ/
noun
A countable (= piece of cloth, towel etc) ●Which of these **cloths** can I wipe the floor with?
B non-countable (= fabric, material) ●His suits are all made of beautiful woollen **cloth**.

clothes /kləʊðz/
noun plural, no singular (= items of clothing, garments) ●She wears expensive **clothes** made of silk.

cold /kəʊld/
adjective
A (≠ hot, = low in temperature) ●The water is too **cold** for swimming in.
B (of food — cooked but not eaten hot) ●There's some **cold** meat and salad ready.
C (= unfriendly, unkind; compare **cool** = calm) ●Her words are friendly but her voice is **cold**.
noun
A (= low temperature — weather) ●I like walking in the **cold** if my feet are warm.
B (= common illness, affecting nose, throat, sometimes causing headache) ●He has (caught) a **cold**, so he's staying indoors today.
❖ **in compounds** ●**cold**-blooded murder (pre-meditated, cruel) ●He's getting **cold** feet. (feeling less brave, more doubtful) ●**cold**-hearted (insensitive, unkind) ●**cold** storage (refrigerated, saved for future use) ●**cold** war (not real fighting, hostility without battle)

colloquial
adjective (= used in conversation, not in formal writing) ●OK is a very common **colloquial** expression.

colloquialism
noun (= informal expression) ●Don't use **colloquialisms** in business letters.

colloquially
adverb (= using informal language) ●Speaking **colloquially**, I told him it was a load of rubbish.

colon [:]
punctuation mark heavier than a semi-colon, but lighter than a full stop
1 before a list ●The following items are for sale: a large table, ten chairs and a bookcase.
2 before a long passage of direct speech ●He began his speech: 'I am glad to . . .'

colour (American spelling *color*) /ˈkʌlə*/
noun
A (= hue) ●There are seven **colours** in a rainbow. ●The film is not in **colour**; it's in black and white.
B (= racial distinction) ●All are welcome, regardless of **colour**.
verb (= paint, apply colour) ●The children are **colouring** their pictures. ●Her opinions are **coloured** by her experience. (affected, distorted) metaphorical

colouring
noun (= complexion, hair-colour) ●She has attractive **colouring**.

discolour
verb (= make dirty, spoil) ●The walls were **discoloured** by mud.

colourless
adjective (= without colour, pale, lifeless) ●He gave a rather **colourless** description of the battle.

colourful
adjective (= bright) ●We need more **colourful** curtains to cheer this room up.

coloured
adjective (= not white-skinned or, in some countries, neither black nor white) ●**Coloured** people/**Coloureds** are more often out of work than whites.

come
verb irregular, **came**, **come**, intransitive (suggests motion towards the speaker or towards the present time, ≠ go) ●I knocked on the door but no-one **came**. ●**Come** here, I want to speak to you. ●The music has **come** to an end; now we can leave.

comings and goings
noun (= activity, bustle) ●There

comma

were many **comings and goings** between the Palace and the Ministry.
❖ *in idioms* ●How much does it **come to?** (What is the total or the end-result?) ●It suddenly **came to me.** (I suddenly had an idea.) ●**Come and see me** tomorrow. (Visit me.) ●Don't **come back** till you can pay me. (return) ●How did you **come by** that information? (acquire, get) ●When the news **came out,** we were all shocked. (was published, was revealed) ●Have short skirts **come in?** (become fashionable) ●Don't throw it away; it might **come in useful.** (prove to be useful) ●**Come on,** children, we must hurry. (Hurry.) ●Buying that business was a big risk but it **came off;** now he's rich. (succeeded) ●I think I'm **coming down with** flu. (becoming ill with) ●I hope this pudding **comes out** well. (results) ●I hope he'll **come up with** a good idea. (produce, invent) ●As the minister in charge, he'll **come in for** most of the blame. (get a share) ●She'll soon **come round** to your way of thinking. (change her opinion) ●He seems weak but he's **as tough as they come.** (extremely tough) informal ●I could take you in my car, or, **if it comes to that,** pay for your taxi. (indeed, in that case)

comfortable
adjective (= at ease, not in pain) ●Are you feeling **comfortable?**

comforting
adjective (= cheering, reassuring) ●It was **comforting** to know the doctor was on his way.

comma [,]
punctuation mark Some commas are necessary; others are optional. Some very simple advice: when in doubt, leave it out.
OPTIONAL commas which simply show pauses ●In the afternoon, heavy rain, with snow in places, may be expected. (Some writers would use no commas at all in that sentence because the meaning is clear without them. However, the commas make it easier to read.)
NECESSARY commas which prevent confusion: (a) to separate items in a list; (b) to separate sentence adverbs from the rest of a sentence; (c) to separate two expressions which refer to the same thing; (d) to separate a dependent clause from the rest of a sentence; (e) to separate direct speech from reporting verbs.
(a) *in a list* ●She wants bread, meat, milk, sugar and tomatoes. ●I'll buy a book for my father, a silk scarf for my mother, lots of fruit and a box of chocolates. ●He writes the plays, acts in them, helps with the costumes, plays the music and organises the publicity; he does almost everything. ●You must provide suitable, cheap, light-weight equipment. (But lists of adjectives do not always need commas: 'Pretty little French girls appeared.')
(b) *separating sentence adverb* ●Fortunately, the stolen money was found. ●The story, however, was not true. ●Many believed him, nevertheless.
(c) *separating two expressions* ●Mr James, her uncle, left her £20,000. ●The problem before us, how to pay for it, can be solved. ●Dr Smith, the medical officer, operated alone. (These commas are used in pairs, like 'lightweight brackets'.)
(d) *separating dependent clause* ●Sophie, who is a fool, forgot the tickets. ●Although they are old, these boots look quite smart. ●If you don't ask him, he won't come. (But if the main verb comes first, the comma is unnecessary: He won't come if you don't ask him.)
(e) *separating direct speech* ●'Now,' she said, 'we can begin.'

common

●'Can you come tomorrow?' she asked, adding, 'I hope so.' ●John replied, 'Yes, if you like.'

The following passage shows these five necessary commas in use: 'Mr Wilson, (c) the head of the department, (c, d) who is responsible for this difficult, (a) imaginative and expensive proposal, (d) will not be here, (b) unfortunately, (e)' said his deputy, (e) 'until next week.'

To understand some of the differences commas can make, try reading these sentences as if there were no commas ●Gentlemen, don't believe him. ●Would you like Bill, or Ben, to come with you? ●He only wants to work, to save money, to raise a family. ●Mary, said John, was a fool. ●However, we pay for it; they don't contribute. ●He didn't tell me, that was the problem.

See also APOSTROPHE, BRACKETS, QUOTATION, RELATIVE, SENTENCE ADVERBS.

common
adjective
A (= usual, often seen) ●Beggars are **common** in many big cities.
B (= ordinary) ●She makes wonderful food from **common** ingredients.
C (= low class) ●Only **common** people speak with their mouths full of food.

uncommon
adjective (= unusual, rare) ●Snakes are **uncommon** in Europe.

commonplace
adjective (= uninteresting) ●I was bored by her **commonplace** opinions.

commonly
adverb (= usually) ●Hydrophobia, **commonly** called rabies, is a very serious illness.

❖ *in idioms* ●In **common with** most old people, he suffers from back-ache. (Like most) ●We don't have much **in common**. (We are not very alike.) ●When we discuss theory, we are **on common ground**; but we disagree about practice. (in agreement) ●She has plenty of **common sense**. (everyday practical judgement) ●It was a **common-sense** decision.

Also note **the Common Market** = the European Economic Community (EEC)

compare /kəm'peə*/
verb
+ *object* + *to* + *something* (= consider similarities) ●He **compared** her to a beautiful, pale flower. (said she was like)
+ *object* + *with (or* + *to)* + *something* (= consider differences) ●**Compare** this real leather with that imitation leather.

comparison
noun ●By **comparison** with/In **comparison** with Grenada, Jamaica is a big country.

comparative /kəm'pærɪtɪv/
adjective ●He's a **comparative** beginner; he began only three weeks ago. ●'Bigger' is a **comparative** adjective.

comparatively
adverb ●You spent a lot of money; I spent **comparatively** little.

comparable
adjective (= of the same kind) ●We need **comparable** statistics for previous years.

incomparable /ɪn'kɒmprəbəl/
adjective (= easily the best) ●Her voice is **incomparable**.

comparison
Comparison may be expressed in adjectival and adverbial phrases and clauses.

adjective
1 Short adjectives and those ending in *-y* form comparatives by adding *-er* (or *-ier*). Long adjectives are modified by *more* ●smaller ●paler ●heavier ●funnier ●more amusing ●more convenient ●more difficult. The opposite or negative idea is expressed by *less* or *not as/so*.

concession

● This is **less** expensive, **not so** dear.
2 Phrases are mostly used predicatively. ● My house is **further away**. ● Your car is **not as big**.
3 They may be expanded by adding *than/as* + *object* ● My house is further away **than yours**. ● Your car is not so big **as that Rover**.
4 They may be expanded by adding *than/as* + *subject* + *verb,* making a subordinate clause ● It's further away **than you think**. ● Your car's not so big **as I expected**.
5 irregular formations ● good – **better** ● bad – **worse** ● far – **further** [away]
adverb One-syllable adverbs add *-er* but most adverbs (all those ending in *-ly* except *early*) are modified by *more* ● He worked hard**er**. ● She came lat**er**. ● We shall finish earli**er/more** quickly if we work **more** energetically. ● Please don't speak **so** quietly. ● He won **less** easily than we had predicted.
expressions of comparison ● This one is/isn't **like** that one. ● This one is **different from** that one. ● This one is/isn't **the same** as that one. ● He is **as** tall **as** his mother now. ● Is she **as** pretty **as** her sister? ● My chair's not **so** comfortable **as** yours.
   These comparisons can be further modified by adverbs of degree such as *much/not much, far* and *no* ● This is **much** easier than the others. ● I'm **no** wiser than I was before. ● Horses are **no** more intelligent than apes. ● He spoke **far** less confidently after that. ● She arrived, **not much** later than she had promised. ● He would be **far** more likely to help if you offered to pay him. ● He's the better-looking of the two, by **far**. ● I'm **far** more worried than he is.
See also **almost, as, fairly, few, hardly, less, little, many, more, much, nearly, quite, rather,**
ADJECTIVES, ADVERBS, SUPERLATIVES.
For more details see CEG 8.18.

concern /kənˈsɜːn/
verb
A not in progressive (= be about, be relevant to) ● This letter **concerns** you; you'd better read it. ● This problem **concerns** us all.
B in passive + *with/about* (= related to) ● The book is more **concerned** with theory than with practice.
C in passive [+ *about*] (= worried) ● I was very **concerned** when he was sick/about his illness.
noun (= business, responsibility) ● His love life is not your **concern**. ● He controls various **concerns** in Austria.
❖ *in idioms* ● **As far as I'm concerned,** you can sell it. (my opinion is . . . but others may feel differently) ● **Concerning your letter,** let me say this. . . (with reference to, regarding)

concession
Expressions of concession include one-word sentence adverbs, phrases and clauses
sentence adverbs ● He doesn't like chocolate cake. **Nevertheless**, he ate it. He likes coconut cake, **however**.
phrases ● **In spite of** her protests, he left. ● They played the match, **despite the bad weather**. ● **Whatever the difficulties**, we must try. ● We'll buy it, **no matter what the cost**. ● **However tired**, you must finish the job.
clauses ● **Although/Though** he had no money, he was cheerful. ● **Even if she were rich** she would not be happy. ● **However hard he tried**, he could not solve the problem. ● **Whatever you do**, don't tell him my secret. ● **Tired as he was**, he went on working. ● I'll do it **even though it's dangerous**. ● **Although it is strange**, it is true. ● It is strange, **yet it is true**.
See also **although, besides, despite, even, however, still, though, yet.**
For more details, see CEG 11.21.

31

condition

1 Expressions of condition include one-word adverbs, phrases and clauses.
adverbs •We have agreed to the sale of the house **provisionally/conditionally.**
phrases •**In that case,** you can make your plans. •Is he here? **If so,** I wish to see him. •**Barring accidents,** they will be there by mid-day.
clauses
pattern I *future + if + present* •He will work if you pay him. (probable)
pattern II *conditional + if + past* •He would work if you paid him. (possible)
pattern III *conditional perfect + if + past perfect* •He would have worked if you had paid him. (impossible because past)
2 The relations remain the same when the sentence begins with *if* •If she loves him, she will marry him. •If she loved him, she'd marry him. •If she'd loved him, she'd have married him. (she had . . . she would)
3 Negatives •He won't work if you don't pay him/unless you pay him.
4 The conditional tense of all verbs is formed by using *should/would + infinitive,* without *to* •I/we should or would (shortened to **I'd, we'd**) you/he/she/it/they would (**you'd, he'd, she'd, they'd**) The conditional perfect is formed by adding *have + past participle* •I shouldn't have known. •Would she have married him if . . .? •He'd have told me . . .
5 Conditions can be made less probable by using different constructions. •If he were to die/If he should die/Should he die/In the event of his death, she would get his money.
See also **if, provided, should, unless, would,** SUBJUNCTIVE.
For more details see CEG 11.20.

conjunctions

These are 'joining words' which make connections between words, phrases or clauses. They can join items of equal weight (co-ordinating) or unequal weight (subordinating).
co-ordinating conjunctions •He sings **and** she dances. •You can come now **or** stay the night. •He likes me **but** I don't like him.
  Some co-ordinating conjunctions work in pairs (co-relatives) •**Either** you come now **or** you stay here. •**Neither** he **nor** my mother understands it. •You can **both** swim **and** sail on the lake. •We **not only** went swimming **but also** went sailing.
subordinating conjunctions •He sings **while** she dances. •**If** you don't come now, you must stay the night. •**Although** he likes me, I don't like him.
  Some subordinating conjunctions are confusing because they can introduce more than one kind of subordinate clause (see **as, since, while**). Some consist of two or more words •**so that** •**except that** •**in order that** •**now** [that] •**supposing** [that] •**as far as** •**as soon as** •**so as** (+ *to* + *infinitive*) •**rather than** (+ *non-finite*) •**as if** •**as though** •**in case**
See also **and, but, for, or, so, that** and separate entries for all subordinators.
For more details see CEG 11.

consent

verb (= agree, give permission) •He **consented** to lend me the car. •I tried to persuade him to pay for the petrol but he wouldn't **consent** to that.
noun (= permission) •They want to marry but her parents will not give their **consent.**

consider

verb
A + *object* [+ *to be*] (= judge, count as) •Tom and I have always

control

considered her a member of the family, though she isn't related. •He is **considered** to be the country's best jazz musician. B + *that* (=think) •Do you **consider** that this job is done? C + *-ing* (=think about) •Will you **consider** selling me your car?

consideration
noun
A (=thoughtfulness) •He treats his staff with great **consideration**, never over-working them.
B (=process of considering) •We must take several factors into **consideration** when choosing a house.

considering
participle 1 used as sentence adverb •She's done very well, **considering**. (when you consider the problems etc)
2 used as a preposition
•**Considering** his illness, he manages very well (allowing for)
❖ *idiom* •**All things considered**, it was a great success. (seen as a whole)

contain
verb (=hold, keep inside) not in progressive •The freezer can **contain** enough food for a month.

content[s]
noun first syllable stressed (=what is inside) •After the power-cut, the **contents** of the refrigerator had to be thrown away. •The style of the letter is beautiful but the **content** is silly. (what it says)

content[ed]
adjective (second syllable stressed) (=satisfied, happy) •He's perfectly **content[ed]** with his little house and moderate salary.

continue
verb (=go on) •The road **continued** for many miles. •Please **continue** your story.
+ *-ing*/+ *to* + *infinitive* •Snow **continued** falling/to fall.

continual/continually
adjective/adverb (=often, over and over again) •We stopped **continually** to take pictures.

continuous/continuously
adjective/adverb (=without a break) •The rain was **continuous**; it never stopped for a moment.
•He talked **continuously** for an hour.

continuous tense
See PROGRESSIVE.

contractions
(short forms)
All the following forms are normally used in conversation and informal written English. •**I'm** (I am) •**you're** (you are) •**he's** (he is/he has) •**she's** (she is/she has) •**it's** (it is/it has) •**we're** (we are) •**they're** (they are)
•**I've** (I have) •**you've** (you have) •**we've** (we have) •**they've** (they have)
•**I'll** (I shall/will) •**you'll** (you will) •**he'll** (he will) •**she'll** (she will) •**it'll** (it will) •**we'll** (we shall/will) •**they'll** (they will)
•**I'd** (I should/would/had) •**you'd** (you would/had) •**he'd** (he would/had) •**she'd** (she would/had) •**we'd** (we should/would/had) •**they'd** (they would/had)
•**aren't** (are not) •**isn't** (is not) •**haven't** (have not) •**hasn't** (has not) •**shan't** (shall not) •**won't** (will not) •**shouldn't** (should not) •**wouldn't** (would not) •**hadn't** (had not) •**can't** (cannot) •**couldn't** (could not) •**don't** (do not) •**doesn't** (does not) •**didn't** (did not) •**mustn't** (must not) •**needn't** (need not) •**oughtn't** (ought not) •**wasn't** (was not) •**weren't** (were not)
•**here's** (here is) •**there's** (there is) •**that's** (that is) •**how's?** (how is?) •**what's?** (what is?) •**when's?** (when is?) **where's?** (where is?) etc.

control
verb (=rule, direct, test) •The police could not **control** the angry crowd. •The amount of water in the river can be **controlled** by dams and drainage schemes. •All our

correct

calculations and experiments are carefully **controlled**.
noun (=power to command, guide) ●The enemy must not get **control** of this area. ●Try not to lose **control** of your temper.
❖ *in idioms* ●You're the driver; the car is **under/in** your **control**. ●The brakes failed and the car was **out of control**. (impossible to steer, direct) ●Don't worry! Everything's **under control**. (working properly, as it should be)

correct
adjective (=right) ●Is that the **correct** word to use?
verb ●(=rectify, make right) ●Please **correct** my mistakes.

cost
noun (=expense, price of production) ●He got rich by reducing his **costs** and raising his prices. ●The **cost** of living varies from country to country.
verb irregular, **cost, cost,** no passive; [+*person object*] +*price* (=have as its price) ●This car **cost** [me] $5000, two years ago. ●How much will it **cost** you to get there? ●The tickets don't **cost** much.

could /kʊd/ /kəd/
verb past and conditional of **can**
1 *past* (=was/were able to) ●He **could** swim when he was only four. (He was able to swim then) but not *He needed to get to the other side of the river and he could swim across. When the meaning is 'managed to', use **was able to**.
●**Could** you understand the lecture? (Were you able to understand it?)
●She **couldn't** hear everything. (She was not able to hear everything)
2 *conditional*
A ordinary use (=would be able to) ●He **could** do it if he tried.
●We **couldn't** have escaped without your help. (We shouldn't have been able to escape if you hadn't helped us)
B to be polite, tentative ●**Could** you tell me your name, please? ●If you **could** just open the door ... (Please would you open it?)

C for logical possibility ●He **couldn't** be her father; he's too young. (It would not be possible)
D (=it would be possible) ●We **could** go to the cinema tonight. (a suggestion implying 'Let's go.')
E for chances, possibilities in the present and future ●You **could** be killed by a bus today. (It is possible, it might happen) ●There **could** be more trouble in that area, the paper says.
F for unrealised possibilities in the past ●You **could** have broken your leg.
G to ask permission ●'**Could** I borrow your bicycle, please?' (May I?) 'Yes, you can.' (not *could)
H to report general permission ●He said we **could** go. ('You can go.') but for particular permission, say 'I was allowed to' not *could.
●The children **were allowed** to stay up late last night.
I after *so that* and *in order that* ●He left early so that he **could** catch his train. ●In order that the food **could** be served hot, it was put into special containers.
See also **able, allow, can, may, might, possible.**
For more details see CEG 6.3.

council /ˈkaʊnsəl/
noun (=assembly, group to discuss matters)●There are two women councillors in our local **council**.
Do not confuse with:
counsel /ˈkaʊnsəl/
noun (=advice, legal adviser) ●His **counsel**'s advice was to admit he was guilty. ●Teachers must be both instructors and **counsellors**.
consul /ˈkɒnsəl/
noun (=representative of foreign country, dealing with immigration, visas etc.) ●You must speak to your **consul** about your passport.

count
verb
A (=enumerate) ●Is it possible to **count** all the stars?
B (=have value, importance) ●Don't listen to her; she doesn't **count**.

countable
See NON-COUNTABLE (nouns).

couple /'kʌpəl/
noun
A (= two things, not necessarily a pair, but of the same kind) •Can you lend me a **couple** of dollars/eggs/stamps/bits of paper?
B (= man and woman together, especially a husband and wife) •There were several **couples** dancing.
See also: **pair**.

course
❖ *in idioms* •**Of course** I remember you. (Naturally, obviously) •Your papers will be sent **as a matter of course** (as a routine piece of business) •They arrived **in due course**. (eventually, after a period of time)

cover /'kʌvə*/
verb
+ **with** (= hide, protect) •The field was **covered** with snow.
+ **up** •He tried to **cover** up the gun.

uncover
verb (reveal) •The police **uncovered** the thieves' plan.

discover
verb (= find) •Columbus **discovered** new countries.

cross
verb (= go from one side to the other) •We must **cross** the road at the traffic lights.
adjective (= angry) •Don't be **cross** with me; I didn't mean to break the glass.
noun (= shape of X or +) •He couldn't write his name so he put a **cross**.

crossroads
noun (= place where four roads meet) •When you reach the **crossroads**, turn left.

across
preposition (= over) •I could see him waiting **across** the road.
adverb •He came **across** to speak to me.

❖ *in idioms* •You have written that wrong; **cross it out**. (delete it) •He **gets his ideas across** to people. (He expresses his ideas well) •I **came across** it by chance. (found, met)

cry /kraɪ/
verb **cried, cried** (= weep, shed tears) •It was a very sad film; it made me **cry**.
noun
A (= shout, loud expression of anger, pain, fear etc) •I heard **cries** of alarm from inside the burning house.
B (= period of weeping) •She felt better after she'd had a little **cry**.

❖ *in idioms* •She **cried herself to sleep**. (went on crying until she fell asleep) •The house is **crying out for** a good clean-up. (in great need of)

cut
verb irregular, **cut, cut** (= sever, pierce with a knife, separate, using sharp tool) •First, **cut** the chicken in half; **cut** it through the middle, then **cut** it up into little bits. •This is a sharp knife; it **cuts** cleanly.
noun •After the fight, he had **cuts** on his face and shoulders. •Your new hair **cut** suits you.

❖ *in idioms* •There is a **short cut** through the park. (a quicker route) •Those dangerous trees must be **cut down**. •**Cut off** his head! •We were **cut off** in the middle of our telephone conversation. •Please **cut** your speech **short**, we're late. They showed the whole film, **uncut**.
•You must **cut out** all the unnecessary details. (remove)

D

dare
verb with both ordinary and modal forms of negative and questions (= be brave enough to) •Do you **dare** to tell him?/**Dare** you tell him? •I don't **dare** to go./I **daren't** go.

❖ *in idioms* •I **dare say** he'll telephone soon. (Probably) •**How dare you** speak to my mother in

dark

that way? (expression of anger) For more details see CEG 4.24.

dark
adjective (≠ pale, ≠ light) •It's too **dark** to see the path. •They wear **dark** blue uniforms.
noun (= darkness/nightfall) •Don't go out after **dark**.

dash [—]
punctuation mark
1 used to show parenthesis, like brackets, but not so heavy •My mother told me — this was twenty years ago — that I should marry someone rich.
2 for afterthoughts and ideas loosely or casually connected •I believed she was wise — well, she was I suppose — in a way.

day
noun (≠ night) •Monday is the first **day** of the week.
adjective •They went on a **day** trip to the sea. •The **day** return tickets are quite cheap. •His ideas are only **day**-dreams. (fantasy)

everyday
adjective (= ordinary, familiar) •He explained in **everyday** language.
❖ *in idioms* •I spoke to him **the other day**. (a few days ago) •**Some day** I'll meet the right girl. (in the future) •Can I visit you **one day**? (some time) •He rang **the day before yesterday**. •He'll ring again **the day after tomorrow**. •He works **all day** and sleeps all night. •It's **made my day**! (made me very happy). •Let's **call it a day**, we've done enough. (stop work) •**Day by day** he became thinner. (Each day, As time passed)

de-
prefix (= do the opposite of, reverse the effect of) •They **de**-activated (or **de**-fused) the bomb. •The dollar was **de**valued.

dead /ded/
adjective (≠ alive) •His father is **dead**; he was killed in the war. •Throw away the **dead** flowers.

adverb (= absolutely) informal •You are **dead** right. •He hit it **dead** centre.

deadly
adjective (= very dangerous) •He killed his **deadly** enemy with **deadly** poison.

death
noun •His **death** was a shock to us all.
❖ *in idioms* •I was **dead-beat**. (tired out) •He's **dead to the world**. (deeply asleep) •This road is a **dead-end**. (no exit) •The **deadline** is tomorrow. (It must be finished by tomorrow.) •He is **deadly serious**. (He really means it.) •I was **sick to death of** his behaviour. (made very impatient by) •He's at **death's door**. (very ill indeed) •They **put** the prisoners **to death**. (executed, killed) •This old car is **a death trap**. (very dangerous thing, place)
See also **die.**

deal /di:l/
verb irregular, **dealt, dealt** /delt/
A + *with* (= manage) •I can't **deal** with this problem; can you manage it?
B + *in* (= buy and sell) •He **deals** in furs.
noun/determiner/adverb (= a lot) •It worried me a good **deal** that Sophie was late.
+ *of* •He has paid a great **deal** of money.

dealer
noun (= trader) •I bought the picture from an art-**dealer**

dear
adjective mainly attributive
A (= beloved) •She is a very **dear** friend of my mother.
B (to begin all letters) •**Dear** Sir, **Dear** Mrs Smith, **Dear** Sophie,
C (= expensive, ≠ cheap) •The grapes were too **dear**, so I bought some bananas.
interjection (expressing disappointment, sadness) •Oh, **dear**! What a pity!

decide
verb (= make up one's mind)

determiners

• Have you **decided** what you're going to do? • She's **decided** on the blue dress. (chosen) • I've **decided** not to go. (I'm staying) • You must **decide** for yourself. (make an independent choice) • The committee **decided** against holding an election. • They **decided** that there should be no election.

decision
noun • Have you made a **decision** yet?

deep
adjective (= profound, ≠ shallow) • The snow is **deepest** in the valley. • He has a **deep** interest in history.
adverb • The lake is 30 metres **deep**. (in depth)

deeply
adverb • He was **deeply** interested in her account of her travels.

depth
noun • The **depth** of the lake is 30 metres.

❖ *in idioms* • Now we get **into deep waters**. (difficult areas of a subject, hard to understand) • He's **out of his depth**. (The subject is too difficult for him.)

degree
Some grammar books refer to *adverbs of degree;* such words as **barely, enough, fairly, hardly, much, only, quite, rather, scarcely, too.** Modern grammar books often use the term *intensifiers,* subdivided into three groups:
emphasisers eg **really, obviously**
amplifiers eg **completely, absolutely**
down-toners eg **slightly, almost**
See also INTENSIFIERS.

delay
verb (= postpone, put off until later, cause lateness, hesitate) • We can't **delay** the decision any longer. • We were **delayed** by a road accident. • Don't **delay**; buy it today!
+ -ing • Could you **delay** going on holiday for a few days?
noun (= delaying, being delayed) • Do it at once; without **delay**.

• Work on the roads is causing serious **delays** to traffic.

demonstratives
These are adjectives or pronouns • **this** singular • **these** plural (near here) • **that** singular • **those** plural (over there) • **That** watch is too dear; I'll take **this** [one]. • I'll take **this** cheaper one. • Are **these** your socks?/Are **these** socks yours?
For more details see CEG 3.9.

deny
verb transitive (= say it is not true) • You say I am a thief. I **deny** it. • He **denied** visiting her house.

depend [on]
verb (= rely) • She **depends on** her husband for money. • You can **depend on** him; he will keep his promise. • 'Can you help me?' 'That **depends [on]** what you want me to do.'

dependent
adjective • She is **dependent** on her father till she is 18.
For dependent clauses, see SUBORDINATE.

independent
adjective • He is grown up and **independent** now, earning his own living.

despite
preposition (= in spite of) • **Despite** the difficulties, they finished the job.

determine /dɪˈtɜːmɪn/
verb (= decide, limit) • The boundaries are **determined** by the mountains and rivers. Especially in passive • He is absolutely **determined** to go. (He has made up his mind.)

determiners
In some grammar books, all words that come before ordinary adjectives, to limit the meaning of the noun they refer to, are called *determiners,* eg
articles **a, the**
demonstratives **this, that**

37

die

> *possessives* **my, his, John's**
> *quantifiers* **each, enough**
> *wh-words* **whatever, whose**
> Most of these are *central determiners* [1] which can be preceded by *predeterminers* [2] such as **all, twice, what** and followed by *post-determiners* [3] such as **two, first, other, more** •**All** [2] **the** [1] **other** [3] young children are here. •**Half** [2] **these** [1] **little** [3] cakes are stale.
> For details of usage, see also ARTICLES, DEMONSTRATIVES, POSSESSIVES, QUANTIFIERS and individual entries.
> For more details see CEG 3.

die
verb (≠ live) •He is **dying**; he will probably die in a few days. •He **died** last year. He's been dead for nearly a year.
❖ *in idioms* •She said she was **dying to** meet him. (very keen to) •When the noise **died down/away** they were able to go on with their conversation.

different
adjective (≠ same) •Men are **different** from women, thank goodness. •I'm getting tired of this food; can't we have something **different**?

difference
noun •The **difference** between 20 and 30 is 10. •I can't see any **difference**; they look the same to me.
in idioms •The law applies to everyone; **it makes no difference** who you are. •We can go on Wednesday or Thursday; **what difference does it make**? (it does not matter which)

difficult
adjective (≠ easy) •I find this exercise very **difficult**. •The theory is **difficult** to explain.

difficulty
noun (= problem) •He had financial **difficulties**. •What is the **difficulty** with your car?

direct
adjective (= straight, straightforward) •Is this the most **direct** route? •He gave me a **direct** look and said, 'No'. •That was a **direct** answer.

indirect
adjective (= evasive) •When I asked where he had been, he gave an **indirect** reply.

directly
adverb/conjunction
(= straightaway, soon) •The nurse is coming **directly**.
(= as soon as) •**Directly** dinner was over, he left the room.

direct
verb
A (= show the way) •Can you **direct** me to the Passport Office, please?
B (= supervise) •He **directs** the whole enterprise: he is the General Director.

direction
noun
A (= way to go) •You are walking in the wrong **direction**; you must go back.
B (= order, instruction) •Follow the **directions** on the packet.

dis-
prefix forms many opposites
•**dis**advantage •**dis**approve
•**dis**believe •**dis**connect
•**dis**contented •**dis**honest etc.

disappoint
verb (= make sad when expectations not met) •He was **disappointed** when he got low marks in the exam.
•I am **disappointed** in/with/by you/your results.

disappointment
noun •What a **disappointment**, not being able to get tickets for tonight's performance! •It was a **disappointment** to me; I had expected something better.

distant
adjective •He is a **distant** relation; my aunt's cousin.

distance
noun •The **distance** from here to

Paris is 9 km. •You can see the church in the **distance**. •She looked prettier from a **distance**.

do

verb irregular, **did, done**; main auxiliary, used to form questions and negatives.
FORMS
(a) *present*
I, you, we, they do[n't]/[not]; he, she, it does[n't]/[not]
(b) *past* (all persons) **did[n't]/[not]**
1 as an ordinary verb (=perform, carry out) •What is he **doing** now? •He doesn't **do** any work at all. •Does she **do** the cleaning?
2 used as an auxiliary
(a) to make the negative and question forms of the *present* and *past simple* tenses •He **doesn't** like coffee and nor **do** I. •We **don't** usually stay late. •**Do** you always go to bed at ten o'clock? •**Does** she walk to work? •**Doesn't** she feel tired? •She **didn't** tell me you had telephoned, so I **didn't** know what to do. •**Did** you meet Sophie last night? •What **did** she say? •Why **doesn't** she write to me? •What **does** she propose to do at the weekend? •**Didn't** she mention her plans?
(b) for negative commands, requests etc and for emphatic positive imperatives •**Don't** walk on the grass. •**Don't** leave the bathroom dirty. •**Don't** tell anyone. •**Do** come in. •**Do** believe me. •**Do** go away.
NB As an auxiliary, **do** combines with all other verbs except the modal auxiliaries. It can be used with **have** and **do** when they are ordinary, not auxiliary verbs •He **doesn't have** much free time. •**Did** he **have** enough to eat? •**Don't have** any more to drink. •She **didn't do** all the work. •I **don't do** much at the weekend. •**Do** you **do** all the cleaning or **do** other people **do** some too? •**Don't do** that now.
3 used to contradict what somebody seems to think •I **do** understand. (you think I don't, so not just *I understand) •In the end, she **did** write to me. (I had almost given up hope of a letter) This distinction can be made only with the voice in negative emphatic statements: *normal* •I don't understand. *emphatic* •I don't understand.
4 used as a *proform* representing a verb that has already been used •She likes you. I know she **does**. (= likes you) •Do you agree? If you **do** [agree], vote for me.
❖ *in common collocations* as an ordinary verb •She has **nothing to do**, so she's bored. •Exercise would **do her good**. (be good for her) •'Have you **done** all **the shopping?**' 'I've **done** some but there's some more **to do**.' (to be done) •'Will you **do** it?' 'I'm **doing something else** tomorrow.' •He hasn't **done** much **work** yet. •She's **doing well** in her new job. •What have you **done with** my book? (where is it?) •What have you **done to** my book? (Why is it dirty, torn?)
❖ *in idioms* •This pencil **will do**, if there's no pen. (will be good enough) •This is bad work. It **won't do**. (it is not acceptable) •The problem is **to do with** insurance. (connected with, concerned with) •I shall **have nothing to do with** it. (I refuse to be involved) •Cost **has nothing to do with** it. (it is irrelevant) •We have no butter, so we must **do without** it. (eat our bread with no butter) •We could **make do with** margarine. (It is not so good, but better than nothing) •I'm thirsty; I **could do with** a glass of cold water. (I should very much like one) •They have **done their house up**; it looks very good now. (improved, decorated) •Let's **do away with** these stupid old ways of doing things! (abolish, get rid of) •I offered him £5 and he said **'Done!'** (He agreed to a price) •'Meet my brother.' **'How do you**

double

do.' (a conventional greeting when introduced, not a real question. The response is 'How do you do.') •Here is a list of **dos and don'ts**. (things you may or may not do) •I shall be glad when my appointment with the dentist is **over and done with**. (finished and forgotten) For more details see CEG 4.12.

undo
verb (=open, untie, unbutton, take to pieces) •I can't **undo** this string. •If they fight, it will **undo** all our good work.

overdo
verb (=work too hard, exaggerate) •He's been **overdoing** it and now he's ill.

double /'dʌbəl/
adjective (=with two parts, for two people etc) •We have a **double** garage but only one car. •They booked a **double** room with two single beds.
noun
A non-countable (=something twice as big, strong, valuable etc) •Rooms are quite cheap in the winter but in the summer you must pay **double**.
B (=someone who looks the same) •Film actors are often replaced by **doubles** for dangerous scenes.
adverb (=together, in twos) •After the bang on my head, I was seeing things **double**.
predeterminer (=twice) •He's **double** the weight he was before.
verb (=make twice as great) •He **doubles** our wages on Sundays. •He was so sure his horse would win that he **doubled** his bet.

❖ *in compounds* •**double chin** (loose fold of skin). •**double**-decker (bus with two floors, sandwich with two layers of filling). •**double**-glazing (two layers of glass for insulation in windows) •**double**-talk (partly incomprehensible way of speaking)

doubt /daʊt/
verb (=consider improbable) +*if/whether* •I doubt whether he will marry her.
+*noun/noun clause* •You cannot **doubt** her sincerity. •Do you **doubt** what he says?
noun (=uncertainty) •We have some **doubts** about the proposal. •If you are in **doubt**, look it up in a reference book. •No **doubt** he will come later. (I'm sure)

doubtful
adjective (=uncertain) •He looked **doubtful** when I suggested buying it.

down
adverb usually adverbial particle forming phrasal verbs, completing the sense of verbs of motion, often with a figurative sense (≠up, =in an inferior position, coming to an end.) •When did he come **down**? (downstairs) •The temperature went **down**. (It got cold.) •In the storm, some buildings fell **down**. (collapsed) •The nurse told me to lie **down**. (not sit) •Turn **down** the heat and let it simmer. •The fire died **down** at last but the house had been burnt **down**. (to the ground) •Take that picture **down**. (remove it from the wall) •The people were kept **down** by their cruel rulers. (oppressed) •The policemen broke the door **down** in order to get in. (destroyed it) •All the trees had been cut **down**. (to the ground) •Bend the wire **down**. (downwards)
preposition (=in a downwards direction) •He fell **down** the stairs. •**Down** the street you'll see a bus stop. •We sailed **down** the river. (towards the sea, downstream) •I'll walk **down** to the station with you. (as far as)

❖ *in compounds and collocations* •Don't be **down-hearted**. (depressed, sad) •The business went **downhill**. (did badly) •They have **their ups and downs**. (good times and bad times) •That last risk **was his downfall**. (the cause of his failure) •Make a **down-payment** and pay the rest later. (deposit) •She has a very **down-to-earth** manner. (practical, unsentimental)

❖ *in idioms* •He **looked down on** his old friends when he became rich.

drop

(despised) •**Put this down** in your book. (write it) •He has **gone down with** flu. (become ill) •**Let's get down to business**. (begin work seriously) •He won't **let you down**; he'll keep his promises. (fail to fulfil a promise) •Don't hold it **upside down**. (the wrong way up) •He's **tied down** by his responsibilities. (restricted) •This wet weather is **getting me down**. (making me depressed) informal

dozen /'dʌzən/
noun determiner (= 12 in a group) •Please buy two **dozen** eggs. (2 dozen/24)
❖ *in idioms* •There were **dozens** [and **dozens**] of people in the room. (lots) informal •They were all talking **nineteen to the dozen**. (fast and continuously)

draw /drɔ:/
verb irregular, **drew, drawn** /dru:/ /drɔ:n/
A (= take, pull) •He **drew** all his money out of the bank. •Please **draw** the curtains. (open or shut them)
B (= make pictures, design) •He **drew** a face in the sand. •Can you **draw** a map of the town centre for me?
withdraw
verb (= retreat, take back, cancel) •They **withdrew**, to discuss the next step in private. •He was asked to **withdraw** his rude remarks.
❖ *in idioms* •I **draw the line at** stealing. (I am not willing to go so far as to steal) •He **drew back** when he saw the gun. (retreated) •The bus **drew in** to the side of the road to allow the faster traffic to pass. •The match was **drawn**. (Nobody won; the scores were equal.) •The only **drawback** in your plan is the expense. (disadvantage)

dress
verb (= put clothes on) •She's old enough to **dress** herself. •People used to **dress** in heavier clothes. •How was the Princess **dressed**? •Wait here while I **dress**/get **dressed**.

undress
verb (= take clothes off) •He **undressed** and had a shower.
dress up
verb (= put on special clothes for fun) •Children like **dressing up** in grown-up clothes.

drink
verb irregular, **drank, drunk** (= swallow liquid) •He **drank** all the milk.
noun (= something to drink, beverage) •Have a **drink** of water or fruit-juice. •What about a **drink**? (an invitation) •After a few drinks, he felt ill.

drive
verb irregular, **drove, driven**
A (= guide) •He **drove** the car carefully along the narrow country roads.
B (= force to go) •The ship is **driven** by large engines. •What **drove** her to do such a terrible thing?
noun
A (= journey by road) •We had a pleasant **drive** in his car.
B (= energy, initiative) •He hasn't got enough **drive** to succeed.
C (private road to a house) •The car was waiting in the **drive**.
❖ *in idioms* •What are you **driving at**? (What do you mean? What are you suggesting?) •You **drive me mad** when you say that. (You irritate me very much.)

drop
verb
A transitive (= allow to fall) •His hands were shaking and he **dropped** the glass.
B intransitive (= fall) •Prices have **dropped**.
noun (= a small amount of liquid) •Could I have a **drop** of milk in my coffee?
❖ *in idioms* •He was so tired, he **dropped off** in the armchair. (went to sleep) •Some students **drop out** of college every year. (leave before the course is over) •Please **drop in** to see us next time you come to London. (visit us)

41

due /dju:/
adjective
A (= owed) •He always pays his bills as soon as they are **due**.
B (= suitable) formal •He was driving without **due** care, the policeman said.
C (= expected) •What time is his plane **due**?
noun (= something one has a right to, often fair judgement, gratitude etc) •I don't like her, but to give her her **due**, I think she is very attractive.
adverb (= directly) + *north, south, east, west* •The house faces **due** west, so we see the sun set.

due to
preposition (= because of, caused by) very much like *owing to,* but some English speakers use **due to** only with nouns. •His failure was **due to** laziness. Some speakers accept: •He failed **due to** laziness.

during /'djʊərɪŋ/
preposition (= in, referring to a point or period of time within another period, answers the question 'When?' not 'How long?') •He stayed here **during** the holidays. •**During** the night, I heard someone scream. •'When was he away? Was it **during** August?' 'Yes, he was away for one week in August.'
See also **for**.

E

each
adjective determiner (compare **every**)
+ *singular verb,* applied to two or more, seen as individuals. •Two men arrived. **Each** man was smoking. (They were both smoking.) •**Each** girl must bring her own notebook. (All girls must bring their own books.)
As a determiner, before other adjectives •**Each** successful attempt wins a point.
adverb (= to/for every one) usually end position. •The tickets cost £5 **each**; that's £15 for all three of us.

pronoun (= every one separately) •**Each** was given his particular orders. •Put **each** of them in an envelope. (several envelopes needed, compare 'Put all of them in an envelope' — one envelope)

each other
pronoun not subject (= one another) •They hate **each other**. (a reciprocal feeling — he hates her and she hates him)
See also **all, both, every**.

easy
adjective **easier, easiest**
A (≠ difficult) •This puzzle is **easier** than it looks. •This dress was **easy** to make.
B (= comfortable, relaxed) •The rich have **easy** lives.

uneasy
adjective (= worried) •I feel **uneasy** about her going alone.

easily
adverb (= with ease) •The door opened **easily**. •She is **easily** the cleverest. (by far) •It's more **easily** (or It's easier) said than done.

ease
noun (≠ difficulty) •He jumped over it with **ease**. (easily)
verb (= make more comfortable, alleviate) •Take an aspirin to **ease** the pain.
❖ *in idioms* •**Take it easy**. (Relax, don't worry.) informal •I'm **easy** about it. (I don't mind what is decided.) informal •He tried to put me at [my] **ease**. (make me feel relaxed) •You ought to **ease up**. (work less hard) informal

eat /i:t/
verb irregular, **ate, eaten** /et/ /i:tən/ (= consume) •Have you **eaten** all the cheese? •Is there anything to **eat**? •He's hungry; he hasn't **eaten** yet.
❖ *in idioms* •She is **eaten up with** jealousy. (dominated by jealous [etc] feelings) •**Eat up** your supper and go to bed. (finish eating it) •He'll **eat his words** when he sees this. (take back what he said, apologise)

emphasis

effect
noun (=result) ● What will be the **effect** of this change? ● The video was full of surprising **effects**.
effective
adjective (=having a [desired] effect) ● The display of red, white and blue flowers was very **effective**.
efficient
adjective (=working well, economically) ● We need an **efficient** system to replace the old wasteful one.
effectively
adverb
A (=to produce an effect) ● She dresses **effectively** in bright colours.
B (=for all practical purposes) ● Money lent at very low interest rates is, **effectively**, almost a gift.
❖ *in idioms* ● The old system will remain **in effect** for another few weeks. (in use, operation) ● The medicine will **take effect** almost immediately. (produce results) ● He said he would help if he could, or **words to that effect**. (something with the same meaning)
See also **affect**.

eg
abbreviation for **exempli gratia** (=for example) ● Evergreen plants, **eg** holly and ivy, are used for Christmas decorations.

either/neither
/ˈaɪðə*/ or /ˈiːðə*/, /ˈnaɪðə*/ or /ˈniːðə*/
adjective determiner, used with singular, countable nouns (=this one or that one, of two) ● You can use **either** side. (It doesn't matter which.) ● **Neither** leg is broken. (Both are OK.)
pronoun [+*of*] ● 'Shall I take the old one or the new one?' 'Take **either** [of them]. **Neither** is very good.' In informal English it is possible to use a plural verb ● Is/Are **either** of the children here?
conjunction [+*or/nor*] ● You must **either** be quiet **or** leave the room. ● I **neither** know **nor** care what he thinks. ● **Either** his mother **or** his father will pay the bill.
adverb end-position (corresponding to *too* in negatives) ● 'I don't like it.' 'I don't like it, **either**.' or 'Neither do I.' ● 'He can't swim.' 'She can't swim **either**.' or: 'Neither can she.' ● He's not tall but not short, **either**. (of average height)
See also **any, both, each, so, too**.

else
adverb after question words and some pronouns
A (=in addition) ● What **else** did he tell you? ● Someone **else** was with him. ● I can't see anything **else**, only this.
B (=instead, in a different way, time) ● I can't come on Friday. When **else** can I see you? ● It's unpleasant but how **else** can we do it?
or else
A (emphasising *or*, =otherwise) ● He can pay **or else** he can leave. ● It's in my purse; **or else** I've lost it.
B (as a threat) ● Pay me now, **or else** . . .

---

emphasis
1 Emphasis — making part of a sentence more than usually important — is often shown by speaking louder or slower. In writing, we can use capital letters or underlining to give emphasis, but not too often in formal writing.
2 Auxiliary verbs, which are normally not stressed, change the whole meaning of a sentence when they *are* stressed. ● She's drinking tea/She <u>is</u> drinking tea. ● You can't swim./I <u>can</u> swim. ● She doesn't drink./She <u>does</u> drink.
3 *Do* can be used when there is no other auxiliary ● **Do** hurry [please].
4 Changing word order also often creates emphasis ● Clever, isn't it! ● This book — you left it in my room. ● What I think is, let's go.
5 Certain 'negative' words such as *never, nor* etc require inversion if they begin a sentence ● **Never** once

did he thank me for my work. •'At no time have I paid her money. •Nor have I.
6 Other words used for emphasis: *certainly, really, -self, so, such, very.* See also **it** (cleft sentences), INVERSION.
For more details see CEG 1.

end
verb (= finish) •What time does the lesson **end**? •The party **ended** at midnight. •How should I **end** this letter?
noun (= final point, ≠ beginning) •He lives at the **end** of the road. •Tell us the **end** of the story.
❖ *in idioms* •He worked hard and, **in the end**, he made good. (eventually, at last) •There's **no end to** his complaints. (He is always complaining.) •It's just **a means to an end**. (a way of reaching an aim) •I'm **at a loose end**. (I have nothing to do at the moment.) •Look in that box of **odds and ends**. (bits and pieces, assorted little things) •Our friendship is **at an end**. (finished) •He can't **make [both] ends meet**. (He's very poor; he can't afford to live well.)

enjoy /ɪn'dʒɔɪ/
verb transitive (= take pleasure in) •Do you **enjoy** reading dictionaries? •Both children and adults **enjoy** swimming in the sea. •I'm **enjoying** myself very much, thank you.
enjoyable
adjective (= pleasant) •Thank you for a very **enjoyable** evening.
enjoyment
noun (= pleasure) •There isn't much **enjoyment** in sitting alone in the dark.

enough /ɪ'nʌf/
adjective determiner (= sufficient) after singular nouns, before or after non-countable and plural nouns. •There aren't **enough** chairs for everyone. •Is he fool **enough** to believe her? •He has food **enough** for an army.
+ *to* + *infinitive* •She's old **enough** to help with the work.
pronoun •Count the chairs. Are there **enough**? •Stop it! That's **enough**! •I've had **enough**, thank you. •She hasn't got **enough** of these cakes for everybody. •Not **enough** is known about this subject.
adverb
A (= sufficiently) •Is the room big **enough** for a party? •He didn't run quickly **enough** to catch the bus.
B (= not very, only rather) •I like him well **enough** but he's not a great friend of mine.
❖ *in idioms* •**Oddly enough/Strangely enough**, we didn't meet, although we were both there. (This seems odd) •'You can borrow the car if you clean it.' '**Fair enough**!' (Agreed, That's reasonable) informal. •He predicted the horse would win and **sure enough**, it won. (as predicted) •He's had **more than enough** to eat. (too much)

enquire (also spelt **inquire**)
verb (= ask) •I don't know; I'll **enquire**. •'How is he?' she **enquired**. •She **enquired** how he was. (She asked how he was.)
+ *about* •She **enquired** about the times of the trains to London.
+ *after* •She **enquired** after your health. (asked how you were)
enquiry
noun (= asking, question, investigation) •Have there been any **enquiries**? •There was an **enquiry** into the accident.

essential
adjective (= necessary, forming the central part of) •Water is **essential** to plants; without it they die. •The **essential** point of the argument is economic.
noun (= necessary, important things) often plural •If you are carrying your own luggage, you take only the **essentials**. •One of the **essentials** of good cooking is a good appetite.

every

essence
noun (=central, best quality) ●I couldn't understand everything but I understood the **essence** of it.

essentially
adverb (=in reality, basically) ●He works in a town but he is **essentially** a country person.

etc
abbreviation for **et cetera** (=and the rest, and so on). ●Remember to bring paper, pencils **etc**.

even
adjective
A (=regular, level) ●The room must be kept at an **even** temperature.
B (=equal) ●We have each won a game so we're **even**. ●2, 4, 6, 8 are **even** numbers; 1, 3, 5 are odd numbers.
adverb
A (=which is more than you might expect) before something surprising ●**Even** a child can understand this. (so of course an adult can understand it) ●**Even** today a few people remember him. ●He must be 70, 80 **even**.
B (=still, yet) ●He tried hard and then tried **even** harder. ●You are **even** more foolish than I knew. (I already knew you were foolish but I didn't know you were so foolish.)
even if
conjunction (=though) ●I like him, **even if** he is a fool.
❖ *in idioms* ●I'll **get even with** you. (get my revenge) ●It's **even chances**. (50/50 probability) ●I saw it and **even now/even so** I can't believe it. (although I saw it)

ever
adverb mostly in negatives, questions and conditionals
A (=at any time, ≠never) ●Has he **ever** been to China? ●Do you **ever** hear from Sophie? ●If I **ever** have time, I'll write that story. ●They hardly **ever** drink coffee. ●You'll be in trouble if you **ever** do that again. ●We worked harder than **ever**. ●'Was it **ever** finished?' 'No, never.'
B (=always) ●**Ever** since that time, nothing has been done. ●It will be the same for **ever**.
C used after question words to add force: ●Who **ever** is that man? (who on earth) ●What **ever** is he doing? ●I wondered how **ever** I could do it. ●Why **ever** didn't you tell me you would be late?

-ever
as part of conjunctions (=it doesn't matter who, what, when, where, how, which etc) ●Wher**ever** he goes, she goes too. ●I'll buy which**ever** is cheapest. ●What**ever** happens, don't laugh. ●I'm not opening the door, who**ever** you are. ●It will take a week, how**ever** we do it. ●How**ever** expensive it is, he'll buy it. ●We can meet when**ever** you like.

❖ *in compounds* ●ever green ●ever-loving ●ever-present etc
❖ *in idioms* ●They lived **happily ever after**. (always afterwards — end of fairy story) ●**Yours ever**, Sophie Smith (used to sign letters, informally). ●It's **ever so hot**. (very hot indeed) informal. ●He's **ever such a rich man**. (very rich) informal
See also **always, however, matter, never, so, such**.

every
adjective determiner, with singular countable nouns. (compare **each**, but always more than two, counted one by one) ●**Every** picture was sold. (They were all sold.) ●He telephoned his mother **every** week. ●**Every** one of the cups was clean.
❖ *in idioms* ●He cleans the house **every now and then/every so often/every now and again**. (sometimes, from time to time) ●He cleans it **every other day**. (every two days)

every-
in compounds, pronouns
●**Every**body/**Every**one is looking forward to the holidays. ●He sold **every**thing in order to pay his debts. ●Why doesn't **every**body look after his/her/their own

45

ex-

money? (*their* to avoid *his/her*)
everywhere
adverb ●These flowers grow **everywhere**; they're very common.
conjunction (= wherever)
●**Everywhere** he goes, she goes too.
❖ *in idioms* ●It is written in easy, **everyday** English. (familiar, colloquial) ●Has she got her papers and pencils **and everything?** (and so on) ●This arrangement is better **in every way**. (from all points of view) See also **all, any(-body), both, each, no(-body), some(-body)** etc.

ex-
prefix (= former, still alive) ●I met her **ex-**husband. (the man she was once married to)
except /ɪk'sept/
preposition (= not including, leaving out, but) ●They invited everybody **except** me. ●Any day will do, **except** Thursday. ●I know nothing **except** what you told me.
except for (= apart from) ●**Except for** the baby, we all drink coffee.
excepting
preposition (= same as **except**, but also used after *always* and *not*)
●They work hard, always **excepting** Sophie. (Sophie is always lazy.)
●Everybody helped, not **excepting** Sophie. (Even Sophie helped.)
exception
noun (= a case which breaks the normal rule or pattern) ●Everyone must pay; we can make no **exceptions**. ●All the players, without **exception**, arrived on time. (absolutely all) ●Plurals usually end in -*s*, *men* is an **exception**.
exceptional/exceptionally
adjective/adverb (= unusual/ unusually [good]) ●This picture is quite **exceptional**/quite **exceptionally** beautiful. ●'Is he clever?' 'Yes, **exceptionally**.'

exclamation mark [!]
punctuation mark following exclamations, ie expressions of surprise, anger, delight etc, but not in indirect speech ●'It's

wonderful!' she exclaimed. (She exclaimed that it was wonderful.)
●Be quick! ●Oh, dear! ●What a shame! ●Look out! ●Oh, hell!
●How lovely you look!

excuse
verb /ɪk'skjuːz/ (= forgive, usually for small faults) ●I hope you will **excuse** the untidiness of this room.
●Please **excuse** me for forgetting your name/**excuse** my forgetting your name.
excuse me!
said before asking a small favour, causing slight inconvenience.
●**Excuse** me, have you got the time?/can you move over a little bit?/would you pass the bread?/I have to walk in front of you/I've lost my way.
noun /ɪk'skjuːs/ (= explanation of small faults) ●You are late. What's your **excuse** this time? ●He has no **excuse** for his bad behaviour. ●She made an **excuse** and left the room in tears. (excused herself, saying, eg 'I'm afraid I must leave you for a moment — **excuse** me.')
expect
verb (= suppose, assume something will happen)
[+ *that*] ●I **expect** [that] your mother is proud of you. ●He says he **expects** a cheque (will arrive in tomorrow's post). ●I **expect** you have only just arrived?
[+ *object*] [+ *to*] ●I don't **expect** them to behave perfectly but I do **expect** ordinary good manners.
●He hopes he'll win the prize but he doesn't really **expect** to [win it].
●She is **expecting** a baby in July.
●It's not a beautiful room but for $100 what do you **expect**?
●She **expects** too much; she even **expects** me to do her washing.
●'Will Sophie be there?' 'I **expect** so/I **expect** not.'
unexpected/unexpectedly
adjective/adverb (= without warning) ●My aunt arrived at our cottage **unexpectedly**. ●It was a completely **unexpected** visit because

her letter had not arrived.
See also **wait**.

explain
verb (= make clear, show) •This booklet **explains** the new tax system. •I don't understand; please will you **explain** [it]? •He didn't **explain** what he wanted. •She **explained** to me what had happened. •I had to **explain** it all to the police.

explanation
noun •What is the **explanation** for/of this strange event?

eye /aɪ/
noun •His **eyes** are weak; he has to wear glasses. •Shut your **eyes** now and go to sleep.

❖ *in idioms* •Will you **keep an eye on** the baby for a few minutes? (watch, look after) •That film really **opened my eyes**. (made me see/realise something) •Something in a shop window **caught her eye**. (attracted her attention) •He took the money **under my very eyes**. (when I could actually see him) •He **has his eye on** the manager's job. (He wants to replace the manager) •**In her eyes**, he is wonderful. (She thinks) •I'm **up to my eyes** in work. (very busy) •She **has an eye for** a bargain. (She's good at finding bargains.) •We **don't see eye to eye**. (We disagree.) •You can **see with half an eye** that she's unhappy. (easily tell) •He **couldn't take his eyes off her**. (He watched her all the time.) •He **closed his eyes to** my mistakes. (He pretended not to notice them.) •There's **more in this than meets the eye**. (It's not as simple as it looks.)

F

face /feɪs/
noun (= front part — of head, mountain, coin building etc)
•When I saw the expression on his **face**, I knew he had passed his exam.
verb (= look towards, confront)

•We are **faced** with difficulties.
•We must **face** them bravely.

❖ *in idioms* •He will **lose face** if he doesn't win. (feel humiliated) •I haven't **the face to** ask him for even more money. (courage, boldness to do something presumptuous or offensive) •How can you **look me in the face** after what you have done? (show no shame) •**On the face of it,** this is an excellent idea, but I have doubts. (Apparently, to all appearances) •He called me a fool **to my face**. (not behind my back, but speaking to me) •At last we met **face-to-face**. (in direct confrontation) •**Face the facts!** (Recognise the truth!) •He is **two-faced**. (a hypocrite, saying one thing, doing another) •**In the face of** their objections, he changed his decision. (confronted with) •This old penny stamp is worth much more than its **face-value**. (one penny, in this case).

fact
noun
A countable (= items of true information) •Is it a **fact** that he married six times? •We must look at the **facts** before we act. •The **fact** that the money has gone does not mean it was stolen.
B non-countable (= the truth)
•This story may be **fact** or fiction.

❖ *in idioms* •**As a matter of fact**, that money is mine. (Actually, if you really want to know) •**In fact**, I have the receipt for it. (To convince you further, indeed). •He did not see, **due to the fact that** he wasn't looking. (because . . .)
See also **actual, indeed**.

fair
adjective
A (= just, equitable) •It's not **fair** to criticise her when she isn't here to defend herself. •**Fair**-minded people want to look at both sides of the question.
B (= light, pale — of skin, hair)
•She has blue eyes and **fair** hair.

fall

C (=good, clear, fine — of weather) •The boat crosses only in **fair** weather.

fairly
adverb
A (=justly) •He described the situation **fairly**.
B (=quite, rather, pretty) usually modifies favourable adjectives and adverbs •I'm **fairly** happy about it. (but not in ecstasies) •He did the work **fairly** well. (but not superbly) •This soup is **fairly** hot. (hot enough)
❖ *in idioms* •**Fair enough!** (That's reasonable, I agree.) •That's not **fair play**. (You are breaking the rules.)
See also **pretty, quite, rather.**

fall /fɔ:l/
verb irregular, **fell, fallen**, intransitive (=drop, descend freely or by accident) •Snow **fell** during the night. •A tree has **fallen** across the road.
noun
A (=descent, decrease) •He broke his leg when he had a **fall**. •The **fall** in supplies has put prices up.
B (AmE =autumn) •Come after the summer vacation, in the **fall**.
❖ *in idioms* •She **fell out with** her family about the money she kept. (quarrelled) •Keep awake; don't **fall asleep**. (go to sleep) •He has **fallen in love** with the Princess. •He told a joke but it **fell flat**. (no one laughed) •He was so dizzy that he kept **falling over/falling down**. (collapsing) •Has she any money to **fall back on**? (to use in emergency, when her usual supply or source fails) •It's a trick; don't **fall for** it. (be deceived by) •It was a splendid scheme but it **fell through**. (came to nothing)

fancy
noun
A non-countable (=imagination) •Is this fact or **fancy**?
B countable (=casual thought, whim) •It's only a **fancy** of mine, perhaps, but I think someone is watching us.

verb
A (=imagine) •**Fancy** spending all that money!
B (=have a liking for, desire for) •Do you **fancy** a drink? •He obviously **fancies** that girl.
adjective (≠plain, =decorated, extraordinary) •I prefer plain ties; these are too **fancy** for me.
❖ *in idioms* •I bought it because it **took my fancy**. (seemed attractive at the time) •She **fancies herself** as an actress. (She thinks she acts well.) •He was dressed as a rabbit for a **fancy-dress** party.

far /fa:*/
adverb farther/further, farthest/furthest
A (=at/to a distance, a long way) mostly in questions and negatives and after *too* and *so*. •He can't walk **far**. •How **far** [away] is it? •I'm afraid it's a long way; two miles away. I think it's too **far** for him. •I'm very tired; I can't go any **farther**. **Farther, farthest** are used with directions and distances but the all-purpose words are **further/furthest:** •He lives in the **farthest/furthest** house.
B (=very much) •He is **far** better now. •I'm **far** too busy to watch television. •You're not **far** wrong. (You are more or less right.)
❖ *in idioms* •I am **far from happy** about it. (I'm unhappy about it.) •She is **by far the prettier** of the two. (much the prettier) •'Is he successful?' '**Far from it!**' (No, he's a failure.) •Shouting is bad, but throwing things! That's **going too far!** (being unreasonable) •He will **go far** if he works hard. (succeed) •**How far** should I believe what he says? (To what degree?) •He has saved $2000 so **far**. (up to now) •**So far as I know**, he is trustworthy. (I have no reason to distrust him.) •**So far as I'm concerned**, you can take the car. (For my part, I don't need it.) •She had **a faraway look** in her eye. (as if she was day-dreaming)
See also **away, long, many, much.**

fast /fa:st/
  adjective (=quick) •This music is too **fast** for dancing. •My watch is five minutes **fast**.
  adverb
  A (=quickly) •Don't go any **faster**; you're driving too **fast** already. (Your speed is too high.)
  B (=firmly) •The paper was stuck **fast** to the wall.
  verb (=eat nothing, usually for religious reasons) •Muslims **fast** during Ramadan.
fasten /fa:sən/
  verb (=fix) •Please **fasten** your seat belt. •I've lost a button; I can't **fasten** my shirt [up]. •He **fastened** his attention on me.
unfasten
  verb (=undo, open) •Can you **unfasten** this hook, please?
fastener
  noun (=clip, zip, etc) •This **fastener** is stuck; I can't do it up.
❖ *in idioms* •He's **fast** asleep. (deeply) •Stay in the **fast** lane. (on motorway)
fault /fɔ:lt/
  noun (=mistake, imperfection) •The little **faults** in the cloth show that it is hand-made. •Everyone has **faults** as well as virtues.
❖ *in idioms* •It's **not my fault**. (I'm not to blame.) •Which of the two drivers was **at fault**? (was in the wrong, made a mistake) •You're always **finding fault with** my cooking. (complaining about it) See also **blame, mistake**.
feed
  verb irregular, **fed, fed** (=give food to) •Your dog is very fat. What do you **feed** him on? •Has she **fed** the baby yet? •There are a hundred guests **to be fed**. •Little streams **feed** big rivers.
❖ *in idioms* •I am **fed up with** waiting for you. (tired of, irritated by) informal •I'm afraid $5000 is just **chicken-feed** when you consider what we really need. (a tiny amount)
feel
  verb irregular, **felt, felt**

A (=sense by touch) •I like to **feel** the wind on my face.
B (=experience generally) •'Do you **feel** cold?' 'No, I **feel** fine.' •I'm not **feeling** worried.
C (=think, believe, usually temporarily and without proof) •I **feel** we ought to go now. •What does he **feel** about Sophie's new plan?
feel as if/as though
  (=seem) •I **felt as if** I was flying.
feel like [+ -*ing*]
  (=want) •Do you **feel like** going to the cinema? •No, I **feel like** a quiet evening at home.
feeling[s]
  noun (=emotion, belief, sensation, understanding, anger) •He spoke of his son with great **feeling**. •My **feeling** is that we have made a mistake. •You will have a **feeling** of excitement. •I wish you had more **feeling** for my problems. •His final speech stirred up **feeling**. •Everyone has strong **feelings** on the subject of death. •You must accept his present or hurt his **feelings**.
❖ *in idioms* •Please **feel free** to say what you really think. (you are permitted, welcome to) •I'm **feeling funny**; can I have some water please? (having strange sensations) •I'd like to come up the mountain with you but I don't **feel up to** it. (feel strong enough)
fetch
  verb (=go and get and bring back) •He's very ill. Please **fetch** a doctor. +*person object* +*object* •I'll **fetch** you your glasses. (for you)
❖ *in idioms* •We **fetched up** in a pub somewhere. (arrived without planning) informal •She spends all her time **fetching and carrying**. (doing little jobs)
few /fju:/
  adjective/noun determiner (≠ many) used only with plurals
  A with no article, emphasis on smallness of number •**Few** students understood the lecture. (because it was difficult)

49

fight

B with article, emphasis on idea of 'at least some' •A **few** students understood the lecture. (although it was difficult) •So **few** people came that the meeting was cancelled. •Explain briefly; use as **few** words as possible. •Very **few** tickets were sold; **fewer** than last year. •A **few** people came, so we held the meeting. (not many, but at least some) •He came a **few** minutes later. •Here are a **few** more glasses. •Only a **few** of us went.

❖ *in idioms* •Quite a **few** glasses were broken. (a fair number, more than you would expect) •A **good few** weeks later, he wrote. (Several)

fight /faɪt/
verb irregular, **fought, fought** (=use violence against)
+ *object* •They **fought** their enemies.
+ *for* •They have **fought** for their independence.
without object •Please stop **fighting!**
noun (=battle, conflict) •There was a big **fight** about it. •Let us join the **fight** against ignorance.

❖ *in idioms* •We **fought our way** through the crowd. (It was difficult) •He didn't win but he **put up a good fight.** (fought well) •If he **fights back** (defends himself by fighting) he has **a fighting chance** of success. (a small but real possibility) •Talking won't work; they'll have to **fight it out.** (settle the argument by fighting)

figurative
adjective of words (=used in a special way, not literally, but making a comparison) •the wind **screamed** •the **fruit** of our labours •an **oily** expression.
See also METAPHOR, SIMILE.

fill /fɪl/
verb transitive or intransitive (=make or become full) •The room **filled** with smoke./Smoke **filled** the room. •Let me **fill** your glass.

❖ *in idioms* •Please **fill in the details** on this form. (supply information) •Is that enough? No, **fill it up.** (make it completely full) •His book **filled a gap,** so it sold well. (supplied a need) •I've **had my fill** of this subject for tonight. (enough, I don't want to discuss it any more)

find /faɪnd/
verb irregular, **found, found**
A (=discover, ≠lose) •Have you seen my pen? I can't **find** it. •At last we **found** the place we were looking for.
B (=decide from experience, feel, consider) •Do you **find** him easy to work with? •I **found** it difficult to understand him.

❖ *in idioms* •How do you **find time** to do so much? (organise your time) •This is secret; nobody must **find out** about it. •If they **find out,** we'll be shot. (get to know) •Cruelty **is found** everywhere. (exists) •You're welcome to stay but you must take us **as you find us.** (accept us in our ordinary way of living) •He was **found guilty** of the crime. (The court said he had committed the crime.)

fine
adjective
A (=high quality, very good) •There's a **fine** view from the top. •I've never eaten **finer** food.
B (=very thin, delicate) •Babies have very **fine** hair. •I need a pen with a **finer** point.
C (=healthy, comfortable, OK) •'How is he now?' 'He's **fine,** thanks.' •'Is the coffee too strong?' 'No, it's **fine,** thanks, just the way I like it.'
D (=bright and sunny) •If it's **fine** tomorrow, let's go out.
E (=grand, impressive) •It was a **fine** speech but we need action.
verb/noun (=take money as punishment/penalty) •He was **fined** $100 for parking the car in the town centre. •That's a very high **fine.**

finely
adverb (=well, carefully, very

first

small) •The actors were **finely** dressed. •The violin was **finely** tuned. •The vegetables must be **finely** grated.
❖ **in idioms** •He was **in a fine state** after that journey! (sarcastic = terrible) •This **suits me fine**. (= well, adverb) •It's six o'clock; you're **cutting it fine** if you want to catch the bus. (risking being late)

finish
verb (= reach, bring to an end) •What time does the lesson **finish**? •Have you **finished** breakfast yet? + -ing •I haven't **finished** cleaning up.
noun A (= end, especially of a race) •It was a very close **finish**.
B (= appearance of something well-made, with care for final details) •I admired the **finish** of her expensive handbag.

final /faɪnəl/
adjective (= last, impossible to change) •The **final** day of January is 31st. •What was his **final** decision?
noun often plural (= last match, exam in a series) •The **finals** will be played next week.
❖ **in idioms** •She's **putting the finishing touches to** her make-up. (attending to the last details) •Can I borrow that paper when you've **finished with it**? (have no more use for it) •Let's **finish up** the milk. (empty the bottle, drink it all) •They **finished up** [the evening] [singing songs] at Tony's.
See also **end**.

finite verbs
The finite forms of a verb are those which show tense and vary according to the subject. Sentences normally contain at least one finite verb. *Non-finite* forms are used as complements and to show aspect but do not 'make sense' alone, eg *infinitives, participles*. In the following examples, the verbs in **bold** are finite forms: •He **decided** to leave as soon as he **could** find the money for his ticket. •Having realised what **was** happening, he **felt** worried about his family, whom he **pictured** waiting for news of him.
See also CLAUSE, INFINITIVE, NON-FINITE, PARTICIPLE, SENTENCE.
For more details see CEG 4.5

fire
noun countable •He has a **fire** in his bedroom.
non-countable •There's no smoke without **fire**. •Paper catches **fire** easily. •The house is on **fire**.
verb (= shoot, explode) •The officer ordered the men to **fire**. •Several shots were **fired**.
❖ **in idioms** •Doing business with him is **playing with fire**. (dangerous, taking risks) •He was **under fire** from all sides. (being attacked, literally or metaphorically) •He was **fired** from his first job for always arriving late. (dismissed)

firm
adjective (= strong, solid, hard) •You can stand on this chair; it's quite **firm**. •He gave me a **firm** handshake. •That is my **firm** belief. •Keep a **firm** hand on that child; he's very naughty.
noun (= a business company) •What **firm** does he work for?

first
adjective/noun determiner ordinal (= 1st, ≠ last) •I was the **first** to arrive. •The **first** explorer to reach this spot died fifty years ago.
adverb
A (= to begin with) •**First**, prepare the meat for cooking.
B (= for the first time) •When I **first** came here, it was different.
C (= before something else) •Don't go! Have a drink **first**.
❖ **in idioms** •**First things first**: where's the money? (get things in order of importance) •**At first** I hated this place but now I like it. (To begin with, in the beginning)

51

fit

•He doesn't know **the first thing** about economics. (even the most elementary facts) •She studied **first aid**, so she was useful when the accident happened. (treatment of the injured by ordinary people) •The book is written **in the first person**. (The writer calls himself 'I'.) •We have to get up **first thing**. (very early in the morning)

fit /fɪt/
adjective
A (=right, suitable) •These old clothes are not **fit** to wear in public; they're only **fit** for gardening.
B (=in good health) •He must be quite **fit**; he climbed the mountain easily.
verb
A (=be the right size or shape) •His coat doesn't **fit** him; it's too tight.
B (=position something exactly) •Can you **fit** this piece in the right place?
noun
A (=sudden, short attack or outburst) •He had a **fit** of coughing and could not speak.

outfit
noun
(=set of clothes, equipment). •She was wearing her party **outfit**, complete with gold handbag.

❖ *in idioms* •She goes to **keep fit** classes. (to do physical exercises) •Do **as you think fit**. (consider right) •**If the cap fits** (American: *shoe*) wear it. (If it's true, admit it.) •I was laughing **fit to burst**. (as if ready to explode) •She's willing to **fit in with** our arrangements. (adapt her arrangements to ours) •If you have toothache, the dentist will **fit you in** very soon. (find a time to see you)
See also **suit**.

fix
verb
A (=fasten, settle firmly, agree) •The pictures were **fixed** to the walls with pins. •Can we **fix** a date for our next meeting?
B (=repair) •Has the washing machine been **fixed** yet?
C (=deal with) •Don't worry; Sophie will **fix** everything.

❖ *in idioms* •They can't **fix on** a date. (decide) •I can **fix you up with** everything you need. (supply, arrange) •I think the election was **fixed**. (settled dishonestly)

flat
adjective
A (=smooth, level) •Some people still believe the earth is **flat**. •Lie down **flat** on your back.
B (=too low in pitch, ≠ sharp) •The music sounds awful; it's **flat**.
noun
(=apartment) •She lives in the **flat** above mine.
adverb
(=completely) •He's **flat** broke. (He has no money at all.) informal

❖ *in idioms* •He gave me **a flat refusal**./He **flatly** refused. (absolutely) •The idea **fell flat**. (didn't work) •This torch won't work: **the battery's flat**. •We were working **flat out**. (as hard as we could)

fly /flaɪ/
verb irregular, flew, flown
A (=move on wings by air) •'Did you go by sea?' 'No, we **flew**.' •A large bird has **flown** onto the pond.
B (=move fast) •The door **flew** open and she rushed in. •I'm late. I must **fly**.

flight
noun
A (=trip by plane) •Did you have a good **flight**?
B (=set of steps) •There are six **flights**; shall we take the lift up?

❖ *idiom* •It's 20km by road, but only 12km **as the crow flies**. (in a straight line)

fold /fəʊld/
verb
(of paper, cloth etc =turn, bend) •Will you **fold** the tablecloth [up] and put it away? •This **folding** chair can fit in a small space.
noun
(=crease, arrangement of cloth) •Iron this again; there are a few **folds** in it.

follow
verb
A (=come, go, arrive etc after)

52

for

•I'll go first, please **follow** me.
B (= understand) •I don't quite
follow; can you explain that again?
following
adjective (= next) •He was sick on
the **following** day.
noun (= what comes next) •The
following have been chosen: Smith,
Brown, Young, etc.
preposition (= after) •**Following**
the performance there will be
drinks served in the hall.
❖ *in idioms* •What about **something
to follow**? (a pudding, fresh fruit?)
•The results are **as follows**: 2−2,
3−1.
fool /fu:l/
noun (= silly person) •Don't be a
fool; do what the doctor says.
verb (= deceive) •This isn't gold:
it's brass — you can't **fool** me.
foolish
adjective (= silly) •It would be
foolish to spend all your money on
chocolate.
❖ *in idioms* •If you dress like that at
your age, you'll **make a fool of
yourself**. (make yourself look silly)
•If you believe that rubbish, **the
more fool you**. (it shows you are a
fool) •**He's no fool**. (He is quite
competent.) •Is your plan
foolproof? (very easy to
work/understand, so that even
fools can use it — it can't go
wrong)
foot /fʊt/
noun plural **feet**
A (= part of the body) •I can't
walk any further; my **feet** hurt.
•Leave it at the **foot** of the bed/
hill/stairs/garden. (figurative)
B (measure = 0.3048 m.) •The
room is about 20 **feet** long. •He's
over six **foot** tall.
❖ *in compounds* •**foot**path, (for
walkers not cars) •**foot**note (at
bottom of page) •**foot**lights (on a
stage)
❖ *in idioms* •It's not far: we can go
on foot. (walking) •You always
feel strange in a new job, but
you'll soon **find your feet**. (get
used to it, know your way about)

•I intended to jump but then I **got
cold feet**. (lost courage) •It will be
nice to go home and **put my feet
up**. (have a rest) •Don't allow him
to behave like that! **Put your foot
down**! (insist on better behaviour)
•Oh dear! I've **put my foot in it**!
(said or done the wrong thing,
usually offended someone
unintentionally) •I've never **set
foot in** Ireland. (visited)

for
preposition
A (= intended to belong to)
•Please take it; I bought it **for**
you. •Don't eat that cake; it's **for**
Sophie's birthday.
B with things + -*ing* (= for the
purpose of) •'What's this money
for?' 'It's **for** buying the tickets.'
(to buy the tickets) •A ther-
mometer is a thing **for** measuring
temperature.
C (= in favour of, ≠ against)
•They're **for** starting all over
again. •Are you **for** or against this
plan?
D *some adjectives* + *for* + *object*
+ *infinitive* (often = that clause)
•She's anxious **for** him to phone.
(that he should phone)
It's + *adjective* + *for* + *object*
+ *infinitive* •It's important **for** you
to arrive early. •Is it necessary **for**
me to pay now? •It's unusual **for**
Sophie to lose her temper.
It's + *adjective* + *for* + *there to be*
•It's unnecessary **for** there to be
any special arrangement. •Is it
important **for** there to be an
opportunity to discuss the problem?
It's too + *adjective* + *for* + *object*
+ *infinitive* •It's too old-fashioned
for me to wear.
It's too + *adjective* + *enough* + *for*
•It's not fashionable enough **for**
Sophie.
E (= during, till the end of) •He
went on driving **for** hundreds of
miles. •She's been living with them
for a year. (She went to live with
them a year ago) •She had known
them **for** about a month before she
agreed to share their house.

With perfect tenses when the period includes the present •I've been feeling slightly ill **for** a week. (since last week) •They haven't written to us **for** ages. •We spoke on the phone **for** ten minutes, but that was months ago.
conjunction after main statement (=because) formal •He died, **for** the wound was deep.
❖ *in idioms* •We went upstairs quietly, **for fear of** wak**ing** the children. (so as not to) •I have never met him. **For all I know,** he may be very pleasant. (but I have no knowledge of him) •He treated her with great kindness and generosity, but **for all that** she refused to visit him. (in spite of that) •This quarrel has gone on long enough; let's settle it **once and for all.** (finally, for the last time) •Sophie's quite big **for her age.** (considering her age) •She works as a gardener **for £2 an hour.** (for a wage of) •He said he was leaving **for good.** (for ever, not coming back) •I hope you know **what you're in for.** (what unpleasant things will happen to you) informal •**If it wasn't for him,** we'd be very poor. (If he hadn't helped us) •They are all rather lazy. **As for** Sophie, she never does anything. (And when you come to consider)

forbid /fə'bɪd/
verb irregular, **forbade, forbidden,** transitive (=prohibit, order not to) •The doctor has **forbidden** him to smoke. •Smoking is **forbidden** in the theatre. •I **forbid** you to open the door. •My mother **forbade** me to speak to men like you. •You're not to do it; it's **forbidden.**
See also **allow, must.**

force
verb (=make somebody/something act against their will or nature) •The prisoners were **forced** to work all day. •We lost the key and had to **force** the door open. •His laughter sounded **forced.** (unnatural)
noun
A (=strength, often violence) •The **force** of the water drives a dynamo. •Their money was taken from them by **force.** •Your argument has great **force.**
B (=military or other trained group) •The police **force** is not usually armed.
❖ *in idioms* •Let us **join forces** to fight them. (unite) •Is that very old law still **in force**? (in operation) •He spoke **from force of habit.** (without thinking, instinctively)

forget
verb irregular, **forgot, forgotten**
A (≠remember) •'What's her name?' 'I **forget**'.
+ *-ing* (=something done but lost to memory) •I shall never **forget** [meet**ing**] her, though.
+ *to* + *infinitive* (=didn't remember in time) •I brought the tomatoes but I **forgot** [to bring] the salt. •Did you **forget** to ask the price?
B (=ignore) •Don't **forget** me when you're rich!
in idioms •'I'm sorry I broke that glass.' 'Oh, **forget it.**' (Never mind, it doesn't matter.) •I quite **forgot myself** and used some very bad language. (lost my self-control.)

forgive
verb irregular, **forgave, forgiven** (=say or feel no longer angry, willing to accept someone/something with imperfections) •I was unkind last night; please **forgive** me if you can. •God will **forgive** you your sins if you are sorry.
+ *person object/possessive adjective* + *-ing* •I cannot **forgive** him/his **calling me a liar.**

forgiving
adjective (=lenient, able to forgive) •She has a sweet, **forgiving** nature.

forgiveness
noun (=act of forgiving, mercy) •If you accidentally step on someone's foot, say you are sorry but don't beg for **forgiveness!**
❖ *in idioms* •It's best to **forgive and forget.** (not be bitter) •**Forgive me, but** what you say is not true.

(Pardon my saying so — a formal version of *excuse me*, usually said before contradicting someone, or being necessarily rude)

form
noun
A (=shape, kind) •She has a woman's **form** but a dragon's nature. •What **form** of government is used in your country?
B (=paper used for recording information) •You must fill in an application **form** if you want to be considered for this job.
verb (=take shape, develop) •The dancers **formed** a circle. •An idea was **forming** in my mind. •Adverbs are often **formed** by adding *-ly* to the adjective.

formal
adjective (=according to convention or rule) •He asked for a **formal** written apology.
•Business letters are usually written in **formal** language.

former
adjective
A (=of an earlier period) •I met the **former** leader. (He is not the leader now.)
B (≠ latter, =first of two) formal •Schoolchildren and students marched, the **former** in uniform. (schoolchildren)

forward[s]
adverb (=towards the front) •The army slowly moved **forward[s]**. (advanced) •It swings backwards and **forwards**. (to and fro)
verb (=pass on to new address) •Please **forward** my letters.
adjective without *s* (=advanced) •He plays in the **forward** line. (front row of players in football etc) •These jobs are not very far **forward**. (not much work has been done)
❖ *in idioms* •Are you looking **forward to** the weekend? (thinking of it with pleasure) •I look **forward to** meeting your family.
See also **back(-wards)**, **home(-wards)**, **in(-wards)**, **on(-wards)**, **out(-wards)**, **to(-wards)**.

free
adjective
A (=not tied, not confined) •He's not **free**; he's in prison. •Are you **free** on Monday or do you have to work? •We're not slaves; we're **free** men.
B (=not charged for) •If you buy a car this month, they give you a **free** radio.
C (=not controlled by rule) •It is a **free** translation, not exactly word for word.
D (=vacant) •'Is this seat **free**?' 'Yes, no one's using it.'
E + *from* (=without, not troubled by) •He is **free** from pain only when he is asleep.
F + *to* + *infinitive* (=allowed) •She's **free** to leave the hospital. •I am not **free** to speak about the plans.
adverb
A (=without payment) •Old people travel **free** on buses.
B (=loose, unattached) •The chickens run **free** in the garden.
verb (=set free, allow to escape) •Let us **free** you from this worry.

-free
suffix (=without) •He has a salt**free** diet. •We live tax**free**.

freely
adverb
A (=willingly, openly) •He told me quite **freely** that he had made a bad mistake.
B (=without limitation, generously) •Please give **freely** to this charity.

❖ *in compounds* •**free** agent (someone who can act independently) •**free** enterprise (trade without much government control) •**freehold** (≠ leasehold, absolute ownership of property) •**free** speech (the right to express ideas in public) •**free** trade (no restrictions or high charges on imports)

❖ *in idioms* •They have a **free and easy** attitude to work. (not serious, relaxed, cheerful) •When I **have my hands free** to help you, I will. (but at the moment, I am too busy)

55

friend

friend /frend/
noun (= someone who shares feelings, interests etc but not a relation) •Sophie and Jane are **friends**. •'Do you know Jane?' 'Yes, she's an old **friend** of mine.' •Diamonds are a girl's best **friend**. (a line from a song) •Can I bring a **friend** to the party?

friendly
adjective NOT adverb, (= warm, accepting in manner, on good terms) •The dog won't bite; he's quite **friendly**. •Are you **friendly** with Sophie? •He spoke to the children in a very **friendly** way and made them laugh.

unfriendly
adjective (= not friendly, unkind) •He did not welcome us; he said very little and never smiled — in fact, he was rather **unfriendly**.

friendship
noun (= friendly relationship) •Real **friendship** is worth more than gold. •Their **friendship** lasted all their lives — they never quarrelled.

❖ *in compounds* •girl**friend**, boy**friend**. •He has a new girl**friend** every week. (companion, close friend.) Possessive adjectives suggest a closer relationship, more exclusive •She's his girl**friend**. •That's my boy**friend** (special partners)

❖ *in idioms* •They quarrelled but now he is **friends with** her again. (on good terms) •She's very sociable; she **makes friends with** anyone she meets. (becomes a friend of)

fright
noun (= feeling of fear) •The sudden noise gave me a **fright**.

frighten
verb (= fill with fear) •He tried to **frighten** me by showing me a knife. •I wasn't **frightened** of the knife. •I was **frightened** [that] he might cut himself. •It wasn't really **frightening**.

frightful
adjective (= shocking, unpleasant) often informal. •What **frightful** weather we're having!

from
preposition
A (= beginning at) •She works **from** morning to night. •He loved her **from** the moment he saw her. •It's 20km **from** here to Paris. •We once lived only 3 km **from** the Eiffel Tower. •Which platform does the train start **from**? •The bank is open **from** nine to three.
  Countable nouns are used without an article in phrases like •**from** shop to shop •**from** head to foot •**from** floor to ceiling •**from** girl to woman
B (= supplied by, originating in) •Who is your letter **from**? •I'm **from** Japan. (I'm Japanese) •Where are you **from**? (What is your nationality?)
C (= judging by) •**From** his appearance, I think he is ill. •**From** what you say, she must be stupid.

❖ *in idioms* •I meet him **from time to time**. (sometimes) •Things went **from bad to worse**. (they deteriorated) •Do you speak **from experience**? (Are your remarks based on experience?) •My experience is **different from** yours. •I can't **tell one from another**. (They all seem the same to me.)

front /frʌnt/
noun
A (≠ back, = part facing forwards) •The teacher stood at the **front** of the class. •The **front** of the house faces East.
B (= battle line) •More soldiers have been sent to the **front**.
adjective (= at the front) •We sat in the **front** row. •Come in by the **front** door. •He was in the **front** line. (of a battle)

❖ *in idioms* •Please go **in front**; I'll follow you. (ahead) •Don't stand **in front of** the TV. (I can't see the screen) •Don't speak in that way **in front of** the children. (in their presence) •You're **at the front of the queue**. (You'll be served next.)

56

fuss

-ful
suffix (used to make adjectives from nouns and verbs) •peace**ful** •event**ful** •master**ful** etc and (to make nouns meaning the amount to fill a container, space etc) •spoon**ful** •room**ful** (of people) •arm**ful** (of flowers).

full
adjective
A (≠ empty, = filled) •My suitcase is **full**; I'll need another bag for the other things. •When the bus came, it was **full** and we had to wait for the next one. •I'm **full**. (I've had enough to eat.) informal + *of* •This work is **full** of mistakes. •Her cooking is **full** of flavour.
B (= complete, greatest possible) •Give your **full** name. •I paid the **full** cost. •He drove at **full** speed.
❖ *in compounds* •**full** board (in hotels etc, all meals) •**full** grown (completely developed) •**full** time (≠ part time, of a job) •**full** moon (seen as a circle)
❖ *in idioms* •He is **full of his own troubles**. (obsessed by, he can't think of anything else) •When the children woke up, they were **full of beans**. (very energetic) •The speech was quoted **in full**. (all of it) •We worked **full out**. (at maximum power)

full stop [.]
punctuation mark A full stop is used to show the end of a sentence. It can be difficult to know how long a sentence should be. See SENTENCE. Full stops are also used to show when words have been shortened, eg Sept. (September) •reg. (regulation). As abbreviations become more familiar, the full stop tends to be omitted. It is no longer necessary after *Mr* (Mister) or *Dr* (Doctor) or most short forms ending with the same letter as the full form eg *regd* (registered)

fun
noun always non-countable (= enjoyment, source of amusement) colloquial •I was working while you were having **fun**. •Washing up dirty saucepans isn't much **fun**. •Are you going out? Well, have **fun!** •Let's ask Sophie to come; she's always good **fun**.

funny
adjective
A (= amusing) •His **funny** stories made everybody laugh.
B (= strange) •Can you hear a **funny** noise?
C (= slightly ill) •I wasn't very ill but I did feel a bit **funny**.
❖ *in idioms* •He's learning Chinese **for fun**. (for pleasure not because he needs to) •He made that remark only **in fun**; it was not serious. (not intended to offend) •It's unkind to **make fun of** people who make mistakes. (laugh at)

furniture
noun non-countable (eg tables, chairs, desks, cupboards, beds) •They haven't got much **furniture**; they sit on boxes and sleep on the floor. •The only real piece of **furniture** is an old chest of drawers.

furnish
verb •The hotel has been expensively **furnished**.

further/farther
See **far**.

furthest/farthest
See **far**.
If in doubt, use *further/furthest*.

fuss
noun singular (= commotion, protest) •What a **fuss** about nothing! •Don't make so much **fuss** about being one minute late.
verb (= worry, act nervously) •Stop **fussing!** There's nothing to worry about.
❖ *in idioms* •She **makes a fuss of** her nephew. (She treats him with special favour.) •He's **a fussy eater**. (If the food is not exactly as he likes it, he won't eat it.) •I'm **not fussy** whether we go or stay. (I don't mind what we do) informal.

57

future

English can refer to future events in several different ways, each with particular shades of meaning. It is difficult to give rules which are both simple and reliable in every case. The following guidelines are helpful but not complete.

FORMS

1 *future simple tense* — called a tense but not really a 'pure' future because it often suggests willingness or promises or threats as well as simple prediction.

I/we **shall/will; you/he/she/it/they will** + *infinitive*. ● I/We **shall** help. (neutral, almost pure future, with no reference to feelings) ● I/We **will** help. (suggests the help is voluntary, offered willingly) ● You/He/She/It/They **will** help. (almost neutral prediction of future events)

It is possible to use *will* for all persons but better especially in negatives and questions, to use *shall* for the first persons ● **Shall** I open the window? ● **I shan't** be at home this evening. ● **Shall** we go now? The problem can often be avoided in speech by using the short form *'ll* which is the same for both *shall* and *will* ● I**'ll** see you tonight. ● We**'ll** get another one. ● They**'ll** be told soon.

2 *be going to* + *infinitive* — the easiest general-purpose expression of future time. With a person as subject it suggests an intention that will be carried out or an existing cause that will certainly produce a result. This idea of inevitability is strongest when the subject is not a person. ● I**'m going to buy** a new bicycle. (I intend to and I am confident it will be bought) ● She**'s going to be** very angry when she sees that broken window. (Her anger will result from a cause that exists now.) ● Look out! That car **is going to crash!** (Nothing can stop it)

When combined with *if,* the *be going to* form can be a main verb (future) or a dependent verb (present): ● He**'s going to be** late if he doesn't hurry. ● If you**'re going to buy** it, you will have to borrow some more money.

3 *present progressive tense* — also used for future events already arranged. An adverb of time or the context make it obvious that the verb refers to the future ● Sophie **is bringing** her boyfriend to the party [tomorrow]. ● When **are** they **getting** married? ● He**'s making** a big mistake. ● They**'re playing** the Beethoven next. ● It **isn't being recorded** until tomorrow. (Not used with STATIVE VERBS.)

4 *present simple tense*
(a) used for future events seen as absolutely certain facts ● Tomorrow **is** Sunday. ● Term **begins** on Monday. ● He **gets** a pension when he retires. ● If you touch this, you **die!** ● We **don't start** work till 9.30.
(b) also used for dependent clauses of time and condition when the main verb is future ● She'll tell you if/when you **ask** her. ● As soon as they **see** it, they'll eat it. ● I shan't take the medicine unless I **feel** ill again. ● As you **go** in, you will see the statue on your left.

5 *future progressive tense*
(a) corresponding to the present progressive, refers to an action which will be in progress at a certain point or for a certain period in the future ● I'm working hard today and I**'ll be working** hard tomorrow. ● Two hours from now you **will be lying** in the sun, enjoying yourself.
(b) also used for the future seen as a 'matter of course'; something that will happen without reference to anyone's personal intentions ● **Will** you **be seeing** him again? ● The guests **will be arriving** in twenty minutes. ● We **shan't be leaving** till late at night.

general

6 *future perfect*
(a) used for looking back from (an imaginary) future time. •By lunchtime he**'ll have finished** the work. •They **will not have built** the new hotel before the celebrations. •By the time he has really learned the language he**'ll have grown** a long grey beard.
(b) the future simple, future progressive and future perfect can be used to express a present assumption •You **will be** Miss Brown. (I suppose) •He **will be working** with me. (I assume) •You **will have met** already? (I think) •You **won't have had** any lunch? (I expect you are hungry — would you like some food?)
7 *am/is/are to + infinitive* — used for plans and instructions •There **is to be** a meeting next week. •We **are** all **to be** there by 7.30. •The details **are to be announced** soon. •This information **is to be kept** secret.
 The past form of this construction is often used in the negative as a past form of *must not* •She **wasn't** [allowed] **to** speak to him. •We **weren't to** open his letters.
future in the past Something that had not yet happened at a past moment was then in the future. Several of the forms above have corresponding forms for this •I'm just going to tell you./I **was about to** (or **just going to**) tell you. [2] •He's leaving for Paris in ten minutes, so he can't talk now./He **was leaving** ... so he **couldn't** talk then. [3] •He hopes you will be happy./He **hoped** you **would** be happy. [1] •We're to be there early./We **were to be** there early. [7]
See also **about to**, **shall**, **will**, CONDITION, TENSE, TIME.
For more details see CEG 5.6.

G

game
noun (= amusement, usually competitive) •They have played six **games** and won five. •Chess is not a **game** for babies. •Let's have a **game** of cards. •Don't get so serious about it; it's only a **game**.

gather
verb
A (= collect) transitive •**Gather** [up] all these toys and put them away, please.
intransitive •A crowd **gathered** to watch the fight.
B (= understand) •I **gather** [that] something has gone wrong. (I have been told, it appears) •What do you **gather** from this information? (What does it mean to you?) •You're a friend of his, I **gather**? (I suppose, from what has been said or shown)

gear
noun
A non-countable (= equipment, clothing) •Do you really need all that fishing **gear**? •I like your **gear** informal
B countable/non-countable (= mechanism for transferring/changing engine-power) •Start the car in bottom **gear**. •His bicycle has six **gears**. •Everything seemed out of **gear**. (disconnected, not working properly)
verb
+ *to* (= connect closely, relate) •Supply must be **geared** to demand.

general
adjective (≠ particular, = concerning all) •Public transport is a matter of **general** interest. •Leave out the details and just give me a **general** idea.

generally
adverb (= usually, in general) •Do you **generally** go to bed with your socks on?

generalise
verb (= make a general statement) •It is difficult to **generalise** about

genitive

the people who live there; they are so varied that **generalisations** are not helpful.

genitive

The genitive **'s** or **s'** or **'** shows possession, relationships, qualities etc. ● 'Who is that?' 'Sophie**'s** boyfriend. They've borrowed his parents' car.' ● 'Whose is that car? Is it Sophie**'s**?' 'No, it's her boyfriend**'s** parents'.'

of + genitive ●Are you a friend of Sophie**'s**? (one of her friends) ●I read it in a book of **yours**. (one of your books)

See also **of**, APOSTROPHE, NOUNS (used as adjectives), POSSESSION. For more details see CEG 2.23.

gerund

A gerund is a verbal noun. That is, a word ending in *-ing*, like a present participle, but used as a noun in a sentence. The words in **bold** in the following examples are gerunds ●**Smoking** is bad for you. ●I like **helping** you. ●I'm tired of **waiting**. ●I don't mind his **being** late. (his lateness)

Modern grammar books often use the term *-ing form* instead of **gerund**. So for more details see also -ING.

get

verb irregular, **got**, **got** or AmE **got**, **gotten**. (Five main meanings: A obtain, receive, acquire; B become — a suggestion of change; C cause to change/become; D with *have* possession; E with *have* + *got* + *to* + *infinitive* — obligation etc)

A *transitive* (= obtain, receive, acquire) ●Can you **get** a lettuce for me? ●I haven't **got** your letter yet.

❖ *in idioms* (A) ●I didn't **get the joke**. (understand) ●He'll **get you in the end**. (He'll catch you, have revenge on you)

B + *adjective*/ + *infinitive* + *participle*/ + *preposition*/ + *adverb* (= become) ●You'll **get** fat if you eat so much. ●Let's **get to work** on this problem. ●I can't **get moving**. ●How did it **get lost**? ●**Get off** the bus near the museum. ●When did they **get back** from America?

❖ *in idioms* (B) ●**Get a move on**! We're late. (hurry) informal ●I hope you **get well/better** soon. (recover from illness) ●They're **getting ready** to leave. (preparing) ●When will they **get there**? (arrive) ●He worked hard but **got nowhere**. (failed) ●Although he has a bad leg, he **gets about/[a]round** quite a lot. (travels, moves) ●A good lecturer can **get** his message **across** to the audience. (communicate) ●You must study if you want to **get ahead**. (succeed) ●How is your work **getting along**? (progressing) ●At last I **got around to** writing the letter. (found time to do it) ●If you leave food on the table, the cat will **get at** it. (reach, attack) ●I don't know what you're **getting at**. (what you mean, what you are implying) ●Sophie is sorry she couldn't come; she couldn't **get away**. (from work etc) ●That's the truth; you can't **get away from it**. (deny, ignore) ●I know you're not paying your taxes but you won't **get away with** it. (succeed in cheating, escape unpunished) ●What time will you **get back**? (return) ●He was standing in the doorway so that I couldn't **get by**. (pass) ●Silly dog! **Get down**! (Don't jump up) ●Now we can **get down to** work. (concentrate, begin serious work) ●He doesn't **get in** till 7.15. (arrive) ●There was a long queue but we **got in** [or **into**] the cinema (etc). ●He opened the door of the taxi and she **got in**. (entered, went inside) ●You'll **get into trouble** if you hit a policeman. (find yourself in difficulty) ●We have to **get off** early. (leave, be off) ●She **got off** her horse to open the gate. (dismounted, descended from) ●Tell him where he **gets off**. (Tell him to behave properly, speak

60

firmly to him.) informal •How is he **getting on** in his new job? (progressing, getting along) •He's **getting on in years.** (rather old) •She and I **get on** very well but I don't **get on with** her husband. (have a friendly relationship) •Please **get on with** your work! (continue) •Shut the door so that the dog can't **get out.** (escape, leave) •I don't want to go to this meeting but I can't **get out of** it. (avoid) •Has he **got over** his illness now? (recovered from it) •I **can't get over** her winning first prize. (I'm very much surprised at it) •This carpet is worn out; let's **get rid of** it and buy a new one. (dispose of, throw away) •It's easy to **get through** to New York. (on the telephone). •He **got through** all his money in a week and now he's broke. (finished, used up) •I don't **get up** early on Sundays. (rise) •What is he **getting up to** now? (doing, with the suggestion that it is something wrong or silly)
C + object + adjective/ + infinitive/ + participle/ + preposition/ + adverb (= cause to change, become) Most of the patterns and idioms listed already can include a direct object, eg •**get** the lid off •**get** your money back •**get** the dinner ready •**get** the harvest in •**get** your clothes on. •How can I **get** this pan clean? •We couldn't **get** the fire going. •I **got** him to lend me the money. (persuaded) •**Get** all this rubbish out of the way!
❖ **in idioms** (C) •Will you **get these shoes mended**? (Take them to a shoe-mender, similar to *have + object + past participle*) •Don't try to do it yourself: **get it done by** an expert. (pay for the service) •**Get this message down.** (write, record it) •The weather is **getting me down.** (It depresses me) •He talked so much, I couldn't **get a word in** [**edgeways**]. (say anything, by interrupting) •I don't want to **get you into trouble.** (cause

problems for you) •Please **get this into your head.** (understand, remember this) informal •Can you **get this letter off** today? (send) •I'll be glad to **get this** difficult operation **over with.** (to have it finished, at an end)
D *have + got* (=possess) •'Have you **got** a stamp?' 'No I haven't **got** any. Sophie's **got** some.' 'How many has she **got?'**
E *have + got + to + infinitive* (=must) •I've **got** to leave early. •Have they **got** to pay for it? •She hasn't **got** to go yet.
The word **got** can be omitted to make the language more formal, especially in positive statements •She has some stamps. •I have to leave early. Formal writers try to avoid using get/got too much, but in speech and informal writing, expressions using get/got are natural and acceptable.
See also **become, have, must.**

give /gɪv/
verb irregular, **gave,** /geɪv/ **given**
A (≠ take, = pass something to) + *1 object* •He **gave** all his money (away).
+ *2 objects* •He **gave** the piano to his sister. •He **gave** his sister the piano. •He **gave** it [to] her. •He **gave** her it.
in passive: •His sister was **given** the piano. •The piano was **given** to his sister.
B (= allow) •**Give** me an opportunity to help!
❖ **in idioms** •This is a secret; don't **give it away.** (reveal it) •She begged and begged until he **gave way.** (relented, agreed, gave in) •Don't stand on the ice; it will **give way.** (break) •He was too strong for me to fight; I had to **give in (to him).** (surrender, yield) •Please **give out** the books, one to each child. (distribute) •Oh dear! Our supply of sugar has **given out.** (come to an end — we have run out of sugar.) •He is trying to **give up** smoking. (stop) •I **give up.** What's the answer? (I can't guess

glad

it.) •I know it's hard but **don't give up!** (keep trying) •In a marriage, there must be **give and take**. (flexibility, willingness to yield) •**Given the chance**, I should do it again. (If I had the chance) •The exam must be done in **a given time**. (certain, specified)

glad
adjective (≠ sorry, = pleased) •I'm very **glad** to hear your good news. •Are you **glad** about his success? •I'm **glad** you're coming tomorrow. •I'd be **glad** to help you if I could.

gladly
adverb •She **gladly** accepted his offer of help. •'Will you do it?' 'Yes, **gladly**.' (willingly) polite

go /gəʊ/
verb irregular, **went, gone**; also **been**

A (≠ come, = leave) •Please stay, don't **go**. •He's **gone** to Sweden. (He's there now) •He's **been** to Sweden. (He has come back; he knows what Sweden is like.)
B (= move, work, be in action) •At first the train **went** very fast; then it stopped and wouldn't **go**.
C + -ing (= do an action) •Can we **go** shopping/swimming/riding?
D (= belong, have a usual place) •Where do these papers **go**?
E (= become/get) •Her skin **went** brown in the sun. •I'll **go** crazy if you don't turn that radio off. •The milk's **gone** off (sour); the meat's **gone** bad; the bread's **gone** stale.
F (= disappear [to]) •Where has all the money **gone**?
G (= progress) •'How did the party **go**?' 'It **went** well.'

going to
form of future (see FUTURE 2.) •She's **going to** pay me on Friday. •She was **going to** pay me on Friday, but she didn't. •'I hope she pays you on Monday.' 'Yes, she's **going to**.'

❖ **in idioms** •This little bit of butter won't **go far** among six people. (be enough) •This old carpet **must/has to/can go**. (be thrown away, got rid of. •**Anything goes**. (People can do what they like.) informal •Of course we shall help; that **goes without saying**. (That is taken for granted.) •The bees **went 'zzzzz'**. (they buzzed) •Her hat doesn't **go with** her dress. (look right, match or harmonise) •**Let yourself go!** (Relax) •**Don't let yourself go!** (Don't lose control). •She isn't well but she **keeps going**. (continues to work etc) •It's quite cheap, **as things go** nowadays. (compared with other present day prices) •Your work is good **as far as it goes**, but it is not complete. (within limits) •He called her a fool. That was **going too far**. (beyond the limits allowed) •Is there **any more food going**? (available or being offered) •I knew it **from the word go**. (from the very beginning) •**Go and buy** some more stamps. (go in order to buy) informal. See **and**. •I can't run fast but I'll **have a go**. (make an attempt, try) informal •You're always **on the go**. (active, busy) informal •How do you **go about** making a paper balloon? (tackle, undertake a job) •It **goes against** my principles to accept money for hospitality. (be opposed to) •We're all listening; **go ahead**. (begin, continue) •My headache **went away** when I took an aspirin. (left, vanished) •Let's **go back** to the beginning. (return, in space or time or line of argument) •He won't **go back on** his promise. (break it) •The years **went by**. (passed) •You can't **go by** what he says; he often makes mistakes. (judge by) •The ship **went down** in a storm. (sank) •His remarks did not **go down well with** the audience. (They did not approve) •When I criticised him, he **went for** me. (attacked) •You must work harder and that **goes for** everybody. (applies to) •Do you **go (in) for** outdoor sports? (enjoy, practise, make a habit of) •We must **go into** this matter carefully. (examine it in detail) •Suddenly the

grand

lights **went off/out.** ●The bomb **went off** as he got into the car. (exploded) ●How did the meeting **go off**? (Was it a success or a failure?) ●**What's going on** here? (happening) ●I'm sorry, but don't **go on about** it! (grumble, nag, complain) ●Please **go on.** (continue, after an interruption) ●Here's some money **to be going on with**; I'll give you some more soon. (to use for the moment, temporarily) ●You can't speak to him; he's **gone out.** (left the building) ●They don't **go out** much. (They stay at home, amuse themselves.) ●The fire's **gone out.** (stopped burning) ●She's been **going out with** him for two years. (She has been his girl friend) ●Can we **go over** the factory? (visit and examine) ●Could we **go over** that paragraph once more? (re-examine) ●There aren't enough books to **go round**; some of you must share. (supply everybody) ●The new plans have **gone through.** (been accepted, made official) ●She has **been through/gone through** a lot of pain. (suffered) ●You promised to do it and now you must **go through with** it. (keep your promise, finish the job) ●She **goes to a lot of trouble/expense/great lengths** to make it perfect. (She spends time/money/energy) ●At last he **went to sleep.** (slept) ●We don't want to **go to war.** (fight) ●The carpet and curtains **go together** well. (harmonise, go with each other) ●His business **went under** when he started borrowing too much. (sank, failed) ●Prices have **gone up** again. (risen) ●Your pink dress **goes with** your eyes! (matches, looks right with) ●If there's no coffee, you **go without.** (don't drink any, do without)

good
 adjective **better, best** (≠ **bad**) ●Read this; it's a **good** book. ●My neighbours were very **good** to me when I was ill. (kind, helpful) ●The children were very **good** and gave us no trouble. (well-behaved) ●That sounds like a **good** idea. (useful) ●Eggs are **good** for you. (beneficial) ●She's **good** at drawing. (skilful)
 Better and **best** are both *adjectives* and *adverbs* ●He speaks **better** English than you. ●He speaks English **better** than you do. ●This is the **best** room. ●It's the **best** designed.
 But **good** is an adjective only; use **well** as the adverb ●He speaks **good** English. ●He speaks English **well.** ●This is a **good** room. ●It's **well**-designed.
❖ *in compounds* ●**good**-looking (attractive) ●**good**-natured (kind) ●**good** sense (common sense)
❖ *in idioms* ●He lives **a good distance** away. (quite large, considerable) ●**A good few** people arrived. (quite a lot of) ●There was **a good deal** of laughter. (quite a lot) ●Have **a good look.** (look carefully) ●'Did he say no?' 'Not exactly but **as good as.**' (He meant no) ●Are you ready? **Good!** (I'm glad) ●Please get here **in good time.** (early) ●He started with nothing and **made good.** (became successful, rich) ●Take the medicine; it's **for your own good.** (It is to benefit you.) ●A holiday would **do her good.** (make her healthier, happier) ●He said he was going **for good** but I bet he comes back. (for ever, permanently) ●It's **no good/not much good** switching it on — there's no electricity. (useless) ●Is this box **any good** to you or shall I throw it away? (useful, of any use) ●**What's the good of trying?** I never succeed. (It's no use trying)

got
 See **get, have (got).**

grand
 adjective
 A (= magnificent) ●What a **grand** occasion! There were speeches and crowds and people in fine clothes.
 B (= [self-]important) ●The President's wife looked particularly **grand** in purple silk and diamonds.

63

grant

❖ *in compounds* (family relationships, two generations apart)
● **grand**parents (parents of parents) ●One has two **grand**fathers and two **grand**mothers. ●**grand**children (children of children). ●One may have any number of **grand**sons and **grand**daughters.

grant
verb (=give, admit) ●I **grant** you that it sounds reasonable, but there are mistakes in it. (I admit) ●**Granted**, but they are not important. (Yes but)
❖ *idiom* ●Don't take his kindness/him for granted. (accept it without question or without gratitude)

grateful /'greɪtfʊl/
adjective (=feeling thankful) ●I am **grateful** to you for your help. ●We should be **grateful** if you would let us know as soon as possible.

gratitude
noun (=thankfulness, gratefulness) ●He asked me to express his **gratitude** to all the people who have supported him.

great /greɪt/
adjective
A (=large, important) used instead of *big* with non-countable words, similar in meaning to *a lot of* ●He made a **great** mistake/change/improvement. ●She spoke with **great** care/sorrow/difficulty/enthusiasm/kindness/candour.
+ *other adjectives of size* ●It's a **great** big river. ●What a **great** fat cat! ●Don't carry that **great** heavy case.
B (=excellent) ●He was the **greatest** thinker of the century. ●No **greater** philosopher existed.

greatly
adverb (=very, much) ●I was **greatly** surprised to see him. ●We weren't **greatly** interested in it.

❖ *in compounds* (family relationships, two or three generations apart)
●My parents' uncles and aunts are my **great**-uncles and **great**-aunts. My parents' grandparents are my **great**-grandparents. My brother and I are their **great**-grandchildren; a **great**-grandson and a **great**-granddaughter.
❖ *in idioms* ●You can come? **Great!** (Good!) informal ●She's a **great** talker/letter-writer/card player. (She talks/writes/players cards a lot [often] or well — an ambiguity) ●He lost a great deal of money/a great many friends. (a lot of/ a good deal/ a good many)

ground
noun
A (=surface of earth, piece of land, outdoors — for indoors, use *floor*) ●We had a picnic, sitting on the **ground**.
B (=base, foundation) ●What **ground[s]** do you have for thinking this? ●Let's go over the **ground** again.
past participle of verb **to grind**, **ground, ground** (=turn to powder) ●Have you **ground** the coffee-beans?
❖ *in idioms* ●We're on common ground. (We agree, share the same experience.) ●I can't cover the ground in a five-minute talk. (explain the main points) ●The plan immediately fell to the ground. (failed) ●I was surprised that it ever got off the ground. (made a successful start) ●I know you're in love but keep your feet on the ground. (remain practical) ●Don't give in; stand/hold your ground. (defend your position) ●Although we gained ground here, we lost ground there. (succeeded, pushed forward, failed, retreated)

grow /grəʊ/
verb irregular, **grew, grown**, transitive and intransitive
A (=develop, get bigger) ●Tomatoes don't **grow** well here, so we're **growing** potatoes instead. ●The village **grew** into a town.
B (=become) ●The room has **grown** dark. ●Soon it will **grow** cold. ●The music **grew** quieter.

growth
noun
A (=development) We're pleased about the **growth** of our company.

B (= unhealthy lump in the body) •There is a small **growth**, which might be cancer.
❖ *in idioms* •Children often bite their finger nails; but they usually **grow out of** the habit. (abandon it naturally as they get older) •Children seem to **grow up** so quickly these days! •What does your daughter want to be when she's [a] **grown up**? (become [an] adult)

guess /ges/
verb
A (= make a judgement without knowing the facts) •Can you **guess** what I've bought for your birthday? •He **guessed** what I was thinking about.
B (= suppose) especially AmE •I **guess** I've got to wait for her.
noun (= attempt to guess, opinion not fact) •I can only make a wild **guess**. •My **guess** is that he'll win the election.
❖ *in idioms* •What happens next is **anybody's guess**. (completely unknown) •She's **keeping us guessing**. (not telling us) •Most of these economic reports are **only guess-work**. (based on inadequate information).

H

had
See **have, had better**.

hair /heə*/
noun countable (hairs grow on heads) •Waiter, there is a **hair** on this plate!
non-countable (= the whole covering formed by separate hairs) •His **hair** is long; he ought to have it cut.

half (½) /ha:f/
noun plural **halves** •The film lasts an hour and a **half**. (1½ hours) •Two and two **halves** to London. (2 adult and 2 children's tickets)
pronoun/predeterminer •Only **half** of them are here. •I'll be ready in **half** a minute. •I'd like **half** a dozen eggs. (6) •We have only **half** as many as you asked for.

adverb (= partly) •This steak is **half**-cooked. •I can **half** believe it.
❖ *in compounds* •**half**-brother (related through one parent) •**half**-hearted (not really interested) •**half**-term •**half**-time (middle of football match) •**half**way (at the midpoint) •**half**wit (fool)
❖ *in idioms* •He doesn't do things **by halves**; he does them properly. (in an incomplete way) •We can buy that if we **go halves**. (share the cost) •Deciding what to take is **half the battle**. (the most difficult part) •**It isn't half** cold! (It's very cold) informal. •Mine **isn't half** as nice as yours. (Yours is much nicer than mine.)

hand
noun (= part of body, part of clock, worker) •My **hands** are cold because I've lost my gloves. •Does your watch have a second **hand**? •The factory has no jobs for machine **hands**.
verb (= give, pass by hand) •Would you **hand** me that pen, please?

handy
adjective (= useful, near) •There is a grocer's shop which is quite **handy**.
❖ *in compounds* •**hand**bag (American *purse*) •**hand**book (short book containing essential information) •**hand**ful (small number, amount) •**hand** luggage (light bags etc which can be carried) •**hand**-out (food etc given free, or information on a printed paper) •**handy**man (workman doing practical jobs in houses) •heavy-**handed** (clumsy, interfering) •left-**hand**ed (tending to use the left hand more than the right)
❖ *in idioms* •Ask Bill; he's **an old hand**. (someone with lots of experience) •Will you **give/lend me a hand** with this heavy box? (help) •This problem is **getting out of hand**. (out of control) •She has **first hand knowledge** of the subject. (direct experience) •He heard it/bought it **second hand**.

hand

65

hang

(He was not the first hearer/owner.) •All the work is done **by hand.** (not by machine) •The house often **changed hands.** (had different owners) •A pilot must practise flying, to **keep his hand in.** (to maintain his skill) informal •**I gave him a free hand.** (I said he could do things in his own way.) •The government **has the upper hand.** (is the stronger of the two opponents) •Did you **have a hand in** this arrangement? (Did you participate in making it?) •**My hands are full.** (I'm very busy.) •We have a little money **in hand.** (ready for use, available, spare) •I leave you **in Sophie's good hands.** (in her care) •My house is **on the left [hand] side.** •A summer holiday would be lovely. **On the other hand,** a spring holiday would be much cheaper. (But, a point on the other side of an argument) •The whole problem is **out of my hands.** (no longer my responsibility) •She has **a lot on her hands.** (great responsibilities, a lot of work) •That child must be **taken in hand.** (disciplined, brought under control) •Let's **shake hands on it.** (agree on a bargain, arrangement) •She **handed round** chocolates with the coffee. (distributed) •The custom has been **handed down** by many generations. (passed on) •We shall **hand it on** to our children. •The stolen money was **handed over** to the police. (given into their control) •**Hands off!** (Don't touch.) •**Hands up** or I shoot! (Put your hands above your head)

hang

verb irregular, **hung, hung**
A (=suspend) •I've **hung** the washing out to dry •Her hair was **hanging** over her face. (suspended, loose)
B regular, **hanged, hanged** (=execute, kill by hanging) •The thief was **hanged** in the market place.
❖ *in idioms* •If you **hang on,** I'll call him. (wait, especially to telephone callers, more formal 'Hold the line') •The boys have no work so they just **hang about/around** in the streets. (waste time, do nothing) informal. •I can't **get the hang of it.** (knack, skill to make something work) •Important people are always followed by **hangers-on.** (parasites) •Please don't **hang up [on me].** (end a telephone conversation by replacing the receiver) •That girl has too many **hang-ups.** (things that make her worried or irrational)

happen

verb (=occur, take place, by accident, chance) •What will **happen** if we miss the plane? •We **happened** to be present when the Queen drove in. •Do you **happen** to know where he is? •The brakes failed. Has that ever **happened** to you?
❖ *idiom* •I saw him only yesterday, **as it happens.** (by chance, surprisingly)

happy

adjective (≠sad, =feeling pleased, lucky, suitable) •He's very **happy** with his new toys. •It was a **happy** day for her when she got that job! •She was **unhappy** to leave it. •Red is not a **happy** choice of colour to wear with your hair.
happily/unhappily
adverbs often sentence adverbs (=fortunately/unfortunately) •**Unhappily,** the best man could not find the wedding ring. **Happily,** he found it in time.
❖ *in idioms* •**Happy** Birthday! •**Happy** New Year! •She's rather **happy-go-lucky.** (careless)

hard

adjective (≠soft, ≠easy, =firm, difficult) •This bed is very **hard** and uncomfortable. •Some languages are **harder** to learn than others.
adverb (=energetically, vigorously) •They are working **hard** to finish the job. •Is she trying **hard** enough? •He hit me **hard** across the face.

❖ *in idioms* •Don't be too **hard on him**; he meant no harm. (strict, unkind) •What **hard luck**, to miss the last train! (misfortune) •They're too **hard up** to pay the bill. (poor) •He's a **hard-hearted** man, treating the poor woman like that! (cruel, heartless) •It was **raining hard** when he told her to go. (heavily) •He learnt his business **the hard way**. (by practical experience) •He feels he's **hard done by**. (badly-treated) •What he needs is **hard cash**, not promises. (ready money) •We were competing but there were **no hard feelings**. (no enmity) •You have to be **hard-headed** in business. (practical and thorough) •She's a bit **hard of hearing**. (a bit deaf) •Leather shoes are more **hard-wearing** than plastic ones. (long-lasting)

hardly
adverb
A (= scarcely, almost not, with difficulty, barely) •I've only just met him, so I **hardly** know him. •It was so dark that I could **hardly** find the path. •He can **hardly** expect me to start work at 6 am! •**Hardly** anyone likes him. (almost nobody)
B (= only just, only rarely) •We had **hardly** started dancing when the music stopped. •I've **hardly** ever eaten caviar. •She's got **hardly** enough money for her bus fare. •He doesn't work hard; in fact, he **hardly** works at all.

harm
noun non-countable (= damage) •It will do no **harm** if he takes some exercise. •He didn't mean any **harm** by his remark. (It was not malicious)
verb (= hurt, damage) •A little cold water won't **harm** you.

harmful
adjective (= dangerous, damaging) •These chemicals are **harmful** to the skin.

harmless
adjective (= safe, not dangerous) •Some snakes are poisonous and some are completely **harmless**.
❖ *in idioms* •Let's put this fragile glass **out of harm's way**. (somewhere safe) •**What harm can it do** to stay? (It is OK, safe)

hate
verb transitive, not used in progressive (≠ love, = dislike strongly) •'Do you like cheese?' 'No, I **hate** it.'
+ *-ing* •I **hate** waiting for buses.
+ *object* + *-ing* •She **hates** me borrowing her clothes.
+ *infinitive* (often = be sorry to) •I **hate** to say this, but . . . •He would **hate** to admit his real feeling.
noun (= hatred, feeling of hate) •You can see the **hate** in her eyes.
See also **like, love**.

have
verb irregular, **had, had**
1 main auxiliary, used to make perfect tenses; 2 as an ordinary verb with three main meanings (= A possess; B = take; C with *to* = must)
FORMS
(a) *present* **I, you, we, they have/ he, she, it has**
(b) *past* **had**
  These positive forms are used when the verb is either an auxiliary or an ordinary verb. The ordinary verb makes negatives and questions with *do*:
I, you, they do[n't]/[not] have
he, she, it does[n't]/[not] have
Do[n't] I, they, you, we have?
I, you, he, she, it, we, they did[n't]/ [not] have
Did I, you, he, she, it, we, they have?
  The auxiliary verb makes negatives and questions with *not* and inversion:
I, you, we, they have[n't]/[not]
he, she, it has[n't]/[not]
Have I, you, we, they? Has he, she, it?
I, you, he she, it, we they had[n't]/ [not]
Had I, you, he, she, it, we, they?

have

1 As an auxiliary, *have* is used to make all the following tenses, given here with both active and passive examples where possible:
(a) *present perfect: have + past participle* •She **has** opened the door. It **has** been opened. (Now it's open) •**Has** she opened it? **Has** it been opened? •She **hasn't** opened it. It **hasn't** been opened.
(b) *present perfect progressive/continuous: have + been + present participle* •She **has** been working since breakfast. (Now she is tired) •**Has** she been working long? •She **hasn't** been working all that time. No passive forms in normal English.
(c) *past perfect: had + past participle* •We **had** already washed the clothes. They **had** already been washed. (so we didn't wash them again) •**Had** she dried them? Had they been dried? •She **hadn't** ironed them. They **hadn't** been ironed.
(d) *past perfect progressive: had + been + present participle* •They **had** been waiting outside for two hours. (so they were cold) •**Had** they been waiting all that time? •They **hadn't** been waiting for more than an hour. No passive forms in normal English.
(e) *future perfect: will + have + past participle* •We shall **have** written the report by six o'clock. The report will **have** been written by six o'clock.
(f) *future perfect progressive: will + have + been + present participle* •On Monday they will **have** been waiting a whole year. No passive forms.

Used as an auxiliary, the verb **have** is frequently contracted. Note that *He's, She's, It's* and *Sophie's* can represent both *is* and *has* •She's coming home. (is) •She's come home. (has) •He's being taught how to do it. (is) •He's been taught how to do it. (has) •Did you say 'Sophie's won' or 'Sophie's one'? (*has* or *is*)

2 As an ordinary verb
A (= possess) **Have** used without *got* is possible but rather formal. •He **has** a car but **has** he a boat? •He **hasn't** enough time. Ordinary conversational English includes **got** •He's **got** a car but **has** he **got** a boat? •He **hasn't got** enough time. Americans especially often use the **do** forms for ordinary possessions •**Does** he **have** a boat? •He **doesn't have** enough time. Older English people use the **do** forms for habitual or repeated possession •**Do** they always **have** coffee in the house? • I **didn't have** such nice teachers as you.
B (= take) Always the ordinary **do** forms without *got* •He **doesn't have** a bath every morning. •'Did you **have** a good time last night?' 'Yes, we did. We **had** a lot of fun.' •'Let's **have** a drink. What are you **having?**' 'I'll **have** a tomato juice.' •She **didn't have** piano lessons till she was twenty. •**Do** you **have** milk in your tea? **Don't** you **have** sugar?
C with *to* (= must) Possible with both ordinary and *do* forms with **got** •He **has** to pay but you **don't have** to/you **haven't got** to pay. American English prefers the **do** form for habitual or repeated obligation •**Do** you **have** to be there at eight every day?/**Have** you **got** to be there at eight tomorrow?

Must and **have to** are almost interchangeable expressions of obligation, though where there is a possible distinction between external and internal obligation, *must* is usually chosen for internal obligation •I must take some exercise. (I feel the need)/I **have to** take exercise. (the doctor says it is necessary)

The alternative expressions are as follows:
(a) for obligation *present/future* •He must go. •He has to go./He will have to go. •He's got to go. •He is to go. *past* •He had to go. •He'd got to go. •He was to go. (suggests 'but he didn't')

(b) for *'not necessary' present/future* •He needn't go./He won't need to go. •He doesn't need to go. •He hasn't got to go. •He won't have to go. •He doesn't have to go.
past •He didn't have to go. •He hadn't got to go. •He didn't need to go. •He needn't have gone. ('but he went')
(c) for *'prohibited, not allowed' present/future* •He must not go. •He is not [allowed/permitted] to go. •He will not be allowed/permitted to go.
past •He wasn't [allowed/permitted] to go.
other structures
having + past participle
A to express past before past:
•**Having** stolen the money he ran away. (As soon as he had stolen it, he ran away.)
B to express cause: •**Having** read his book, I knew his opinion. (Since/As I had read his book, I knew) •Not **having** met him, I cannot tell you what he's like. (I can't tell you what he's like because I haven't met him.)
to have + past participle (perfect infinitive) •I'm sorry not **to have** told you. (that I didn't tell you)
•I'm happy **to have** been able to help. (that I have been able to)
•His leg seems **to have** been broken. (It seems that his leg has been broken.)
have + object + past participle
A (= have something done) to express arranging or paying for a service: •'Does she **have** her clothes made?' 'No, she makes them herself.' •I must **have** my hair cut soon. •'Have you **had** the car repaired yet?' 'I've **had** the plugs changed but I haven't **had** the engine tuned.'
B simply to cause something to be done to somebody: •I'll **have** you put in prison for this!
C with present participle (= to cause or refuse to accept a situation) •They soon **had** us doing exercises. (got us doing exercises)
•I won't **have** him opening my letters.
❖ *in collocations* •**have** a word with (speak to)/a lie down (rest)/a bath (wash oneself in a bath)/a swim (go swimming) a go/a try (attempt)/a baby (give birth to)/your own way (get what you want)/something in mind (think of, remember)
❖ *in idioms* •I **have** it!/I've got it! (I know the answer) •**Have a drink?** (an offer) •**What will you have?**/**What are you having?** (Choose your drink) •We **had some friends in** for dinner. (invited them as guests) •She's **got her new hat on.** (She's wearing it) •He **hadn't got anything on.** (He was naked or possibly he had no previous engagements; he was free) •I must **have it out with** her and settle the matter. (discuss it fully and openly) •**He's had it!** (he has no hope, he's finished) informal •**You'd better** go home. (It would be better for you if you went home) often a threat •**What had we better/best do** now? (What is our best course of action?) •**I've had enough** [of this]. (Let's stop, leave, go etc)
See also **better, must,** ASPECT, PERFECT, TENSE.
For more details see CEG 4.13.

he

pronoun 3rd person singular, subject, masculine. •A male person is referred to as *he*. An animal may be *it* or *he/she*, depending on whether the speaker thinks of him, her or it as having a personality or not.
He can also be used to mean *he* or *she*. •If somebody arrives late, **he** should sit at the back. Some people see this as unfair to females and use *they* instead or begin the sentence with *you* or *one*. •If **you** arrive/**one** arrives late **you/one** should sit at the back.
It is polite to refer to oneself last in a series of pronouns •**He** and I can do it together. (but do not use *he* for objects — not *They saw he

69

head

and I, but ●They saw **him** and me.) ●Who's **he**? I've never seen **him** before.
But it is unnatural to say *That's he. The normal word in such emphatic positions is **him, her** etc. See also **her, him, his, one, she,** CONTRACTIONS, PRONOUNS.

head /hed/
noun (= part of body, brain, leader) ●This noise makes my **head** ache. ●He can't get it into his **head**. ●My father is the **head** of the family.
❖ *in idioms* (mainly figurative) ●Write your name **at the head of the list**. (top) ●Sit **at the head of the table**. (top) ●The restaurant bill will be about £20 **a head**. (per person) ●Do you have **a good head for** figures? (Are you good at arithmetic?) ●I was **shouting my head off** but nobody heard me. (very loudly) informal ●All this political detail is **over my head**. (beyond me, too difficult for me) ●Success **went to his head**. (made him proud) ●Try to **keep your head** when you're frightened. (stay calm) ●Don't **lose your head**. (panic) ●He's **off his head**. (mad) ●We **put our heads together** and thought of a plan. (co-operated, consulted) ●Let's **head for** home. (go towards home.)

hear /hɪə*/
verb irregular, **heard, heard** (= be aware of sound, get news) ●Could you speak louder? I can't **hear**. ●Have you **heard** the results yet? ●I **hear** from her occasionally. ●Nobody had **heard** of him until he won the prize. (He was unknown, not famous)
+ *object* + *-ing* ●I **heard** him starting the car. (he was in the process of starting it — not necessarily successful).
+ *object* + *infinitive* ●I **heard** him start the car. (completed process)
overhear
verb (= hear by accident) ●I wasn't listening but I **overheard** a woman talking to her friend.

hearing
noun (= sense by/distance at which one can hear) ●My **hearing** isn't perfect. (I'm a little deaf.) ●Don't say things like that in his **hearing**. (when he can hear you) See also **listen to**.

heart /ha:t/
noun
A (= part of the body which pumps blood) ●Don't frighten her; she has a weak **heart**.
B (= centre of feelings) ●She has a kind and generous **heart**.
C (= centre or most important part) ●Now we come to the **heart** of the problem.
❖ *in compounds* ●**heart**-ache (sorrow, misery) ●**heart** attack (sudden coronary thrombosis — heart not working properly) ●**heart**breaking (terribly disappointing) ●big-/warm-/kind-**hearted** (generous) ●cold-/hard-**heart**ed (cruel)
❖ *in idioms* ●Don't **lose heart**. (Don't be discouraged) ●**Take heart!** (Cheer up! Be encouraged) ●I **haven't (got) the heart to** tell him. (It would be cruel, so I don't want to) ●It will **break his heart** to leave this house. (make him very unhappy) ●She enjoys living in a town but she's a countrywoman **at heart**. (essentially) ●**My heart was in my mouth**. (I was very frightened.) ●**My heart was in my boots**. (I was very sad/worried) ●**Her heart is in the right place**. (She is kind) ●Try not to **take it to heart**. (to be deeply upset by it) ●She's **set her heart on** going to Africa. (she wants to go very much and is determined that she will) ●What a **heartless trick!** (cruel)

heavy /'hevɪ/
adjective (≠ light, = weighty, serious, sad, difficult, unusually large) ●That suitcase is too **heavy** to carry. ●There has been **heavy** fighting near the border. ●I'm a **heavy** sleeper, especially after a **heavy** day's work.

help
verb intransitive (= aid, assist, do

70

high

some of the work) ●Do the children **help?**
+ *object* ●Do they **help** you?
+ *object* + *infinitive* ●They **help** me (to) clean the house.
noun non-countable (= aid, assistance) ●The children are a great **help.** ●It's not much **help**, telling me I'm silly.

helpful
adjective (= willing to help) ●The receptionist was very **helpful;** she made the arrangements and took trouble to help us.

helpless
adjective (= unable to do things without help) ●When he was sick, he was as **helpless** as a new-born baby.

helping
noun (= portion of food) ●Please could I have another **helping** of ice cream?

❖ *in idioms* ●I **can't help laughing** when I think of her silly mistake. (I have to laugh) ●I'm sorry I'm late, but **I can't help it;** the bus didn't come. (It's not my fault) ●**Help!** (Please bring help. I'm in danger) ●Please **help yourself** to sugar/butter etc. (Take what you want, serve yourself.)

hence
adverb (for this reason) formal ●They keep the gold in here; **hence** the double locks.

her
pronoun 3rd person singular, object, feminine ●Where's Sophie? I want to speak to **her.** ●I haven't seen **her.**
Also emphatic ●That's **her!**
adjective possessive, determiner ●Sophie's sister is here but **her** brother couldn't come.
See also **herself, hers, she,** etc. PRONOUNS.

here
adverb (≠ there, = in this place) ●'Come **here** and sit by me.' 'No, I'll stay **here,** thank you.'
+ *verb* + *noun* ●**Here** comes the teacher. (I can see the teacher coming in this direction.)
+ *pronoun* + *verb* ●**Here** it is. (indicating something near)

❖ *in idioms* ●He left his belongings **here and there.** (scattered around) ●**Here's to** your happiness! (drinking a toast) ●**Here you are.** (offering, giving something) ●His age is **neither here nor there.** (It's irrelevant, not connected with the subject) ●**Look here,** that's my car. (Listen to me, pay attention to what I say)
See also **there.**

hers
pronoun possessive, 3rd person singular, feminine ●'Does that book belong to your sister?' 'No, it's not **hers,** it's mine.' ●Do you know Alice? I'm a friend of **hers.** (one of her friends) ●His books are here. **Hers** are over there on that shelf.

herself
pronoun reflexive, 3rd person singular, feminine ●She can please **herself.** (do what she likes) ●She considers **herself** better than other people.
Also emphatic ●She told me this **herself.** (She herself, not somebody else, said so)

❖ *in idioms* ●She's **by herself** today. (alone, on her own) ●She can do it **by herself.** (without help) ●She's **not herself** today. (in her usual healthy state)
See also **own, self,** PRONOUNS.

high /haɪ/
adjective (≠ low, used like *tall* but not for people or animals) ●'How **high** is that building?' 'It's about 100 metres high.' ●You need oxygen to climb the **highest** mountains.
adverb (after verb) ●Balloons can fly **high,** but aeroplanes fly **higher.**

highly
adverb especially before adjectives formed from verbs (= to a high degree) ●They were **highly** pleased by it.

height /haɪt/
noun (= extent upwards) ●The tower is 100 metres in **height.**

him

❖ *in compounds* ●at **high** speed (fast) ●**high** office (important position) ●**high**-brow (with intellectual tastes) ●**high** class (good quality, or of high social position) ●**High** Commission (-er) (like an embassy or ambassador, in a Commonwealth country) ●**high** life (the life of rich, fashionable people) ●**high**lights (most important parts) ●**high**-powered (forceful) ●**high** season (busiest, most expensive time for travel, hotels etc) ●**high** tide (the moment when the sea reaches furthest inland) ●**high**-priced (expensive)

❖ *in idioms* ●They searched **high and low**. (everywhere) ●It's **high time** he got married. (He ought to have married before now.)

him
pronoun 3rd person singular, object, masculine ●She agreed to marry **him**.
Also emphatic ●That's **him**!

himself
pronoun reflexive, 3rd person singular, masculine ●He has hurt **himself**. ●He feels sorry for **himself**.
Also emphatic ●The President **himself** signed the letter.

❖ *in idioms* ●He was **by himself**. (alone) ●He did it **by himself**. (without help) ●He **wasn't quite himself**. (not in his normal state)
See also **he, his, self,** PRONOUNS.

hire
verb
A (=pay for the use of something, usually for short periods, rent) ●Is it expensive to **hire** a car for a week? ●You needn't buy skis; you can **hire** them.
B (=sell the use of something, let) ●'Will you **hire** your boat to me for one day's fishing?' 'Sorry, I never **hire** it out.' ●Bicycles for **hire** here.
See also **let, rent.**

his
adjective possessive, determiner, masculine ●Anthony has left **his** money on the table. ●Each student must write **his** own notes.
pronoun prossessive, 3rd person singular, masculine ●That money isn't **his**; it's mine. ●Are these notes hers or **his**?
See also **he, her, him,** etc, PRONOUNS.

hit
verb irregular, **hit, hit**
A (=strike) ●The brakes didn't work and the car **hit** the wall.
B (=have a bad effect on) ●The high price of petrol is **hitting** drivers.
noun (=a stroke, action of hitting) ●It was a good **hit** right in the middle.

❖ *in idioms* ●He's **hit the nail on the head**. (He's quite right in what he says) ●That new play will be **a hit**. (success) ●I hoped they would be friends but they didn't **hit it off**. (get on well together) ●At last we **hit on** a good idea. (chanced to find) ●The arrangements were rather **hit-and-miss**. (casually planned, careless) ●Don't accept everything he says: **hit back**. (defend yourself — physically or in words)

hold
verb irregular, **held, held** (=keep, carry, contain, control) ●She was **holding** a baby in her arms and **holding** another child by the hand. ●**Hold** your head still while I take your photograph. ●The main cities are **held** by the enemy. ●How much water will the bath **hold**?
noun (=grip, control) ●Keep a **hold** on your wallet, in case there are thieves about.

❖ *in idioms* ●**Hold on!** (Wait a moment) ●Don't let the baby **get hold of** the matches. (find, handle) ●I'll make some bookshelves if I can **get hold of** some wood. (acquire) ●She seems to be a delicate little girl but she can **hold her own** against strong men. (defend her position, show herself capable) ●He behaved badly but we shan't **hold that against him**. (blame him for it, allow it to influence us against him) ●We must not **hold back**, we must go forward and attack. (be unwilling to do something) ●There isn't much petrol; I hope it **holds out** till we reach a petrol station. (lasts) ●The workmen refused the new pay offer and **held out for** more money. (demanded and waited for) ●I think they will **hold to** that decision. (stick to, keep to) ●The building work was **held up** by bad weather. (delayed) ●I hope there aren't any more **hold-ups**. (delays) ●Your argument doesn't **hold water**. (It is not valid, doesn't make sense)

holiday
noun
singular (= free time, fairly short — a day or two, longer if specified) ●Don't forget Monday is a **holiday**. ●He gets three weeks' **holiday** per year. ●She's on **holiday** this week, so don't ring her at the office.
plural ●Where are you going in the **holidays**? (long, eg school holidays)

home /həʊm/
noun (= house or place one lives in, comes from, base) ●She has lived in New York for several years but she still thinks of Florida as her real **home**.
adverb No preposition used before *home* in these expressions of movement ●We're going **home**. (not *to home) ●She left **home** when she was 18. ●What time does he come **home**? ●How often do you write **home**? ●Will he be **home** before you?
At used when there is no movement ●We'll be **at home** tonight. ●She has to stay **at home** all day.

homely
adjective (British English = simple; American English = not good-looking) ●We had a **homely** supper of bread and cheese. ●She's a pleasant girl, but **homely**.
❖ *in compounds* ●**home**made bread, clothes etc (made at home) ●**home**sick (wanting to be at home when abroad or away from home) ●**home**work (studies, preparation for school work done at home)
❖ *in idioms* ●The new arrivals soon felt **at home**. (comfortable, relaxed) ●**Make yourself at home**, please. (Behave freely, as if you were at home — a polite invitation to guests) ●Seeing the problem for myself really **brought it home to me**. (made me realise the facts, understand)
See also **house**.

hope
verb (= wish and expect)
+ *infinitive* ●He **hopes** to study in London.
+ *(that)* ●I **hope** (that) she likes chocolates.
+ *(that)* + *subject* + *negative verb* ●He **hopes** you won't forget. (not *He does not hope you will forget)
+ *so/not* ●'Will Anthony be there?' 'I **hope** so/I **hope** not.'
in the past perfect ●She had **hoped** to visit her sister but it was impossible. (suggests she was disappointed)
noun (= expectation) ●Do you have any **hopes** of success?

hopefully
adverb (= with hope) ●The children were looking **hopefully** at the box of biscuits.
sentence adverb (= I, we hope) ●**Hopefully**, he is no longer in danger.

hopeless
adjective (= without reason for hope) ●The case seems **hopeless**; we cannot win.
❖ *in idioms* ●This arrangement/recipe/repair doesn't look very good but we must **hope for the best**. (be optimistic) ●These old shoes are **past/beyond hope** (of repair); throw them away. (useless) ●I wrote to him **in the hope of** persuading him to lend me money. (hoping to persuade)

hot
adjective
A (≠ cold, = at a certain temperature) ●'How **hot** is the

73

water?' 'It's not **hot** enough to make tea.'
B (of food = spicy, peppery) ●Do you like really **hot** curry?
C (of temper = angry) ●She's very **hot**-tempered; don't annoy her.
❖ *in idioms* ●She looks good but her arithmetic is **not too hot**. (She is bad at arithmetic.) ●His speech was all **hot air**. (meaningless) ●They are considered **hot-blooded** people. (passionate, with strong feelings) ●I fear war may start in one of the **hot spots**. (places troubled by unrest) ●The fighting was **hotting up**. (getting more intense, exciting) ●I hope you don't **get into hot water** for doing this. (suffer, get punished)
See also **cold**.

hour /ˈaʊə*/
noun (= 60 minutes) ●'How long were you waiting?' 'An **hour** or maybe an **hour** and a half.' ●I saw him an **hour** ago. ●I haven't seen him for **hours**. (a long time) ●The trains go on the **hour**. (at exactly two o'clock, three o'clock etc.) ●We leave at two hundred **hours**. (0200)
❖ *in idioms* ●Doctors must be ready to work **at all hours**. (at any time) ●She often had to work **out of hours/after hours**. (at times not normally part of a working day)

house
noun (= building for living in) ●They have put their own furniture in the **house** and it seems more like home.
verb (= provide accommodation, storage) ●It will be difficult to **house** all the family/equipment.
❖ *in compounds* ●**house** agent (someone who arranges sales of houses) ●**household** (all the people in one house) ●**house**keeping money (money for regular household expenses) ●**house**-proud (very clean and tidy, keen on housework) ●**house**wife (woman who looks after house, family) ●**house**work (cleaning, other domestic work)
❖ *in idioms* ●He earns the money and she **keeps house** for him. (looks after domestic matters) ●Drinks are **on the house**. (provided free by the hotel etc)

how
adverb
A (= in what way) ●I don't know **how** to make pancakes. ●**How** did you get here? By car? ●**How** will they know what it is?
B (= to what degree) questions + *adjective/adverb* + *inverted verb* ●**How** long will it take? ●**How** much does it cost? ●**How** well do you know the chairman?
C indirect questions — no inversion ●She doesn't know **how** long it will take ●I wondered **how** old he was. ●He asked me **how** heavy I was.
D exclamations + *adjective* + *subject* + *verb* ●**How** beautiful she is! ●**How** very unkind he can be!
+ *subject* + *verb* (usually = how much) ●**How** he worked! ●**How** she worried!
+ *adjective/adverb* ●**How** wonderful! ●**How** slowly [time passed]!
See also WHAT and compare '**How** nice she is!'/'What a nice girl she is!'
❖ *in idioms* ●**How do you do?** (formal greeting on being introduced. Answer, 'How do you do?') ●**How are you?** (enquiry about health, general well-being. Answer, 'Very well, thank you. And how are you?' ●**How are you getting on?** (enquiry about progress in job etc) ●**How do you like your coffee?** (Black or white? With sugar or without?) ●**How is your boy friend?** (Is he well? an enquiry about health. Not the same as 'What is your boy friend like?' — a request for a description) ●**How's life?** ●**How's** the weather? ●**How's** your omelette? ●**How was** the party last night? (All asking for a personal reaction more than an exact description) ●**How can I ever**

idea

thank you? (Thank you very, very much) ●**How about** going to the pictures? (What about ... a suggestion — let's go) ●**How on earth** can you afford it? (How ever; it is very surprising that you can afford it) ●'Don't do it like that!' '**How else** can I do it?' (in what other way?)
See also **ever, however, what.**

however
adverb (= in whatever way, no matter how, it makes no difference how) ●**However** she does her hair, it looks awful. ●I'll never understand this, **however** hard I try.
sentence adverb (= nevertheless) ●He said he was certain. **However,** he was wrong. ●'Goodbye' he said. The car, **however,** would not move. ●He's an idiot. I can't help liking him, **however.** (= though)
See also **ever, whatever, whoever,** etc, CONCESSION.

hurry
verb
A intransitive (= move [too] quickly) ●We must **hurry** if we want to catch the bus, so please **hurry** up.
B transitive (= make someone/ something move quickly) ●The stewardess **hurried** the passengers onto the plane.
noun (= haste) ●Drive slowly; there's no **hurry** — we're not late. ●I can't talk about it now; I'm in a **hurry.**
❖ *in idioms* ●I shan't forget it **in a hurry.** (I'll always remember it) informal ●He's **in no hurry** to marry her. (not eager)

hurt
verb irregular, **hurt, hurt**
A intransitive (= ache) ●Does your head **hurt?**
B transitive (= cause pain) ●These shoes are lovely but they **hurt** my feet. ●His feelings were **hurt** by what you said. ●Physically, one may be badly or seriously **hurt;** emotionally, very much **hurt.**
In negatives and questions ●It won't **hurt** (you) to take a little more exercise. (It will do you good) ●Will it **hurt** if I miss supper? (Will it matter?)

hyphen [-]
punctuation-mark (between words) It is not always easy to know if a word needs a hyphen between two parts of it or if it is really one word or two separate words. There is a difference between a *black bird* (any bird with black feathers) and a *blackbird* (a species of bird) but there is no *black-bird; however, if you wrote the word like that with a hyphen, it would be understood as the species, because the hyphen makes it clear that you mean something different from the two separate words. When there is a hyphen, you stress the first part ●paper-boy (boy who brings papers)
Also use hyphens for compound adjectives, used attributively ●It's an out-of-the-way place. and adjectives formed from participles ●fair-haired ●old-fashioned.

I

I
pronoun first person singular, subject. Note short forms (see CONTRACTIONS) **I am/I'm, I shall, I will/I'll, I have/I've.** In 'tag' questions there is no form *amn't I'; instead, we say **aren't I?'** ●I'm coming too, **aren't I?' I'd** can mean either *I had* or *I should/ would* ●**I'd** already paid, hadn't I? ●**I'd** be wrong to go, wouldn't I? See also **me,** CONTRACTIONS, PRONOUNS.

idea
noun can be both countable and non-countable
A (= picture in the mind) ●Do you have any **idea** what it's like? ●I have a good **idea** for a short story.
B (= understanding, opinion) ●I have a good **idea** what he wants.

75

ideal

●She has her own **ideas** about politics. ●How did you get the **idea** that he wanted to marry you?

ideal
adjective (=perfect, ≠real) ●In an **ideal** world no one would be poor. *noun* (=perfect example, belief in high standards) ●They believe in the **ideals** of perfect honesty and justice.

ideally
adverb sentence adverb (=if things were perfectly arranged) ●**Ideally**, students should have quiet, private rooms and no worries.

idealist
noun (=person with unrealistically high standards) ●He was once an **idealist**.

idealism
noun (=system of living according to ideals) ●Now he has lost his **idealism**.

idioms
Idioms are phrases with meanings that are not obvious from the meanings of the individual words. They are often typical expressions of users of a particular language, expressions not translated word for word. In this book the word *idiom* is used to include many common expressions including phrasal verbs, which cause difficulty to some learners of English.

ie
abbreviation for Latin *id est* (that is) used to put something into other words (=that is to say) ●All available accommodation, **ie** houses, flats, hotel rooms, will be in use.

if
conjunction subordinate
A (=on condition that, supposing that) not usually with a future tense following ●**If** she asks me, I'll tell her. ●**If** she asked me, I'd tell her. ●**If** she had asked me, I'd have told her.
+ *so/not* ●Has the letter come? **If** so, read it. **If** not, please telephone for news.
B in indirect questions ●He asked/enquired/wondered/wanted to know **if** the letter had come. (whether the letter had come or not)
C (=that) ●I'm sorry **if** you don't like it. ●Nobody minds **if** you behave like that.
❖ *in idioms* ●**If I were you** I'd say I was sorry. (My advice is: 'Say you're sorry.') ●We can go now, **if you like.** (if that's what you want to do, if it pleases you) ●He didn't steal it; he took it without asking, **if you like.** (if I may use that expression) ●I should like to lend him the money but **it's not as if** I'm well-off. (it isn't true that, the situation would be different if) ●**If only I knew** her name! (I don't know her name; I very much want to know it.) ●**If only I had known** her name! (I didn't know her name then; it is a great pity that I didn't.) ●**Even if** she laughs at him, he adores her. (Although) ●Give names of children, **if any.** (if you have children) ●There are few people nowadays, **if any**, who remember him. (perhaps nobody does)
See also **provided, should, unless, whether, would,** CONDITION, SUBJUNCTIVE.

ignore
verb (=not to take notice of, pretend not to see) ●When I spoke to him, he **ignored** me and went on with his work.

ignorant
adjective (=without knowledge, sometimes without civilised manners) ●With no good schools, many children grow up **ignorant** of basic skills.

ill
adjective **worse, worst**, predicative (≠well, =sick) ●She was **ill** on Monday and **worse** on Tuesday; she's staying in bed today. ●Are you feeling **ill**? (Do you want to vomit/drink some water etc?) ●Are you **ill**? (Do you have an illness, an identifiable disease?)

improve

adverb usually in compounds, formal (= badly, not enough) •She was **ill**-dressed, **ill**-informed, and **ill**-mannered.

❖ **in compounds** •It was an **ill**-advised thing to do. (unwise) •She fell **ill** at ease in his company. (uncomfortable, embarrassed) •**ill**-tempered (bad-tempered) •**ill**-timed (at the wrong, inappropriate time)
See also **sick**.

immediately /ɪˈmiːdɪətlɪ/
adverb (= at once) •Call a doctor **immediately!**
conjunction (= as soon as) •**Immediately** he arrived, he started telling us what to do.

immediate
adjective (= extremely fast, nearest) •The effect of the medicine is **immediate**. •Send an **immediate** reply to this letter. •We must inform his **immediate** relations.

imperative
Verbs in the imperative form express commands, orders or polite requests to do things.
FORMS
1 Positive — same as *infinitive*, without *to* and without *subject*
•**Come** here. •**Stop.** •**Look** at this. •**Be** quiet. •**Sit** down. •**Relax.** •**Go** away. •Always **tell** the truth.
2 Negative — *do not/don't* + *infinitive* •**Do not** walk on the grass. •**Don't** be late. •**Don't** tell her. •**Don't** cry. •**Don't** worry.
NB (a) Imperatives can be made more polite by adding *please*. •**Please** have this seat! •**Please** don't go yet. •Give me your money, **please**.
(b) Question tags can be added to make an order into a more polite request. •Help me with this, **will you?** •Have a biscuit, **won't you?** (Won't you have a biscuit?) •Post this letter, **can you?** •Stop complaining, **can't you?** (The meaning of these phrases depends very much on intonation.)
(c) Positive requests, complaints, apologies etc become more forceful by adding *do*. •**Do** sit down. •**Do** have a drink. •**Do** forgive me for being late. •**Do** stop shouting.
(d) A subject can be supplied when needed. •**Sophie**, leave the room; **the others,** stay here.
3 Some imperatives are really strong suggestions, not real orders. If they apply to a group including the speaker, we use *let's* (let us) + *infinitive* •'I'm tired; **let's** go home.' 'OK. **Let's.**' •'**Let's** not quarrel about it./Don't **let's** quarrel about it.' 'OK, **let's** not.'
4 Passive imperatives are possible. •**Be** warned! •**Don't be** disappointed! The same idea is often expressed by *get*. •**Get** washed! •Don't **get** left behind!
5 The imperative form can be used to express condition. •**Touch** that and you die! •**Say** that again and I'll hit you!
6 Reported imperatives (indirect): *tell, order, request, ask* + *object* + *to* + *infinitive* •'Go away!'/**She told him to go away.** •'Please go.'/**She asked him to go.** + *not/never* •'Don't sit on my papers.'/**She asked me not to sit on her papers.** •'Never do that again.'/**I told him never to do it again.** •'Please supply this information.'/**The letter requested [me to supply] the information.**

improve /ɪmˈpruːv/
verb transitive or intransitive (= become better, make better) •Her English is **improving**. •I hope the weather **improves** before the week-end. •This isn't quite good enough; can you **improve** [on] it? •The room was much **improved** by re-painting.

improvement
noun (= process or result of getting better) •There has been a great **improvement** in his health since he stopped smoking.

77

in

in
preposition (= contained by, within)
●The money's **in** the bank/**in** my purse. ●There are plenty of fish **in** the sea.
in + *countries, large towns, seas* (not *at) ●**in** the Atlantic ●**in** Tokyo ●**in** America
in + *periods of time* (= at some time during) ●**in** March ●**in** 1999 ●**in** the past
❖ **in idioms (preposition)** ●There are 20 **in all**. (altogether) ●He's **in business**. (a businessman) ●Everything is **in doubt**. (uncertain) ●He was **in difficulties**. (having trouble) ●She said it only **in fun**. (as a joke) ●They **fell in love**. (started to love each other) ●He says one thing **in public** (publicly) and another **in private**. (privately, to friends) ●What can I give you **in return**? (as payment) ●**In reply**, he gave an example. (to make an answer). ●At the end of the film, I was **in tears**. (weeping) ●**In the end**, he agreed to pay. (finally, at last) ●You will forget it **in time**. (eventually, as time passes) ●I hope we'll be **in time**. (not late) ●He is **in hospital** (as a patient)/**in prison** (as a prisoner)/**in church** (as a worshipper) ●I like him, **in a way**. (but not in every way) ●Don't get **in my way**. (keep out of my path) ●Take it **in turns**. (first one, then the other).

adverb (= away from the outside)
●It's cold out here; let's go **in**.
●Don't forget to put the salt **in**.
●Open the door and let me **in**!
●Your exam papers must be [handed] **in** at five o'clock. ●My mother isn't **in**; I think she'll be **in** in five minutes.

❖ **in idioms (adverb)** ●Is the tide **in**? (high — of the sea) ●Fur hats were **in** last year. (fashionable) ●She works hard **day in, day out**. (continuously) ●They were **running in and out** of the rooms. (coming and going, changing direction) ●Look at those black clouds; I think we're **in for** a storm. (going to suffer) ●She **asked him in**. (invited him into the house or room) ●Thieves **broke in**. (entered by breaking a door or window) ●Do **call in** when you're passing this way. (visit) ●You must **fill in** this form. (write details on it) ●I shall never **give in**. (surrender) ●Please **get the milk in**. (fetch from outside) ●Everybody can **join in**. (participate) ●Can I **look in** [on you] before you go? (visit briefly) ●The house is ready, we shall **move in** next week. (start living in it) ●The police car told them to **pull in**. (drive to the side of the road and stop) ●The dog must be **shut in**. (confined)

inner
adjective attributive only (≠ outer, = inside) ●His **inner** feelings are hidden.

inside
adjective/adverb/preposition
(≠ outside) ●Slow cars should stay in the **inside** lane. ●My money is in my **inside** pocket. ●It looks ugly from the road but lovely [when you go] **inside**. ●Look **inside** the box.
noun ●The **inside** of the box is lined with silk. ●Write your name on the **inside**.

indoors
adverb (= in/into the building)
●Please come **indoors**; it's raining.

indoor
adjective (= suitable for indoors)
●In the winter, they play **indoor** games. ●Please wear **indoor** shoes when you are indoors.

inwardly /ˈɪnwədlɪ/
adverb (= secretly, invisibly) ●I was outwardly calm, but **inwardly** angry.
See also **at, by, into, on, with, within,** PREPOSITIONS.

into
preposition (= to the inside of) used mainly for movements, not positions, but with some verbs there is not much difference between **in** and **into**. ●Go and jump **in/into** the river. ●He threw it **in/into** the waste-bin.
However there are real differences

indirect speech

of meaning in the following examples ●He went **into** hospital last week./He was **in** hospital last week. ●He was walking **into** (entering)/**in** (within) the garden.
❖ *in idioms* ●Can you **make** this cloth **into** a blouse? ●The prince **turned into** a frog. ●Please **translate** it **into** Arabic.

in a sense
See **sense**.
in case
See **case**.
in fact
See **fact**.
in front of
See **front**.
in mind
See **mind**.
in other words
See **other, words**.
in place of
See **instead, place**.
in spite of
See **spite**.
in use
See **use**.
in view of
See **view**.

in-
prefix also **il-, im-, ir-** (= non-, un-, not) There are many words beginning with **in-** which do not have a negative meaning ●**in**come ●**in**crease ●**in**dustry ●**in**spect ●**in**sure but these prefixes are used freely to make, especially, negative adjectives ●**in**definite ●**in**flexible ●**il**legal ●**im**mature ●**im**perfect ●**ir**regular ●**ir**resistible.

indeed
adverb
A (= certainly) ●'It's a lovely day'. '[It is] **indeed**'.
very + adjective + indeed
(intensifier) ●She is very beautiful **indeed**. (extremely)
B (= in fact) ●He's rich; **indeed**, he's a millionaire.

indirect speech
(= reported speech) This is different from **direct speech**, which is written within quotation marks:
direct speech ●'I'm tired.'
indirect speech ●He says he is tired./He said he was tired.

In this example the reporting verb is *say*. Other possible reporting verbs include (for statements) *suggest, think, tell [someone that], point out [that], report [that], announce, agree [that]*.
direct questions may begin with question words or inversions (*yes/no* questions) ●'**Who** is he?' ●'**Is he** your father?'
indirect questions ●She wants to know who he is./She asked [me] who he was. ●She is wondering if/whether he is my father./She asked if he was my father.
direct commands in the imperative ●'Stay here.' ●'Don't go away.'
indirect commands ●He told/asked/commanded/begged/ordered her to stay there and told (etc) her not to go away.

Reporting what people say often means showing their intentions, which may be expressed by intonation, gesture or context; eg these words may be spoken in several different ways and situations: 'Are you a fool?' 'Don't imagine you can escape.' 'She will deal with it.' They might be reported using verbs such as *think, warn, threaten, promise, assure, wonder, hope, agree* etc.
TENSES
When the reporting verb is past, we need to use the tenses which make sense. ●'I **work** hard.'/She said she **worked** hard. ●'I **don't** smoke.'/She said she **didn't** smoke. ●'He's **waiting**.'/She said he **was waiting**. ●'**Are** they ready?'/She asked if they **were** ready. ●'I **saw** him last night.'/She said she **had seen** him the night before. ●'I **have known** him for ages.'/She said she **had known** him for ages. ●'He **was waiting**.'/She said he **had been**

infinitive

waiting. •'I **hadn't seen** her before.'/She said she **hadn't seen** her before. •'He **will come** late.'/She said he **would come** late. •'**I'll help** you.'/She said she'**d help** me. •'**Can** you **swim**?'/She asked if I **could swim.** •'**Do** you **like** it?'/She asked if I **liked** it. •'Where **is** it?'/She asked where it **was.** •'**Did** he **pay**?'/She asked if he'**d paid.** •'**Would** he **pay**?'/She asked if he'd **pay.** •'What **did** you **do**?'/She asked what I'**d done.** •'What **have** you **done**?'/She asked what I'**d done.** •'I **must** go.'/She said she **had to** go.

If the conversation reported is not 'here' and 'now', other changes may be needed, eg a conversation which took place on a Sunday in York: *direct* 'Do you live in York?' 'No, I'm on holiday; I arrived here yesterday.'/*indirect* He asked her if she lived in York. She said she didn't; she was on holiday and had arrived there the day before (or in York on Saturday).

Other changes sometimes needed:
•this — **that** •these — **those**
•now — **then** •tomorrow — **the next/following day** •last night — **the night before/the previous night** •come — go •ago — **before**
See also **ask, can, could, say, tell, that** TENSES.

infinitive

We usually refer to verbs by their infinitive forms — the basic word which you find in a dictionary. Infinitives are used in many English constructions but they cannot form complete sentences without the 'help' of a finite verb.
FORMS with *to* and without *to* (sometimes called 'the bare infinitive')
1 With *to* eg *to clean, to do* •I asked him to clean it/to do the work.
negative •I told her not to clean it.
progressive •He expects to be doing it all day long.

perfect •I hope to have done it by eleven o'clock
passive •There are a lot of clothes to be cleaned. •What is to be done?
passive perfect negative •He was angry not to have been informed. (that he had not been informed).

These infinitives are used (a) as the subject of a sentence, usually introduced or represented by *it,* (b) after certain verbs which can be followed by other verbs only as infinitives with *to,* (c) after verbs with objects, (d) after adjectives, (e) after nouns, (f) to express purpose, (g) after question words.
(a) as a subject •**To find** your way can be a problem. •It can be a problem **to find** your way.
•It would be nice **to see** him again.
•It was hard **to understand** her.
•It makes me sad **to see** him suffer. •Would it give you pleasure **to see** it? •It's a pity not **to use** your skills.
(b) after certain verbs •I can't **afford** to buy it. •They have **agreed** to co-operate. •She **appears** (seems) to know already. •We can **arrange** to pay by credit card. •I **asked** to be seen privately. •I don't **choose** to work; I have to. •At last she **consented** to marry him. •I don't **dare** [to]/dare not jump off. •She **decided** to leave immediately. •He **has/is determined** to buy the car. •We **expect** to be told soon. •Sophie **will** not **fail** to post it. •We **happened** to meet [by chance]. •Can you **help** [to] pack this case? •I **hesitated** to disturb him. •We're **hoping** to take a holiday soon. •I'd **learn** to speak Japanese in Japan. •Can you **manage** to lift this weight?
•Anthony didn't **mean** to offend you. •You have **neglected** to sign the cheque. •Don't **offer** to lend him any more cash. •Let's **prepare** to welcome them home. •She **pretended** not to recognise me.

infinitive

• I **promise** to say nothing. • He always **refuses** to do the washing-up. • He **seems** to have eaten too much. • He **swore** to stay in tonight. • Don't **trouble** to lock the door. • Do you **want** to go out tonight? • I **wish** to speak to the manager, please.

(c) after verbs with objects • I **advised her** to see a doctor. • You are not **allowed** to smoke here. • I **asked the children** to keep quiet. • She **begged him** to change his mind. • The heat **causes the metal** to expand. • The officer **commanded the men** to fire. • Were you **compelled** to answer? • I **shall encourage the boys** to cook. • We **expect it** to be a complete success. • They **forbid people** to feed the animals. • The soldiers **forced the enemy** to turn. • Can you **get the bank manager** to agree? • They'll **help you** to go to sleep. • She **instructed the children** to leave. • Do you **intend us** to wait all day? • I **invite you** to inspect the room. • I **leave you** to solve the problem. • You don't **need a book** to explain it. • Everyone is **obliged** to pay tax. • You can't **order us** to go. • Perhaps you'll **permit me** to explain. • Try to **persuade him** not to marry her. • I **prefer the children** to play indoors. • I **recommend you** to read this book. • Would you **request your son** to come in? • Please **remind me** to buy some eggs. • He **taught me** to ride a horse. • I **want you** to show me how to do it. • They **warned us** not to swim there. • I **wish you** to understand this.

(d) after adjectives • She is **easy** to talk to. • It was **surprising** to meet him here. • He was **sorry** not to see you.

Especially after *enough* and *too*: • It's **too dirty** to wear. • The children are **old enough** to travel by themselves.

(e) after nouns • He has no **wish** to live. • Her **promise** to write was forgotten.

Frequently, the basic idea is purpose: • Give me a **bag** to put it in. • I need **something** to do. • She won't have **anywhere** to live. • Has she got a **goal** to reach? • Here's the **money** to pay for it.

General observations may be made using *for* + *-ing* with the same meaning • Money is to spend/Money is **for** spen**ding**. • This cloth is to clean the windows/**for** cleaning the windows [with]/This is a cloth with which to clean the windows. formal

(f) to express purpose (in order to/so as to) • He came specially **to see** me. • At the top we stopped **to look** at the view.

Negative purpose: use *in order not to* or *so as not to* • We spoke quietly **so as not to** wake the baby. • Please reply at once **in order not to** lose this opportunity of a lower price.

(g) after question words • He asked me **what** to do. • Please show me **where** to leave it. • I can't find out **how** to open it. • You must decide **whether** to tell her or not. Question words do not begin sentences using infinitives with *to*. Not *Who to pay? but 'Who shall I pay'? See next section for questions using infinitive without *to*.

The word *to* often represents a whole infinitive expression: 'Will you come?' 'I'd like **to** but I can't'. • He'll tell me when he's ready **to**, but just now he doesn't want **to**.

2 Without *to*

Perfect and progressive forms of the infinitive without *to* exist: • He can **have done** it by tonight. • I'd rather **be talking** to you than working.

The passive form is *have + been + past participle* • It can't **have been done** yet. These infinitives are

81

-ing forms

used (a) after the modal auxiliaries (b) after certain other verbs, often with objects (c) after why/why not . . .?

(a) after modal auxiliaries •I must/shall/will/can/could/may/might/should/would **clean** the car today. •They won't **help** me. •You needn't **lock** the door.

(b) after certain verbs (with objects) •He'**d rather** study than come to the party. ('d = would — He prefers to study./He prefers studying to coming out.) •She'**d better** not wait any longer or she'll miss her train. ('d = had — It would be better for her not to wait . . .) •Don't **let** him borrow my bicycle. •**Let** me help you. I'll **help** you [to] do it. •She **made** me promise. •I can't **make** him understand.

The following verbs can also be used with -ing forms but the meaning with an infinitive is that the complete action is perceived: •I **watched** her drive the car into the garage. (but if it was a long process you could say 'I **watched** her driv**ing** — or try**ing** to drive — the car in.') •Did you **see** him take the diamonds? •I **felt** a cold hand touch[ing] me. •I didn't **hear** him say 'yes'. •They will **notice** my hand tremble/trembling.

(c) after *why/why not* •Why **suffer** unnecessarily? Take an aspirin. •Why **ask** her? She won't know. •Why not **have** another drink? (It is silly to suffer/ask her/to refuse a drink.)

Do is often explained by an infinitive •What he does is [**to**] **collect** money.

For more details see CEG. 7.15.

-ing forms

These are sometimes called *gerunds,* which are verbal nouns, or *present participles,* which are parts of verbs, often used as adjectives.

The *-ing* form is used (a) to make progressive tenses (b) as an adjective (c) like a noun, with articles and, formally, possessives (d) after certain verbs (e) with a passive meaning (f) after all prepositions and certain fixed phrases.

(a) progressive tenses
present progressive (continuous) •He is/isn't **waiting**. •Is it **raining**?
past progressive •She was **cooking** supper when I arrived.
present perfect progressive •I've been **trying** to eat less meat this week.
future progressive •Will you be **working** next Saturday morning?
conditional progressive •We'd be **living** in luxury now if I were rich.

(b) as an adjective •His **smiling** face irritated me. •He seemed to be a **working** man. •Hand me a **polishing** cloth, please.

(c) like a noun •**Eating** in bed is nice but messy. •I love **getting** up late. •The **re-painting** of the house (redecoration) cost us a fortune. •I was surprised at his **asking** for it.

(d) after certain verbs •Did he ever **admit** stealing the money? •He **appreciates** being free to comment. •Try to **avoid** driving on the grass. •Would you **consider** lending me $20? •It's silly to **delay** going to the dentist. •She **denied** opening the safe. (said she didn't open it) •He really **dislikes** touching wet fish. •I **enjoy** swimming in the sea. •Nobody **escapes** dying. •We can't **excuse** lying. •**Finish** telling your story; I want to know the end. •**Forgive** my mentioning this, but . . . •He has **given up** smoking. •We couldn't **help** laughing. •I can't **imagine** [myself] being a spy. •You **mentioned** having a drink. •Do you **mind** waiting a minute? •We all **miss** seeing your happy smile. •She is **practising** speaking German. •I can't **resist** eating one more cake. •Don't **risk** being late

intensifiers

for the plane. •I can't **stand** listening to her voice. •Let's **suggest** putting some music on. •I can't **understand** his having forgotten my birthday. •On holiday, you can **go** fishing/boating/dancing/shopping/riding/skiing etc.
(e) with passive meaning •Your hair needs/wants **cutting** (to be cut) •Do the plants need **watering**? •The oil requires **changing** frequently.
(f) after prepositions and certain fixed phrases •They're talking **about** leaving school. •He died **from** eating too much. •This room is **for** reading in. •**After** hearing/having heard his story, I felt sorry for him. •I can't move him **without** waking him.
NB •We **look forward to** meeting you. •She's **not used to** getting up early. •I **prefer** writing to telephoning. •Let's do something nice, **like/such as** going out to dinner. •Telephoning is **easier than** writing. •**It's no good** pretending; I know what you want. •**It's not much use** trying to dry the dishes with a wet cloth. •These shoes are **not worth** buying; they wear out so quickly. •I don't **feel like** working today. •He **has a liking for** singing in the bath, as well as playing the radio.
See also the following verbs which can be followed by either *-ing* or an infinitive but have different meanings: **forget, hear, remember, see, stop, try, watch** and **would** for the difference between •I like eating./I'd like **to eat**. Other words which change meaning slightly.
•**afraid** to jump/of falling
•**certain/sure** to succeed/of succeeding •**interested** to see/in seeing •**used** to do it/**be used** to doing it.
See also ADJECTIVES, PREPOSITIONS, TENSES.
For more details see CEG. 7.22.

inquire
See **enquire**.
insist [**on**]
verb
A (= declare firmly) •He **insisted** [that] I was wrong.
B (= order something) •I said I didn't want to go but he **insisted**. •Then he **insisted** on [buying] the best seats.
insistent
adjective (= determined in making demands) •He was so **insistent**, it was difficult to refuse.
instead /ɪnˈsted/
adverb sentence adverb (= in place of that) •There was no coffee so we had tea **instead**.
instead of
preposition (= in place of) •We had tea **instead** of coffee. •**Instead** of helping me, he made my work more difficult.
intend
verb (= plan, mean [to do/to be]) •I **intend** to leave tomorrow. •What do you **intend** [to do/doing]? •He didn't **intend** any harm.
+ *person object* + *to* + *infinitive*
•I **intend** you to realise what this means. •You are **intended** to be a fairy in this play, so please try to act like one! •That fish you are eating was **intended** for the cat.
intention
noun (= determined plan) •His firm **intention** is to leave today.
intentional
adjective (= done on purpose)
•'Was that final explosion **intentional**?' 'No, quite **unintentional**; somebody dropped a match on the fireworks.'

intensifiers
These are a large group of adverbial expressions used to show how strong the feeling of an adjective or verb is. For details of the way the most important ones are used, see the words given in

interest

bold in the following lists of the main types of intensifier.
EMPHASISERS **actually, certainly, clearly,** definitely, **fairly,** for **certain,** for **sure,** frankly, honestly, **indeed, just,** literally, of **course,** obviously, plainly, **really, simply, surely**
AMPLIFIERS
(a) maximising: absolutely, **altogether,** completely, entirely, **fully,** in all respects, **most, quite,** thoroughly, utterly
(b) putting high on a scale: a good **deal,** a great **deal,** a **lot, badly,** by **far, deeply, greatly,** heartily, **much, so,** violently, **well**
DOWN-TONERS lowering the forcefulness
(a) slightly: **kind** of, **more** or less, **quite, rather, sort** of
(b) considerably: a **bit,** a **little, at all, barely, hardly,** [not] in the **least,** [not] in the **slightest,** in **part, little, partly, scarcely, slightly, somewhat,** to some extent
(c) giving a rough approximation: **almost, all but, as good as, nearly**
For more details see CEG 9.22.

interest
noun
A countable and non-countable (= [cause of] willing attention) ●I have no **interest** in his problems. ●Her **interests** include knitting and jazz. ●He showed some **interest** when I mentioned that you would be at the party.
B (= money paid for the use of money) ●Can you get 12% **interest** in a savings account?
verb (= attract attention from) ●Does this subject **interest** you?
interested /ˈɪntrestɪd/
adjective/past participle (≠ bored)
●Are you **interested** in jazz? ●I am **interested** by your last remark. ●He looked **uninterested** and sleepy.
interesting /ˈɪntrestɪŋ/
adjective/present participle
(≠ boring) ●I've always found history **interesting.** ●What an **interesting** face he has!

disinterested
adjective (= impartial, not involved) ●In order to be fair, a judge must be **disinterested.** Some people use this word to mean **'uninterested'.**
❖ *in idioms* ●It is not **in his interest** to help you. (Helping you will not help him.) ●A garden can repay your hard work **with interest.** (more than repay it) ●He doesn't **take much interest in** politics. (doesn't concern himself with)

interrogative
(= asking questions)
For interrogative sentences, see QUESTIONS. For interrogative pronouns (**who, whom, whose, which, what**) see individual words and PRONOUNS.

intransitive
of verbs (= not taking an object) The verbs in these sentences are used intransitively ●She's **sleeping.** ●He **waited.** ●Have you **recovered?** ●They haven't **arrived** yet. Many verbs can be used either transitively or intransitively ●They're **leaving.**/They're **leaving home.** ●Can you **dance?**/Can you **dance the tango?**
See also TRANSITIVE.
For more details see CEG 7.3.

inversion
The verb can sometimes be put before the subject: this is called inversion
1 Its most important use is forming questions, with auxiliary verbs or with *do* ●Can he swim? ●Has she arrived? ●Would you help me? ●Does your teacher speak Japanese? ●Did the President agree? ●What is he expecting? ●Where do they go? ●May I?
2 Another use is in statements saying something is the same (after *so, nor* and *neither*) ●'My coffee's cold.' 'So is mine.' (My coffee is cold, too) ●'I shan't drink it.' 'Neither/Nor shall I.' (I shan't drink it either.)
3 After *here* and *there* — calling

84

attention. •Here lies the body of a great king. •There goes the bus!
4 Other uses of inversion are usually formal or literary:
(a) meaning *if* •Had you told me, I could have helped. (If you had told me) •Should he ask for money, please contact me. (If he asks/should ask . . . but it is improbable)
(b) after *hardly, no sooner, never, only, not once,* etc at the start of a sentence: •Hardly/Scarcely had I arrived when she began to complain. (I had no sooner arrived than she began to complain) •Never/Not once/At no time will they allow you to touch that switch. •Only in dreams have I seen such wonderful flowers. •Not only do we want to be paid, but we also want some holidays.

invite
verb (= ask, offer entertainment) •He has **invited** me [to dinner]. Has he **invited** you, too? Who else has been **invited**? •The audience is **invited** to ask questions at the end.
invitation
noun (= written or spoken offer of hospitality, etc) •Thank you for your kind **invitation**.
iron /ˈaɪən/
noun non-countable/*adjective*
A (metal) •The bars were made of **iron**. •She has **iron** determination. (figurative — strong)
B countable (= thing for pressing clothes) •Is the **iron** (switched) on?
verb (= press, do the ironing) •'What are you doing?' 'I'm **ironing**.' •'Will you **iron** my shirt for me?' 'It doesn't need **ironing**; it's a non-**iron** shirt.'
it
pronoun 3rd person singular, impersonal, subject or object. (= that thing) Used 1 as a simple pronoun, 2 to begin sentences in which **It** represents or introduces abstract ideas, phrases or clauses.
1 •I've lost my book; where is **it**?

•'Whose is this sweater.' '**It's** not mine.' •'Who's that outside?' '**It's** Sophie!'
2 •**It** isn't raining now but **it'll** be raining soon. •**It's** too late to change our plans. •**It** would be better to stay at home, wouldn't **it**? •Well, **it's** no use grumbling. •Let's get on with **it**! •**It's** important/difficult/impossible [for me] to find the right book. •**It** would be unusual/amazing/ interesting to meet somebody 120 years old. •**It's** probable/a pity/ true/inevitable that we shall be a little late. •**It** seems/appears/occurs [to me] that he has forgotten the date. •Does **it** suit you/matter to you/please you to get here early? •**It** was no good/useless/pointless/ not worth saying it all again.
'Cleft' sentences look similar but are used to emphasise one item in a sentence. •**It** was my grandmother who gave me the emerald ring. •**It** was me that my grandmother gave the emerald ring to. •**It** was the emerald ring that my grandmother gave to me.
❖ *in idioms* •**It can't be helped**. (We can do nothing about that) •Now **it's my turn**. (The time has come for me) •**If it weren't for/If it hadn't been for** the problems with visas, we'd have gone. (If there had been no problems . . .) •**That's it**. (I've finished/There's no more) informal. Also (That's right, good.) •I'm afraid **he's had it**. (he has failed.) •**Look at it this way**. (Consider the matter from this point of view.) •**Have it your own way**. (I think you're wrong but I can't change your mind.) •Don't stop; **keep at it**. (continue working)

its
adjective possessive, determiner (Not *it's = it is.) •The horse broke **its** leg and was shot. •It's an ugly table; **its** legs are too short.
itself
pronoun reflexive, 3rd person singular, impersonal •The heating switches **itself** on automatically.

job

Also emphatic ●At last we saw the holy place **itself**.
❖ **idiom** ●The car won't start **by itself**. (without turning the key) ●The statue stands **by itself** in a large room. (alone, prominent)

J

job
noun (= a piece of work, paid employment) ●Can you do this little **job** for me? ●He has an important **job** in the UN.
❖ **in idioms** ●He's been **out of a job** since they closed the factory. (unemployed) ●It's **a good job** he didn't catch you! (It is lucky/a good thing) informal ●They find **jobs for the boys**. (appoint their supporters) informal
See also **work**.

join /dʒɔɪn/
verb (= connect, unite) ●Mark the place where the lines **join**. ●This road **joins** the main road further on. ●When his girl friend said goodbye, he **joined** the army. ●We can mend it if we **join** all the pieces together.
noun (= place where things join) ●It's mended so well, you can't see a **join**.

joint
noun (= place where parts, bones, join) ●This furniture has strong, well-made **joints**. ●His arm isn't broken; it's only out of **joint**. ●She bought a **joint** of meat for dinner.
adjective (= belonging to two people) ●Married people often have a **joint** bank account.

adjoining
adjective (= next [door]) ●The **adjoining** land is used for growing corn.
❖ **in idioms** ●I hope everybody will **join in**. (take part) ●If we **join forces** [with each other] we can win the battle. (act as allies)

joke /dʒəʊk/
noun (anything said or done to make people laugh) ●Don't be upset; he only said it as a **joke**.

●I'm afraid the office system here is just a **joke**. (ridiculous)
verb (= tell a joke) ●Were you **joking** when you said he could drive a car?
❖ **in idioms** ●It's **no joke** waiting for buses in the rain. (It's not fun) ●Your rude remarks are **beyond a joke**. (too unpleasant to laugh at) ●He **can't take a joke**. (He won't laugh if someone teases him.) ●I **don't see the joke**. (It doesn't seem funny to me.)

journey /'dʒɜːnɪ/
noun (= trip, time spent travelling) ●Do you have a long **journey** to work? ●I hope you have a good **journey**!
See also **travel**.

judge
verb (= assess, decide, use judgement) ●I can't **judge** whether he's telling the truth or not.
sentence adverb/participle ●**Judging** from/by her face, she thinks she is very clever. (I believe she thinks). ●He is quite rich, **judging** by his expensive clothes. (I believe he is rich)
noun (= person who makes/gives judgment). ●The **judge** sent him to prison.

jump
verb (= spring over, leap, rise quickly) ●This horse can easily **jump** (over) a gate. ●I can't understand her ideas because she **jumps** from one to another so fast. ●Quick, **jump** on to that bus before it goes.
noun (= leap, transfer) ●We'll have to make the **jump** from the old methods to the new ones.

jumpy
adjective (= nervous) ●Those strange noises in the night make me feel **jumpy**.
❖ **in idioms** ●When I was offered the chance to act, I **jumped at** it. (accepted eagerly) ●Don't try to **jump the queue**: I was here first. (go to the front of the line) ●Don't **jump down my throat**; give me a chance to explain. (interrupt angrily)

keep

just
adjective (= fair, right, equitable)
• Is it **just** that men earn more than women? Or is it unjust?
adverb usually positive only
A (= exactly) • Your present to me is **just** what I want. • It happened **just** here, in this place. • **Just** then, he fell over. • **Just** as I said that, everyone stopped talking. • You look **just** like your sister.
B (= absolutely, simply) • It's **just** perfect/wonderful/ridiculous.
C (= hardly, almost not) • He (only) **just** passed the exam; he almost failed. • 'Can you see it?' 'Yes, **just**; it's very small.'
D mid-position, usually + *perfect tense*, not *past* (= very recently)
• I've **just** heard the news: I'm very sorry. (Compare 'I just heard the news.' — ambiguous; perhaps 'I only heard it.') • He'd **just** begun to get better when his troubles began again. • Have you **just** come to this country?
E focusing, mid-position (= only)
• She's **just** trying to help. • I **just** wash up; I don't do the cooking.
• Could you **just** pass me that pen?
❖ *in idioms* • That's **just my luck**; the toast fell butter side down! (said when something unfortunate happens) • 'She works very hard.' 'Yes, that's **just the thing**: she works much too hard.' (that is exactly what I meant) • I can't see her **just now**. (right at this moment) • I think I saw him **just now**. (a moment ago) with past tense • **Just in time!** (almost late)
• You **might just as well** talk to a wall. (the effect would be similar)
• I'd **just as soon/happily** stay at home. (I'd be equally ready to — I don't mind.) • I can't say **just yet**. (but quite soon) • **Just shut the door**. (Please — will you?) • **Just a minute/a moment!** (Wait.) • The clothes were **just about dry** when it started raining. (so they didn't quite dry) • I **just about got the clothes dry** before the rain started. (I almost failed, but I was in time)

K

keen
adjective (= sharp, sensitive, enthusiastic) • He has a **keen** eye/mind/sense of humour. • He wants to buy a motorbike but she's not [very] **keen** [on the idea].
• Why are you so **keen** to learn Russian?

keep
verb irregular, **kept, kept** (= hold, maintain, guard, retain) • She **keeps** her money in a sock under the bed.
• They're planning to **keep** fish in a pond. • Where are the prisoners **kept**? • Please **keep** to the left.
• We must **keep** calm, and not panic.
+ *adjective* • We all **kept** quiet.
+ *-ing* • **Keep** working, don't stop.
+ *object* + *adjective* • My coat **keeps** me warm.
+ *object* + *-ing* • **Keep** the fire burning.
+ *object* + *adverb* • Her illness **keeps** her at home.

-keeper
noun (= someone who guards, looks after) • He is a shop-**keeper**/door**keeper**.

keeping
noun (= care) • Is your jewellery in safe **keeping**?

❖ *in idioms* • This cheese **won't keep**; let's eat it now. (won't stay fresh)
• **Keep this [secret] to yourself**. (Don't tell anyone) • I've **kept my promise**. (done what I promised to do) • **Keep an eye on** my bag. (watch it) • Let me stay; I'll work **for my keep**. (my food and accommodation) • Tell me everything. Don't **keep anything back**. (withhold anything) • He can't **keep his food down**. (he is sick) • Try to **keep the expenses down**. (under a certain limit, under control) • If you **keep in with** the butcher, you'll get good meat. (stay friendly with) informal • **Keep off the grass! Keep your hands off me**. (Don't walk on it/Don't touch)
• He **keeps on [talking]** about the

87

kill

past. (continues to talk etc) •**Keep out!** (No entry) •**Keep out of my way.** (Don't obstruct me) •The slaves were **kept under** by cruel masters. (oppressed, subjugated) •I'm working hard now but I can't **keep it up.** (maintain the rate, quality, speed.) •I hope I'm not **keeping you up.** (stopping you from going to bed) •Slow down: I can't **keep up (with you).** (go at the same speed [as you])

kill
verb (= cause to die, destroy) •Her husband was **killed** in the war.
  killer
  noun (= one who kills, murderer) •The police have not found the **killer.**
❖ *in idioms* •We had missed the train so, to **kill time,** we drank coffee. (pass the time) •He **made a killing** by selling at the right time. (a lot of money, suddenly)

kind /kaɪnd/
  noun (= sort, variety) •A parrot is a **kind** of bird. •What **kind** of food do parrots eat? •I think they eat all **kinds** of fruit.
  adjective (= helpful, caring) •Children should be taught to be **kind** to animals. •Would you be **kind** enough to open the door/get off my foot/sign here? (formal request) •That's very **kind** of you. (thanks)
  unkind (= spiteful, unhelpful) •How **unkind** to mention his dirty hands!
  kindly
  adjective (= kind-hearted, kind) •What a **kindly** old soul she is!
  adverb
  A (= in a kind way) •Speak to him **kindly** or he'll be scared.
  B (= please) •**Kindly** leave the bathroom clean.
❖ *in idioms* •One is not any good; we need **two of a kind.** (two similar ones, a pair) •'Are you working here?' 'Well, **kind of.** I'm not doing much and I'm not being paid.' (in a way, in a manner of speaking, not exactly) informal •It's **kind of** embarrassing, asking for a reference. (sort of, rather) informal. •That child does not **take kindly to** work. (undertake it willingly)
See also **like, sort.**

knock /nɒk/
verb (= hit, strike) •Please **knock** and wait for an answer. (on a door) •He accidentally **knocked** the lamp off the table.
❖ *in idioms* •His sudden accident **knocked all his plans on the head.** (made it necessary to abandon them) •The bang on his head **knocked him out.** (he was unconscious) •She's been **knocking about/around** [with him] for years. (friendly, partners) informal •Let's **knock off** early today. (stop work) informal

know /nəʊ/
verb irregular, **knew, known** usually not in progressive tenses (= have, accept information, be acquainted with) •'Do you **know** who he is?' 'Yes, but I don't **know** him; we've never met.' •I **knew** [that] he was a friend of yours. •How long have we **known** each other? •Do you **know** how to make scrambled eggs? (Can you? Have you learnt the technique?)
  knowledge /ˈnɒlɪdʒ/
  noun (= what is known, understanding) •I have no **knowledge** of his early history. •She sold the house without his **knowledge.**
  knowledgeable
  adjective (= well-informed) •He's very **knowledgeable** about plants.
❖ *in idioms* •He **knows his business/what he's talking about.** (He has useful practical knowledge) •I hope she **knows her own mind.** (knows what she really wants) •She's very unhappy, **you know.** (I hope you realise/I suppose you understand) •You say he's honest but **I know better.** (I know more about him.) •I never really **got to know** him. (became a real friend of his) •How can you **know the good**

from the bad? (distinguish between them) ●To the best of my knowledge, he's French. (As far as I know) ●It's well-known that he was born here. (a generally recognised fact) ●Hydrophobia, also known as rabies, is a dangerous disease. (called)

L
lack
verb (=not have, be without) formal ●He lacks the capital needed to develop the business. ●He's not lacking in confidence. ●Lacking a leader, they lost the battle.
noun (=being without, want) ●There is no lack of interest in building a swimming pool, but the project may fail for lack of funds.
land
noun non-countable (≠sea, =territory, ground) ●The land near the coast is fertile. ●Good farming land is being used for building. ●Fish can't live on land.
verb (=deliver to a destination on land, arrive by air, ≠ take off) ●The plane will land in ten minutes. ●They landed the goods in Dover/a big fish/a large order.
large
adjective (≠small, =big) slightly more formal than big ●A large loaf please. ●The house isn't large enough for us all. ●Larger sizes are available.
largely
adverb (=to a great degree, considerably) ●Their supplies are largely imported. ●The visitors, largely Europeans, love it.
enlarge
verb (=make larger, give more detail) ●We could easily enlarge the room by taking that wall down. ●Please enlarge [on] that idea.
❖ in idioms ●There he was, [as] large as life. (real, unmistakable) ●By and large, I dislike sweet food but this pudding is delicious. (On the whole, in general)

last
adjective determiner
A (≠first, =final, at the end) ●Will the last person to go to bed please turn off the lights? ●He smoked his last cigarette, and died.
B (=only remaining) ●She smoked my last cigarette, and left me with none.
C (=most recent) ●You mentioned it in your last letter.
with no pre-determiner ●Last night/week/year/month, he telephoned to say goodbye. (Not *last day, say yesterday)
Not used with a perfect tense ●Did he pay you last night?/Has he paid you? but not *Has he paid you last night?
With the, perfect tenses are possible ●In the last month he has telephoned me five times. (one month counting back from now, including now) ●Have you seen him in the last few days? (recently)

learned /ˈlɛ:nɪd/
adjective (=scholarly) ●Many priests are very learned men.
adverb (=after all others) ●My horse finished last.
verb (=endure, survive, continue) ●How long will this meeting last? ●I didn't expect that coat/marriage/cease-fire/good luck to last. ●Will the water supply last [out] till we reach land?

lastly
adverb/sentence adverb (=in the last place, finally) ●Lastly, let me thank you for listening.
❖ in idioms ●We waited for hours and at last the bus came. (after a long time) ●Last but not least, thank you to the cook. (At the end, but important) ●She stayed with him to the last. (till the end/death) ●On top of all my other problems this is the last straw. (the final difficulty, which makes everything seem impossible) ●He always has the last word. (in an argument, he sums up, speaks last)

89

late

late
adjective
A (=after the right time, ≠early) •The bus was twenty minutes **late**. •**Late** arrivals will be welcome. B (=before now) •I knew her **late** husband. (now he is dead)
adverb (=after the right time, (≠early) •Why did he arrive **late**? These flowers come out **later** than those. •I'm tired; I went to bed **late**. •I'll speak to you **later** [on]. (not now)

lately
adverb mainly in negatives and questions (=in the recent past, recently) •I haven't written to her **lately**. •Have you done any painting **lately**?

latest
adjective/noun (=most recent thing, news etc) •Have you heard the **latest** [news]? •She always wears the **latest** fashions.
❖ *in idioms* •**Sooner or later**, he'll come back. (I don't know when but it is certain that) •It must be ready by Tuesday **at the latest**. (and no later)

laugh /la:f/
verb (=show amusement, happiness with the voice, smiling)
•Everybody was **laughing** and singing. •We were **laughing** about the story he told us; we weren't **laughing** at him.
noun (=moment of laughing, joke) •We had a **laugh** about what had happened.

laughter
noun non-countable (=sound of laughing) •We could hear the **laughter** while we were outside.
❖ *in idioms* •Don't worry about it; **laugh it off**. (laugh and forget it) •It's **not a laughing matter**. (It's serious.) •He **burst out laughing** when I told him. (started laughing loudly)

lay
verb irregular, **laid, laid** always transitive (=place, put, set) •He **laid** the clothes on the bed. •Will you **lay** the table for supper? (put plates, knives etc on it) •They haven't **laid** the carpet properly; it's not flat. •Chickens **lay** eggs. •These eggs are new-**laid**. (fresh) See also **lie** (**lay, lain**) and **lie** (regular).

lead /li:d/ /led/
verb irregular, **led, led** (=be in front, take charge [of]) •The dog **led** the policemen to the body. /led/ •If you **lead**, I'll follow. /li:d/
noun
A /li:d/ (=act of leading, first place) •When he gave us a **lead**, we all followed. •He took the **lead** in the discussions. •Look! My horse is in the **lead**!
B /li:d/ (=electric cable, string to control a dog) •We need two **leads**: one for the kettle and one for the iron. •You must keep the dog on a **lead**.
C /led/ uncountable (=metal, very heavy) •Bullets were made of **lead** once.

leader /'li:də*/
noun (=person who leads) •Only the **leaders** were arrested.
❖ *in idioms* •He **led** me to believe he was rich. (persuaded me without actually saying so) •Don't let that young man **lead you astray**. (tempt you to do wrong) •What are all these kind words **leading** [up] to? (introducing, preparing the way for) •Too much money **leads** to trouble.

lean /li:n/
verb [ir]regular, **leant/leaned, leant/leaned** (=slope, tend, not be upright) •The famous tower of Pisa **leans** to one side. •When he **leaned** over to pick something up, he hurt his back. •**Lean** back on this cushion and relax. •Don't **lean** the ladder against the window.
adjective (=not fat) •His face is **lean**, like a hungry man's. •**Lean** meat is nicer than fat meat.

leaning
noun (=favourable feeling, tendency) •He has socialist **leanings**.

learn /lɜːn/
   verb [ir]regular, **learnt/learned, learnt/learned** (=absorb knowledge, understand) ●He **learned** more from his friends than from his teachers. ●He **learnt** very fast. ●He **learnt** how to drive a car in a week. ●I've never **learned** [any] Japanese. ●I **learned** of his death with great sorrow.
   learner
     noun (=student, beginner) ●Don't copy me; I'm only a **learner**.
   learning
     noun (=scholarship, academic knowledge) ●My teacher was a man of real **learning**.
   See also **teach**.

least
   adjective superlative of **little** (=smallest, ≠most) ●The **least** noise will wake him up. ●Which is the **least** expensive drink? (the cheapest)
   noun (=the smallest thing, etc) ●The **least** I can do, after all your help, is pay for the petrol.
   adverb (=in the smallest degree, ≠most) ●It happened when I **least** expected it. ●He's the **least** popular man in the room.
  ❖ **in idioms** ●I haven't the least idea (I don't know at all) ●It's dirty but **at least** it's dry. (one good thing . . . if nothing else) ●A decent car costs **at least** £3000. (not less than) ●I'm not worried **in the least**. (at all) ●Nobody should be hurt, **least of all** the children. (especially not)

leave /liːv/
   verb irregular, **left, left** (=go away from, deposit, not touch, not use, bequeath) ●'When does the bus **leave** here?' 'It's already **left**.' ●You can **leave** your luggage with me. ●She **left** her husband for another man. ●There's nothing **left** in my money-box. ●If there's any food **left** [over], give it to the dog. ●He **left** all his money to his children.
   noun (=permission [to take a holiday]) ●You can't speak to him; he's [away] on **leave**. ●How much **leave** do you get each year?
  ❖ **in idioms** ●It's too difficult; let's **leave it**. (not do it) ●I **leave** everything to you: the planning, the buying and the final details. (I make you responsible for it.) ●We'll **leave it at that**. (say no more about it) ●**Leave the cat alone!** (Don't bother it) ●Don't **leave your umbrella behind**. (go without it) ●Please **leave go** of my arm. (don't hold) ●At last, we **took our leave** and left. (said goodbye and departed) ●He has **left off** smoking in bed. (stopped doing it) ●Put everything in: don't **leave anything out**. (omit) ●**Leave me out of this discussion**. (Don't ask my opinion) ●As he is a little deaf, he sometimes gets **left out** of the conversation. (excluded)

left
   adjective (≠right) ●Can you write with your **left** hand?
   noun (=left side) ●Drive on the **left**. ●In politics, he's on the **left**, but not a communist.

lend
   verb irregular, **lent, lent** (=allow someone to borrow) +1 or 2 objects ●He asked me to **lend** him £5, but I've only **lent** him £3, because he was **lent** £5 yesterday. ●Libraries don't usually **lend** reference books. ●**Lend** your dictionary to me.
  ❖ **in idioms** ●Can you **lend a hand** with the preparation? (help) ●This room **lends itself** to parties. (is specially suitable for)
   See also **borrow**.

less
   adjective/pronoun determiner, comparative of **little**, with uncountable nouns only. With countable nouns, use *fewer* — but many people use **less** with all nouns (≠more, =not so . . .), ●If you eat **less** (food) you'll get slim. ●I have fewer clothes than you, and **less** money. ●**Less** noise please! ●He earns **less** than two pounds an hour.
   adverb (=not so . . ., to a smaller

-less

degree) •He worries about it **less** than he did. •She's **less** beautiful than I expected. •When she saw his face, she spoke **less** angrily. •He's **less** likely to agree if you shout.
preposition (= minus, not counting) •His salary, **less** tax, is £14,000 a year.
❖ *in idioms* •This one is **more or less** the same. (almost, practically) •It will cost $3000, **more or less**. (about) •Anyway, **not less than** $2000. (at least) •I don't even like him, **much less** love him. (certainly not, let alone) •**The less** you eat, **the** thinner you get. •She ate **less and less**, and got thinner and thinner. •He's a fool but I don't love him **any the less for that**/but I love him **none the less for that**. •He's a fool. **None the less**/ **Nevertheless** I love him. (however) See also **least, more, most,** COMPARISON.

-less
suffix for making nouns into adjectives (= lacking, free from, without) •a child**less** marriage •a pain**less** operation •end**less** waiting •home**less** refugees.

lest
conjunction (= in case, so that . . . not) formal •Here is your money, **lest** you [should] think I had forgotten it. •**Lest** we are interrupted, listen now to my secret plan.

let
verb irregular, **let, let**
A (= allow) not so formal as *allow* and *permit*
+ *object* + *infinitive* •**Let** me buy you lunch. •Don't **let** him go. •Will the police **let** the thief escape? •She won't **let** the cat get the meat.
+ *object* + *adverb* •Please **let** me in/out/through.
in imperatives •**Let** them all decide; **let** each man have a vote; **let** there be no mistake; **let** us be certain about this question.
Making suggestions, including the speaker •**Let's** have a party. •**Let's** forget all that.
B (= hire, allow the use of a house, room etc for money) •He **let** me the room for £40 a week. •Are there any more rooms to **let**?
❖ *in idioms* •I can't ride a bicycle, **let alone** drive a car. (even less, certainly not) •**Let him/it alone**. (Don't interfere.) •**Let him/it be**. (Don't interfere, leave it.) •Hold tight and don't **let go**. (stop holding on) •**Let go** of my hand. (Don't hold it.) •She never **lets herself go**. (relaxes) •Please **let me know** what you decide. (tell me) •The party's cancelled! What a **letdown**! (disappointment) •I rely on you so don't **let me down**. (fail to do what you've agreed to) •I hope you know what you're **letting yourself in for**; it's a big job. (undertaking, accepting) •As you seem to be sorry, I'll **let you off** this time. (forgive, not punish) •Terrorists **let off** a bomb on the train. (exploded) •It rained/He worked/The music continued for hours without **letting up**. (lessening pausing, resting)

lie /laɪ/
verb irregular, **lay, lain** intransitive (= be in resting position, flat, remain still) •Last week he **lay** in bed, sick. •Your clothes are **lying** all over the floor. •The papers were found where they had **lain/been lying** for a hundred years. •My hair won't **lie** flat, even if I brush it.
B regular (= tell lies) •I think you're **lying**. •Don't **lie** to me.
noun (= what is not true) •It's a lie! Don't believe it.

liar /laɪə*/
noun (= person who tells lies) •I don't want to call you a **liar** but please explain why you said something that isn't true.
❖ *in idioms* •What **lies behind** that remark? (What is the real reason for it?) Compare 'The garden **lies** behind the house.' (is, is located) •He won't **lie down** under such

like

treatment. (He will protest; not accept it)

lift
verb (=raise, go up, put up) ●It's too heavy; I can't **lift** it [up]. ●Can you **lift** this box onto the table? ●The clouds **lifted** and the sun shone. ●**Lift** the lid [off] and see what's inside.
noun
A (=elevator) ●Take the **lift** to the third floor.
B (=a ride in someone's car) ●I'm going near there. Can I give you a **lift**?

light /laɪt/
noun countable and uncountable (=brightness, illumination, lamp) ●**Light** from the sun is reflected from the moon. ●I can't see; turn the **light** on.
verb (ir)regular, **lighted/lit**, **lighted/lit** (=illuminate, start burning) ●It's cold; will you **light** the fire? ●He **lit** another cigarette.
adjective
A (=pale, ≠dark) ●I'd prefer a **lighter** colour; what about cream or pink? ●The big windows make the room **light** and airy.
B (=with little weight, ≠heavy) ●Let's have a **light** lunch, just a salad. ●It's **light** entertainment, not serious art. ●Her health is delicate; she can do only **light** work.

alight
verb (=settle, get down) ●Do not **alight** from the bus until it has stopped. ●The butterfly **alighted** on a flower.

lighten
verb (=make lighter, less dark or less heavy) ●Her face **lightened** when she heard the good news.
●**Lighten** the eggs by beating lots of air into them.

lightly
adverb (=slightly, not heavily, without due respect) ●She touched him **lightly** on the arm. ●Don't speak **lightly** of death.

❖ *in compounds* ●**light**-hearted (happy, cheerful) ●**light**-headed (not thinking clearly, dizzy, drugged) ●**light**-fingered (with a delicate touch, inclined to steal small items) ●**highlight** (draw attention to important parts)

❖ *in idioms* ●Now he sees things **in a different light**. (from another point of view) ●That story of his generosity shows him **in a good light**. (favourably) ●In the end, the whole plan **came to light**. (was discovered) ●**In the light of** the new information, we have changed our minds. (having considered, taken into account) ●**Have you got a light, please?** (request for match, lighter for cigarette)

like
verb transitive, not used in progressive (=be fond of, enjoy) would **like** (=wish, want) ●I'm hungry; I'd **like** some hot food. ●I **like** this restaurant. ●Would you **like** steak?
+object +complement ●'How do you **like** your steak [done]?' 'Do you **like** it well done?' 'I like steak medium but I don't like it rare.'
+-ing, +to +infinitive ●He **likes** making me laugh./He **likes** to make me laugh.
These two sentences mean almost the same but to refer to *habitual*, general preferences we normally use *+-ing*. ●Old people **like** sitting still and drinking tea; they don't **like** noisy dancing.
For *specific* preferences, on a particular occasion, we use *would like +infinitive* ●If you would **like** some coffee now, I'll ask the waiter.
+object +to +infinitive ●He would **like** me to pay him now. ●Would you **like** coffee to be served in the garden?
preposition (=in the same way as, with the same qualities as) ●She is **like** her mother in appearance, but not **like** her in character. ●In character, she is more **like** me. ●'Don't look at me **like** that!' '**Like** what?' '**Like** a cat with a mouse.' ●Animals, **like** human beings, need company.

93

likely

noun
A (=similar things) •They eat vegetables; lettuce, cabbage and the **like**.
B always plural (=preference) •She has many **likes** and dislikes.
conjunction colloquial only, not universally accepted, but commonly heard. (=as, in the way that) •Do it **like** I do it. (=as I do it, like me) •It looks **like** he's feeling sick. (as if)

dislike
verb (stronger than *not like*) •I **dislike** people who shout. •I don't **dislike** tennis but I prefer squash.

alike
adjective/adverb predicative only (=similar) •We look **alike**, my sister and I, but we don't think **alike**. •These two flowers are exactly **alike**.

unlike
preposition (=not in the same way as) •**Unlike** you, I work for my living. •Riding a bicycle, **unlike** driving a car, is good for you.

liking
noun (=fondness, taste) •He has a **liking** for weak tea. •I hope this tea is to his **liking**.

-like
suffix forming adjectives from nouns (=similar to) •This is a workman**like** job. •He spoke with child**like** innocence. •Jam is a jelly-**like** food made from fruit.

❖ *in idioms* •How do you **like** living alone? (What are your feelings, thoughts, about it?) •**What is it like?** (Describe it) •What does it **look like/sound like/seem like/feel like?** (describe these aspects) •It **looks like** rain. (I think it will rain.) •I **feel like** a hot drink (should like, want) but I **don't feel like** making it. (want to [bother to] make it) •She talks **like** mad. (a lot, excessively) •I like coffee but **it doesn't like me**. (it gives me indigestion, keeps me awake) •You can borrow my bicycle, **if you like**. (if you want to) •**I like that!** You say I'm lazy and you never help at all! (Sarcastically — I am irritated by your remark, I don't like it) •**I'd like to see you** get it done as fast as that! (I don't believe you could) •It weighs **something like** 200 kilos. (about, roughly)
See also **as, want, wish**.

likely
adjective usually complement (=probable) •Rain is **likely** this afternoon.
+ *to* + *infinitive* •Is it **likely** to stop the game? •Are we **likely** to get wet?
+ *that* •It's quite **likely** that the game will be cancelled.
attributively •The most **likely** result is a draw. •That's a **likely** story! (sarcastic — I don't believe you)
adverb (=probably) •They'll very **likely** cancel the game.

unlikely
adjective (=improbable, not likely) •You're **unlikely** to get the truth from him. •Manchester is an **unlikely** place for a honeymoon.

likelihood
noun (=probability) •There is no **likelihood** of delay. •The **likelihood** of such an accident is about 1,000 to one.
See also **probability**.

line
noun (=a thin mark, limit, boundary, row) •I can't draw a straight **line** without a ruler. •The first to cross the **line** is the winner. •Children, please stand in [a] **line**.
verb (=cover the inside, be on the sides of) •Her coat is **lined** with silk. •People **lined** the streets to watch the Queen go by.

outline
verb/noun (=[show] the main design, plan without detail) •Let me just **outline** my proposals. •I have prepared an **outline** on one piece of paper. •This is only an **outline**.

❖ *in idioms* •Please **hold the line**. (on the telephone; wait, don't hang up) •**Drop me a line**. (Write me a short letter) informal. •He was **in the front line** [of battle]. (He was exposed to the strongest attack.) ●You're **on the right lines**. (likely to find the right answer that way) ●**What line will you take?** (What will be the main idea of what you say?) ●We must **take a strong line with** the rebels. (treat them strictly) ●I agree with you **all along the line**. (completely) ●I'll tell white lies but I **draw the line at stealing**. (that's going too far) ●His ideas are **not in line with** party doctrine. (don't correspond, match) ●He's **not in line**, doesn't **accept the party line**, doesn't **toe the line, keep in line**. ●You must **read between the lines**. (think about what is not written, see hidden meanings)

listen /lɪsən/
verb [+ *to*] (= give attention to sound) ●**Listen!** I can hear him coming. ●I wish he would **listen** when I speak to him. ●Don't **listen** to her; she's trying to mislead you. (believe)

❖ *in idioms* ●You should not **listen in to** other people's conversations. (eavesdrop) ●She's **a good listener**. (sympathetic, allows people to talk to her)
See also **hear**.

little
adjective mainly attributive; no comparative or superlative forms: use **smaller, smallest** ●[The] **little** apples are sweeter than [the] big ones.
Small refers only to size; **little** often suggests an attitude to smallness. ●Poor **little** boy! He's lost. ●She has lovely **little** feet. ●He's a stupid **little** fool.
adverb
A (= not much, to a small degree) rarely used alone; use *not much* ●His work is **little** known.
B + *verbs of feeling, knowing* (= not at all) ●He **little** realised what would happen. (He didn't know at all)
C *a* + *little* [*bit*] (= slightly) ●Can you move along a **little** [bit]?
●Let's wait a **little** longer. (a short time) ●I'm a **little** [bit] annoyed

with you. ●We learned how to manage, **little** by **little**. (gradually)
adjective/pronoun determiner (= not much, a small amount [of] ≠ few, a few) **less, least** with non-countable nouns ●He has **little** money. (not enough) ●He has a **little** money. (some, at least) ●She has a **little**, too. (Compare 'She has few friends./He has a few.')
●There is [very] **little** time for discussion. (not enough)/There's a **little** time for discussion. (some) ●I can do **little** to help you. (not much)/I can do a **little** to help you. (something) ●We have very few/only a few oranges and **little** cheese, so buy a few more oranges and a **little** cheese at the shop.
See also **any, few, plenty, some**.

live /lɪv/
verb (= be alive, have a place as home) ●I'll remember this as long as I **live**. ●He didn't **live** long enough to see the results of his work. ●Where do you **live?** (Where is your present home?) ●I **live** quite near you.
adjective /laɪv/ usually attributive (= alive, living) ●Snakes eat **live** mice. ●Don't touch the **live** connection. (electric)
living /'lɪvɪŋ/
adjective (= alive, live) ●For many people, **living** people/the **living** are more important than the dead.
noun (= livelihood, means to live) ●He earns /makes/gets his **living** by cleaning windows.
alive /ə'laɪv/
adjective always predicative (= live, living) ●Is this fish **alive** or dead? ●Try to keep the party spirit **alive**.
lively /'laɪvlɪ/
adjective (= quick-moving, active) ●Do your exercises to **lively** music.
life /laɪf/
noun plural **lives**
A countable (= time between birth and death, or present) ●He had a long and exciting **life**. ●All his **life**, he's been a fool.
B non-countable (= energy, animation) ●There is no **life** on the

moon. •There's not much **life** in my part of town.
❖ *in compounds* •The TV's in the **living**-room. (family room) •He has to feed his **live**stock. (animals on a farm) •He wrote his **life** story. (autobiography) •The **life** history of a butterfly is complex. (development) •He's drowning; throw him a **life** belt. (floating ring to hold on to)
❖ *in idioms* •You can't **live on** £10 a week. •Cows **live on** grass. •Does the cook **live in**? (live in the house or hotel where she works) •He **lives off** his girlfriend. (depends on her for money) •He has been **living with her**/They have **lived together** for a long time. (lived as if married, though not married) •When the sun shines, the world **comes to life**. (wakes up) •He **took his own life**. (killed himself) •They don't have a high **standard of living**. (life style)

lonely /ˈləʊnlɪ/
adjective (= unhappy because solitary) •Nobody visits her; she has a **lonely** life.
  alone
  adjective/adverb predicative (= solitary, without company) •She is/lives **alone** but I don't think she is lonely. •She **alone** understands this machine. (No one else does)
  lone
  adjective attributive (= solitary) formal •A **lone** tree stands at the top of the hill.

long
adjective refers to space and time **longer, longest** (≠ short) •It's a **long** walk from here to school. •We waited a **long** time for the bus. •My hair is **longer** than yours.
adverb
A (= for a long time) •He won't wait much **longer** for his money. •He hasn't been back **long**. (He's only just come back.)
B after measurements (= in length) •The table's 2 metres **long**. •That film is 3½ hours **long**.
verb
+ *for*/ + *to* + *infinitive* (= want very much, look forward to) •I'm **longing** for news of him/to hear what he's been doing.

length
noun (= extent, distance measured) •The **length** of the pool is 100 metres, but it is only 25 metres wide.
❖ *in compounds* •**Long**-distance phone calls (not local) •I'd like a **long** drink. (in a big glass, eg made with water, fruit juice) •Don't be so **long**-winded; say what you mean. (verbose, using too many words)
❖ *in idioms* •I **shan't be long**. (I shall come back soon.) •**It won't take long**. (It will soon be finished.) •It won't stay there **for long**. (for a long time) •We'll see it **before long**. (soon) •**As/So long as** you need me, I'll stay. (While) •You can borrow it **as long as** you don't treat it roughly. (if, provided that) •**In the long run/term**, there are more serious problems. (When we look a long time ahead) •He **no longer** lives here. (He doesn't live here now/any more.)

look
verb (= use the eyes, try to see, attend to) •If you **look** carefully you can just see the place where it has been mended.
+ *at* + *object* •He **looked** at me with surprise.
+ *adverb phrase* •**Look** under the table.
+ *adjective* •This cake **looks** delicious. •You don't **look** well. (You look ill.) •You don't **look** good in brown. (Brown doesn't suit you.)
noun (= act of looking, aspect) •Have a **look** at this photograph. •He has the **look** of a confident man/a confident **look**. •He's very confident, by the **look** of him.
interjection (= Listen! What I'm going to say is important) •**Look!/Look** here! Don't try to fool me.

❖ *in idioms* •We must be **on the lookout** for trouble. (watchful, ready to see) •The **outlook** for tomorrow is bright and sunny. (forecast, view ahead) •My cousin **isn't much to look at** but she is very amusing to be with. (not pretty) •Will you **look after** the children while I'm away? (take care of, see to) •If you **look ahead** you can make better preparations for the future. (think what will happen) •May I **look around?** (in a shop; inspect the things displayed) •Old people naturally **look back** to their childhood. (remember, think of the past) •He became proud and **looked down on** his old friends. (scorned, held in contempt) •I've been **looking for** a really nice card to send her but I can't find one. (search) •Are you **looking forward to** seeing him again? (thinking about with pleasure) •I'll try to **look in** again this week. (call on, visit briefly/watch TV) •If there is cause for complaint, we must **look into it**. (investigate it) •Can we **look on** while these terrible things happen? (watch, as mere spectators) •**Look out!** (Watch! a warning of danger) •**Look out for** pickpockets. (Be on your guard against/keep an eye open for) •He is tall enough to **look over** the wall. (direct his look over, across etc) •Please **overlook** the mistakes in my work. (pretend not to see) •If you **look through** the window, you'll see the sea. (look out of) •Can I **look through** these photographs, please? (look at them all briefly) •I can't remember his number; you'll have to **look it up** in the phone book. (find by reference to a list, catalogue etc) •Children should be taught to **look up to** their grandparents. (respect) See also **see**.

loose /luːs/
   adjective (= free, uncontrolled, ≠ tight) •This shirt is too big; the collar feels **loose**. •Shut the gate. The dog's **loose**.

loosen
   verb (= make looser) •I've eaten too much; I'll have to **loosen** my belt.
❖ *idiom* •If you're **at a loose end**, come and have a drink with me. (with nothing to do)

lose /luːz/
   verb irregular **lost, lost**
   A (= fail to find, mislay) •Have you seen my glasses anywhere? I've **lost** them. •He's **lost** his way./He's **lost**. (He doesn't know where he is.)
   B (= fail to win) •If you bet on horses, you usually **lose** money. •You can't **lose** by putting your money in a savings account.

loss /lɒs/
   noun (= act of losing, sometimes = death, sometimes ≠ profit) •The **loss** of his father was a shock to him. •In the end, he made a **loss** on the deal.
❖ *in idioms* •Don't **lose your head**. (do something silly) •Don't **lose your temper**. (get angry) •Ask at the **lost property office**. (for something you have lost)

a lot of/lots of
   adjective determiner used with countable and non-countable nouns (= many, much, plenty of) •We have **a lot of/lots of** eggs and **a lot of/lots of** milk. •There isn't **a lot/lots of** milk. •There aren't **a lot/lots of** eggs. •Was there **a lot/lots of** trouble? •Were there **a lot/lots of** fights? •Take some of mine. I've got **a lot/lots**.

a lot/lots
   adverb informal (= very much) •Thanks **a lot**. •I love you **a lot**. •I love you **a lot** more/**lots** more. •This one is **lots/ a lot** bigger than that one, but that one over there is the biggest of the **lot**.

loud
   adjective of sound (= high in volume, ≠ quiet, ≠ soft) •The **loud** music kept me awake.
   adverb •Now, sing **loud!** You can sing **louder** than that.

loudly
   adverb often unpleasant (= noisily)

love

●He swore **loudly** when he hurt his finger.

aloud
adverb (= loud enough to hear) ●Say it **aloud** please; don't whisper.

love
verb not used in progressive tenses; — compare *like, hate*. (= feel strong affection/liking, for) ●Sophie doesn't **love** me any more. ●I **love** Elton John's records.
+ *-ing* ●I **love** listening to his music. (general)
+ *infinitive* ●I'd **love** to meet him. (particular)
noun (= strong affection, liking, physical attraction) ●I've never been in **love** before. ●My **love** for you will never change. ●He has a great **love** of/for history books. ●Please give my **love** to Grandmother. (in a letter)

lover
noun (= one who loves) ●Art **lovers** go to Florence. ●Is he Sophie's **lover**?

low
adjective not used for people (≠ high) ●The oil level is rather **low**: put some more in. ●If you do bad work, you'll get **low** marks. ●He is in very **low** spirits. (depressed)
adverb (= to a low level) ●He has sunk very **low**. (morally or physically)

lowly
adjective (= humble, not grand) ●The **lowly** people would not dare even to speak to someone so important.

lower
verb (≠ raise, = put down) ●They promised to **lower** taxes on petrol.

luck
noun (= chance, fate) ●It was bad **luck**, you losing that game. ●Better **luck** next time. ●Good **luck**/I wish you **luck** with/in your examination. ●You're in **luck**; there's just one chocolate left.

lucky
adjective (= fortunate) ●You're **lucky** to have/having such a nice brother. ●I hope tomorrow is my **lucky** day.

luckily
adverb (= fortunately) ●**Luckily**, he was at home when I phoned.

M

main
adjective no comparative or superlative (= most important, chief) ●What were the **main** points in his talk? ●Keep to the **main** road and you won't get lost. ●Don't get ill, that's the **main** thing.

mainly
adverb (= chiefly, mostly, on the whole) ●The island's food is **mainly** imported. ●I'm **mainly** interested in practice not theory.

mains
noun/adjective (= major water/gas/electricity supply [line, pipe]) ●We don't have **mains** gas so we use bottled gas.

make
verb irregular, **made, made** (= produce [the effect of]) unlike *do*, used in expressions where the result is something new or different. ●'What are you doing?' '**Making** supper.' ●'What are you **making**?' 'An omelette.'
+ *object* ●Can you **make** an omelette?
+ *object* + *infinitive* ●Can you **make** him cook one?
+ *object* + *object* ●He will **make** you a beautiful omelette. Then he'll **make** himself a better one.
+ *object* + *adjective* ●Too many eggs **make** you sick. ●Alligators don't **make** good pets. ●10 and 10 **make** 20. ●Can you **make** this paper into a hat? ●He **made** a hat out of/from a newspaper. ●Bread is **made** from flour. ●My shirt is **made** of cotton.
noun (= brand name, sort) ●What **make** of car was it? A Renault?
❖ *in idioms* + nouns/adjectives/adverbs/other

98

1 *+ nouns* •Let's **make friends**. (stop quarrelling) •You must **make a choice/a decision**. (choose, decide) •He **made a fool of** me. (made me look/seem foolish) •The South **made war on** the North. (attacked) •**Don't make a noise**. (Be quiet) •She **made a face** when she took the medicine. (showed her distaste on her face) •It **makes a difference to** the result. (affects) •I think you have **made a mistake**. (erred) •She **made fun of** his new pink shirt. (ridiculed) •Please **make room for** him to sit down. (move to leave a space) •You don't **make money** writing books. (get rich) •**How much does he make?** (earn) •I **made** [her] **an offer** for her car. (offered a price) •Have you **made your bed** yet? (put it in order, ready to sleep in)

2 *+ adjectives* •**Make certain** the door is locked. (Check, Confirm) •I've **made sure** of it, already. (checked) •He was once very poor but he **made good**. (succeeded in business etc) •It was **made plain/clear/obvious** to me that I was not welcome. (shown, explained) •It **makes** me **mad/wild/angry/furious** (etc) to see him waste all that money. (angers)

3 *+ adverbs* •Let's **make for** home. (go towards home) •I don't **know what to make of him**. (I cannot understand him.) •Can you **make anything of** this message? (understand something by it) •He **made off** [with the money]. (He escaped [taking the money with him]) •I can't **make out** his writing. (decipher) •He **made out** that he was ill. (pretended) •Please **make out** the cheque to me. (write) •They constantly quarrel and then **make up**. (become friends again) •I don't believe you; you're **making it up**. (inventing a story) •Wait while I **make up** [my face]. (put cosmetics on, apply make-up.) •We must **make up for** the time we lost. (compensate, by working harder now)

4 *other* •She's a star **in the making**. (She's going to be a star.) •If there's no cream, **make do with** milk. (use milk instead) •He **makes believe** she loves him. (pretends, indulges in a fantasy)

manage /'mænɪdʒ/
verb
A (= control, supervise) •He **manages** the business and she **manages** the household.
B (= cope, deal with a problem etc) •Can you **manage** that heavy case?
+ to + infinitive •Could you **manage** to do the washing before Tuesday? •If you can't **manage**, I'll help you.
C (= succeed in taking, using) •Could you **manage** another slice of cream cake?

manageable
adjective (= easy to hold, control) •I need a dog of a **manageable** size.

manager
noun (= person who controls a business, or a household) •When food is so expensive, you have to be a good **manager**. •Please could I speak to the **manager**? [or **manageress**]

management
noun
A (= process of managing) •I leave the **management** of the accounts to my accountant.
B (= people in charge, employers) •There must be discussions between workers and **management**.

---

manner
Adverbs answering the question *How?* are sometimes called *adverbs of manner*, but modern grammar books often use other terms, especially for adverbial phrases describing means or instruments. The words in **bold** below are various ways of expressing the idea of manner. •'How does she approach her work?' **'Carefully/In a careful way/With care.'** •The

many

speech was given **in a formal manner.** •The Chairman replied **without hesitation.** •My wife cooks rice **the way I like.** •Can you cook **like my mother?** •You talk to me **as if you were my mother.** •He talks **as though he were a fool.** •He talks **foolishly, in a foolish way, like a fool, as if he were a fool.** •'How do you go to work?' **'By bus/On a train/By train/On foot.'** (means) •'How do you cut leather?' **'With a knife/By machine/With scissors.'** (instrument)
See also ADVERBS.

many /'menɪ/
adjective/noun determiner used with plurals, in negatives and questions **more, most** (≠ few, = a lot) •'Are there **many** people waiting for the bus?' 'No there aren't **many**./Yes, there are [a lot].' •'How **many**?' 'About twenty.' •There were so **many** people on the bus already that we couldn't get on. •There are too **many** people in the world. •**Many** people say that, but it isn't true. •There are **many** more [people] than there were a hundred years ago.
❖ *in idioms* •**Many a man** has made that mistake. (Many men have) •**Many's the time** I've told the story. (There have been many times that) •**A good many** children go to bed hungry. (Many, A considerable number of) •You've given me **three too many**. (three more than I need) •He didn't invite me **in so many words**; but I know he wants me to come. (in actual words, clearly)

marry
verb transitive or intransitive (= get married [to someone]) •'I wonder why he never **married**.' 'Perhaps nobody wanted to **marry** him.'

marriage /'mærɪdʒ/
noun
A (= wedding, ceremony) •I was at their **marriage**.
B (= state of being married) •I hope the **marriage** will be long and happy.

married /'mærɪd/
adjective (≠ single) •**Married** life doesn't suit him.

match
noun
A + *for* (= person who is as good, strong etc as) •He's a good fighter but not a **match** for my brother.
B (= two things that go together, harmonise) •This hat is a good **match** for your scarf.
C (= a contest in sport) •Are you going to watch the big **match** on TV?
D (= little stick for making fire) •Don't put used **matches** back into the box.
verb
A (= be equal to, as good as) •Nobody can **match** my mother's cooking.
B (= be the same, eg in colour) •Her blue hat **matched** her eyes. •She wore a green satin dress with **matching** shoes.

matter
noun
A non-countable (= material, tangible stuff, ≠ mind) •**Matter** cannot be created or destroyed.
B non-countable (= subject, content, ≠ style, manner) •The style of his writing does not suit the subject **matter**.
C countable (= business affair, concern) •These **matters** can be discussed after dinner. •It's not a private **matter**.
D non-countable (= pain, trouble) •You're crying. What's the **matter**?
verb (= be important) •Nothing **matters** to him except money. •'Will it **matter** if I'm late?' 'No, don't worry. It doesn't **matter** at all.'
❖ *in idioms* •I'm afraid he will die; **it's only a matter of time**. (when some time has passed, nothing can be done) •Come quickly! It's **a matter of life and death**. (If you don't come somebody may die.) •That is **a matter of opinion**. (not

100

necessarily a fact, open to question) ●**As a matter of fact**, it cost £5321. (To be exact, Really) ●'Let me introduce you.' 'Well, **as a matter of fact**, we've already met.' (I ought to tell you) ●They will send you the information **as a matter of course**. (routine; you needn't ask for it) ●The police have **let the matter drop**. (allowed it to be forgotten) ●She poured water on the burning oil, and it just **made matters worse**. (made the situation more difficult to deal with) ●She says she'll follow him **no matter where** he goes/**no matter what** he says/**no matter who** tries to stop her. (wherever/whatever/whoever) ●He has a very **matter-of-fact** way of talking but he's a romantic at heart. (realistic, practical, down-to-earth)

may
verb auxiliary, modal (= A be likely to, in some degree; B have permission)
FORMS
(a) *present* **I, you, he, she, it, we, they may[n't]/[not]**
(b) *past/conditional* all persons **might[n't]/[not]**
(c) no *infinitive*, no *future* form.
A (= be likely to) ●She **may** telephone tonight. (Perhaps she will) ●It **may** be too late, or it **may** not. ●She **may** have decided to wait. (I don't know what she has decided to do) ●You **may** not recognise her with her hair cut.
+ *perfect infinitive* ●He **may** have missed the bus. (Perhaps he has missed it; that is why he's late) Compare 'He might have missed the bus.' (Perhaps he missed it; that's why he was late/It would have been possible for him to miss it; then he would have been late)
B (= have permission) ●She **may** telephone tonight. (She is permitted to) ●The medicine **may** be taken at any time. (Patients are allowed to take it) ●You **may** decide for yourself. (I allow you to decide) ●He **may** not come in with his dirty shoes on. (dirty shoes are forbidden) ●'**May** I help myself to coffee?' 'Yes, of course you **may**/can.' In all these examples of meaning B, *can* could replace **may** and would sound more natural in informal circumstances. ●'**May** I borrow it?' (in reported speech: He asked if he might/could borrow it.)

maybe
adverb (= perhaps) not very formal ●**Maybe** she'll phone tonight. ●You're feeling tired, **maybe**?
❖ *in idioms* ●You **may be** my mother, but you can't rule my life. (Although you are my mother) ●**May you be** very happy in your new job! (I wish you happiness) ●She looks so different with her hair cut that you **may well** not recognise her. (you are very likely not to) ●She **may well** be a princess. (perhaps she is; it's possible but I don't know) ●He never listens; you **may as well** talk to the wall. (It would be the same if you did) informal ●You **may as well** help me if you've got nothing else to do. (Why not?)
See also **allow, can, could, might, perhaps, permit, probably,** AUXILIARY VERBS, MODALS.

me
pronoun 1st person singular, object ●He spoke to **me**. ●He told **me** what you said. ●This is mine; it belongs to **me**. ●You're even fatter than **me**.
As an emphatic pronoun in ordinary conversation ●It's **me** he loves, not you — **me**!

mean /miːn/
verb irregular, **meant, meant**
A (= have the sense, meaning of) ●'What does "brief" **mean**?' 'It **means** "short".' ●His work **means** a great deal to him.
B (= necessitate — logically) ●Here comes the boss; that **means** trouble.
+ -*ing* ●He wants to catch the early train, which **means** getting up at 6.15.
C (= intend) ●I'm sorry I called you a fool; I didn't **mean** it.

101

means

+ *to* + *infinitive* •Does she really **mean** to leave home? •Are we **meant** to wait here or go in? •The exploding cigar was **meant** to be a joke.
adjective
A (≠ generous) •He is so **mean**, he uses teabags twice.
B (= malicious) •The older children are sometimes a bit **mean** to the younger ones.
noun/adjective (= average) •The **mean** of 5, 6 and 10 is 7.

meaning
noun (= idea intended, sense, value) •What's the **meaning** of his behaviour? •He says life has no **meaning** without his wife.

meaningful
adjective (= with meaning) •That statement is not **meaningful**: it is meaningless/nonsense.

meanwhile/in the meantime
adverb (= in the interval, at the same time) •I'm working hard. **Meanwhile**, you're watching TV.

❖ *in idioms* •He says unpleasant things but he **means no harm**. (is not malicious) •Don't try to stop him; he **means business**. (has serious intentions) •She **means well** . . ., but she is a nuisance. (intends to help, but)

means
noun
A (= method) •In those days, a horse was the only **means** of travel.
B (= money to do something) •Do you have the **means** to support a family, young man?

❖ *in idioms* •'May I borrow your pencil?' **'By all means.'** (Of course, Please do) •The door was opened **by means of** an electric control panel. (by using) •Sophie is **by no means** clever. (not at all clever) •It is silly to live **beyond your means**. (spend more than you can afford on your way of life) •He's not exactly — **I mean** — he's rather — you know — **I mean** — I don't like him. (used to fill gaps when the speaker cannot find the right words)

meet
verb irregular, **met, met**
(= encounter, come together)
•Shall we **meet** [each other] at the station? •I haven't **met** him. What's he like? •I'll **meet** you off the plane/at the airport/when you arrive. •This path **meets** the road soon. •Their eyes **met** and she knew he understood. •If you **meet** [with] any problems, please let me know.

meeting
noun (= gathering of people for a purpose) •We held/had a **meeting** to discuss it.

memory
See **remember**.

mention
verb (= say something about, briefly) •I know the owner of that shop; you can **mention** my name to him. •He talked about some wonderful plans but he didn't **mention** paying for them. •Did he **mention** my visit/[my] coming to stay/bringing his dog? •He just **mentioned** it, that's all.
noun usually non-countable (= brief reference) •Was there any **mention** of the fight in the newspaper?

❖ *in idioms* •We have to supply all the food and equipment, **not to mention/without mentioning** the travel costs. (and in addition, there's) •'I'm extremely grateful to you.' **'Don't mention it'**. (polite reply to thanks and apologies) •This restaurant **gets a mention** in the 'Good Food Guidebook'. (is mentioned)

---

metaphor
A metaphor is a phrase making a comparison without using words such as *like* or *as* to introduce it. Metaphorical or figurative language is not to be understood literally. Some metaphors are so familiar that they become clichés. The phrases in **bold** in the following sentences are metaphors. •The hills were **under a blanket** of cloud.

• Her cruel words **pierced his heart**.
• She **sailed** into the room. • The engine **coughed** and **came to life**.
• Put the steak on a **bed** of lettuce.
• His rise to fame was **meteoric**.
• The information **fed** into the computer is stored in its **memory**.
• My Arabic is a bit **rusty**.

middle
noun (= centre, central part) • Put a cherry in the **middle** of each little cake. • He woke up in the **middle** of the night. • I'm getting very fat round the **middle**.
adjective (= in the centre, or nearly) • Take the **middle** path, not the left or right extreme.
❖ *in compounds* •**middle**-aged (between 40 and 60) •**Middle** Ages (AD 1100 – 1500) •**middle**-sized (neither large nor small) •**middle** class (social group between extremely wealthy and manual workers)

might
verb auxiliary, modal (= A to be [slightly] likely to; B have been to some degree likely to; C conditional/reported past form of *may* = be likely to; D reported past form of *may* = have permission; E could [be expected to], should)
A (= be [slightly] likely to) • 'Do you think she may phone?' 'Well, she **might**, I suppose.' (less likely than *may*)
B (= have been . . . likely to) • She **might** have decided to wait. (but I think it unlikely) • He **might** have been King if his father had died earlier. (but he never was King)
C conditional/reported past form of *may* (= be likely to) • He may fall if he runs too fast./He **might** fall if he ran too fast. (He would be likely to fall) • He said that he **might** fall.
D Reported past form of *may* (= have permission) • She said I **might**/could borrow it. ('You may borrow it.')
E (= could [be expected to],

should) • If you're going out, you **might** post this letter for me. (You could; I hope you will) • I don't mind you leaving early, but you **might** have asked me. (almost 'you should have asked'; it would have been a normal courtesy)
❖ *in idioms* •**You might be my father**, but you can't tell me what to do. (Although you are) • She **might well have** died if the doctor hadn't arrived quickly. (It was very likely that she would) • This steak is terrible; you **might as well** eat cardboard. (may [just] as well; it would be the same)
See also **can, could, may, probable**, AUXILIARY, VERBS, MODALS.

mind /maind/
noun (= thought, intellect, memory, opinion) • Use your **mind** to solve the problem. • The idea suddenly came into my **mind**. • To my **mind** he is a great artist.
verb (= be concerned, care [for], object to) • Do you **mind** if I smoke? • He doesn't **mind** waiting. • I'll phone this evening, if you don't **mind**. • Will you **mind** the baby for a minute? •**Mind** your head! (Don't hit it on the low ceiling, etc.) •**Mind** you don't fall! (Be careful not to)
❖ *in compounds* • absent-**minded** (tending to forget little things) • broad-**minded**/narrow-**minded** (tolerant/intolerant) • single-**minded** (with one aim) • child-**minder** (someone who looks after children) •**mind**-reader (someone who knows what others are thinking) •**mind**less (stupid, without interest/without thought)
❖ *in idioms* • This music **brings to mind** my childhood. (makes me remember, reminds me of) • I can't **call to mind** the exact occasion. (remember) • Your face **puts me in mind of** a film star. (makes me think of) •**Put** your worries **out of your mind**. (Don't think about them.) • He believes in **speaking his mind**. (saying what he thinks, being frank) • I'm **in two minds about**

mine

taking the day off. (undecided) ●Please **make up your mind**. (decide) ●I shan't **change my mind**. (think or decide differently.) ●**I've a good mind/half a mind** to stay at home today. (I feel tempted to) ●She doesn't **know her own mind**. (know what she really wants, what to decide) ●She must learn to **have a mind of her own**. (to think independently) ●I hope you will **bear this idea in mind**. (not forget it, keep it in mind) ●You will understand it if you **give/set/put your mind to it**. (think hard) ●Do you **have it in mind to** go shopping today? (Do you intend to) ●His danger is constantly **on my mind** (it worries me) so that I can't **keep my mind on** my work. (concentrate) ●He's **set his mind on** buying it. (decided he really wants to buy it) ●The dreadful news almost drove him **out of his mind**. (mad) ●Nobody **in their right mind** would drive a car without brakes. (sane) ●He must have **lost his mind**. (gone mad) ●I intended to phone you but **it went out of my mind**. (I forgot about it) ●I think she works hard to **take her mind off** her worries. (distract herself) ●**I wouldn't mind a drink**. (I'd quite like one; I could do with one) ●Please **mind your own business**. (don't interfere in/ask questions about mine) ●He does not play this game well; **mind you**, he has not been playing long. (take this fact into account) ●Let's have some caviar and **never mind** the expense! (not trouble about it) ●**Would you mind** waiting here? (Please wait here.) ●'**Mind out!** You nearly knocked me over.' (Look where you're going; be careful) 'Sorry.' '**Never mind.**' (It doesn't matter.)
See also **care, think**.

mine

pronoun possessive, 1st person singular ●I bought that book. There is my name in it; it's **mine**. ●A friend of **mine** told me about it. (One of my friends)

noun
A (= underground hole from which coal, gold etc is dug) ●The miners bring up coal from very deep **mines**.
B (= sort of bomb, exploded by contact) ●His ship hit a **mine** and he was killed.

minute /ˈmɪnɪt/

noun (= 1/60 of an hour) ●He stayed under water for three **minutes**.
adjective /maɪˈnjuːt/ (rhyming with *cute* = very small, detailed) ●You need a microscope to see the **minute** sea creatures.
❖ *in idioms* ●**Just a minute!** (Wait a moment, I wish to comment) ●**The minute he saw her** he fell in love. (As soon as he saw her)

mis-

prefix (= badly, wrongly) ●I hope the children don't **mis**behave. ●The government **mis**handled the crisis.

miss

verb
A (= fail to hit, catch, hear etc) ●He threw a bottle at me; fortunately, he/it **missed** [me]. ●You'll **miss** your train if you don't run. ●I'm afraid I **missed** what you said at the beginning; would you repeat it? ●You can't **miss** the Cathedral; it's huge.
B (= notice, feel unhappy for lack of) ●I lost my purse on Friday but I didn't **miss** it till Saturday. ●He gets very homesick; he **misses** his wife and his own country.
noun
A (= failure to hit etc) ●The car didn't hit me but it was a near **miss**. (it nearly did)
B (= title of unmarried woman) ●**Miss** Brown has decided she would like to be called Ms Brown. (Ms = a title used for both married and unmarried women)
❖ *in idioms* ●I've sold the last ticket; you've **missed the boat**. (lost your opportunity) ●There's a button **missing** from this coat. (lost, not there) ●Please write the date; you've **missed it out**. (omitted it) ●'Do you want to go to this

more

party?' 'I don't — let's **give it a miss.**' (not go).

mistake
verb irregular, **mistook, mistaken** often passive (= misunderstand, fail to recognise) •I thought I heard the telephone but I was **mistaken.** •He **mistook** the directions and went to the wrong place. •You can't **mistake** my house; it's bright blue.
noun (= error, wrong thought) •There are several spelling **mistakes** in this letter. •If you think I shall help you, you've made a **mistake.** •Everyone makes **mistakes.**
❖ *in idioms* •Great acting is immediately recognisable; **there's no mistaking it.** (You cannot fail to notice it) •I sent the other letter **by mistake;** what a muddle! (accidentally, carelessly) •He is dishonest; **make no mistake about that.** (Don't trust him; be sure I'm right) •I **mistook her for** her daughter: she was very pleased. (I thought she was/looked like)

Mister
noun (= usual title for men of all ages, married or single, written **Mr**)

mix
verb transitive or intransitive (= blend, put together) •Oil and water don't **mix.** •If you **mix** yellow paint with blue, you get green.
noun• (= mixture, combination) •It's easy to make a cake if you buy a cake **mix.** •There was a **mix-up** in the arrangements and we went to the wrong hotel. (confusion)
❖ *in idioms* •He's a bit **mixed up** about it. (emotionally confused) •That group is rather **a mixed bag.** (assortment of different people, things) •I have **mixed feelings** about it. (partly glad and partly sorry)

modals
1 Modal auxiliary verbs are used to talk about events which are expected, possible, impossible, probable, improbable, necessary or unnecessary. They are: **can, could, may, might, will, would, shall, should, must, ought,** and **need.** Like the three major auxiliary verbs *(be, have* and *do)* they form questions by inversion and negatives without *do:* •'**Can** they swim?' 'No, they **cannot/can't.**' •'**Should** we pay?' 'No we **shouldn't.**'
2 They have no *-s* in the third person singular •he **can** •she **will** •it **must** •she **may.**
3 They have no infinitives and no past forms. Instead, other expressions are used •I hope **to be able to** help you. (I hope I can) •He didn't expect **to have to** pay for it. (He didn't know he must pay) •You **should have** written to her, or she **ought to have** written to you.
See also **necessary, possible, probable,** AUXILIARY VERBS, FUTURE.
For more details see CEG 6.

moment /ˈməʊmənt/
noun (= short space of time) •Wait for me. I'll only be a **moment.** •Just a **moment**/half a **moment**/one **moment;** I wish to ask a question. •I never for a **moment** thought him guilty. •He's busy at the **moment;** please ring again later. •She arrived, as usual, at the last **moment.**

money /ˈmʌnɪ/
noun (= coin, notes, wealth) •Have you got enough **money** to buy the tickets? •I've spent all my **money;** have you got any? •We must save **money** by drinking less.
❖ *in idioms* •He made a lot of **money** from buying land. •There's no **money** in writing books. (not much profit) •He gets his **money's** worth. (value for what he pays)

more
adjective/pronoun determiner, comparative of **much, many** used with countable and non-countable

nouns (≠ less, ≠ fewer, = in greater degree or quantity) •I'd like some **more** cake, please. •**More** than a hundred people came. •It's **more** difficult than I expected. •We like what we've seen; let's see **more**. •'Is there any **more**?' 'Yes, there's some **more** in the kitchen. There's no **more** left here.'
adverb (= in greater degree) •You must exercise **more**. •Sing it once **more**. (again) •He has a few **more** friends than I have and a great deal **more** money.
Making comparative forms of adjectives and adverbs of more than one syllable •She's **more** patient than her sister, and **more** reliable. She works **more** carefully and arrives **more** punctually.
❖ *in idioms* •Tell me **more**! (I'm interested in what you say) •He found it **more and more** difficult to get jobs. (increasingly) •The house next door is **more or less** the same as this one. (roughly) •**The more** you work, **the more** you earn. (proportionately) •He used to go dancing on Saturday night but he doesn't go **any more**. (any longer) •We'll have a party and **what's more** I'll pay for it. (more importantly) •He's **no more able** to earn his living than a child of three. (quite unable)
See also **fewer, less, most,** COMPARISON.

moreover
adverb sentence adverb, formal (= in addition, besides, corresponding to informal phrase 'what's more') •He's a fool and, **moreover**, a thief.

most /məʊst/
adjective superlative of **much, many** (= greatest, ≠ least, ≠ fewest) •He has the **most** need of the money, so give it to him. •**Most** children enjoy outdoor games. •Which is the **most** difficult question? (the hardest)
noun (= the greatest amount/thing) •We wanted to save it all, but the **most** we could do was keep the house; the garden was sold.
adverb A •Where he **most** wanted to succeed, he failed. •I like all your family, but I like you **most** of all. •The little stones are expensive; the medium-sized ones more expensive and the large stones **most** expensive.
B (= very) with subjective words referring to feeling, not fact •I am **most** happy to say . . . •He will **most** certainly be told.

-most
suffix forming superlative adjectives •the upper**most** card (the one on top) •his inner**most** feelings (most private, hidden)

mostly
adverb (= mainly, usually) •Their clothes are made **mostly** of wool.
❖ *in idioms* •**For the most part**, I agreed with him. (mostly, but not entirely) •It will cost you £30 **at the [very] most**. (not more than £30) •Let's go out and **make the most of** this lovely weather. (use it most profitably)

move /mu:v/
verb (= change position [of]) transitive or intransitive •Please don't **move** the papers on my desk. •If the birds don't **move**, it's difficult to see them. •Would you **move** your car, please; I can't get mine out. •Let's get things **moving**.
noun (= movement) •Then he made a good **move**. (in chess or in arranging his business etc)

movement
noun
A non-countable (= act of moving) •**Movement** is painful if your back is injured.
B countable (= group with a purpose) •He has joined a **movement** which tries to persuade the government to change its defence policy.
C countable (= a general change in thought/feeling) •In most countries there has been a **movement** towards greater informality.

moving
adjective (= causing strong emotion) ●His story was so **moving** that we were all in tears.
❖ **in idioms** ●His job takes him abroad; they are always **moving house**. (changing houses) ●**Get a move on** or we'll be late. (Hurry up) informal ●**Move along**, please. (especially in a bus; move further in to make room for others) ●We can't **move off** till the doors are all shut. (depart) ●I think we've said enough about that; let's **move on**. (change the subject) ●He was so miserable in the house that in the end he **moved out**. (left)

Mrs /ˈmɪsɪz/
noun (= usual title for married women) ●**Mrs** Jones will be coming with her daughter, Miss Jones.

much
adjective/pronoun determiner; comparative **more**, superlative **most**, used with non-countable nouns, mainly in negatives and questions (= a large quantity [of]) ●There isn't **much** time to change trains. ●Has he got **much** money saved up? ●'How **much** does he need?' As **much** as you do? ●I can't stop now; I have [far] too **much** work to do. ●She isn't doing **much**; ask her. ●It doesn't make **much** sense. ●He has so **much** money that he buys a new aeroplane every year. ●**Much** research has been done on this subject and **much** has been discovered.
adverb (= to a great degree, often) ●That book won't help **much**; it's very **much** out of date. ●I don't **much** like eating out of doors./I don't like eating out of doors **much**. ●Don't talk so **much**! ●He smokes too **much**. ●You very **much** surprise me/You surprise me very **much**/I'm very **much** surprised by what you say.
+ *comparative* ●She's feeling **much** better now. ●**Much** more expensive ones can be found.
+ *the* + *superlative* ●She's **much**

the prettiest of all. (clearly, easily) + *too, rather* ●It's **much** too late to go now. ●He'd **much** rather stay here.
❖ **in idioms** ●He did as **much** as he could. (what was possible) ●It's as **much as I can do** to pay the rent. (I can't pay for anything else) ●So he'd stolen it! **I thought as much.** (I suspected it) ●Can you understand this message? I can't **make much of** it. (understand) ●This **isn't much of a place** for a holiday; there's nothing to do here. (is not a good place) ●I agree, it's **not up to much**. (not good) ●I don't **think much of** it. (don't like) ●How **much** cheese do you want? About that **much**? (as much as I'm demonstrating) ●**Much to my surprise/pleasure/disgust** [etc] he fell in the mud. (I was greatly surprised/pleased/disgusted when) ●I felt **much the same as you**. (almost) ●'What's happening?' 'Nothing **much**.' (very little) ●He's **not much good at** football. (He's rather a poor footballer.)

must
verb auxiliary, modal (= have to)
FORMS
(a) *present* **I, you, he, she, it, we, they must**[**n't**]/[**not**] (= is/are [not] allowed to); **need**[**n't**]/[**not**] (= is are [not] required to)
(b) no *infinitives*, no *participles*.
Expressing the ideas of A it is necessary; B it is permitted/forbidden; C it is unnecessary; D logical necessity.
A (= it is necessary) ●You **must** open it. ●You have to open it. ●You've got to open it. ●You are to open it. *past* ●You had to open it. ●You'd got to open it. ●You were to open it.
B (= it is forbidden) ●You **must not** open it. ●You are not to open it. *past* ●You were not to open it.
C (= it is unnecessary) ●You **needn't** open it. ●You haven't got to open it. ●You don't have to open it. ●You don't need to open it. *past* ●You **needn't have** opened

107

it. (but you did) •You hadn't got to open it. •You didn't have to open it. •You **didn't need** to open it.
D logical necessity •I can't open it; it **must** be locked. •I don't believe you; you **must** be joking. •You have no coat; you **must** be cold. *past* •You had no coat; you **must** have been cold. *negative* (use **can't**) •The lock is broken; it **can't** be locked. •I don't believe it; you **can't** be serious. •I told her just now; she **can't** have forgotten already.

questions
A (=it is necessary) •**Must** you/Have you got to/Are you to/**Need** you/**Do** you **need** to/Do you have to? *past* •Had you got to/Were you to/Did you have to/**Did** you **need** to?
B (=it is permitted) •Are you [allowed] to open it? •Can you open it? *informal* •May I open it? •Were you [allowed] to open it? •Could you open it?
C (=it is necessary) •**Need** you/**Do** you **need** to/Have you got to? *past* •Did you have to/**Did** you **need** to/Had you got to?

FURTHER EXAMPLES
A (=it is necessary) •I **must** leave early. (will have to)
In reported speech •She said she had to/she'd got to/she would have to leave early. •He said he had had to leave early. ('I had to leave early')
B (=it is forbidden) •You **must** not leave early.
In reported speech •She said he was not to leave early/**mustn't** leave early/She told him not to leave early. •She said he was not [supposed] to have left/shouldn't have left early. (but he had left early, disobeying; 'You were not [allowed] to leave early.')
C (=it is unnecessary) •You **needn't** wear a tie. (don't have to/will not have to)
In reported speech •She said he **needn't/didn't need** to/didn't have

to/hadn't got to/**wouldn't need** to/wouldn't have to wear a tie. •She said he **needn't have** brought a coat./She said he **hadn't needed** to bring a coat. (but he had brought one; 'You didn't need to bring a coat.')
D logical necessity •He has a private aeroplane; he **must** be rich. In reported speech •She said he had an aeroplane; he **must** be rich. (and still is) •He said she **must** be/have been surprised to see him there. ('You must be surprised to see me here.')
See also **allow, can, could, have, may, might, need, permit,** AUXILIARY VERBS, MODALS.

my
adjective possessive, determiner, 1st person singular (=belonging to me) •Don't sit there; that's **my** place. •**My** hair needs cutting.

myself
pronoun reflexive, 1st person singular •I don't need you; I can look after **myself**, wash **myself** and dress **myself**. Also emphatic •I shall come **myself** to inspect the work.
❖ *in idioms* •I cooked it [all] by **myself**. (alone, without help).

N
name
noun (=what somebody/something is called) •His first **name** (or Christian **name**) is Edward, his sur**name** (or family **name**) is Edwards, and his middle **name** is Engelbert, so his full **name** is Edward Engelbert Edwards. His nick**name** is Ted.
verb (=call, give a name to) •He **named** his dog Humperdink.
❖ *in idioms* •I know him **only by name**. (I haven't met him; only heard of him) •He entered the country **under the name of** David Jones. (calling himself David Jones — not his real name) •He **made his name** as a dancer, then became a singer too. (became famous) •They constantly **call each other names**. (insult one another)

nasty /ˈnɑːstɪ/
adjective **nastier, nastiest,** not formal (= unpleasant, ≠ nice) ●Don't be **nasty** to your little brother. ●'Is your pudding nice?' 'No, I'm afraid it's rather **nasty**.' ●As he became poorer, the rooms he lived in became **nastier** and **nastier**.

nature /ˈneɪtʃə*/
noun
A (= character, natural quality, sort) ●He is by **nature** a mild and gentle man. ●It's human **nature** to be greedy; all human beings are greedy. ●They enjoy dancing and entertainments of that **nature**.
B (= the world, not changed by people) ●He loves to admire the beauties of **nature**.

natural /ˈnætʃrəl/
adjective (≠ artificial, = happening in an ordinary way) ●He died a **natural** death. ●She is a **natural** musician. ●There is a **natural** explanation for these strange events; they are not magic.

naturally
adverb (= in a natural way) ●She spoke **naturally**, with no nervousness.
sentence adverb (= of course) ●**Naturally**, we expect hotel guests to lock their doors.
❖ *in compounds* ●super**natural** powers, spirits etc (beyond normal experience, derived from gods or unknown worlds) ●**natural** history (popular biology) ●**natural** resources (land, minerals etc possessed by a country) ●Helping people is second **nature** to her. (completely natural)

near
adjective/adverb/preposition (= close, ≠ far [away from]) ●Where is the **nearest** telephone? ●As we came **near** [the kitchen] we could smell something burning. ●Our house is **nearer** [to] the sea than yours. ●He was **near** death. (almost died) ●It will happen in the **near** future. (soon)
verb (= come, go near, approach)

●As the plane **neared** its destination, the passengers became anxious.

nearby
adjective/adverb (= near, a short distance away) ●There's a telephone **nearby**, just down the road. ●We went to a **nearby** café for lunch.

nearly
adverb (= almost) ●This bottle's **nearly** empty. ●I **nearly** forgot to tell you.
❖ *in compounds* ●She gave a **near**-perfect performance. (almost perfect) ●It was a **near** miss (almost a hit). ●My **near**side headlight is broken. (lefthand side, BrE) ●The **Near** East (eastern Mediterranean countries, Arabic-speaking countries of North Africa)
❖ *in idioms* ●She's **nowhere near** as good a cook as my mother. (nothing like as good/not nearly as good) ●Choose two apples **near enough** the same size. (more or less) informal
See also **almost, close, far.**

necessary
adjective (= needful, needed, which must be) ●Water is **necessary** for all living things. ●Tea is **unnecessary**, except for me. ●If **necessary**, we can drive all night.

necessarily
adverb (= unavoidably, in a way that must be so) ●Good food is not **necessarily** expensive.

necessity
For ways of expressing necessity, see **have to, must, need.**

neck
noun (= part of body between head and shoulders) ●**neck** of land (narrow piece, used figuratively)
❖ *in idioms* ●Don't **break your neck** to get it done; there's no great hurry. (work very hard) ●The two horses/competitors/players are **neck and neck**. (with an equal chance) ●He's not afraid to **stick his neck out**. (say or do potentially

need

unpopular, risky things when necessary) informal •I'm **up to my neck in it**. (in trouble or overworked) informal

need

verb 1 modal auxiliary; 2 regular verb
1 *modal auxiliary* mainly used as negative and question form of *must* (=be necessary) •You **needn't** pay now. •**Need** he go yet? But the regular forms are also possible •You don't **need** to pay. •Does he **need** to go yet? *past forms* •You **needn't have** paid. (but you did pay) •You **didn't need** to pay. (we do not know whether you paid or not)
2 *regular verb* used for positive statements (=have a need for, lack, want for a purpose, require) and negatives and questions • I **need** a holiday. •Does the soup **need** more salt?
+ *to* + *infinitive* [+ *object*] •I **need** to go away. •He **needs** to take a holiday. •He doesn't **need** to rest. ('internal' need) •He **needn't** stop. ('external' requirement)
+ *-ing* •My hair **needs** cutting.
+ *-ed* •I **need** my hair trimmed/cut/washed. (by someone else) **Did/Does** the car **need** cleaning/to be cleaned?
noun (=lack[ing] or want of something necessary) *non-countable* •The **need** for great care is obvious. •There is no **need** for/of extra laws. *countable* •Water is one of their greatest **needs**.
❖ **in idioms** •He **needs** to be punished. (We ought to punish him) •You should help a friend **in [time of] need**. (when he needs your help) •He **has need of** advice. (needs it) •I'll help him **if the need arises/if need be**. (if necessary) •You can take money from this account **as/when the need** arises. (according to the need at any time)
See also **get [something done], have to, lack, must, necessary,**
AUXILIARY VERBS.
For more details see CEG 4.25.

negative

Positive sentences can be made into negative ones usually by adding *not* to the verb.

1 *Not* comes after an auxiliary verb •We **must not** be late. •She **has not** seen it •It **is not** true. These are usually short forms: **mustn't, hasn't, isn't.** See CONTRACTIONS. In sentences without auxiliary verbs, use *do* + *not*.
•I **do not/don't** understand. •He **doesn't** explain it clearly. •She **didn't** tell me.
2 Questions can be made negative, often suggesting that the answer expected is *Yes*. •**Isn't** it a lovely day? (not a real question but a way of starting a conversation) •**Isn't** this the right bus? (I thought it was; I hope it is) •**Can't** you come earlier? (Please try) •**Don't** they like their pudding? (I thought they would like it) •**Didn't** you bring your books? (I expected you to bring them)
More polite — negative statement with positive question tag •You **didn't** bring your books, **did you**?
3 Commands (imperatives) can be made negative by beginning with *do not/don't*. •**Do not** walk on the grass. •**Don't** forget to write. •**Don't** be silly. Plural imperatives — with *let's* — add *not* •**Let's not** tell anyone. Or •**Don't let's** tell anyone. informal
No + *-ing* (mainly in notices) •**No smoking.**
4 Infinitives are made negative by putting *not* before them, and *-ing* forms work in the same way. •I told him **not** to walk on the grass. •It is difficult **not** to feel angry. •I enjoy **not** knowing what will happen.
Certain verbs used to introduce negative ideas — *think, expect, believe, suppose, imagine* — are usually made negative instead of the following verb: •He **doesn't think** she will see you. •I **don't**

never

believe we've met before. ●I don't imagine you're enjoying this. These verbs can also be used in tags: ●'Will she see us?' 'He **thinks not.**' ●'Have we met?' 'I **believe not.**' ●Are you enjoying this? I imagine **not.**
  Other negative words besides *not* are: *never, seldom, rarely, scarcely ever, hardly ever.* They are not used with *do.* ●She **never** says 'thank you'. ●He **seldom/rarely** has any spare time. ●I **scarcely/ hardly ever** eat any bread. Question tags following such statements are positive ●She never says 'thank you', **does she?** ●He seldom has time, **does/has he?** ●I hardly ever eat bread, **do I?**
  Some words are used mainly in negatives and questions. They are often called 'non-assertive' words: *any, anything, anybody, ever, yet* ●'I can see something.' 'I can't see **anything.**' ●There isn't **anybody** there. (is nobody) ●He isn't **ever** late. (is never) ●I've seen it already but she hasn't seen it **yet.**
  See also **do, neither, never, no, nor, not.**

neither /ˈnaɪðə*, ˈniːðə*/
  adjective determiner used with singular countable nouns (= not one and not the other) ●There are two secretaries working for him and **neither** girl can spell. (both girls are bad at spelling)
  pronoun
  + *of* ●**Neither** of his two secretaries can spell. **Neither** is competent. (Both of them are bad spellers and incompetent)
  conjunction
  + *nor* Compare *either . . . or.* ●**Neither** his mother nor his father came to the wedding. (Both were absent) ●They **neither** wrote, telephoned nor sent a card.
  adverb initial position + inversion, in answer to negative statements (= nor, also . . . not) ●She doesn't like it. **Neither** do I. ●He didn't pay. **Neither** did my brother. ●I won't eat it. **Neither** will you. ●'I can't swim.' '**Neither/Nor** can I./I can't either.'
  See also **any, both, each, either, or, so, too.**

nerve
  noun (= part of system carrying messages to the brain, courage, impudence) ●It was very painful when the dentist's drill touched a **nerve** in my tooth. ●I don't have the **nerve** to ask for more money so soon after my last request.

nerves
  noun plural (= patience, self-control) ●My **nerves** are always bad before an exam.

nervous
  adjective
  A (= excited, worried, frightened, naturally tense) ●He is very **nervous** about speaking in public. ●Don't be **nervous** of the dog; he won't bite you.
  B (= related to the system of nerves) ●They say the spots on his hands result from a **nervous** illness.
  ❖ *in idioms* ●I intended to jump off the high wall but at the last moment, I **lost my nerve.** (My courage failed; I was not brave enough) ●Watching children play with dangerous toys is very **nerve-racking.** (makes one feel tense and worried) ●The constant noise from the radio **gets on my nerves.** (irritates me) ●She had **a nervous breakdown.** (an illness — she was very worried, depressed, tired, unable to work)

never
  adverb (= not ever, not at any time, not, ≠ always)
  1 Mid-position ●He **never** has any money to pay for his drinks. ●'I've **never** been to America. Have you ever been there?' 'No, **never.**'
  2 Usual position, before the verb but after the verb *to be* ●She **never** shouts and **never** weeps. ●She is **never** angry. Otherwise, usually after the first auxiliary but this is not a reliable rule ●He has **never**

111

been seen paying for a drink. •You **never** have to ask him twice. •I shall **never** come back.
3 Initial position + inversion •**Never** have I seen him so unhappy. Making a negative imperative, formal •**Never** go to sleep with your shoes on. (Don't ever)
nevertheless
adverb sentence adverb (= in spite of that, however) •He is 92. **Nevertheless** he looks after himself. •It's rather expensive but I'll buy it, **nevertheless**.
❖ **in idioms** •It would **never do** to meet the Queen wearing dirty shoes. (It would not be right at all — so you must clean them) •'My shoes are dirty.' '**Never mind**!' (Don't worry about them.) •The speech seemed **never-ending**. (very long) •I've heard him sing once. **Never again**. (Once is enough; he sings very badly)

new
adjective (≠old, = fresh) **newer, newest** •He spent all his money on a **new** coat. •Is your car **new** or second-hand? •**New** potatoes taste better than old ones.
❖ **in compounds** •a **new**-born baby (just born) •a **newly**wed couple (just married) •a **new**comer (someone recently arrived)
❖ **in idioms** •It looks **as good as new**. (though it is old) •I'm **new to the job** so I work rather slowly. (I've only just started)

news
noun non-countable (= information about recent events) •Have you read the **news** today? •The **news** is that there will be no buses tomorrow. •Do you have any **news** of your daughter?
❖ **in compounds** •Papers get the news from **news**agencies such as Reuter. •We get our **news**papers from **news**agents (shops).
❖ **in idioms** •That's **news to me**. (I didn't know that before) informal •I had to **break the bad news** to him. (tell him something unpleasant) •He's often **in the news**. (mentioned in newspapers, on television, in public)

next
adjective determiner (≠ first, = nearest, following) •He lives in the **next** house/**next**-door. •They discussed it at the **next** meeting. •He will be 22 **next** year. •Who's **next**? Please come forward. •He was ill on Monday and the **next** day he died. (on Tuesday)
adverb (= afterwards, subsequently) •I remember the first verse of the song but what comes **next**? •First you wash it, **next**, you dry it.

next to
preposition (= in the closest place to) •Could we have the table **next to** the window?
adverb (= almost) informal •It's **next** [door] **to** impossible to find what you need in all this muddle. •He has **next to** nothing in the bank.

nice
adjective (≠ nasty, = pleasant, good, kind) best replaced by a more precise adjective in writing, such as *enjoyable, kind, pretty* etc. •'If the weather's **nice**, I'll read a **nice** book, lying in my **nice** little garden, with a **nice** box of chocolates supplied by my **nicest** friend.' 'That sounds much **nicer** than driving to the seaside.'
❖ **in idioms** •This looks **nice and clean**. (Its cleanness makes it nice) •**nice and fresh, nice and warm, nice and peaceful** etc.

night /naɪt/
noun (≠ day, = time of darkness between days, sometimes used to include evening or time after work) •What are you doing to-**night**? (this evening) •What about tomorrow **night**? •I saw that film last **night**. (yesterday evening) •I lay awake all **night** thinking about it. •He works in an office during the day, and studies at **night**. •He worries about his girl friend **night and day**. (all the time)
❖ **in compounds** •**Night**-clothes are worn in bed. (pyjamas, nightdresses

112

— 'evening dress' is formal dress for social evenings) •We can go to a **night** club after dinner, and dance. •He has **night**mares (bad dreams) if you don't leave the **night**light on. (little light left burning all night)

no
adverb
A plural **noes** (negative reply, ≠ yes) •'Does Sophie drive well?' '**No**, she doesn't.' •'Doesn't Sophie drive well?' '**No**, she doesn't.'
B to give an adjective the opposite meaning •She's **no** great driver. •She's **no** better than me. •**No** fewer than a thousand people came to watch. (There were really as many as that) •**No** more than six people allowed in the lift. (six or less)
adjective determiner used as negative of 'any' in same positions (= not any, not a)
+ *noun* •There's **no** time. (not any time)
+ *-ing* •You must do **no** [heavy] gardening. •**No** smoking. (Smoking is not allowed)
+ *adjectives* (especially comparatives) •This chair is uncomfortable and this one's **no** better. That one's **no** different. But *not* is more often used before adjectives without nouns: 'This chair is not comfortable.'

nobody, no one
pronoun (= not anybody) •I saw **nobody** come in. I'm sure **no one** came in. (I didn't see anybody, anyone) •**Nobody** else was there. (no other person)

nothing /ˈnʌθɪŋ/
pronoun (= not anything) •I've got **nothing** to do. (I haven't got anything to do) •**Nothing** else matters. (This is the only thing that matters) •You can have it for **nothing**. (free)

nowhere
adverb (= not in any place, not anywhere) •The road seems to lead **nowhere**. •We must sleep here, there's **nowhere** else.

❖ *in idioms* •It's **no trouble**. (not a bother) •We had **no choice**. (There was only one possibility) •It **makes no difference** which way you do it. (The result will be the same) •There's **no harm** in asking the price. (no expense, no damage) •**No doubt** you're right. (I'm sure) •**This must go no further**. (Don't tell anybody else) •**No sooner** had he spoken **than** everyone was silent. (As soon as he spoke) •There's **no such thing as** free service. (It doesn't exist; you always pay some way or another) •**It's no good crying/Crying does no good**. (It's not helpful/useful to cry) •There's **no saying/knowing/telling** what will happen next. (It's impossible to say etc) •There's **no more** milk [left]. (It's gone) •**No through road**. (not connected with another road, dead end) •**Nobody but you** would think of that! (Only you) •It's **nobody's business but mine**. (It does not concern anyone else) •'I'm sorry I broke your pencil.' 'Oh, **that's nothing**.' (Never mind) •Don't be embarrassed; **it's nothing to be ashamed of**. (not a matter for shame) •It will take a very long time, **to say nothing of** the expense. (not mentioning, let alone) •He is so rich he **thinks nothing of** spending $1000 on a pair of shoes. (He hardly notices) •Your remarks have **nothing to do with** the problem. (They are irrelevant, not connected with it) •I'll **have nothing to do with it** if it involves stealing. (I shall not join in) •He had wonderful plans but they all **came to nothing**. (had no result) •His new girl friend is **nothing like** his old one. (They are quite different) •She's **nothing like as** pretty. (not nearly as pretty) •Her car is **nowhere near** as new as his. (Her car is much older) •He was wearing **next to nothing**. (very few clothes) •The car won't move; there's **nothing for it** — we must walk. (no other way) •'What's on the news?' '**Nothing much**.' (very

113

little) informal ●'I think he's a fool.' 'No, he's **nothing of the kind**; he's very clever.' (not at all) ●'Have you heard the story about his adventure in Spain?' 'Yes, but there's **nothing in it**.' (it's not true) ●'Can you water-ski?' 'Yes, there's **nothing to it**.' (it's very easy)
See also **any, none, some**.

non- /ˈnɒn/
prefix used to make nouns, adjectives and adverbs negative (=not) ●**non**-resident ●**non**-smoker ●**non**-violent ●**non**-iron ●**non**-profitable ●**non**-stop
See also **un-**.

non-countable

Non-countable, or uncountable or mass nouns are words with no plurals, not used with *a/an* and followed by singular verbs. Some of the most common are: **advice, anger, beauty, behaviour, bread, conduct, courage, dancing, furniture, hair, harm, health, information, intelligence, knowledge, luggage, money, news, parking, poetry, progress, research, safety, spaghetti, travel, violence, wealth, weather, wine, work**
●Their **health** is good. ●Give me some **information**. ●Is good **weather** expected? ●Let me give you some/a piece of **advice**. ●She has lots of dark curly **hair**. ●The **furniture** needs polishing. ●The **spaghetti** is nearly cooked. ●Our **research** has shown we need more fertiliser. ●Their **intelligence** was surprising. ●No/Little/Not much **progress** has been made. ●Give me some more **bread**/another loaf of **bread**.
NB Many nouns can be used both as non-countable and countable nouns: ●He sells many **cheeses**. (different sorts of cheese, but *cheese* is more often thought of as non-countable) ●There's some **cheese** in the cupboard. Is there enough? ●You eat too much **cheese**.

Unit nouns are used to refer to subdivisions of non-countable nouns. The most common are: **bit, part, piece** ●[a] **part** of his education ●a **bit** of paper ●a **piece** of chocolate.
Nouns of measure are more precise: ●a **ton** of rubbish ● a **metre** of cloth.
See also **any, many, much, some,** ARTICLES, NOUN.
For more details see CEG 2.4.

non-finite

Non-finite clauses have non-finite verbs such as (a) an *-ing* participle, (b) an *-ed* participle or (c) an infinitive. The clauses in **bold** below are non-finite and do not make complete sense without the rest of the sentence.
(a) *an -ing participle* ●**Entering the church,** you see the altar straight ahead. ●**Not having my glasses on,** I can't see it. ●**The baby being asleep,** we moved quietly.
(b) *an -ed participle* ●**Frightened by the noise,** she screamed. ●**The bill paid,** we left the restaurant.
(c) *an infinitive* ●The answer is **to pay by cheque.** ●It would be better **for you to pay cash.**
See also FINITE, INFINITIVE, -ING, PARTICIPLE.
For more details see CEG 7.15.

none /nʌn/
pronoun determiner used with non-countable nouns (=not any, no part) and countable nouns (=not any, not one) ●'**None** of that bread is fresh.' '**None** at all?' '**None**. Have a biscuit.' ●**None** of his friends will tell him. (but 'Neither of his parents is alive.') ●**None** of us knows for certain.
❖ **in idioms**
+ *the* + *comparative* + *for* ●He's **none the better for** his time in hospital. (Perhaps he's worse)
+ *too* + *adjective/adverb* ●My coffee's **none too hot**. (rather cold) ●He speaks English **none too well**. (badly) ●**Nonetheless,** you'll

noun

understand him. (nevertheless, all the same, however)
See also **any, either, neither, no, some.**

nor
conjunction compare *either . . . or* (neither . . . + **nor**) ●Neither my mother **nor** my father told me.
adverb (= also . . . not, neither, in answer to negative statements) ●'She didn't tell me.' '**Nor** did he.' See also **either, neither, or.**

not
adverb used to make verbs and other words negative; in speech, usually contracted to *-n't* after auxiliary verbs ●You must **not**/must**n't** smoke. ●He's **not** arriving till tomorrow. ●He's **not** here yet. ●You were silly **not** to take the opportunity. ●It's mine, **not** yours. ●**Not** everyone will believe your story. ●He dared **not** speak. ●She used **not** to be silly.
proform Compare *so.* ●'May I smoke?' 'I'm afraid **not**' ●'Is this mine?' 'I think **not**'. (I don't think so) ●'Will he recognise me?' 'I hope **not**.' ●'She doesn't know.' 'I suppose **not**.'
❖ *in idioms* ●He is **not without** friends. (He has friends). ●He paid **not a penny**. (nothing) ●'Thank you very much.' '**Not at all**.' (polite reply to thanks or apologies) ●'Are you angry?' '**Not in the least**.' (not at all) ●She is **not his girl friend** but his wife. (She is his wife, not his girl friend) ●She is **not only his wife but also** his business partner. (She is his partner as well as his wife) ●**Not that it really matters** . . . but how did you know my name? (Although it does not really matter . . .)
See also **neither, never, no,** CONTRACTIONS, NEGATIVE.

note /nəʊt/
verb (= pay attention to, write down) ●Please **note** that the arrangements have been changed. ●Have you **noted** the new address? ●If you don't **note** it [down] you will forget it.

noun
A (= musical sound, written sign for it) ●She sang every **note** perfectly.
B (= a written record or comment) ●Did you make/take **notes** of his speech? ●There's a **note** added at the bottom of the page.
C (= a short or informal letter) ●It is polite to send a **note** saying thank you for hospitality.
D (= paper money) ●He paid me in £20 **notes**.
❖ *in idioms* ●**Take note of** what I say! (remember it) ●**Make a mental note**. (remember it) ●I'd like to **compare notes** with you about our experiences in Africa. (talk about something we both know)

noun
Nouns are words which can be used as the subject or object of a verb. They are usually the names of people, things, qualities, actions etc.
noun phrases Words or groups of words acting as subject or object of a verb. In the following examples, the words in **bold** are noun phrases: ●**Brothers and sisters** always argue. ●**The fat woman with glasses** is **my aunt**. ●**My aunt's car** wouldn't start. ●**The ignition key** was stuck. ●My father said **something unpleasant**. ●**Auntie Flo** suggested **calling a garage**. ●She didn't know **the number of the garage**. ●So we all had **a three-mile walk**. ●**What he wants** is your money.
plurals Most nouns can be made plural by adding *-s:* **keys, troubles, notes, ideas, girls, houses**. The most common irregular plurals are:
●**man — men** ●**woman — women**
●**child — children** ●**foot — feet**
●**tooth — teeth** ●**wife — wives**
●**knife — knives** ●**leaf — leaves**
●**life — lives** ●**shelf — shelves**
non-countable nouns (mass nouns) have no plural. They are often the names of substances: **wood, iron,**

> glass, butter, milk, rice, ice, paper, hair, dust, rubbish. Some nouns can be both countable and non-countable/•wood = a wood (forest)/wood (timber)

now
adverb
A (=at this time, ≠then) •Once I lived in the country but **now** I live in London.
B (=very soon, immediately) •Please, doctor, come **now**.
sentence adverb discourse marker, to attract attention •**Now**, listen to me. •**Now** then, we'll begin.
noun (=the present time) •**Now** is the moment to ask him. •From **now** on it will be downhill. •Up to **now**/Till **now**/Until **now** we have walked uphill. •By **now** you must be tired. (At or before this moment)
now [that]
conjunction (=as a result of the fact that) •**Now** that I know him better, I like him more than I did.

nowadays
adverb (=in modern times, now, compared with the past) •Not many people employ private servants **nowadays**.
❖ **in idioms** •We meet **now and then**. (occasionally) •**Now and again**, he rings up for a chat. (Occasionally, From time to time) •He was on the phone **just now**. (a moment ago) •We've answered question 1. **Now for** question 2. (Let's turn our attention to) •I do remember, **now [that] you mention it**.
See also PRESENT.

number
noun
A countable (=part of counting system, written sign, figure, digit) •What's the **number** of the page? •Do you have his [phone] **number**? •The houses on this side have even **numbers**.
B often plural form with singular meaning (=quantity) •A large **number**/Large **numbers** of students gathered in the street. •The **number** of students in this university *is* 3000. •3000 *is* a large **number**. •3000 students *are* listening to him.

numberless
adjective (=too many to count) •There are **numberless** poems about love.

numerous
adjective attributive and predicative (=many, widespread) •**Numerous** people have mentioned it. •Insects became more **numerous**. (there were more of them)
❖ **in idioms** •**A number** of us asked questions. (some) •**Any number of** books have been written about it. (many) informal •He does everything **by numbers**. (as if by machine, in strict order) •**His days are numbered**. (He will not live/last much longer) •He thinks only of **number one**. (himself) informal. •That's our **number one problem**. (most important)

O

object
noun /ˈɒbdʒɪkt/
A (=thing) •He took several **objects** out of the box.
B (=aim, purpose) •Our **object** is to reach an agreement.
verb /əbˈdʒekt/ (=be against, protest) •I don't **object** if you want to smoke, but my mother **objects** to smoking.

object
In grammar, a word or phrase can be
(a) the direct object of a verb •The dog chased **the cat**.
(b) the indirect object of a verb •He gave **me** the money. (to me)
(c) the object of a preposition •I threw a stone at **him**.

occasion
noun
A (=time, [important] moment) •Their wedding was a very happy **occasion**.

B (= need) ●If the **occasion** arises, I'll ask the bank for more money. — formal
occasional/occasionally
adjective/adverb (= infrequent/infrequently) ●We get an **occasional** letter./He writes **occasionally**.
odd
  adjective
  A (= strange, out of place) ●It's rather **odd** that he hasn't phoned. ●He is wearing **odd** socks, one red, one grey. ●If you have any **odd** moments with nothing to do, I have some **odd** jobs for you.
  B (= and a little more) *number* + **-odd** ●He weighs 80-**odd** kilos. (80 – 90 kg)
  C (= not divisible by 2) ●1, 3, 5, 7, 9 are **odd** numbers.
oddly
  adverb
  A sentence adverb (= surprisingly) ●**Oddly** [enough] we have met before.
  B (= in a strange way) ●He spoke **oddly**, as if he were drugged.
odds
  noun (= chances of something happening) ●The **odds** are 10 to 1 that he will win.
❖ *in idioms* ●He's often the **odd man out**. (someone left out of a group; someone who doesn't make friends easily) ●It makes no **odds** whether you pay now or later. (It makes no difference) ●The **odds are against** her arriving early. (It is unlikely that she will) ●They are **at odds with each other** about money. (They disagree about it) ●I found the right button in this little box of **odds and ends**. (assorted oddments)
of /ɒv, əv/
  preposition
  A (= belonging to) ●the lid **of** the box ●the taste **of** honey
  B (= containing) ●a box **of** letters ●a jar **of** honey
  C (after measurements, dates, unit nouns) ●two grammes **of** powder ●the first **of** May ●a piece **of** cardboard ●a loaf **of** bread
  D (= from among) ●a member **of** the club ●one **of** my friends ●the bigger **of** the two ●the most important **of** all ●a type/sort/kind **of** animal ●Three **of** us want to go
  E (= for, by) ●The love **of** a mother for her child. ●A child's love **of** his mother.
  F (= possession — mainly for inanimate nouns) ●the leg **of** the chair (compare 'the boy's leg') ●the history **of** the world ●the point **of** his remark ●the cost **of** tea
  G + *no* + *noun* (= without the quality) ●a book **of** no interest (an uninteresting book) ●a stone **of** no value (a valueless stone)
❖ *in collocations* ●She dreams/speaks/thinks/talks **of** no one else. (about) ●I am certain/sure/convinced **of** it. ●How kind/clever/nice/silly/wise etc **of** you to do that! ●I'm fond/proud/ashamed/tired/glad **of** it. ●He died **of** hunger. ●Can we cure her **of** this disease? ●They robbed him **of** his money. (stole his money from him) ●Do you know **of**/Have you heard **of** him?
See also **because** [**of**], **by way of, for the sake of, in reach of, in search of, in spite of, instead** [**of**], **make a fool of, make fun of, out** [**of**].

off /ɒf/
  adverb (= away [from], ≠ on) ●They went **off** early in the morning. ●Take your shoes **off** before you go in. ●Please turn/switch/put **off** the light. ●Goodbye, I'm **off**. ●Take Monday **off**; have a holiday. ●Communications failed; we were cut **off** from the rest of the world.
  preposition (= [away] from, ≠ on) ●Keep **off** the grass. ●Cut a piece **off** the end to make it shorter.
  adjective predicative only
  A (= cancelled) ●The party's **off**.
  B (= not fresh enough to eat or drink) ●Throw that milk away; it's **off**.
  C (= not connected, working) ●'Is the electricity on?' 'No, it's **off**.'
    attributive ●It's one of his **off**

off

117

offend

days. (not as good as usual) ●Hotels are cheaper in the **off** season.

❖ **in compounds** ●well/badly **off** (rich/poor) ●better/worse **off** (in a better or worse state) ●**off**-white (not quite white, slightly grey or yellow) ●**off**-colour (not quite well, slightly ill) ●**off**-putting (unpleasant: see **put off**)

❖ **in idioms** ●I watched TV **on and off/off and on**. (from time to time, not continuously) ●He answered me **right/straight off**. (immediately) informal ●The street I live in is **off the High Street**. (a turning from) ●He's **gone off** [drinking] tea. (lost his appetite, taste for it) ●This is **off the record**. (not to be made public, secret) ●Those remarks are **off the point**. (irrelevant) ●Are you **off your head?** (mad)

See also **break off, clear off, come off, cut off, drop off, fall off, get off, go off, keep off, set off, show off, wash off, wear off, write off**.

offend

verb (= make angry, cause hurt feelings) ●He didn't mean to **offend** you, he was only joking. ●Some people are easily **offended**.

offence

noun (= crime, wrong, cause of hurt feelings) ●It is not an **offence** to smoke in the street, but it gives **offence** to some people. ●Don't take **offence** if I tell you this.

offensive

adjective (= unpleasant, hurtful) ●It is always **offensive** to call someone a liar.

noun (≠ defensive, = attack) ●The enemy is now on the **offensive**.

offender

noun (= guilty person) ●**Offenders** [against this rule] will be punished.

offer

verb (= present something for acceptance or refusal, say you are willing to do something) ●She **offered** us coffee/coffee to us/to bring [us] coffee ●Let me **offer** [you] some advice. ●How much will you **offer** [me] for my car?

noun (= something offered) ●Thank you for your **offer** of help. ●He made an **offer** of £1000 for the car. ●You should accept his **offer**. ●There was cheap food on **offer**.

often /'ɒfən/

adverb (= frequently, ≠ seldom) ●'How **often** do you wash your car?' 'Not very **often** — once a month.' ●Old cars are **often** very comfortable.

❖ **in idioms** ●She sends me a card **every so often**. (now and then, from time to time) ●He comes home late **more often than not**. (more than 50% of the time)

old

adjective (≠ new and ≠ young) ●**Old** shoes are more comfortable than new ones. ●**Old** people are less energetic than young ones. ●'How **old** is he?' 'Not very **old**; about 35.' ●He is exactly 35 [years **old**]. ●She's an **old** friend, I've known her a long time. ●When I grow **old**, I'll sit in a rocking-chair all day and read. ●My brother is **older** than I am. ●The **older/elder** of the [two] brothers is a politician. ●The **oldest/eldest** son inherits the land. ●This is the **oldest** part of the building.

❖ **in compounds** ●**old**-age pensioner (person past working age) ●**old** boy/**old** girl (former pupil of a school) ●**old**-fashioned (out of date, no longer common, ≠ modern)

on

preposition

A (= touching, supported by, ≠ off; the usual word is *on; upon* is more formal) ●Put the money **on** the table. ●The cat's **on** the roof. ●He kissed me **on** the cheek.

B (with times — days, dates) ●He'll come **on** Wednesday/**on** the second of April/**on** the day after tomorrow/**on** time.

C + *-ing* or + *noun* (= after) ●**On** hearing his voice, I knew who he was.

D (with methods of travelling) ●He goes to work **on** the train/**on** the

bus/**on** foot/**on** a bicycle. (But also 'by train', 'by bus')
E (=about) •He is writing a book **on** nuclear physics.
F (=by means of) •They live **on** rice and fish. •Cars run **on** petrol.
•We spoke **on** the telephone.
adverb/adjective (=continuously, forward, in use) •Let's move **on**.
•We walked **on** and **on**. •Please drive **on** to the next garage. •Send my letters **on**. •Turn the light/fire/radio [etc] **on**. •Is that film still **on**?

onto
preposition (=to a position on) •He jumped on/**onto** the horse. •She came **onto** the stage.
❖ *in idioms* •Where on earth is it? (I can't find it anywhere) •**On my/the way** here, I met Sophie. (As I was coming here) •Is he here **on business** or **on holiday**? (for reasons of) •Whose side are you **on**? (Who do you support?) •Did he arrive late **on purpose**? (intentionally, purposely) •**On the contrary**; he intended to arrive early. (No, that is not the case at all) •**On the whole**, it was a success. (in general, taken all in all) •I'll buy the red one . . . . No, **on second thoughts**, the blue one. (having reconsidered) •The red one is stronger. **On the other hand**, the blue one is prettier. (However) •She took her pens, pencils, papers **and so on**. (etc) •We must work now; we can relax **later on**. (later, some time afterwards) •The chimney was **on fire**. (burning) •The miners are **on strike**. (refusing to work) •Drinks are **on me**! (I'm paying for them) •He's **on his own**. (alone)
See also **carry on, come on, get on** [with], **go on, hold on, keep on, look** [down] **on, put on, run on, take on, try on, wait on**.

once /wʌns/
adverb
A (=one time) •I've seen him only **once**. •Tell me **once** more/again. •Take the pills **once** a day.
B (=some time ago) •He was **once** a poor man but now he's rich.
conjunction (=from the moment that) •**Once** you understand it, it seems very easy.
❖ *in idioms* •I told him once [and] **for all**: he must go. (for the last time) •I see her only **once in a while**. (now and then, infrequently) •Please give it to me **at once**. (immediately) •Everybody spoke **at once**. (at the same time, together) •**All at once**, it went dark. (suddenly) •[**Just**] **for once**, let me pay. (I don't usually pay but I want to this one time) •**Once upon a time** there was a princess . . . (A long time ago — beginning of a story) •Stir the mixture **once or twice**. (a little, a few times)

one
adjective determiner (1, a single, a certain, the same) •There's only **one** way to do it. •Start on page **one**. •It cost **one** dollar twenty-five. ($1.25) •She died at a hundred and **one**. (aged 101) •She died at **one** thirty. (1.30, half past one) •I need **one**/a third of a litre. (⅓ litre) •**One** of my friends gave it to me. •I saw her **one** day in the supermarket. •I'd like to go to India **one** day. •They all face **one** way.
pronoun
A (used instead of a noun referring to a single thing or person) •I need a doctor/telephone/pencil/drink; is there **one** here? (indefinite) Compare 'I need bread/information. (non-countable) *Is* there *some* here?' and 'I need eggs/details. (plural) *Are* there *some* here?' and 'I need your bicycle/your co-operation; can I have *it*?' (specific, definite)
B as subject + singular verb (=any person, including speaker) •**One** should not wear red at funerals. •**One** must do **one's** best to help. formal; compare 'We must do our best/You must do your best . . .' •Talking to **one**self is a sign of madness.

only

ones
plural •I need six eggs. Are there any brown **ones**? •Which **ones** can I take? •I've got some little brown **ones** here.

the one/the ones
pronoun •Talk to the manager; he's **the one** who decides. •Give me **the ones** [that] you don't want.

❖ *in compounds* •**one**-eyed •**one**-legged •**one**-armed (with only one eye, leg, arm) •a **one**-man business (with no employees) •a **one**-horse town (small, boring) •a **one**-sided argument (biased, incomplete) •a **one**-way street (traffic in one direction only) •some**one** •any**one** •every**one** •no **one** (-body)

❖ *in idioms* •This is the **one and only** Count Basie! (unique) •I can't **tell one** jazz player **from another**. (distinguish) •Who wants to go? I do, **for one**. (and I suppose there are others) •It's a knife and a tin-opener [**all**] **in one**. (combined, in a single object) •They like **one another**. (each other) •They are often in **one another's** houses. For more details see CEG 3.29.

only /ˈəʊnlɪ/
adjective (= with no others in the same group) •I was the **only** woman wearing trousers. •The **only** food pandas eat is bamboo. •The **only** animals I saw were sheep.
adverb (= and nothing more, and no one else) •I **only** want to say 'hello'. •There are **only** little ones left. •Ladies **only**. (Only ladies are allowed in.) •She **only** laughed at me. (Several possible meanings, according to intonation — She didn't take me seriously/Others did not laugh/She didn't talk to me/She did not laugh at anyone else)
+ *inversion* beginning a sentence •**Only** after long study did I understand.
   In writing, put the word **only** directly before the word it concerns. •John lent me **only** half the money. •John **only** lent me the money. •**Only** John lent me money. •John lent me **only** money.
conjunction (= but) informal •I'd like to help, **only** I shall be away.

❖ *in idioms* •Is he **an only child**? (with no brothers or sisters) •**If only** I could understand! (I wish) •Don't walk there; I've **only just** cleaned the floor. (I cleaned it a moment ago) •He'll be **only too pleased** to help. (very) •He **not only** spoke to me; he gave me a kiss too.
+ *inversion* •**Not only did he** speak to me; he gave me a kiss, too.
See also **alone, else**.

open

adjective (≠ shut, ≠ closed) •Come in! The door's **open**. •Is the bank **open** yet? •I have an **open** mind about that question.
verb (= cause to open, start) •Please **open** the window. •The opera **opens** with a chorus. •New possibilities **open** [up].
noun (= the outdoors, public knowledge) •He enjoys camping, living in the **open**. •At last, we can bring our opinions into the **open**.

opening
noun
A (= start, inauguration) •The **opening** of the new library will be next month.
B (= space, hole) •There is a small **opening** in the fence.
C (= opportunity for a job, business) •Are there many **openings** for young musicians in television?

openly
adverb (≠ secretly, = willingly) •He told us **openly** of his past crimes.

❖ *in compounds* •**open**-ended (without a time-limit) •**open**-hearted (generous) •**open**-minded (willing to consider new ideas) •**open**-eyed (surprised, or with full knowledge)

❖ *in idioms* •He welcomed me **with open arms**. (generously) •**It is open to you** to refuse. (That is an option, a possible choice)

other

opportunity
noun (= chance, favourable moment) ●He was offered the **opportunity** of working abroad for a year and he took it. ●Most of us waste our **opportunities**.
See also **chance, possibility**.

or
conjunction co-ordinating (marking an alternative) ●Are you going **or** staying? ●Is he old **or** young? ●He never writes **or** telephones. ●Hurry **or** [else] you'll be late. ●This coffee — **or** [rather] coffee-flavoured water — tastes awful. (more like water than coffee.) ●He'll be here in a minute **or** so/**or** two. (about a minute, not much more) ●Give it to me, **or** else . . . (a threat, suggesting 'or you will suffer')
either . . . or
●You can **either** go **or** stay.
whether . . . or [not]
●I don't know **whether** he's here **or** there. ●I don't know **whether** he's here **or not**.

order
noun
A non-countable (= state of neatness, ability to work, arrangement, sequence) ●**Order** is important in hospitals. ●He put his work in **order** before he went on holiday. ●The books are arranged in alphabetical **order**, but some may be out of **order**. ●You can't ring him up; the phone's out of **order**. ●Teachers must keep **order** in a classroom.
B countable (= command, request for supply of goods) ●You must obey **orders**. ●Business is good; we have plenty of **orders**.
verb (= command, arrange) ●The officer **ordered** the men to fire. ●He **ordered** the attack. ●If we have guests, we **order** extra milk. ●He **ordered** [the waiter to serve] coffee. ●Coffee was **ordered**. The waiter was **ordered** to serve it. ●It would be better if we **ordered** things differently.

orderly
adjective (= neat, tidy) ●Her books are arranged in an **orderly** way.

disorder
noun
A (= confusion) ●After the party, the room was in **disorder**.
B (= slight disease) ●He suffers from a **disorder** of the liver.

disorderly
adjective (= confused, uncontrolled, violent) ●The police arrested him for his **disorderly** behaviour.
❖ *in idioms* ●No parking. **By order of** the police. (This is an order from the police) ●**In order to** make it easier, I've drawn a map. (With the purpose of making it easier, [so as] to make it easier) formal ●He spoke slowly, **in order that** everyone should understand. (so that) ●His shoes/suits/shirts are **made to order**. (specially for him) ●Your books are **on order** but they have not arrived yet. (ordered, asked for) ●She **orders her husband about/around** as if he were a child. (gives [him] orders in an unpleasant way)
See also **so as to, so that,**
IMPERATIVE.

other /ˈʌðə*/
adjective/pronoun determiner (= remaining, additional, different; use *another* — one word — not *an other*) ●This foot is bigger than the **other** [one]. ●He thinks he's cleverer than all the **other** students/than all the **others**. ●I don't like these; do you have any **others**?/any **other** colours? ●You can swim across if you like but there are **other** ways. ●I like watching **other** people work. ●No **other** woman can cook like you. ●Is there any **other** reason [than that]?

other than
preposition (= except, anything but) ●He has no relations, **other than** his aunt. ●We can't say [anything] **other than** 'sorry'.

otherwise
adverb (= differently, apart from that, in different conditions) ●Stay there until I say **otherwise**. (change the order) ●**Otherwise**, you will be

121

ought [to]

punished. (If you don't) •The paint was scratched in the accident but **otherwise**, the car is fine.

❖ *in idioms* •He comes **every other day**. (on alternate days, eg Monday, Wednesday, Friday) •He telephoned **the other day**. (a few days ago) •He's dishonest. **On the other hand**, his work is good. (However, But) •They understand **each other**. (one another) •Her troubles came **one after another/the other**. (in succession, not all at once) •**Someone or other** will be there. (but I don't know who) •I can't **tell one from the other**. (see the difference between them) •Your friend Sophie was there, **among others**. (and there were other people present)

See also **another, else, rest**.

ought [to] /ɔːt/
verb modal

A (= have a duty, obligation [to], should)

FORMS

(a) *present* •I, you, he, she, it, we, they **ought** to write more letters.
(b) *past* all persons •I (etc) **ought** to have written more letters.
(c) *questions* •**Ought** we (etc) to leave now? / **Ought** we to have left?
(d) *negative* •We **ought** not to leave. / We **ought** not to have left. (short form: **oughtn't**)

B expressing probability •He **ought** to get here before mid-day. •There **ought** to be some new potatoes soon.

See also **should**.

For more details see CEG 6.12.

our
adjective possessive, determiner 1st person plural (= belonging to us)
•We can change **our** money here.
•**Our** children need **our** care.

ours
pronoun possessive, 1st person plural •This house is **ours**; we bought it with our own money. •A friend of **ours** is coming to stay.

ourselves
pronoun reflexive, 1st person plural
•We must ask **ourselves** what we really intend to do. Also emphatic •We saw it **ourselves**, with our own eyes.

❖ *in idioms* •We built the wall **ourselves**. (without help) •We did it **by ourselves**.

out
adverb

A (= away [from inside], absent, to different people, in different directions) •Don't let the dog come in; shut it **out**. •I'm afraid the manager is **out**, can I give him a message? •They live right **out** in the country. •Please give the books **out**. •The message went **out** to the world.

B (= completely, until gone) •She cleaned the cupboard **out**. •Can you wash these marks **out**?

C (= so as to be seen) •The sun/The secret/The flowers came **out**.

adjective (= impossible, incorrect) •That idea's **out**; it wouldn't work. •These calculations are slightly **out**.

out of
preposition

A (= from inside, away from, ≠ into) •I can't get the cork **out of** the bottle. •He flew **out of** the country last night.

B (= from among) •He got 9 [marks] **out of** 10 [possible].

C (= because of) •He asked **out of** politeness, not interest.

D (= from [a material]) •The statue is carved **out of** stone.

outright
adverb (= completely) •She won the race **outright**. (no doubts) •The shot killed him **outright**. (immediately)

adjective (= complete, clear) •She was the **outright** winner.

outside
noun (= outer part) •The **outside** of the house is painted white.

adjective/adverb (≠ inside, = [on the/from the] outside) •We need **outside** help; we can't do it ourselves. •Come **out**[**side**] and look at the garden. (not far)

preposition (≠ within, = on the

outside of) •The dogs sleep **outside** the house. •This problem is **outside** my experience.

outsider
noun (=someone not accepted in a social group, not likely to succeed) •That club does not welcome **outsiders**.

outward
adjective (=away, towards/on the outside) •The **outward** journey was easier than the return journey. •Although his **outward** appearance is frightening, he is a gentle person.

outwards
adverb (=towards the outside) •Forget your own problems and look **outwards** at other people.

outwardly
adverb (=on the outside, superficially) •**Outwardly** I smiled but inwardly I wept.

❖ *in compounds* •**out**break (sudden appearance of disease, trouble) •**out**building (subsidiary building in a group; shed, barn etc) •**out**come (result) •**out**-dated/**out**-of-date (no longer in use) •**out**door (games, shoes etc used outside) •**out**fit (set of clothes/equipment) •**out**last (last longer than) •**out**line (shape, drawing, main ideas summarised) •**out**look (point of view, future probabilities) •**out**number (be more numerous than) •**out**-of-the-way (ideas, places; not commonly known) •**out**patient (sick person attending but not staying in a hospital) •**out**put (production) •**out**set (beginning) •**out**size (very big) •**out**spoken (frank) •**out**standing (important, very good, not yet done)

❖ *in idioms* •I'm **tired out**. (very tired) •**Short skirts are out** [of fashion]. (unfashionable) •Don't trust him; he's **out for/out to get** your money. (trying to get, after) *informal* •He's an **out-and-out** idiot. (complete) •They were **on an outing** to the seaside. (trip, day out) •She gets **out of breath**. (breathless) •He's **out of work**. (unemployed) •He **went out of his**

way to help us. (took special trouble) •You must be **out of your mind**. (mad)
See also: **break out, carry out, come out, cross out, cut out, find out, get out, give out, go out, have [it] out, hold out, keep out, knock out, leave out, let out, look out, make out, mind out, miss out, pick out, point out, put out, set out, sort out, speak out, take out, think out, try out, watch out, work out.**

over
adverb
A (=down, to the other side) •She was knocked **over** by a bicycle. •Turn the toast **over**.
B (=across) •They came/went **over** to Paris from London.
C (=remaining, not used) •Was there any food **over**, after the party?
D + *adjective/adverb* (=too, more than is good) •She's **over** careful about money.
preposition
A (=above, higher than, ≠ under) •Hold the umbrella **over** his head.
B (=so as to cover) •Put a patch **over** the hole.
C (=to the other side of, especially *up/down*) •The elephants went **over** the mountains. •How did they go **over**/across the rivers? •My aunt lives **over** the road.
D (=more than) •It cost **over** £10.
E (=throughout, in many parts of) •The pain spread **over** his body. •We travelled [all] **over** Africa.

❖ *in compounds* •The boat will **over**turn! (be upset) •At noon the sun is **over**head. (directly above) •I need an **over**draft. (permission from bank to take out extra money) •I'd like a room **over**looking the sea. (with a view of) •Please **over**look my mistakes. (forgive, pretend not to see) •**Over**all, I agree. (On the whole) •Try to **over**come your fear. (defeat, master) •We travelled **over**night. (during the night) •**Over**seas students are welcome. (from foreign countries). •He lives

owe

overseas. (abroad) •Don't try to overtake another car in a narrow road. (pass) •Give the leftovers to the dog. (food remaining after a meal.)
Meaning 'too much'. •overcharge •overcrowded •over-dressed •overgrown •overload •over-simplify (etc)

❖ *in idioms* •Your troubles are [all] over now. (ended) •He didn't understand, so I said it [all] over again. (once more) •Half a kilo, please, or **a bit over**. (more) •Let's do it now and get it **over and done with**. (finished). •The acting was a little **overdone**. (exaggerated)
See also: **get over, leave over, look over, put over, take over, talk [it] over, think [it] over, turn over.**

owe /əʊ/
verb (= be in debt for, have to pay) •Please give me the £5 you owe me. •I don't owe you £5. •I lent you £5 last week, so you owe me £5. •I'll give you £3 and there will be £2 owing. •He owes his success to his teachers.

owing to
preposition (= because of) •Owing to the dry weather, we must save water. •They arrived late, owing to traffic jams.

own
verb
A (= possess) •Do you own this house?
B (= admit, confess) •He owned up to his mistake.

owner
noun (= person who owns [possesses]) •Are you the owner of the house or the tenant?
adjective/pronoun determiner
A (intensifies idea of possession) •'Is it your own house?' 'No, it's not my own; I pay rent for it.' •They treat me as if I were their own son. •The washing machine has its own heater. •He has a room of his own. (to himself)
B (= produced without help) •He makes his own breakfast. •She makes her own clothes.

❖ *in idioms* •Don't leave me on my own. (alone, by myself) •It is my very own room. (nobody else's) •He owned to his mistake. •Please own up; we know you did it.

P

pain
noun
A non-countable (= suffering) •The wounded man was in [a great deal of] pain.
B countable (= feeling of discomfort, hurt) •Where is the pain? •Do you have any pains in your legs?

painful
adjective (= very uncomfortable) •My headache was so painful that I took pain-killers.

pained
adjective (= with hurt feelings, offended) •He looked pained when you refused his invitation.

painless
adjective (= not painful, easy) •The operation is painless. •There are no completely painless ways of learning a new language.

pains
noun (= trouble, effort) usually **take pains** •She takes great pains with her work. (tries hard)

painstaking
adjective (= very careful) •The exhibition was arranged with painstaking precision.

❖ *in idioms* •Don't be **a pain!** (nuisance) informal •He won't **go to great pains** to help. (bother much)

pair
noun (= couple, matching parts [two]) •I want a new pair of trousers/scissors/shoes/socks/sunglasses/gloves etc. •Gloves are always sold in pairs.

pair [off]
verb (= make into a pair) •Stop trying to **pair me off** with Sophie; you know I don't like her.

paper
noun
A non-countable (=material used for writing on) •You can't make shoes out of **paper**. •Have you got a piece of **paper**?
B countable (=document) •May I look at your **papers**, please?
C countable (=newspaper) •Have you seen today's **paper**?
❖ *in compounds* •**paper**back (book, without hard cover) •wall**paper** •drawing-/writing-/wrapping-**paper** (etc)

pardon
verb (=forgive, excuse) •I hope you will **pardon** my mistakes. •**Pardon** me. (sorry, for a small fault, such as touching or pushing someone accidentally or for interrupting someone's conversation)
noun (=forgiveness) •I beg your **pardon**. ('Sorry', as above, but more polite. Also used to ask for a phrase to be repeated.) •'My name is Xzyrcsy.' 'I beg your **pardon**?' (Also used, in an unfriendly voice, to mean 'I disagree with what you say')
See also **excuse [me], sorry.**

part
noun (=piece of a whole) •[A] **part** of the puzzle is missing. •**Parts** of the city are very old. •Is it easy to get [spare] **parts** for your old car?
verb transitive/intransitive (=separate) •Nothing will **part** her from her friend. •The time has come to **part**.
partly
adverb (=not wholly) •What you say is only **partly** true.
partial
adjective
A (=not complete) •My cake is only a **partial** success.
B (=prejudiced in favour) •Of course, I am **partial**; he is my son.
impartial
adjective (=fair, disinterested, unbiased) •Judges must be **impartial**.

❖ *in idioms* •**For my part**, I think it's a bad idea. (as far as I'm concerned) •It was so wet that we stayed indoors **for the most part**. (most of the time, mostly) •Fashion **plays an important part** in the cotton trade. (has an influence on) •I hope everyone will **take part in** the campaign. (participate, join in) •She would never **part with** her wedding ring. (let it go) •He works **part-time**, not full-time. (less than a full working week)

participle
Participles are parts of a verb. Present participles end in *-ing*. Past participles of regular verbs end in *-ed*.
present participles (-ing) used
(a) in all progressive (continuous) tenses: •She is/isn't **smoking**. (present progressive) •She was/wasn't **listening**. (past progressive) •They will/won't be **eating** soon. (future progressive) •He would/wouldn't be **lying** in the sun if it were possible. (conditional progressive) •He has/hasn't been **working** all day. (present perfect progressive)
(b) like adjectives when they describe permanent characteristics: •Go through the **revolving** door. (the door which always revolves) (Compare 'Can you see the wheel revolving?' — main interest is in the action)
past participles (-ed, -en, etc) used
(a) in all simple perfect and passive forms •He has/hasn't **cleaned** the car. (present perfect) •He had/hadn't **cleaned** it. (past perfect) •He will/won't have **found** it yet. (future perfect) •He'd/He wouldn't have **known** if you hadn't told him. (conditional perfect) •The car is **cleaned** regularly./It is being **cleaned** now. (present simple/present progressive passive) •She was **followed**/being **followed**. (past simple/past progressive passive)

particular

No progressive passive for the following •He'll be **told**. •I'd be **punished**. •They'd have been **seen**. •The house has been **painted**. •We had been **warned**.
(b) *like adjectives* when the appearance or state of the thing described is more important than the action which caused it: •He's using a **broken** stick. •He had a very **surprised** look on his face. •We need highly-**trained** teachers. •She was a much-**loved** friend. •It is kept in a **darkened** room.
See also ASPECT, -ING, NON-FINITE, PASSIVE, PERFECT, PROGRESSIVE, TENSE, VERBS.
For more details see CEG 7.15.

particular
adjective
A (=special, specific) •It has a **particular** interest for me, because it comes from my home town. •Do you want any **particular** kind of tea?
B (=very careful, fussy) •He's very **particular** about punctuality, so don't be late.

particulars
noun (=facts in detail) •The police noted all our **particulars**.

particularly
adverb (=specially, in particular) •I hate getting up early, **particularly**/in particular on cold mornings.

pass
verb
A transitive/intransitive (=go by, go past, go through, overtake) •What time will the procession **pass** [this corner]? •Don't try to **pass** that lorry until you can see the road ahead. •We **passed** the time talking and drinking.
B (=give, by hand, or in a game) •Would you **pass** [me] the salt, please? •The ball was **passed** up to the forwards.
C (=succeed, get approved, ≠ fail) •I hope you **pass** your exam. •A law should be **passed** to prevent this.

noun
A (=way across mountains) •Can we use that **pass** in winter?
B (=movement of ball etc in sports) •He made an excellent **pass**, resulting in a goal.
C (=written permit) •You can't get into that building without a **pass**. Compare *passport*.
❖ *in idioms* •I only **passed a remark** about it. (said something, mentioned it) •**Let it pass**! (Let's not argue, trouble about it) •If you take this pill, the pain will **pass away/off**. (slowly go, die away) •Life has **passed him by**. (gone past, left him out) •She's 50, but she can **pass for** 35. (be seen as, be mistaken for) •If she sees blood, she **passes out**. (faints)
See also **past**.

passive
Passive verbs and passive sentences are used a great deal in English, mainly to put the emphasis of a statement in the appropriate place. In an active sentence the person who does the action (the agent) is the *subject* and the person he does it to is the *object:* •He killed the woman. (subject — verb — object) In a passive sentence, the emphasis is changed: •The woman **was killed**. (subject — verb) or •The woman **was killed by him**. In this case, the agent is mentioned when the information is important, but can be omitted when it is not, particularly in impersonal, scientific reporting •The water **was heated**. Not *by me.
FORMS
tenses appropriate tense of *be* + *past participle* •He writes it./It **is written**. •He's writing it./It's **being written**. •She'll tell you./You'**ll be told**. •They lost it./**It was lost**. •He has found it./**It has been found**. •They had taken it./**It had been taken**. •He would pay you./You **would be paid**. •She would have seen

you./You **would have been seen**.
NB (a) *be + present participle* = active, past progressive ●He was writing.
(b) *have + past participle* = active, present perfect simple ●He has written. Intransitive verbs cannot have passive forms.
infinitives [to] be/[to] have been + past participle ●He'd like to teach [her]./She'd like **to be taught** [by him]. ●She expected him to leave the parcel./She expected the parcel **to be left**. ●He was sorry **to have been forgotten**. (that they had forgotten him)
Used especially with modals:
●He has **to be believed**. ●**Can he be trusted?** ●He might not **have been told**. ●He ought **to be paid** now. ●He ought to **have been paid** last week.
-ing forms being + past participle ●He likes talking [to her]./She likes **being talked to** [by him]. ●He resents **having been forgotten**.
●**Having been given** the paper, they started to discuss it. (When they had been given it . . .)
Active sentences with two objects can be made passive in two ways, but usually the person is the subject: ●My mother sent me a card./I **was sent** a card by my mother. or ●A card **was sent** to me by my mother. Active sentences with an object and a complement are made passive by making the object − usually a person − the subject ●They thought him a fool./He **was thought** [**to be**] a fool. ●I made the box bigger./The box **was made** bigger.
For more details see CEG 4.18.

past
adjective (= earlier than the present) ●In **past** times, there was no TV. ●For the **past** few days, she's not been feeling well.
●He remembers his **past** successes.
Do not use *passed*, the past participle of *pass* as an adjective.

preposition (= after, farther than)
●It's half **past** two. (2.30) ●That's long **past** my bed-time. ●The school is just **past** the church.
noun (= past time) ●The **past** can be forgotten but not changed. ●I bet that woman has an interesting **past**.
adverb (= by, in time or space)
●Hours went **past** before we knew.
●Buses go **past** the door.
❖ *in idioms* ●He was a good player once, but now he's [a bit] **past it**. (too old, weak) informal ●This shirt is **past** mending. (too old, worn-out to be mended) informal

past
English refers to the past in several ways, with several different verb tenses and an important difference between the past tense and the present perfect tense.
(a) The past tense refers to a definite time in the past (= then). Sometimes an adverb such as *once* or *last week* makes this clear but sometimes we know it only from the context or circumstances. ●My boy-friend **went** home at eleven o'clock. He **phoned** me from his flat. **Did you hear** the phone ring?
(b) If the speaker is really concerned with the present or the effect of the past on the present, we expect the present perfect: ●My boy-friend **has gone** home. (He isn't here *now*.) He **hasn't phoned** me yet. (I don't know if he is in his flat by *now*) **Have you heard** the phone ring? (during the time between his leaving and *now*)
Some adverbial expressions can be used only with past tenses, not with perfect. ●I saw him **last week/night/month/year**. ●He wrote a week/month/year **ago**.
FORMS
1 Regular verbs form the *past simple* tense by adding *-ed* to the infinitive: ●**cleaned, walked, waited, loaded, moved**. *Questions and negatives* are made with *did*

+ *infinitive* •**Did** he wait? •She **did not**/**didn't** move. •'**Did** they clean the car yesterday?' 'No, **didn't** you clean it?' •We **didn't** know who he was.
2 The *past progressive* tense is formed by the past of *be* (*was*/*were*) + *-ing:* •He **was waiting** while they **were loading** the car. •He **wasn't helping** them. •**Weren't** they **getting** angry? •**Were** you **talking** to him? •**Were** they **being paid** by the hour?
3 Tenses with perfect aspect can also be past: *past perfect* made with *had* + *past participle* •He **had cleaned** the car before I told him to. •Was she tired because she **hadn't slept?** •**Had** she **finished** the work by then?
4 The *past perfect progressive* tense is made with *had been* + *-ing:* •He **had been waiting** for an hour when I finally arrived. •What **had** you **been doing** all that time? •Well, I **hadn't been having** fun; I'd **been driving** through London. I'd **been told** it would be a bad journey and it was.
NB The form of the past and the *subjunctive* are the same in almost every case. When a past tense seems not to refer to the past it may be subjunctive: •I wish I **knew** her name! •If [only] we **had** enough money, we'd buy it now. •It's time we **went** home. See SUBJUNCTIVE.

Modal verbs have no past forms. For ways of expressing the past of *can, must, may, need* and *ought,* see those words. *Could* and *would* are sometimes used with past meanings, but not for definite past events.

Past ideas can be expressed without past tenses. In stories, particularly, the present tense can be vivid: •He **picks** up his gun, but he **is** too late! We also say: •I **hear**/I **am told**/My friends **say** you **want** to sell your car.

For *future perfect* (past in the future) and *future in the past,* see FUTURE.
See also INDIRECT SPEECH, MODALS, PERFECT, SUBJUNCTIVE, TENSE.
For more details see CEG 5.7.

patient /ˈpeɪʃənt/
adjective (= able to wait/work/suffer calmly, without getting angry) •Try to be **patient** with the children, although they are irritating.
noun (= somebody receiving medical advice from a doctor or hospital) •There are several **patients** in the waiting room for Dr Brown.
patience
noun (= ability to be calm) •You need **patience** to teach children.
impatience
noun (= inability to keep calm) •You must never show **impatience** with them.
patiently
adverb (= with patience) •I waited **patiently** for hours but in the end I lost my patience/temper and became very angry.

pay
verb irregular, **paid, paid**
A (= give money for things bought, services provided)
+ *person object* •How much will you **pay** me?
+ *money object* •I'll **pay** £5.
+ *person* + *money* •You must **pay** me £10. •Who's **paying** [the bill]?
B (= be profitable) •Writing books doesn't **pay**.
noun non-countable (= wages, salary) •He works hard for very little **pay**.
payment
noun (= paying, money paid, reward) •**Payment** is due at the end of the month. •You can make the **payment** by cheque. •What do I get in **payment** for my effort?
❖ *in idioms* •I must **pay a visit to** my grandmother. (visit) •Please **pay attention to** these instructions. (take

notice of) ●The business **pays its way** but doesn't make big profits. (is worthwhile, not in debt) ●He was **in the pay of** the enemy. (employed by) derogatory ●Because there was no work for them, the men were **paid off**. (paid and dismissed) ●If I win this bet, will you **pay up**? (pay — probably unwillingly)

people /ˈpiːpəl/
noun plural (= persons) ●How many **people** were invited? ●Business **people** are interested in money.

the people
noun non-countable (= members of a nation, common folk) ●Democratic governments need **the people's** support.

a people
noun countable (= race, nation) ●The Chinese are **a** hard-working **people**. ●Do the **peoples** of Africa understand each other?

per
preposition (= for, during each) ●Apples are 45p **per** pound. ●The car was doing 100 km **per** hour. (kph). ●He earns £90 **per** week/a week.

perfect
adjective non-gradable — not *more, very perfect (= best possible, with nothing wrong or missing) ●The weather was **perfect** that day. ●I have the **perfect** present for his birthday. B (= complete, utter) ●I can't ask a **perfect** stranger for money.

perfection
noun (= [an example of] being perfect) ●She cooked the beef to **perfection**. ●This soup is absolute **perfection**.

perfect
In English grammar, the word *perfect* refers to aspect. Perfect tenses can be present, past and future and always make a connection between the action of the verb and the 'now' or 'then'

perhaps

the speaker is mainly concerned with: ●**I've seen** him before, so [**now**] I know who he is. ●**I had seen** him before, so [**then**] I knew who he was.

Some expressions are used only with perfect tenses: ●He has/had waited **since** four o'clock. ●Have you **already** eaten your supper?
FORMS All perfect tenses are made with *have + past participle*. Progressive perfect tenses are made with *have been + -ing*. Regular past participles, exactly like the past simple, are made by adding *-ed* to the infinitive.
1 *Present perfect (simple)* ●He **has cleaned** the windows. ●**Has** she **washed** the clothes? ●We **haven't locked** the door.
2 *Present perfect (progressive)* ●He **has/He's been working** in the garden all day. ●**Have** you **been helping** him? ●She **has not/hasn't been** sleeping well recently.
3 *Past perfect (simple)* ●He **had/He'd finished** the job, so he stopped. ●She **hadn't done** anything. ●**Had** they **had** a quarrel when you saw them?
4 *Past perfect (progressive)* ●He **had/He'd been working** hard, so he was tired. ●She **hadn't been helping** him. ●**Had** they **been quarrelling** when you saw them?

Only simple perfect tenses can be passive: ●The windows **have been cleaned**. [1] ●The job **had been finished**. [3]
For *future perfect*, see FUTURE.
See also ASPECT, INDIRECT SPEECH, MODALS, PAST, TENSE.
For more details see CEG. 5.8.

perhaps
adverb all positions (= possibly, maybe) ●'Will Sophie be there?' 'Perhaps.' ●**Perhaps** Anthony will telephone later. ●That lady could **perhaps** be Sophie's mother. ●**Perhaps** you would take this suitcase for me./? (polite request)
See also **maybe**.

129

permit /pə'mɪt/
  verb (=allow, make possible) ●We do not **permit** cigarettes/smoking. ●Smoking is not **permitted**.
  +*person object* +*to* +*infinitive*
  ●He **permits** his friends to call him Sam. ●**Permit** me to say how lovely you look. ●His poor health will not **permit** him to walk very far.
  noun /'pɜ:mɪt/ (=written note giving permission) ●You can't fish here without a **permit**.
permission
  noun (=agreement, consent) ●If I can't get my father's **permission** to use his car, I'll have to hire one.
permissible
  adjective (=allowed/allowable) ●Some mistakes are **permissible** in learners' work.
permissive
  adjective (=allowing [too] much freedom ●Your generation is more **permissive** than mine.
  For more details see CEG 6.3.
person
  noun plural, **people** or **persons** — but **persons** sounds formal and impersonal (=human being with an individual character) ●It was the same **person** I spoke to before. ●A **person's** voice is usually quite easy to recognise.
personal
  adjective (=for one particular person, private, rude because too intimate) ●My secretary doesn't open my **personal** letters. ●He said I was getting fat, which I thought was a rather **personal** remark.
personally
  adverb
  A (=directly, not through a representative) ●The Minister will deal with it **personally**.
  B (=speaking for myself) sentence adverb ●Many people think him funny, but, **personally**, I think he's boring.
  C (=in a private way) ●Please don't take this criticism **personally**; it is about your work, not you.
personality
  noun (=character, nature, particularly strong, exciting qualities) ●His mind is energetic but his **personality** is weak. ●She hasn't got enough **personality** to be a successful actress.
personnel
  noun (=people employed, work force) ●The **personnel** department looks after problems connected with the staff.
impersonal/impersonally
  adjective/adverb (=not showing feelings, not human/humanly) ●Computers are efficient but rather **impersonal**. ●'It' is an **impersonal** pronoun.
❖ *in idioms* ●I once saw the Beatles **in person**. (face to face, not on TV etc) ●Do you have any money **about your person**? (in your pocket, with you)
  See also **people**.
persuade /pə'sweɪd/
  verb (=cause [someone] to do something or think something by arguing, begging etc)
  +*person object* +*to* +*infinitive*
  ●Sophie **persuaded** me to lend her £10. ●I wish I could **persuade** you not to lend her money whenever she wants it.
  +*that* +*clause* ●She **persuaded** me that she had a good use for it. (convinced)
persuasion
  noun (=act of persuading, belief) ●With a little **persuasion**, she will agree. ●People of different [religious] **persuasions** united in this campaign.
persuasive
  adjective (=influential in making people think or act differently) ●**Persuasive** advertising encourages us to spend too much.

---

phrasal verbs
  Phrasal verbs are verbs made from two or more words, usually an 'ordinary' *verb* +*an adverb* or +*a preposition*. In this book, the more important ones are shown under

the sub-heading *in idioms* under separate verbs and listed at the end of entries for adverbs and prepositions. They can be used in slightly different ways. The main patterns are shown below, but it is best to look at the examples for normal usage.
1 Some phrasal verbs are *intransitive* •What time do you **get up**? (rise) •The car has **broken down**. (failed to work) *Transitive* phrasal verbs can usually be kept together or separated by the object •'We can **put off** the party till next week.' 'Yes, let's **put it off**.' (postpone, delay) •'I think he **made** that story **up**.' 'Could he **make up** something so clever?' (invent)
2 Pronouns always go before the adverb particle •Of course he made **it** up. •Don't let down your friends/let your friends/**them** down. (break promises to)
3 A *verb + adverb/preposition* is not always a phrasal verb •The end of the wire **turns up**. (points upwards — *verb + adverb*) •I hope the doctor **turns up** soon. (arrives — *phrasal verb*, idiomatic) •We **turned down** the road. (changed direction and went into the road — *verb + adverb/preposition*) •He **turned down** a good job./He **turned** a good job **down**. (refused it — *phrasal verb*)
NB Some verbs are used with particular prepositions, but are not phrasal verbs •You can depend **on** him. •Allow **for** delays. •Don't part **with** your money. •Refer **to** a dictionary. •She laughs **at** all his jokes.
See also PREPOSITION, VERB.
For more details see CEG 10.20.

phrase
A phrase can be simply a group of words but in most grammar books it means a group of words without a finite verb, contrasted with a clause. Thus, an adverb might be one word •**hastily** or a phrase •**in haste** •**in a hurry** •**at great speed** or a clause •**as fast as he could** •**the moment he saw me.**

pick
verb
A (= select, choose) •I don't know which one to **pick**; they are all lovely.
B (= cut, gather) •The apples are nearly ripe; we'll be able to **pick** them soon.
noun (= choice, the best one) •Take your **pick**! •This one is the **pick** of the bunch. (best of the lot) informal
pick up
verb
A (= collect together, gain, get) •He **picks up** ideas here and there. •Where did you **pick up** that information? •Please **pick up** your luggage and leave!
B (= improve, increase) •Business is **picking up**; we're selling more. •The car **picked up** speed and left us behind.
C (= understand, acquire a skill) •I found the game difficult at first but I soon **picked** it **up**.
D (= collect somebody/something, fetch) •My car will **pick** you **up** at the hotel. •Could you **pick up** my letters for me?
pick-up
noun
A (on a record-player = needle and arm) •Is the **pick-up** faulty?
B (= van with open back) •He can carry the equipment in his **pick-up**.
❖ *in idioms* •The cat has **picked holes** in the chair-covers. (made holes) •She's always **picking holes** in my work. (criticising) •She **picks it to pieces**. •He is trying to pick a **fight/quarrel**. (provoke, start) •Say what you want; there's no time to **pick and choose**. (think about the choice) •He has no appetite; he just **picks at** his food. (touches it but without interest) •On a clear day you can **pick out** the church twenty miles away. (see, discern)

place

•Beware **pickpockets**. (thieves who steal from your pocket)

place
noun (=a particular location, spot, position) •Show me the **place** where you saw him. •Father's **place** is at the head of the table. •Let's meet in my **place**. (where I live)
verb
A (=put, arrange) •The seats were **placed** so that we could admire the view.
B (=remember, recall accurately) •I know the name but I can't quite **place** him.
❖ *in idioms* •It's **not his place** to tell me what to do. (duty, right) •**In the first place**, it's too far and **in the second place**, I don't want to go. (One reason is . . . another reason is . . .) •After the party, the furniture was **all over the place**. (spread about, in disorder) •After the first game, the players **change places**. (exchange positions) •Old ideas have to **give place to** new ones. (yield, be replaced by) •I felt **out of place** wearing a suit on the beach. (inappropriate, unsuitable) •You can use milk **in place of** cream. (instead of) •When he was rude to her she really **put him in his place**. (showed her low opinion of him, made him feel small) •When will the wedding **take place**? (happen) •Nobody can **take her place**. (replace her)

place
Adverbs answering the question *Where?* are sometimes called adverbs of place. They include **here, there, anywhere, everywhere, nowhere, somewhere** and many phrases and clauses using such prepositions as **at, to, [away] from, on, off, across, over, along, through, in [to], out of, inside, outside, above, below, under, by, beside, on top of, in front of, underneath, between** and **among**. For examples of use, see these headings.

plan
noun (=arrangement for future activity, diagram/map of room, machine etc) •What are your **plans** for tonight? •The **plans** of the house show a door here.
verb (=make a plan) •The royal visit was **planned** in detail. •It's better to **plan** [ahead] if you want arrangements to be really efficient.
❖ *in idioms* •They're **making plans** to leave/for leaving. (planning) •Everything went **according to plan**. (as planned, as arranged)

play
noun
A non-countable (=activity for amusement, fun) •He didn't intend to hurt you, he only pushed you in **play**.
B countable (=drama, dramatic performance) •Have you seen any of his **plays**?
verb
A (≠work, =amuse oneself) •While we talked, the children were **playing** [games]/with their toys.
B (=act, pretend to be) •A great actor can **play** many parts. •She likes **playing** the grand lady.
C (=produce sound, music) •His radio was **playing** early today. •Can you **play** the piano/some jazz?
❖ *in idioms* •Stop **playing the fool** and get on with your work. (acting foolishly) •It wouldn't be **playing the game** to change the rules now. (acting honourably) •Are my eyes **playing tricks on** me? (deceiving me, giving me false impressions) •They aren't serious; they're just **playing about/around** [with the idea, work, etc]. (having fun) •First we'll record it, then **play it back**. (listen to the recording) •We'd better **play down** the cost when we discuss it with him. (make it seem unimportant, ≠emphasise) •We can **play up** its advantages. (emphasise) •My bad leg is **playing** [me] up. (causing trouble, pain.)

please

verb
A (= make happy) ●He is very hard to **please**. ●It would **please** her to know he's here.
B (= choose) ●You can borrow all the books you **please**.
interjection (making a request polite) ●**Please** don't telephone before 8 am. ●'Two cups of coffee, **please**?' 'With sugar?' 'Yes, **please**.' (but 'No, thank you.')

pleased [with] [to]

adjective (= satisfied, willing, glad) ●I'm **pleased with** your work. ●Are you **pleased to** see him again? ●We shall be **pleased to** answer your questions.

pleasing /ˈpli:ziŋ/

adjective (= likeable, satisfying) ●What a **pleasing** young man! ●The results of the exam were very **pleasing**.

pleasant /ˈplezənt/

adjective (= enjoyable, friendly) ●Lying in the sun is very **pleasant**. ●Please try to be **pleasant** to the boss. ●What a **pleasant** surprise!

pleasure /ˈpleʒə*/

noun (= happiness, satisfaction from something you like) countable ●It is a great **pleasure** to welcome you. ●Reading is his greatest **pleasure**.
non-countable ●I shall welcome him with **pleasure**. ●He takes **pleasure** in gardening/gets **pleasure** from gardening. ●'Thank you for helping me.' 'A **pleasure**.' (polite response to thanks, not at all)
❖ **in idioms** ●He wants me to say I'm sorry, **if you please**, when it's all his fault. (can you believe this?) ●He's very ill. **Please God** he'll get well again. (I hope) ●You don't have to come. **Please yourself**. (Do what you like — I don't mind) informal ●He's always rather **pleased with himself**. (self-satisfied, over-confident) ●'Are you here on business?' 'No, **for pleasure**.' (for fun, recreation)

plenty [of]

pronoun determiner used with both countable and non-countable nouns (= [more than] enough) ●There's **plenty of** room. ●There are **plenty of** seats. ●Twelve is **plenty**. ●She gave us **plenty** to think about.
noun (= state of being well-supplied) ●People who live in **plenty** cannot imagine real poverty.
adverb (= quite) informal ●This house is **plenty** big enough for two people.
See also **enough**.

plurals

In English, nouns can normally be singular or plural if they are countable. Regular verbs have different forms for 3rd person singular present tense: ●**A cat** looks after **itself**. ●**Cats** look after **them**selves.
FORMS
nouns add -*s* ●girl(s), house(s), ring(s) and sometimes -*es* ●watch(es), church(es).
For important exceptions see NOUN (plurals). Some nouns are found only in the plural: **trousers, scissors, pants**.
verbs change their form to mark singular only in the present simple tense, 3rd person: ●He **goes**/They **go**. In other tenses plural is marked by the auxiliary ●He **doesn't** go/They **don't** go. ●He **is** leaving/They **are** leaving. ●He **was** waiting/They **were** waiting. She **has** seen it/They **have** seen it.
pronouns different personal pronouns and corresponding possessive adjectives are used for all persons except *you* in the plural: ●**I/we** ●**me/us** ●**he/they** ●**him/them** ●**my/our** ●**his/their**.
demonstratives also vary: ●**this/these** ●**that/those**
See also ARTICLES, PRONOUNS, VERBS.
For more details see CEG 2.12.

point [at/to]

verb (= indicate, show direction) ●His finger **pointed at** the blackboard.

possession

noun
A (= sharp end) •The **point** of my pencil has broken.
B (= small spot, mark) •A line joins two **points**. •This line is two **point** five centimetres long. (2.5 cm)
C (= main idea, relevance) •Is there any **point** in running if you can't possibly win? •I think you missed the [whole] **point** of his lecture.

❖ **in compounds** •power **point** (electricity socket) •**point** of view (way of seeing/considering something)

❖ **in idioms** •He was **on the point of** leaving. (about to leave, preparing to leave) •He was **at the point of** death. (almost dead) •Please **come to the point**. (Say what you mean, don't waste time on irrelevancies) •That remark is **off the point/beside the point**. (irrelevant) •Rich people are often greedy; your uncle is **a case in point**. (relevant example) •**In point of fact**, he's quite generous. (As a matter of fact, Really) •I mentioned an example **to make my point**. (to make my idea clear) •He **made a point of** thanking her publicly. (took particular care to) •She always tries to **score points**. (in an argument, defeat an opponent by clever answers) •**When it came to the point**, I couldn't tell him. (when the moment came) •He **pointed out** my mistakes/that I had made some mistakes. (indicated, drew my attention to them)

possession

The idea of possession can be expressed
(a) by verbs such as **have, own, belong to** •John **has/owns** a car.
•The car **belongs to** John/him.
(b) by using **'s** (genitive) or possessive pronouns or adjectives
•It is John's car. •**Whose** is it?
•It's John's. It's **his**. It's **his** car.

FORMS
possessive pronouns **mine, yours, his, hers, its, ours, theirs**
possessive adjectives **my, your, his, her, its, our, their** [car]
See also GENITIVE, **of** and individual pronouns and adjectives. For more details see CEG 3.32.

possible

adjective (= that can be, happen, be done) •'Is it **possible** to live for a month without water?' 'No, it's impossible.' •Please reply as soon as **possible**.

possibly

adverb (= perhaps, it is possible that) •He could, **possibly**, have taken the money by mistake.

possibility

noun
A countable (= chance, potential) •There is still a **possibility** that he will win, but not a probability.
•This room has **possibilities**.
B non-countable (= quality of being possible) •The **possibility** of space travel was once doubted by everyone.

possibility

The idea of possibility can be expressed by the verbs **can, may, could, might**. Do not confuse the ideas of 'ability' and 'permission' with 'possibility' because they can be expressed by the same verbs.
•Let's ask him if we **can** swim in his pool. (permission) She says he **can/is able to** swim although he's only two. (ability) **Can** it be true?/It **can't** be true. (possibility) I don't know; he **may/might** swim very well. (possibility) He **may** swim in my pool. (permission) He **might** find it rather cold. (possibility)
•Terrible accidents **can** happen when people are careless./There **could** be an accident now if you're not careful./You **could have been** in a terrible accident if he hadn't warned you. (possibility)

- This is too small; it **can't** be the right size. (logical necessity) ●She **can't** have gone; her car's still here. (logical necessity)
See also **ability, able, can, may, might, opportunity, perhaps.**
For more details see CEG 6.2.

post
noun
A (=system of delivering letters, mail) ●Has the **post** come yet? ●Send this parcel by **post**. ●Put it in the **post**, at the **post** office.
B (=job, position) ●He has been offered an important **post** in a large company.
C (=strong upright pole, support) ●The tent is supported on a central **post**. ●My horse was first past the **post**.
verb
A (=send by post, mail) ●Did you remember to **post** my letter?
B (=place someone in a position) ●Guards were **posted** at the gates.

post-
prefix used to make adjectives (=after) ●**post**-war ●**post**-graduate

practice
noun
A (≠theory, =real use, exercise of a skill) ●You can't improve your tennis without more **practice**. ●What a good idea! Let's put it into **practice**.
B (=habit, custom) ●They have a **practice** of cutting off the hands of anyone who steals.

practise
verb (=exercise regularly, make use of) ●She **practises** [playing] the trumpet every night. ●I believe she **practises** magic.

practical
adjective (=concerned with actual results, ≠theoretical; useful, ≠decorative) ●You must wear **practical** walking boots for climbing; pretty shoes are impractical.

practicable
adjective (=possible [to use]) ●Is it **practicable** to carry all your equipment on your back? ●The road is **practicable** only in summer.

practically
adverb
A (=in a practical way) ●She worked out the costs **practically**.
B (=almost, not quite) ●She did **practically** all the work.
❖ **in idioms** ●We are supposed to start at 8.30 but **in practice**, it's usually 8.45. (in reality) ●I'm rather **out of practice** at speaking German. (not in training, without recent experience)

predicative
See ADJECTIVES.

prefer [**to**] /pri'fɜ:*/
verb not in progressive tenses (=like one thing/person more than an another) ●'Which sort of biscuits do you **prefer**?' 'I **prefer** chocolate ones to plain ones.' (I'd rather have chocolate than plain)
+ -*ing* ●Frogs **prefer** swimming to walking.
+ *to* + *infinitive* ●They can walk but they **prefer** to swim. ●'Would you like to go by taxi?' 'Yes, I'd **prefer** to.'
+ *object* + *infinitive* ●I [should] **prefer** you to come tomorrow. (I'd rather you came tomorrow)

preferable [**to**] /'prefərəbəl/
adjective (=better [than]) ●A taxi would be **preferable** [to a bus].

preferably
adverb (=for preference, if possible) ●You must pay soon, **preferably** today.

preference [**for**]
noun (=a liking for one [thing] rather than another) ●He eats all fruit but has a **preference** for apples. ●The selectors will give **preference** to candidates with previous experience.

prefix
Prefixes are parts of words, joined on at the beginning. Some can be

135

prepositions

used very freely to make new words. The prefixes most worth knowing are:
anti- (=against) •anti-American •antiseptic
bi- (=two) •bilingual •bilateral •biannual
co- (=together) •co-operate •co-author
counter/contra (=against) •counter-revolution •contradict •counter-productive
de- (=reversing a process) •de-colonise •de-centralise •de-frost
dis- (=negative/opposite) •disbelieve •displace •disadvantage •disagree •dishonest
ex- (=formerly) •ex-wife •ex-Prime Minister
il-/im-/in- (=negative) •illegal •immoral •incapable •impossible •illogical •indirect
non- (=negative) •non-smoker •non-political
post- (=after) •postwar •postgraduate
pre- (=before) •pre-war •pre-paid •prehistoric
pro- (=in favour of) •pro-Russian •pro-Islam
re- (=again) •re-write •repaint •re-build
sub- (=below) •sub-heading •sub-committee
super- (=above) •super-human •super-powers
un- (=negative) •unhappy •undo •unaware •untruth.

Use a dictionary to check meanings of words beginning with these prefixes; there are many alternative senses.

prepositions

Prepositions are words mostly showing position or direction in space or time. They go before nouns and object pronouns (*me, you, him, her, it, us, them*). Verbs after prepositions are always -*ing* forms (gerunds, not infinitives). The words in **bold** in the following examples are prepositions. Many of them can also be used as adverbs.
•He went **to** the door **with** his gun **in** his hand and took the money **from** her, **without** saying a word. **For** a moment, she waited, then **by** hitting his hand, she made him let go **of** the gun. She picked it up and pointed it **at** him.

Some prepositions are used with certain verbs, adjectives and nouns in an idiomatic way. It is sensible to learn both words together. The most common and important *prepositional idioms* are listed and exemplified below:

verbs + prepositions •He was **accompanied by** his wife. •Can you **account for** this strange event? •They **accused** me **of** stealing it. •He **apologises for** the delay. •He **approved of** my decision. •Do you **believe in** magic? •This book **belongs to** me. •**Beware of** offending him. •**Borrow** £5 **from** him. •She **depends on** me for help. •What have you **decided on**? •He **died of** cold. •Please **dispose of** the rubbish. •Can you **explain** it **to** me? •She **finds fault with** all my work. •We **hope for** better weather tomorrow. •I think they'll **laugh at** me. •No, they'll **listen to** you. •He **insisted on** paying. •I **mistook** you for your daughter. •I **prefer** her **to** him. •We **object to** these absurd proposals. •The pain **prevented** me **from** sleeping. •She **quarrelled with** her parents and left. •Don't **rely on** getting more money that way. •It will **remind** me **of** you. •**Stick to** your original plan. •Will he **succeed in** reaching it? •He **suffers from** indigestion.

adjectives + prepositions •I'm not **accustomed to** [meeting] people like him. •Is she **afraid of** ghosts? •Don't be **angry with** me **about** my mistake. •Are you **anxious about** being late? •You must be **aware of** the problem. •I'm very **bad at** English. •But I'm quite **clever at** cooking. •I wasn't **conscious of** the

present

change. •My ideas are **different from** (AmE **than**) yours. •Are you **familiar with** this subject? •He is **ill with** bronchitis. •I am **interested in** the job you advertised. •She's very **kind to** animals. •She isn't **nice to** me. •That party is **opposed to** putting up tax. •He's **pleased with** his new radio. •I am not **responsible for** your difficulty. •Photographic film is **sensitive to** light. •Your camera is **similar to** mine. •This cheese is **typical of** the region. •What's **wrong with** wearing a grass skirt?
nouns + prepositions •This is an **account of** his life. •His **belief in** God is unshaken. •He says he has **confidence in** me. •**Congratulations on** your engagement! •He was having **difficulty with** his car. •**Dozens of** children came along. •Your new friend has a bad **effect on** you. •Can you give me an **example of** the process? •There is no **evidence of** damage. •I have no **faith in** medicine. •There's no **lack of** money. •What's **the matter with** this machine? •The **prevention of** crime is difficult. •Do you have **proof of** his guilt? •There must be a **reason for** changing it. •I hate the **thought of** going back to work.
See also individual entries for **about, above, across, after, along, as, at, behind, beside[s], between, beyond, but, by, down, during except[ing], for, from, in[to], inside, instead of, like, near, next to, of, off, on, other than, out of, outside, over, owing to, past, since, till, to, until, upon, with, without.** For more details see CEG 10.

present

We divide time into 'past', 'present' and 'future'. Present tenses of verbs can refer to a point or a period of time called 'now' but they are also used in other ways.
FORMS AND USAGE
present simple Regular verbs: same as the infinitive (except 3rd person singular which adds *-s*). Negatives and questions: use *do* •I **clean** the house. •He **cleans** the car. •He doesn't **clean** the house. •Do you **clean** it? Passive: *be + past participle* •It **is** often **cleaned.**
(a) habit (regularly, every day, once a month, each week, on Sundays, always)
(b) in a time or conditional clause (eg after *when* or *if*) when the main verb is future or imperative. •He'll tell you when/if he **wants** to. •Come when/if you **like.**
(c) in stories, to make them dramatic. •She **goes** to the window, she **jumps**; her body **falls** into the lake.
(d) Some verbs are never used in progressive tenses (stative verbs) The most important are **like, dislike, love, hate, want, wish, prefer, satisfy, surprise, impress, please, believe, doubt, feel** (have an opinion) **think** (have an opinion), **guess, imagine, know, mean, realise, recognise, remember, suppose, understand, hear, see, taste** (have a flavour) **smell** (produce a smell), **sound, weigh** (have weight), **belong to, concern, consist of, contain, depend on, deserve, fit, include, involve, lack, matter, need, owe, own, possess, appear resemble, seem, have** (possess)
present progressive be + -ing •I'm **watching** you. •I know (not *am knowing, see (d) above) what you're **doing.** •'Are you **waiting** for somebody?' 'No, I'm not [waiting].'
(a) at this moment (as I speak, right now, during the present period of time)
(b) suggesting temporary activity. •He's **working** at home this week.
(c) fairly definite future actions, by intention •She's **bringing** her friend tonight. 'Is he **staying** here?' 'No, he isn't **sleeping** here; he's **getting** the last bus.'

137

pretend

(d) in time and conditional clauses, with a future or imperative main verb, when a specific time is 'interrupted'. ●When/If it's **raining**, [you will] take an umbrella. ●If you **are being followed**, change direction.
present perfect simple *have* + *past participle* ●'I've **washed** your socks.' '**Have** you **mended** them?' 'No, they **haven't been mended**.' 'I've **worn** the others for two days.'
(a) actions begun in the past, continuing in the present ●He's **lived** in London a long time. ●How long **have** you **worked** here?
(b) finished actions related to the present, (= so now) ●I've **seen** that film, so I don't want to come to the cinema. ●**Have** you **had** supper? (Are you hungry?) ●The bed **hasn't been made**. (It's a mess)
(c) with stative verbs (listed under present simple, above) ●He **has had** his new car since Tuesday. ●She **has wanted** to leave for some time.
(d) with *ever, never, already, yet* ●**Have** you ever **read** it? ●She's never **met** him. ●We've **discussed** it already/before. ●**Have** you **made** up your mind yet?
present perfect progressive *have been* + *-ing* ●She's **been waiting** for an hour/since early this morning. ●He **hasn't been working**. ●What **has** he **been** doing? Used with the same meaning as the present perfect simple, (a) but not (b), emphasising the continuity of action. ●It's **been raining** since eight o'clock. ●**Has** he **been writing** letters all day? ●I've **been looking** forward to meeting him for ages. See also **if**, ASPECT, PERFECT, PROGRESSIVE.
For more details see CEG 5.1.

pretend

verb (= give an appearance, intending to deceive or in a game) ●I **pretended** to be asleep but I heard everything you said. ●It's no good **pretending** you understand when you don't. ●Now children, **pretend** to be soldiers and march away.

pretence

noun (= false appearance, show, deception) ●He made a **pretence** of enjoying himself but really he was miserable. ●They lead a simple life, with no **pretence** to sophistication.

pretentious

adjective (= claiming importance, making an unpleasantly false show) ●His grand style of dressing and speaking seemed **pretentious** to the people who shared his rather ordinary work.

pretty /ˈprɪtɪ/

adjective (= attractive, delicately designed) ●I liked that **pretty** pink dress you wore.
adverb (= rather, fairly) informal ●He's a **pretty** good/bad tennis player. ●She plays **pretty** well/badly.
❖ *idiom* ●This butter is **pretty well** finished. (almost)

prevent

verb (= stop from happening) ●We can **prevent** accidents by being careful.
+ *object* [+ *from*] + *-ing* ●We can't **prevent** her [from] marrying him.

probability

Probability can be expressed by using an adverb, adjective or a verb such as *ought to* or *should* ●He'll **probably** (adverb) be here before dark. ●He's **likely** (adjective) to be here soon. ●He **should** be/**ought to** be here by six o'clock.
See also **likely, may, might, ought, should**.

progressive

Progressive aspect puts the emphasis on the duration of the action of a verb.
FORMS
present progressive be + *-ing* ●She **is helping** me at the moment. ●Are you **leaving** now? ●We **aren't doing** anything at all. ●Everything **is** slowly **being changed**.

138

past progressive be (was/were) +-ing •They **were waiting** outside when I came in. •**Was** she **cooking** supper when you saw her? •It **wasn't raining** so hard then.
present perfect progressive has/have been +-ing •**I've been waiting** here for an hour/since half past four. •He **hasn't been working** all day. •**Have** you **been enjoying** it?
past perfect progressive had been +-ing •**I'd been waiting** an hour when the bus came at last. •How long **had** you **been waiting?**
future progressive shall/will be +-ing •**I'll be waiting** when you arrive. •He **won't be arriving** till mid-day.
conditional progressive should/would be +-ing •**I'd be studying** hard if my exams were going to be tomorrow. •**Would** you **be working** here if you were a millionaire?
conditional perfect progressive should/would have been +-ing •**He'd have been waiting** at the airport if he'd known what plane she was on.

Stative verbs — see **present simple** (d) — are not used in the progressive.

Always, continuously used with a progressive verb imply unexpected or irritating actions. •She's **always/continuously** forgetting my name. See also ASPECT, PERFECT, PRESENT. For more details see CEG 5.3.

promise /ˈprɒmɪs/
  noun (= statement which may be trusted) •If you make a **promise** you must keep it. •Life is full of broken **promises.**
  verb (= make a promise) •'Please write.' 'Yes, I **promise.**'
  [+*person object*] +*clause*
  •I **promise** [you] I will.
  +*to* +*infinitive* •He **promised** to write soon.
promising
  adjective (= showing signs of future success) •He's young but already a **promising** chess player.

pronoun
Pronouns are words used instead of nouns.
personal pronouns **I, you, he, she, it, we, they** (for subjects) and **me, you, him, her, it, us, them** (for objects). These are easily confused with the possessive adjectives, which are **my, your, his, her, its, our, their.**
possessive pronouns stand for the idea of *adjective +noun*. They are **mine, yours, his, hers, its, ours, theirs.**
reflexive pronouns/emphatic pronouns **myself, yourself, himself, herself, itself, ourselves, yourselves, themselves.**
relative pronouns introduce relative or adjectival clauses: **who, whom, whose, which, that.** The first four are also *interrogative pronouns*, used in questions (another interrogative pronoun is: **what**).
demonstrative pronouns are: **this, these, that, those.**
quantifier pronouns are numerous: **all, each, both, half, some, any, either, many, much, more, most, enough, [a] few, [a] little, fewer, less, fewest, least, several, one, none, neither, every-/some-/any-/no-body/one** and **every-/some-/any-/no-thing.**
indefinite pronoun **one** formal and often replaced by the more ambiguous but less formal **you.** Compare •**One** must try to maintain **one's** standards./**You** must try to maintain **your** standards./People must try to maintain **their** standards.

In modern English, we often use **they** instead of **he** or **she** for a singular subject, though in many contexts **he** is understood to mean a person of either sex.
For examples of these pronouns in use, see individual entries and see also DEMONSTRATIVE, POSSESSIVE, QUESTIONS, RELATIVE.
For more details see CEG 3.27.

proper
  adjective
  A (=right, correct) •Is this the **proper** word to use? •Will she get **proper** medical help if she doesn't go to hospital?
  B (=real) •You're a **proper** fool if you believe it.
  properly
  adverb (=in the right way) •I can't type **properly**: I use only one finger.
  ❖ *compound* •A **proper** noun is a real name, with a capital letter.

proud
  adjective
  A (=with a proper self-respect, feeling of satisfaction in achievement) •I am **proud** to have been a part of this great enterprise. •She was **proud** of her daughter's success.
  B (=arrogant, with too high an opinion of oneself) •She's too **proud** to be seen in an ordinary bus.
  pride
  noun (=self-respect, gladness, arrogance) •He has too much **pride** to ask anyone for help. •He takes great **pride** in his appearance.
  verb
  +*on* (=be pleased with [oneself] about) •He **prides** himself on his ability to grow beautiful roses.
  ❖ *in idioms* •I had to **swallow my pride** and admit I needed help. (forget my proud feelings) •His roses are **his pride and joy**. (what he cares most about among his possessions)

prove /pru:v/
  verb
  A (=show that something is true) •I know he took the money but I can't **prove** it.
  B (=show itself/oneself to be) •We expected a difficult journey and so it **proved** [to be].
  proven
  past participle (alternative to **proved**, used more in AmE and in law)

proof
  noun
  A (=evidence to establish truth) •What **proof** can you give of your identity?
  B (=first print, copy of writing or picture) •The **proofs** must be inspected carefully.
  adjective (=impervious, safe against) •The bank is **proof** against thieves.
  -proof
  suffix used to form adjectives (=impenetrable by) •water**proof** •sound**proof** •**foolproof** (even fools can use it without harm)

provide
  verb (=supply) •The local shop **provides** everything we need.
  +*person object* + *with* + *object* •Can you **provide** us with some eggs?
  provided [that]/providing [that]
  conjunction (=on condition that, if) •**Provided that** you keep quiet, you can come to the concert. •**Providing** you promise not to tell anyone else, I'll explain the secret.
  provision[s]
  noun
  A (=condition) •There is a **provision** in the contract to prevent cheating.
  B (=providing) •The **provision** of children's playgrounds will be necessary.
  C plural (=supplies of food) •Do we have enough **provisions** for a week?
  provisional/provisionally
  adjective/adverb (=temporary/temporarily) •We have made **provisional** travel arrangements; you are booked into the hotel **provisionally** for two nights, but it could be three.

pull
  verb (≠push, =draw towards/behind/into another position) •The horse **pulled** the cart. •**Pull** your chair nearer the fire. •When I **pulled** the handle, it came off.
  noun (=action of pulling) •Give the rope a **pull**.
  ❖ *in compounds* •**pull**over (sweater, jumper) •**pull**-in/**pull**-up (place where cars may stop for snack meals by the side of the road/lay-by)

put

❖ *in idioms* •She enjoys gossiping, **pulling people['s characters] to pieces**. (criticising unkindly) •If you work here, you'll have to **pull your weight**. (do your fair share of work) •She **pulled a face** but she drank the medicine. (showed distaste) •I'm only **pulling your leg**. (joking, telling lies for fun) •His father **pulled strings** to get him the job. (used personal influence) •The other car was faster and soon **pulled ahead/pulled away** from the police car. (got in front [of]) •The old houses are being **pulled down** to make room for new ones. (destroyed) •The car/train **pulled in/up**. (stopped at the side of the road/station) •We can **pull off** the road for our picnic. (stop on the roadside, not on the road) •He **pulled over** to the fast lane. (moved) •She was so ill we thought she would not **pull through/round**. (recover) •**Pull yourself together** and behave properly! (control yourself)

punctuation
Punctuation exists only in writing, of course. It is an attempt to represent some of the information we can communicate in speech but not in written words. 'Pieces of information' are separated from each other by changes in intonation, pauses etc in speech and by punctuation marks in writing.
See also 's, APOSTROPHE, BRACKETS, COLON, COMMA, CONTRACTIONS, DASH, EXCLAMATION MARK, FULL STOP, GENITIVE, HYPHEN, INTERROGATIVE, QUESTION, QUOTATION, SEMI-COLON.

purpose
noun (=intention, aim, determination) •What is the **purpose** of your visit?
purposeful/purposefully
adjective/adverb (=with determination) •His **purposeful** expression made me realise that he meant what he said.

purposely
adverb (=with intent, on purpose) •I didn't hit you **purposely**; it was an accident.

purpose
Purpose (or intention) can be expressed by [*in order*] *to* + *infinitive, for* + -*ing, so that* + *clause*. •He killed her [**in order**] **to steal** her money. •Money is **for spending**. •Knives are **for cutting** [with]. •Beds are **for sleeping** [in]. •He killed her **so that he could steal her money**. •They put him in prison **so that he wouldn't be able to kill anyone else**.
See also **so as** [**to**], **so that**, INFINITIVE (1), ORDER
For more details see CEG 11.19.

push
verb (≠ pull, = press, move [something] away from/to another position) •Be careful! You almost **pushed** me into the water. •Stop **pushing**! •When you **push** this button, the machine is on. •Her mother **pushed** her to marry him.
noun (=action of pushing) •If you give it a **push**, it will fall over.
❖ *in compounds* •**push**-bike (pedal cycle, not motor bike) •**push**-chair (child's folding chair on wheels; AmE *stroller*) •**push**-over (something very easy) informal
❖ *in idioms* •I can finish it in a week or, **at a push**, four days. (if really necessary) informal •If you don't work, you'll **get the push**. (sack, be dismissed) informal •I've got a lot to do, so I must **push on/along/ ahead/forward**. (continue, get on with it, make progress) •If there is a queue, don't **push in**. (try to go first, interrupt) •He told me to **push off**! (go away) slang

put
verb irregular, **put, put**
A (=place, set in position) •Where did you **put** my newspaper? •They are **putting** new curtains up.
B (=express in words) •I feel — how can I **put** it? — very sad.

quantity

- ❖ *in compounds* •**in**put/**out**put (what goes into a process/what comes out, production)
- ❖ *in idioms* •It's a difficult idea to **put across/over**. (make clear, explain) •He **put aside/by** some money for a holiday. (saved) •Please **put the books away** on the shelf. (return to the proper storage place) •I had to **put back/off** the meeting till next week. (delay, postpone) •Let me **put down** your phone number. (write) •What do you **put your success down to?** (What is the cause of it?) •Could I **put forward** a suggestion? (offer) •Can we **put the party forward**? (have it earlier) •I **put in** only three hours' work today. (did, spent time) •You must just **put in an appearance**; you needn't stay late. (go to an occasion briefly) •He **puts me in mind of** Charlie Chaplin. (reminds me of, makes me think of) •I hope you'll **put in a good word for** me. (support me by speaking in my favour) •He really **put his heart/back into** the job. (worked hard, with enthusiasm) •I didn't say that! Don't **put words into my mouth!** (claim I said something that I didn't say) •He often asks her to visit him but she always **puts him off** [with an excuse]. (She makes an excuse to say no.) •The horrible smell of cooking oil **put me off** my food. (made me lose my appetite) •His manners are rather **off-putting**. (unpleasant, repulsive or distracting) •She doesn't normally behave like that; she's **putting on an act/putting it on**. (pretending) •What shall I **put on** for the party? (wear) •Please **put the television on**. (switch it on) •I wouldn't **put money on it**. (bet on it, think it likely) informal •He asks her to do so much; she feels **put upon**. (taken advantage of) •What time must we **put the lights out?** (turn, switch off) •Would it **put you out** if I brought my friend to supper? (trouble you, upset you)

•He never **puts himself out for** anyone. (takes trouble) •Please **put this call through** to the main office. (telephone — transfer, connect) •The criminal was **put to death**. (killed) •He has more money than all of us **put together**. (combined) •Let's **put our heads together**. (combine our ideas, discuss something) •He soon **put two and two together**. (worked out what was happening etc) •Can you **put me up** if I need to stay two days? (provide a bed) •I refuse to **put up with** your bad behaviour. (tolerate, bear) •'Why can't he sleep?' 'I **put it down to** too much coffee.' (explain it by)

Q

quantity

When we ask about quantity, we ask about the amount (of a non-countable noun) or the number (of a countable noun) •**How much?** or **How many?** The answer may be in measurements, such as **1000 square meters, 365 days**, or in expressions using *quantifiers*, which may be adjectival determiners or pronouns, such as: **all, every, each, some, any, many, more, few, several, enough, one, no, none, either** etc. We may also use *pronouns* such as **everybody, everything**, and *adverbs* of frequency, duration and degree, such as: **often, sometimes, never, [for] a while, not [for] long, absolutely, very, rather, quite, not . . . at all,** and *nouns* such as **a lot, masses [of], a [little] bit, a [large] supply, an immense quantity [of] . . .**

See also COMPARISON, NON-COUNTABLE, and separate entries for common determiners.

For more details see CEG 3.12.

questions

It is possible, in speaking, to ask a question using the same words as a statement, but changing the

quite

intonation: •You've seen it? •He likes them? •Coming? Most questions are distinguished from statements by *question words* (*wh-questions*) or by a change in *word order* (*yes – no questions*) or both.
QUESTION WORDS
pronouns •Who telephoned? •What's happening? •Which is the most expensive?
adverbs •Where are you? •When must we go? •Why are you awake? •How shall I send it?
WORD ORDER changes by inversion, that is putting the subject after the verb if it is an auxiliary/modal verb or using **do**, also inverted, for 'ordinary verbs': •He can swim. **Can he swim?** •They know./**Do they know?** •He loves her./**Does he love her?** •They went./**Did they go?** •She will wait./**Will she wait?**

Modal verbs often change their meanings in questions so see examples of **must, need, will, would** etc.

Some questions do not really ask for information; they are
(a) *polite responses:* •'I'm not coming.' 'Aren't you? How sad.' •'I'm tired.' 'Are you?' 'Yes, tired out.' •'John doesn't like tea.' 'Doesn't he? I'll give him coffee, then.'
(b) *requests for confirmation:* •You're coming, aren't you? •John doesn't like tea, does he? •She told you, didn't she? •He didn't like it, did he? •You can't swim, can you?

Negative statements + question tags are often requests for help or information: •You **couldn't** give me a lift, **could you?** •I'm **not** on the wrong train, **am I?**

Intonation is very important in showing the exact meaning of question-tags, and cannot be explained in a book like this.
See also **do**, INDIRECT SPEECH, REQUEST.
For more details see CEG 4.8.

quick
adjective/adverb (= swift, not wasting time) •We have time for a **quick** drink. •Come **quick!** I've hurt myself.
quickly
adverb (used more than **quick**) •She works **quickly** and accurately.
❖ *in compounds* •**quick**-tempered (easily made angry) •**quick**-witted (clever, bright)
quiet /ˈkwaɪət/
adjective (≠ noisy, = calm, not noticeable) •I need a **quiet** room to study in. •He spoke in a **quiet** voice. •Film stars don't have a **quiet** life. •He wore a **quiet** grey tie and white shirt.
noun (= state of being quiet, quietness) •Sick people need peace and **quiet.**
quieten [down]
verb (= make, become, quiet) •After the party, everyone **quietened** down.
disquiet
noun non-countable (= anxiety) •There is some **disquiet** about the possibility of a strike by the bus-drivers.
quite /kwaɪt/
adverb
A + *non-gradable adjectives and adverbs* (= completely, perfectly); B + *gradable adjectives and adverbs* (= rather, fairly); C + *a/an + noun* (= rather a special, more than average example); D in response to a statement (= I agree, that's quite right.)
A (= completely, perfectly) •The weather was **quite** perfect; it was **quite** impossible to imagine a better day. •We went **quite** far enough and I'm **quite** exhausted. •Are you **quite** sure this is the road?
B (= rather, fairly) •The weather was **quite** nice; everyone was **quite** happy. •We went **quite** a long way and I'm feeling **quite** tired myself. •He seems **quite** confident about the route, **quite** surprisingly. His map-reading is **quite** a lot better than mine.

quotation

NB **Quite** can be ambiguous with certain adjectives because they can be either gradable or non-gradable. •It is **quite** different from mine. (rather different or entirely different?) **Quite** is also ambiguous because it can mean both *rather* (=more than usually) and *fairly* (=to some degree, not particularly). You may need to know more about the situation to decide whether 'It's **quite** warm' means 'a little too warm' or 'almost warm enough'. This happens with verbs too: •'Do you like him?' 'Er, . . . quite. (only fairly well) I **quite** like her, though.' (I like her rather well) C (=rather a special, more than average example) •He's **quite** a cook. •It was **quite** a feast. D (=I agree, that's right) •'We ought to do something.' '**Quite**.'
❖ *in idioms* •I **quite** understand. (am not offended, puzzled, surprised) •That's **quite enough**. (Stop it) •They made **quite a few** changes. (several) •It's **not quite** polite. (either as an understatement 'it's rude' or 'it is a little less than polite') •I'm **not quite ready**. (nearly ready)
See also **fairly**, **rather**, COMPARISON.

quotation

Quotation/quoting is repeating the words of another speaker or writer. In writing, these words are enclosed in *quotation marks* ('. . .', ". . .") also called inverted commas. Indirect or reported speech does not use actual quotation and does not have quotation marks: •Sophie said, 'I've crashed the car.'/Sophie said she'd crashed the car. •'Why are you here?' he asked me./He asked me why I was there.

We also use quotation marks when we talk about a word or use it in an unusual way: •Can you 'talk' about something in writing? •We can use the word 'talk' to mean 'discuss'.
See also INDIRECT SPEECH.

R

raise /reɪz/
verb transitive
A (=lift, set upright, make higher) •**Raise** the lid and look inside. •They have decided to **raise** taxes.
B (=bring up, breed [a family, animals]) •He **raises** horses now he's stopped riding.
noun (=increase in pay, etc) AmE (BrE **rise**) •If you don't ask for a **raise**, you won't get one.

rare
adjective
A (≠common, =unusual) •A royal visit is a **rare** event. •She collects **rare** stamps.
B (=very lightly cooked) •He likes his steak **rare**, not well-done.
rarely
adverb (=seldom, ≠often) •Sophie **rarely** writes letters.
rarity
noun (=rare thing, quality of being rare) •This book is a **rarity**; there are very few copies in existence. •Its **rarity** makes it valuable.
See also **scarce**.

rate
noun (=value, cost, speed) •At a **rate** of £5 per hour, he can earn £55 in 11 hours. •He rushed off at a fantastic **rate**.
verb (=value, judge) •'How do you **rate** him as a writer?' 'I **rate** him very high[ly].'
❖ *in idioms* •He's a **first-rate** musician. (in the top class of musicians) •**At any rate**, we can go for a walk. (whatever happens, in any case, even without a car) •We are not saving much money. **At this rate** we won't be able to buy a car till we're very old. •What's the **exchange rate/rate of exchange** for American dollars?

rather /ˈrɑːðə*/
adverb predeterminer
A (=quite, slightly, more than you would expect)
+ *adjectives* with unpleasant meanings •The water's **rather** cold for swimming. (too, to an

144

unpleasant degree) •He drives **rather** fast; I feel nervous. Compare 'He drives fairly fast; we shan't be late.'
+ *comparatives* •It's **rather** worse than I thought.
+ *adjectives* with pleasant meanings •It was **rather** exciting to meet my hero. (particularly, to a pleasant degree)
+ *a/an* + *noun* •He's **rather** a fool. (rather foolish) •Yes, but he has **rather** a lot of money.
+ *verb* •That **rather** surprises me. (somewhat)
B (= it would be better to say) •I shall marry her — or **rather**, I shall ask her to marry me.

would/had (= 'd) **rather** [than]
verb (= prefer) •'Shall we dance?' 'I'd **rather** sit and talk.' 'I'd **rather** dance than talk.' •What would you **rather** be; a cat or a mouse? •I'd **rather** not think about it.

rather than
prepositional phrase (= instead of, sooner than, more than) •**Rather than** climb the stairs, he'll wait for the lift. •She is pretty **rather than** beautiful.

See also **fairly, pretty, quite**.

re-
prefix (= again) used to make verbs pronounced with emphasis to make a difference between **re-** and other verbs beginning with *re* •**re-**cover (put a new cover on)/recover (get better) •**re-**count (count again)/ recount (tell)

each
verb
A (= stretch out [and touch]) •He **reached** across the table. •I'm too short to **reach** the books on the top shelf.
B (= arrive at/in) •Can we **reach** Paris before this evening?
noun (= accessible distance) •The house is within easy **reach** of shops and buses.

ready
adjective
A (= prepared, fit for use) •Supper isn't **ready** yet. •Is everything **ready** for the meeting?
B + *to* + *infinitive* (= willing) •She's always **ready** to give a hand.
adverb used with past participles (= in advance) •She buys **ready**-prepared chickens.
❖ *in compounds* •**ready**-made (clothes, shoes, ≠ tailor-made) •**ready**-to-wear (as above) •**ready** money/cash (money in real currency, not cheques etc)

real /rɪəl/
adjective (= actually existing, true) •Is your ring **real** gold?

really /ˈrɪəlɪ/
adverb
A (= in fact, truly) •Did you **really** push him in the pool? •I **really** don't like him. (emphatically not)/I don't **really** like him. (I am not enthusiastic)
B (= very) •I was **really** angry.
C (in response to conversational remarks, showing interest, surprise, disapproval)
•'I met the Queen once.' '**Really**?' •'I've broken it.' 'Oh, **really**! You fool!'

reality /rɪˈælɪtɪ/
noun
A non-countable (= real existence) •He believes in the **reality** of ghosts.
B countable (= real fact) •You can't escape from the **reality**/ **realities** of life.

realism
noun (= determination to face and deal with facts) •Only **realism** can solve our problems; we must look at the facts realistically. Realists are practical people, but it is possible to be too realistic and forget about the imagination.

realise/realize
verb
A (= understand [a fact]) •I didn't **realise** it was so late.
B (= make into something real/money) •He **realised** his dreams at last.
❖ *in idioms* •Are they fighting **for real**? (seriously) informal, AmE

reason

●We trusted him but **in reality** he was a spy. (in actual fact, in spite of expectation)

reason
noun
A (= explanation, cause)
+ *for* ●What's the **reason** for all this noise?
+ *why* (+ *clause*) ●Tell me the **reason** why [they're shouting].
+ *infinitive* ●They have [good] **reason** to protest.
+ *that* + *clause* ●The **reason** that they're shouting is that they need higher wages.
B (= power to understand, think) ●Animals do not have **reason**, as human beings do. ●There's **reason** in what you say.
verb (= use your brain, argue logically) ●He is so angry that it is impossible to **reason** with him.

reasonable
adjective (= sensible, fair) ●If you can't be **reasonable** it's no good talking about it. ●Is $300 a **reasonable** price?

unreasonable
adjective (= not sensible, not fair) ●It would be **unreasonable** to expect them to do everything.

reasonably
adverb (= sensibly, fairly, quite) ●We talked about the problem **reasonably**. ●The kitchen is **reasonably** clean.

❖ **in idioms** ●She tells lies. **For that reason**, you can't trust her. (That's why) ●Have you **lost your reason**? (gone mad) ●We can do anything **within reason**. (that is not too much to expect) ●**It stands to reason** that he won't work for nothing. (It's obvious, logical) ●I wish he would **listen to reason**. (be persuaded by sensible advice like mine)

For **reason** as a category in grammar, see also CAUSE, PURPOSE.

For more details see CEG 11.18.

reckon
verb
A (= consider, regard) ●Anthony's reckoned [to be] one of the cleverest economists around.
B (= suppose, calculate roughly) ●I **reckon** he's been working here 5 years.
C (= calculate) ●You have to **reckon** your pay from May 1st.

reckoning
noun (= calculation) ●According to my **reckoning**, he's been here 6½ years.

❖ **in idioms** ●You can **reckon on** him to help you. (rely on) ●There are a number of difficulties **to reckon with**. (face, take into account) ●On **the day of reckoning**, he will regret his wicked wasteful habits. (when he has to pay/be punished for them) ●His plan nearly worked, but he **reckoned without** the bad weather, which ruined it. (failed to take account of)

recognise/recognize /ˈrekəgnaɪz/
verb
A (= know again, admit to be real) ●My aunt didn't **recognise** me with my hair cut short. ●This is the **recognised** method of cleaning leather.
B (= see clearly, agree)
+ *object* + *to* + *infinitive* ●Everyone **recognises** this to be the best.
+ *that* + *clause* ●We all **recognised** that he was the cleverest.

recognisable /ˈrekəgnaɪzəbəl/
adjective (= able to be recognised) ●The town has changed so much, it is scarcely **recognisable** as the same place.

recognition /ˌrekəgˈnɪʃən/
noun (= acknowledgement, reward) ●His work received no **recognition** while he was alive; now a statue has been put up **in recognition** of his achievements.

❖ **idiom** ●Age had changed her **beyond/out of all recognition**. (so much that she was unrecognisable)

refuse
verb /rɪˈfjuːz/ (= not accept, not do, not give)

+ *object* •He **refused** my offer/my gift/my invitation.
+ *to* + *infinitive* [+ *object*] + *object* •He **refused** to lend [her] his car. •When he asked her to go, she **refused** [to/to go].
+ *person object* + *object* •He **refused** us permission./We were **refused** permission. •She **refused** them their rights.
But compare 'He declined/rejected my suggestion.' (not *refused) 'He rejected my plan/proposal, denied the story.'
noun /ˈrefjuːs/ (= rubbish, waste material) •Put the kitchen **refuse** in a plastic bag.

refusal /rɪˈfjuːzəl/
noun (= act of refusing) •Her **refusal** to marry him was a great shock to his pride.

regard
noun (= respect, consideration) •He has no **regard** for other people's feelings. •Please give my [kind] **regards** to your wife.
verb + *as* (= look on, consider) •He **regards** me as a mother, not a secretary. •Sophie is not **regarded** as a good driver.

regarding
preposition (= on the subject of, with reference to) formal •I have your letter **regarding** credit.

regardless of
preposition (= without worrying about) •**Regardless of** expense, he ordered brandy.
❖ *in idioms* •**As regards** your other problem, I can't help you. (on the subject of, regarding) •Sophie may not be very good **in that regard** but she's a good cook. (in that way, that respect)

regret
verb (= be sorry about, miss) •If you don't take this opportunity, you will always **regret** it.
+ *-ing* •I **regret** calling her a fool. (I'm sorry I called her a fool)
+ *to* + *infinitive* •I **regret** to say she's a fool. (I'm sorry it is necessary to say so, but she is)
+ *that* + *clause* •Mr Fowler **regrets** that he is unable to be present.
noun non-countable (= unhappiness) •We left our home with great **regret**.

regrets
noun (= note refusing an invitation) •Oh dear! Mr Fowler sends his **regrets**.

regrettably
sentence adverb (= [and] it is a pity) •We quite forgot to send him a card, **regrettably**.

regretfully
adverb (= with feelings of sadness) •**Regretfully**, we said good-bye to our home.
❖ *in idioms* •We **regret to inform you** that we cannot grant permission. (We are sorry) formal •It was a difficult decision but I **have no regrets**. (I do not wish it had been a different one)

regular
regular verbs follow the normal rules of verb formation. If you know these rules, you need to know only the infinitive of a verb to use it in every possible way, eg regular verb **look**, to make past tense and past participles, add -*ed*; to make present participles, add -*ing*.
irregular verbs have to be learnt individually. They are listed in three parts: *infinitive, past simple, past participle* eg **see, saw, seen**: *present participle* seeing *past tense* he saw/he didn't see, *perfect* he has/hasn't seen.

relative
Relative clauses are adjectival expressions, telling us more about a noun or noun equivalent, usually beginning with a relative pronoun or relative adverb.
  Some relative clauses define or identify a noun, others merely provide extra information, which may be between commas acting like brackets.
defining relative clauses in **bold**:
•The car **that's parked outside** is

147

remember

mine. •The man **who sold it to me** is a crook. •The price **I paid for it** was ridiculous. •Several people **I've spoken to** agree. •Will the man **whose car is in the way** please move it? •Put it **where you like.**

In ordinary speech, defining clauses referring to people or things as subjects usually begin with *that* •the parcel/the messenger **that** arrived. But *which* and *who* are normal too: •the parcel **which**/the messenger **who** arrived. When they refer to objects, defining clauses usually have no relative pronoun; they are 'contact clauses': •The person **I asked** didn't know. •An old picture **I found** was sold for £1000. *That* could be used but is not necessary. *Whom* and *which* are also possible and more formal.

In speech, prepositions usually come at the end of a clause; in writing, or formal speech they might come at the beginning, particularly of a long clause. •The problem we have to make a decision about . . ./about which we have to make a decision . . .

non-defining relative clauses used mostly in writing or slightly formal, careful conversation. They add extra information and are enclosed in commas: •That beautiful car, **which is wonderful to drive,** is a Porsche. •Sophie, **who is the world's worst driver,** is not allowed to touch it. •Her mother, **whom I have never met,** is the world's second worst driver. •Sophie's mother, **to whom you referred just now,**/**whom you referred to just now,** is standing beside you. •Your car, **which I noticed outside,** has been hit by another one. •This lady, **whose daughter is a friend of mine,** may be able to explain. •Paris, **where I'm going tomorrow,** is my favourite city.

See also **that, which, who, whom, whose, when, where,** COMMAS. For more details see CEG 11.27.

remember
verb
A (≠ forget, = keep in the memory) + *object* •I shall always **remember** your kindness. •Can you **remember** your childhood?
B (= recall) +*-ing* •I can't **remember** being a baby, but I can **remember** learning to read. [+*that*] +*clause* •She **remembers** [that] he visited her but she can't **remember** when.
C (= take care not to forget) + *to* + *infinitive* •Did you **remember** to lock the back door? •**Remember** to buy some stamps, won't you?

memory
noun
A (= ability to remember) •My **memory** is not as good as yours.
B (= something remembered) •We have wonderful **memories** of the past.

remind [of]
verb (= tell, cause, to remember) •This music **reminds** me of a wedding. •I must lock the door. Please **remind** me [to lock it/to]. •He **reminded** me to lock it/that I should lock it.

reminder
noun (= letter or something else making one remember) •The shop has sent a **reminder** because we haven't paid the bill.

rent
noun (= money paid for use of room, house, TV set, etc) •What's the **rent** for your flat?
verb
A (= pay rent for) •We **rented** a car for a week when ours was out of order.
B (= let, take rent for) •Why don't you **rent** [out] that room?

reported speech
See INDIRECT SPEECH.

request
noun (= polite demand) •He made a **request** for more money.
verb (= ask for, demand politely)

right

- He **requested** us to stop talking.
- He **requested** silence.

requests
There are many ways of making a request. They include expressions using **please will, would, can, could, may** and **might**, as well as idiomatic expressions such as **Is it all right if . . .?, if you wouldn't mind . . ., . . . let me have . . ..** If you want something, you can ask for it in all these ways, beginning with the least polite and ending with the most polite • Coffee, [please]. • Can I have coffee, please? • Could I have/Could you let me have some coffee, please? • I'd like some . . . • Will you give me . . . please? • Would you . . . • Could you . . . • May I have some coffee, please? • I'd like some coffee, if you wouldn't mind,/if you'd be so kind . . . Extreme politeness can easily sound sarcastic.

rest
noun
A (= relaxation, sleep) • I'm tired; I need a [good night's] **rest**. • Let's stop working and have a/some **rest**.
B (= remainder, what is/are left) • Eat what you need and leave the **rest** [of the food] on the table.
• We got there first. The **rest** were following us.
verb (= relax, take a rest) • She usually **rests** after lunch. • **Rest** your head on my shoulder.

❖ *in idioms* • Set your mind **at rest**; everything will be all right. (Don't worry) • I can tell you about what I saw but **for the rest**, I don't know. (as for everything else) • [May he] **rest in peace**! R.I.P. (a prayer for the peace of someone dead)

result
See CAUSE, **so that**.

right
adjective
A (≠ left) • Most people write with the **right** hand.
B (≠ wrong, = correct, moral) • 'Is your name Puddlefoot?' 'That's **right**.' • You are **right** to be cautious.
noun
A non-countable (= what is right) • Do babies know the difference between **right** and wrong?
B countable (= legal claim, moral claim) • We have both a **right** and a duty to speak the truth. • You have no **right** to open my letters.
• Women seem to have fewer **rights** than men. They certainly have less **right** to family money.
adverb
A (= towards the right) • Turn **right** at the lights.
B (= exactly) • Put the cross **right** in the middle.
C (= directly, straight) • You must phone **right** after breakfast.
D (= correctly) • Am I doing this **right**?
E (= completely) • Go **right** to the top.

rightly
adverb
A (= correctly) • If I remember **rightly**, we turn left now.
B (= justly) • She complained, quite **rightly**, when the steak was burnt.

❖ *in compounds* • **Right** wing (politically to the right) • **right** angle (90°) • **right** away/off (immediately) • **right**-minded (sensible)

❖ *in idioms* • I put my watch **right** this morning. (corrected it) • He's **not quite right in the head**. (a bit mad) • Perhaps he wasn't **in his right mind** when he made his will. (sane, mentally healthy) • 'See you at ten!' 'Yes, **right you are/all right**!' (OK) • She is a rich woman **in her own right**. (because of an independent claim) • What a mess! How can we **set it [all] to rights**? (make it all right again) • You would be **within your rights** if you refused to pay the rent if the roof leaks. (justified) • You're trying to **get on the right side of me**, aren't

149

ring

you? (win my favour) •There is a **right of way** through the wood. (path which anyone can use)

ring
verb
A irregular, **rang, rung** (=make a sound with a bell, make a telephone call [to]) •**Ring** the bell before you go in. •He **rang** me early this morning. I told him to **ring** again later/**ring** back. •I **rang** round all my friends to ask them to the party.
B regular transitive (=make a circle round) •He's **ringed** all my mistakes in red ink.
noun
A (=sound of a bell) •There were three loud **rings** at the door.
B (=circle, circular band) •The children danced round the tree in a **ring**. •Does your husband wear a wedding **ring**?
C (=place used for performance, especially circus, boxing) •The fighters were already in the **ring**.
❖ *in compounds* •**ring**-binder (file for holding papers by means of rings through holes) •**ring**-leader (chief of a group of trouble-makers) •**ring** road (AmE 'beltway', road avoiding town centre)
❖ *in idioms* •That name **rings a bell!** (reminds me of something) •What he says **rings true**. (sounds true) •**Give me a ring!** (Phone me) •He can **run/make rings round** me. (He is very much more skilful than me.) •Don't **ring off**. (put the telephone down)

rise /raɪz/
verb irregular, **rose, risen**
intransitive (=go up, come up, get up) •The sun **rises** in the East, and sets in the West. •He **rose** to greet his guests. •Prices have **risen** recently but they may fall again.
noun
A (=increase) •The **rise** in taxes affects everyone.
B (=small hill) •The house is built on a little **rise**.

arise
verb **arose, arisen**
A (=rise, get up) formal •The goddess **arose** at dawn.
B (=happen, appear) •A difficulty has **arisen** about your visa.
❖ *in idioms* •Their dirty surroundings **give rise to** disease. (cause, lead to) •If nothing is done the people will **rise against** their leaders. (start a rebellion, rising)

risk [of]
noun (=danger, chance of something bad) •There's always a **risk** of fire in a wooden building.
❖ *verb* (=take a chance, face [a danger]) •He **risked** [losing] his life by trying to save her from drowning.

risky
adjective (=dangerous) informal •It's a bit **risky**, overtaking on a hill.
❖ *in idioms* •You can leave your car here, but **at your own risk**. (nobody else is responsible for its safety) •If you're in business you must sometimes **take/run risks**. (do things which might turn out badly)

rob
verb
+ *object* [*owner*] [+ *of* + *thing*]
(=take someone else's property, unlawfully, steal) •They **robbed** the bank. •He'll **rob** you of everything you have.

robber
noun (=person who steals) •Bands of **robbers** used to wait here for rich people to pass by.

robbery
noun (=act of stealing) •There were many **robberies** in the area.

round
adjective (=circular, spherical, fat) •Plates should be **round**, not square. •This ball is not perfectly **round**. •Her **round** red cheeks make her look very healthy.
adverb also **around** (=with a circular movement, surrounding a central point, all about, in the other direction) •The earth goes **round** on its own axis and also goes **round** in a circle with the sun at the centre. •Hand these cups **round**. •We walked **around** looking

run

at the sights. •Turn **round** and go back to the start.
preposition
A also **around**; corresponding to use as adverb •The earth goes **round** the sun. •I'm so fat I can't get this belt **round** my waist. •Put the chairs **round** the room. •We wandered **round** the town.
B (= on the other side of) •Leave it **round** the back of the house. •They went **round** the corner too fast.
C (= near) •She lives somewhere **round** here.
noun
A (= regular journey to deliver something to different houses etc) •He did a paper **round** to earn money.
B (in sport = one period of a game etc) •He started well but he was beaten in the second **round**.
❖ *in compounds* •**round** trip (journey there and back) •**round**about (carousel, traffic circle)
❖ *in idioms* •These trees stay green **all the year round**. (permanently) •Try turning it **the other way round** if you can't get it through the doorway. •This is **the wrong way round**. (in a different, wrong position) •It's my turn to **buy a round**. (buy drinks for everyone present)

rule

noun (= regulation, law, way something usually happens, domination) •The **rules** of tennis are easy to learn. •In this house the **rule** is that everyone helps with the washing up. •They were under Chinese **rule** for many years.
verb (= have and use power over) •Does the King really **rule** the country?
❖ *in idioms* •She comes at 8.30 **as a rule**. (generally) •She **rules** her husband **with a rod of iron**. (very severely) •It's not likely to happen but we can't **rule it out**. (say it's impossible)

run

verb irregular, **ran, run**

A (= go [fast] on your feet, take part in a race, competition for election) •If you **run**, you'll catch the bus. •We **ran** races round the garden. •Can you **run** a mile in 4 minutes, Daddy? •Do you think he'll **run** for President?
B (= [cause to] advance quickly) •He **ran** the car into a wall. •Thoughts **ran** through my mind.
C (= organise [work, business]) •The shop is very well-**run**.
D (= go regularly) •Buses **run** every twenty minutes.

noun (= action of running, a short journey for pleasure in a car, etc) •He tried to get fit by going for a **run** before breakfast. •Let me take you out for a **run** in the car.
❖ *in compounds* •**run**-down (tired, ill, decaying) • **run**way (landing strip for aircraft)
❖ *in idioms* •I'm **run off my feet**. (very busy, tired) •We're **running it fine** if we want to catch that train. (have little time) •He's had **a run of bad luck**. (a series of unfortunate events) •**In the long run** it may be better to buy the more expensive furniture. (in the end) •I **ran across her** in the street the other day. (came across, met by chance)
•He **ran away** from home because his father was cruel to him. (escaped) •The clock has **run down**; it needs a new battery. (become slow, stopped) •If you talk to people so rudely you'll soon **run into trouble**. (have problems)
•He's **in the running for** promotion. (likely to be promoted) •He has won the competition three times **running**. (consecutively) •He **ran away/off with** the money (stole it) •We've **run out of** bread. (there's none left) •If you don't look before you cross the road, a bus will **run you over**. (kill you)
•Let's **run through** this lesson once more. (examine briefly, go over)
•We can afford a second-hand car, but my salary doesn't **run to** a new one. (allow the luxury of)

S

's
See APOSTROPHE.
For more details see CEG 2.23.

safe
adjective (=out of danger, not hurt, not vulnerable, not risky) •Is it **safe** to swim here? •You will be quite **safe** if you keep to the path.
noun (=special box/cupboard for keeping money and valuable things in) •You can't open the **safe** without a special key.

safely
adverb (=without accident, without risk) •We arrived **safely** at our destination. •I can **safely** say it will be finished before the weekend.

safety
noun (=state of being safe) •The children's **safety** is more important than anything else.
❖ *in compounds* •**safe**-guard (means of protection) •**safety**-belt (seat-belt in car or to prevent falling etc) •**safety**-pin (pin with protected point, used, eg, for babies' nappies) •**safety** valve (part of machine allowing steam etc to escape safely)
❖ *in idioms* •We'll take a little extra money **to be on the safe side**. (taking no risks) •He's not very adventurous; he always **plays safe**. (takes no risks)

sake
noun (=the good or advantage [of someone or something]) •He changed his way of life for her **sake**. •For the **sake** of his country, he fought and died. •I'm doing this for my own **sake**, to help myself. •We can use an example simply for the **sake** of argument.
❖ *in idioms* •**For goodness sake**, be quiet. (please, an expression of impatience) •What can I do about it, **for God's/Christ's sake**? (I challenge you to answer) strong expressions — use with care.

same
adjective usually **the same** (≠ different) •He always sits in the **same** chair. •Have you lived in the **same** house all your life?
+ *as* + *object/clause* •She was wearing the **same** dress as me. •We'll meet in the **same** place as we met before. •He is not better; he is much the **same**.
pronoun (=the identical/similar thing) •Are you having an omelette? I'll have the **same** [as you].
adverb (=in the same way) •I think it's lovely. I hope you think the **same**. •They look the **same** [as each other] but really, they are different.

similar/similarly
adjective/adverb (=of the same kind, alike) •Our tastes in music are **similar**; my preferences are **similar** to yours. •Birds build nests; **similarly**, rabbits makes holes to live in.
❖ *in idioms* •He's very silly but I love him **all the same**. (nevertheless) •You can pay in dollars or sterling — but **it comes to the same thing**. (makes no real difference)

satisfy
verb (=make someone happy, please, fulfil a need, persuade) •I hope this work will **satisfy** you. •My hunger was not **satisfied** by one small biscuit. •I am **satisfied** that he can do the job.

satisfying
adjective (=filling [a need]) •One biscuit is not a **satisfying** meal.

satisfactory
adjective (=good enough) •If you haven't got a pen, a pencil is **satisfactory** for the purpose.

satisfaction
noun (=contentment, fulfilment) •It gives me great **satisfaction** to know the job is well-done.

satisfied [with]
adjective (=content) •Are you **satisfied** with your new car?

save
verb
A (=rescue, make safe) •He **saved** his friend from drowning.
B (=keep, not spend or waste

money or time etc) •It's hard to **save** [money] when you don't earn very much. •Going by car **saves** time, but not money.
preposition (=except) formal •She knew all the answers **save** one.
savings
noun (=money saved) •It's better to keep your **savings** in a bank than in an old sock.

say /seɪ/
verb irregular, **said, said** /sed/
A (=utter, pronounce)
+ *words* '. . .' •He **said**, 'You're quite wrong.'
+ *indirect speech* •He **said** I was quite wrong.
B (=express an opinion) •'Will he agree to the proposal?' 'I can't **say**.'
C (=indicate) •This letter doesn't **say** when he's coming. •What time does your watch **say**?
D (=assume) •If 20 people, **say**, paid £1, we'd get £20! •**Say** you were ill, who would take care of you?
noun (=right to decide, participate in decisions) •Children don't usually have much **say** in business matters.
saying
noun (=proverb, well-known wise statement) •Do you know the **saying** 'Half a loaf is better than no bread'?
❖ *in idioms* •It goes without **saying** that everyone will help. (Of course, There's no need to say) •There's **not much to be said for** that idea. (little in its favour) •He works all day — **that is to say** from 9 to 5. (in other words, put another way) •His work is unsatisfactory **not to say** bad. (or even, to be truthful)

scarce
adjective (=hard to find) •Good English apples are **scarce** at this time of year. (not *rare, which suggests 'precious, because there are few', like jewels)
scarcely
adverb (=hardly, almost not) •He spoke so quietly I could **scarcely** hear him.

B (=almost certainly not) •There is **scarcely** a better man for the job.

second /'sekənd/
adjective/adverb determiner, ordinal (=in position two, 2nd)
•Do it now, you may not get a **second** chance!
noun/pronoun
A (=second thing, person) •His first wife was lovely; have you met his **second**?
B (=1/60 of a minute) •Just wait a **second**, I'm coming.
secondary
adjective
A (=subsidiary, less important) •Besides the main question, we must discuss a few **secondary** matters.
B (of schools for children over 11) •Some **secondary** schools are very crowded.
❖ *in compounds* •**second**-hand (not new, used) •**second** nature (well-established habit) •**second**-rate (inferior)
❖ *in idioms* •He agreed and then **had second thoughts**. (changed his mind) •She may have to be **content with second-best**. (ready to accept something less than ideal)

secret
adjective (=hidden, not known about) •They found a **secret** door behind the wardrobe. •I had a **secret** passion for chocolate biscuits.
noun (=something kept hidden) •This must be a **secret** between us. •I've found the **secret** of successful slimming!

see
verb irregular, **saw, seen**
A not in progressive (=perceive, experience, using eyes) •It was dark; we couldn't **see** [the path]. •Do/Can you **see** that little bird? •The old man had **seen** a lot of life.
+ *object* + *infinitive* (whole action) •I **saw** him fall off the wall.
+ *object* + *-ing* (at a moment during the process) •I **saw** him walking to the station.

153

B progressive possible (=meet, visit, interview, give or take advice, go and look at) •I haven't **seen** you for ages. •I'm **seeing** him tomorrow; I'll give him your message. •I must **see** a doctor about this headache. •When can the doctor **see** me? •Have you **seen** the Alps in summer?
C (=notice, understand, take care [that], find out) •'I **see** you have bought a new bicycle.' 'Actually, it was a present.' 'I **see**.' •You can fold it up like this, **see**? •**See** [that] you don't hurt your fingers. •I'll go and **see** if/whether the doctor is in.

seeing [that]
conjunction + true fact (=since, considering the fact that) •**Seeing that** you have no money, you can't buy it.

sight
noun
A (=something seen) •The gardens in spring are a wonderful **sight**.
B (=sense of seeing, vision) •My **sight** isn't good; I have to wear glasses. •Are the children in **sight**?
❖ *in idioms* •**See you later**! (goodbye for now) •**Let's/let me see** . . . (I'm thinking) •We **see little/less/ nothing of you** nowadays; we ought to **see something/more of** each other. (see, be in company with) •When he came to the door, I was so surprised, I thought I was **seeing things**. (dreaming, having hallucinations) •I can't buy it, I have no money, **you see**. (that's the explanation) informal •I must go and **see about** [cooking] supper. (attend to, deal with) •Come and **see him off** at the airport! (say goodbye, accompany to the station etc) •I can **see through** your lies; you can't fool me. (recognise the reality) •You must be busy with so many patients to **see to**. (take care of, attend to) •They fell in love **at first sight**. (when they first saw each other). •I **caught sight of** him for only a moment. (glimpsed) •I know him **by sight**. (not by name)

•Don't **lose sight of** your main purpose. (forget)

seem
verb not used in progressive (=appear [to be])
+ *adjective* •You **seem** [to be] worried; can I help?
+ *to* + *infinitive* •That woman **seems** to know you. Who is she? •We **seem** to have made a mistake. •This room doesn't **seem** to have been cleaned.
+ *like* + *object (noun or -ing)* •It **seems** like years but it's only weeks. •If you're really tired, sleep **seems** like going to heaven.
It + **seems** + *to* + *infinitive* •It **seems** to have started raining again. (it has started raining again, I think)
It seems [+ *as if*] + *clause*/[*that*] + *clause* •It **seems** [as if] they have forgotten it. •Yes, it **seems** so; it isn't here. •It **seemed** [that] they were in a different world.
See also **appear**.

seldom
adverb (≠ often, = infrequently, rarely) •We **seldom** visit that place. •Such places are **seldom** visited. •**Seldom** have I heard such a lovely voice. (inversion in formal style after a negative word beginning a sentence)
There is no adjective corresponding to **seldom**: use *rare* or *infrequent*.

self
noun (= natural character) •I'm recovering from my illness: I'll soon be my old **self** again.

-self
part of reflexive/emphatic pronouns •my**self** •your**self** •him**self** •her**self** •it**self** •our**selves** •your**selves** •them**selves** •one**self**

selfish
adjective (= thinking of oneself, not others) •Don't be **selfish**; share your chocolate with your friends.

unselfish/selfless (≠ selfish)
adjective •**Unselfish** people usually have lots of friends. •Her life was one of **selfless** devotion to the poor. (extremely unselfish)

self-
: *prefix* used to form adjectives and nouns, often with participles •**self**-addressed envelope (SAE) •**self**-assured •**self**-confident (sure of oneself) •**self**-centred (selfish) •**self**-conscious (aware of oneself, nervous) •**self**-control (personal [self] discipline) •**self**-explanatory (obvious, explaining itself) •**self**-important (pompous) •**self**-respect (personal pride, not seen as a bad thing) •**self**-satisfied (complacent) •**self**-service (system where customers select goods from shelves or operate petrol pumps themselves)

sell /sel/
: *verb* irregular, **sold, sold**
A (≠ buy, = give something to someone else for payment) •He **sold** his car because he needed money.
+ *person object* + *object* •Will you **sell** me your bicycle?
B (= be sold, used like a passive) •Bad fruit won't **sell**.

seller
: *noun/suffix* (= person who sells) •Orange **sellers** sell oranges. (but street sellers don't sell streets)

sale /seɪl/
: *noun*
A (= selling) •The **sale** of these goods is prohibited.
B (= occasion when goods are sold competitively/cheaply) •He buys all his clothes in **sales**.
❖ *in idioms* •I tried to get tickets but they had **sold out**. (all been sold) •The shops **sold out of** summer clothes long before the summer started. (sold all) •He'd **sell his soul/grandmother for** fame. (do anything, however dishonourable).

semi colon [;]
: *punctuation mark* A semi-colon is lighter than a colon but heavier than a comma. It can be used (a) to separate two complete sentences when they are very closely linked in sense, (b) to separate complex items in a list, often because commas are already used for another purpose.
(a) *two complete sentences* •The noise went on and on; it made my head ache. •I had never met anyone like him; he was quite astonishing. •Don't touch it; it's hot. •This is lovely; how can I ever thank you enough? •I'm ready; let's go.
(b) *in a list* At the beginning of the report is a summary, concentrating on the problems, possible solutions and conclusions; in the centre is a full account of the factors considered, the relative costs, advantages and disadvantages; at the end there is a detailed description of the chosen solution.

send
: *verb* irregular, **sent, sent** transitive
A (= cause to go) •Please **send** the parcel to me. •Please **send** me the parcel. •She **sent** the child out to buy eggs.
B (= put in a particular state) •His voice will **send** me mad!
❖ *in idioms* •He'll **send word** if he needs help. (send a message) •He **sent the beggar away** with no food. (made him go) •The referee decided to **send the player off**. (not allow him to continue playing) •After he moved, we **sent his letters on**. (re-addressed them to his new home) •The king **sent for** the dancing girls. (ordered them to be brought in)

sense
: *noun*
A countable (= intended meaning) •I was using the word in a different **sense**. •There seems to be no **sense** in this argument; it is nonsense.
B countable (= one of the ways we perceive) •His **sense** of hearing is poor but his sight is excellent.
C non-countable (= understanding, judgement) •I hope you've got enough **sense** to accept a good offer. •Is there any **sense** in waiting longer?

senseless
adjective
A (= without sense, stupid) ●It is **senseless** to make unnecessary journeys.
B (= unconscious) ●A stone fell on his head and knocked him **senseless**.

sensible
adjective (= reasonable, practical). ●She's a **sensible** girl. She wears **sensible** clothes for climbing mountains. (She has ordinary common sense)

sensitive
adjective (= responsive, easily affected by outside influences, hurt by criticism) ●Photographic paper is **sensitive** to light. ●She's a **sensitive** girl; she gets sad if she sees unpleasant things. (She has great sensitivity/sensibility)

sensuous
adjective (= causing pleasure to the senses) ●He admired the **sensuous** line of the woman's body.

sensual
adjective (= related to, dependent on physical pleasure) ●The instincts of an animal are **sensual** not spiritual.

sensation
noun
A (= physical feeling) ●A **sensation** of cold can sometimes be the result of fear.
B (= [cause of] excitement) ●Her transparent dress was a **sensation**.

sensational
adjective (= over-excited in style) ●Newspapers make **sensational** stories out of anything that seems unusual.

❖ *in idioms* ●It's a matter of **common sense**, not intellect. (ordinary reason, practical judgement) ●I suppose you can say he's a doctor **in a sense** but not what we usually mean by a doctor. (if you are not very precise) ●Your proposal **doesn't make sense**. (It is illogical or impractical) ●Come on! **Talk sense!** (Be reasonable) informal

sentence
A sentence is a group of words, which, in writing, begins with a capital letter and ends with a full stop, question mark or exclamation mark. It usually has a subject and a verb.
EXAMPLES OF SENTENCES
simple one main clause ●He left. ●He left the house. ●The sad old man, with the box under his arm, containing all his possessions, left his daughter's house.
compound more than one main clause ●He climbed the hill and waited for a bus. ●He was very sad but he didn't complain.
complex includes subordinate clause(s) ●When he had picked up his belongings, he left the house. ●Although he felt sad, he said nothing. ●He left because he had to.
SENTENCE ADVERBS
Adverbs which apply to a whole sentence. ●**Unfortunately**, he missed the bus.
See also ADVERBS.
For more details see CEG 1.1.

set
verb (= put in position, fix, arrange, start) ●The table was **set** for a formal meal. ●The diamond is **set** in a gold mount. ●The teacher **set** exercises for the class. ●His jokes **set** us all laughing.
noun (= group of connected things) ●Is this a complete **set** of china?
adjective
A (= placed, settled, determined) ●His mind was **set** on finishing the job. ●They work **set** hours: 9 – 5.
B (= ready, prepared) ●Are we all **set**? Then let's go.

❖ *in compounds* ●**set**-back (a reverse [of fortune, progress]) ●**sunset** (going down of the sun) ●hair **set** (lotion/process to make hair dry in a particular style/shape) ●television **set** (monitor, receiving apparatus) ●**upset** (turn over, spill by accident *verb*, disturbance *noun*) ●**outset** (beginning [of journey, project])

❖ *in idioms* ●How can we **set them**

free? (get them out of prison) •She has **set her heart on going** to Paris. (she really wants to go very much) •When will the ship **set sail**? (leave) •The sound of his fingers on the blackboard **sets my teeth on edge**. (gives me an unpleasant physical sensation) •Now we must **set about** getting this room clean. (start the job energetically) •If you **set aside** a little money each week, you'll soon have enough. (save) •**Setting aside** our disagreements for a moment, let's make a decision. (Disregarding, Not considering) •Progress was **set back** by bad weather. (delayed) •We want to finish before the winter **sets in**. (begins, gets established) •Before we **set off/out** make sure you haven't forgotten anything. (start on a journey) •The bomb can be **set off** by a very slight touch. (exploded, made to work) •I didn't **set out to** annoy him but he's easily annoyed. (intend to)

settle
verb
A (= arrive and stay, live [in]) •They liked the place so much that they decided to **settle** there.
B (= come to rest) •Dust had **settled** on the furniture.
C (= make steady, comfortable) •The nurse **settled** the old man into bed and gave him some medicine to **settle** his nerves.
D (= bring to agreement) •So it's **settled** that we leave at nine o'clock. •In the end they **settled** the argument by referring to a dictionary.
settlement
noun
A (= place where people [settlers] have started living) •The USA began as a few small **settlements**.
B (= agreement by law/payment of money or property) •It took a long time to arrange the **settlement** of all his property.
❖ *in idioms* •I'm glad it's **all settled**. (arranged) •'I've got no money.' 'Well, **that settles it** — we can't

buy a ticket.' (That has decided the matter) •She wants the very best and she won't **settle for** less. (agree to, accept) •You need a little time to **settle into** a new job/house. (feel comfortable in) •Can I **settle up** [with you] later? (pay my share of the bill)

several
adjective determiner (= a reasonable number) •**Several** people asked questions at the end. •We could see **several** hundred birds on the rocks.
pronoun •**Several** of them seemed to be hurt and **several** more were obviously dead.

shall /ʃæl, ʃəl/
verb modal auxiliary; negative **shall not/shan't**; used with 1st person (*I/we*) instead of *will* for simple future in many cases and always for questions and offers:
•**Shall** I lend you my pen? (not *will I.) •**Shall** we watch television tonight? •I **shall** be 29 tomorrow. •I hope we **shall** be paid for this work.

Especially for older English speakers, *will* seems inappropriate in these sentences, suggesting the idea of willingness or intention. But in modern English *will* is increasingly used with very little difference in meaning. Some people also use **shall** with the 2nd and 3rd persons to express the idea 'I am determined that you/he/she etc will . . .'
•Don't worry, you **shall** be paid.
•She **shall** never hear about it.

In ordinary speech both **I shall** and *I will* become shortened to **I'll**, so we usually hear no difference between them except in response to such questions as •'Will you take/Will you be taking your mother with you?' (a request for information = Is that part of your plan?) 'Yes, I **shall**/Yes, I am.'
•'Will you take me with you [please]?' (a request = Are you willing to?) 'Yes, I **will**.'
See also **should**, **will**, **would**, FUTURE.

shame

shame /ʃeɪm/
  noun
  A (= feeling of guilt, failure)
  • I feel no **shame** because I did nothing wrong.
  B (= something disappointing)
  • What a **shame** [that] your mother couldn't come today!
shameful/shamefully
  adjective/adverb (= disgraceful, very bad) • His **shameful** behaviour embarrassed all of us; he really behaved **shamefully**.
ashamed [of]
  adjective
  A (= full of shame) • You should be **ashamed of** yourself/of the way you behaved. • A little untidiness is nothing to be **ashamed of**.
  B + *infinitive* (= embarrassed) • I am **ashamed** to say I have never read your book. • Don't be **ashamed** to admit you're wrong.

shape
  noun (= form, organisation) • This room is a rather odd **shape**, like a letter D. • It's hard to imagine the **shape** of society in the future.
  verb (= make in a particular form) • When you make a pie, you **shape** the pastry into a large circle/**shape** a large circle from pastry. • It is the headmaster of a school who really **shapes** its development.
shapely
  adjective (= attractive in shape) • She liked to show her **shapely** legs.
❖ *in compounds* • heart-**shaped** biscuits • pear-**shaped** figure • well-**shaped** • bowl-**shaped**.
❖ *in idioms* • 'How are you feeling?' 'I'm **in very good shape** (fit, well) but I was **out of shape** before I started doing exercises.' (unfit) • I have to **get my ideas into shape**. (organised) • The new building gradually **took shape**. (became a definite form)

share /ʃeə*/
  noun (= part belonging to someone) • If I do my **share** of the work, do I get a **share** of the profits? • I don't like chocolates; give my **share** to somebody else.
  • Will you buy **shares** in this business? (an equal part of the profits)
  verb
  A (= have part of the use of, etc)
  • There aren't enough books so you two will have to **share** [one book].
  B (= divide between two or more)
  • When he dies, his money will be **shared** [out] among the children.
  C (= to be one of a group with)
  • I'm afraid I can't **share** your opinion/optimism/excitement.

sharp /ʃɑ:p/
  adjective (≠ blunt, = keen, cutting, pointed, often used figuratively)
  • This knife isn't **sharp**; it won't cut. • Your eyes are **sharper** than mine. • There's a **sharp** right-turn.
  • This photograph isn't very **sharp**; I can't see the detail.
  adverb (= exactly at a particular time) • You must be there at seven o'clock **sharp**.
sharply
  adverb (corresponding to **sharp**, in an unfriendly way) • He spoke **sharply** to the naughty child.
sharpen
  verb (= make sharp, sensitive)
  • Please **sharpen** the meat-knife.
  • A little lemon **sharpens** the taste.

she
  pronoun 3rd person singular, subject, feminine • Where's Mary? Is **she** upstairs?
  She can be used of boats, cars etc to give them personality • **She**'s an old boat but **she** still sails well.
  See also **her**, PRONOUNS etc.

shine /ʃaɪn/
  verb irregular, **shone**, **shone** (= give light, be bright) • Get up! The sun's **shining**. • He didn't **shine** at languages, but he was a wonderful card-player.
  noun (= brightness) • What a beautiful **shine** there is on this polished wood!

shop
  noun (= place where things are bought and sold, AmE store; workshop/[small] factory) • There's

should

a good book**shop** in the village.
●The petrol station has a little repair **shop** at the back.
verb (=visit shops in order to buy) ●Do you **shop** in the village? ●Do you like [going] **shopping**? ●We went **shopping** for shoes but we did not find any we liked.
❖ *in compounds* ●**shop**-assistant (AmE *sales clerk*, staff selling goods) ●**shop**-keeper (proprietor of small shop) ●**shop**-steward (trade union representative) ●**shop**-soiled (slightly dirty from being on display) ●**shop**-lifting (stealing from shops) ●window-**shopping** (looking, not buying)
❖ *in idioms* ●If two experts meet, naturally they **talk shop**. (talk about their work) ●It's worth **shopping around** for the best bargain in video. (comparing prices in different shops) ●I've got **a lot of shopping to do**. (I have to buy a lot of things)

short

adjective
A (≠ tall, ≠ long) ●Tall men need long trousers but **short** men need **short** trousers.
B + *of* (=without enough) ●'We're **short** of fruit; will you buy some?' 'Sorry, I'm a bit **short** of money this week.'
adverb (=suddenly, abruptly) ●He stopped **short** when he saw who it was. ●I must cut **short** my speech, as it's late.

shortly
adverb
A (=soon) ●He's out but he'll be back **shortly**.
B (=impatiently) ●He answered me very **shortly** when I asked how long he intended to stay.

shorts
noun (=short trousers, AmE = underpants) ●'Must I wear **shorts** to play tennis?' 'Yes, I'll lend you a pair.'

shorten
verb (=make shorter) ●Please could you **shorten** the sleeves?
❖ *in compounds* ●**short**-tempered (irritable, easily angered) ●**short** cut (quicker, more direct route) ●**short**hand (system of rapid writing) ●**short**-listed (put in the group from which a final choice is made) ●**short**-sighted (with poor sight at a distance — figuratively, unable to see future effects)
❖ *in idioms* ●My name is Elizabeth, 'Liz' **for short**. (as a shorter way of saying it) ●He said he would be most happy . . . **in short**, yes. (briefly, he meant) ●I think we're **running short of** oil. (our oil supplies are getting low)

short forms
See CONTRACTIONS.

should /ʃʊd/ /ʃəd/
verb modal auxiliary; negative **should not/shouldn't**
1 corresponding to *shall* in indirect speech, and as main verb in conditional sentences (1st person, *I/we*)
(a) *indirect speech* ●I said I **should** go./He said he would go. ('I shall go.')
(b) *conditional* ●We **should** see it if it came this way./We **should** have seen it if it had come this way. (We shall see it if it comes this way.)
NB *would* is possible in these sentences but carries the idea of willingness. So questions beginning 'Shall I' must be reported with **should** ●He asked if he **should** phone me. ('Shall I phone you?')
2 corresponding to *shall* but more polite/tentative because it implies a condition (often = if you agreed) ●I **should** like some sugar, please. ●We **shouldn't** want to be a nuisance.
3 after *in case* and *if* to make something less probable ●What would happen if he died? (He may)/What would happen if he **should** die? (He might) A more formal structure with the same meaning uses inversion ●**Should** he die, who would follow him?
4 after *so that* and *in order that*

159

show

●We spoke quietly so that we **shouldn't** wake the baby. ●In order that everyone **should** be comfortable, cushions are provided.
5 after certain verbs and adjectives ●He insisted/requested/commanded/asked/suggested/advised/recommended/demanded/desired/intended that we **should** leave. ●He was anxious that we **should** go at once. ●I'm sorry you **should** think him a fool. ●It's astonishing/normal/a shame/shocking/interesting/surprising that they **should** make this decision. (The decision has been made.)
6 I **should** — offering advice ●I should/I'**d** do what the doctor says [if I were you]. ●'Shall I pay by cheque?' 'Yes, I **should**.' ●'I forgot to put the date on it.' 'I **shouldn't** worry; they'll fill it in.'
7 meaning almost the same as *ought to* ●He **should** write to his mother more often. ●You **shouldn't** eat so much. In the first person, ambiguity is possible ●I **should** write to my mother (**a** if I needed her advice; **b** I ought to) ●We **should** have told you. (**a** if you had asked us; **b** we ought to have told you) ●Why **shouldn't** he marry her? ●How **should** we organise this party?

The slight difference between **should** and *ought to* is that **should** suggests more that the speaker's personal opinion matters while *ought to* puts more emphasis on objective regulations/duties/obligations ●I think you **should** buy that hat; it suits you./You ought to save some money for the future. 'Would you lend me $10 if I needed it?' 'Yes, I would.'
See also **ought, shall, will, would,** CONDITION, FUTURE.
For more details see CEG 6.10.

show

verb irregular, **showed, shown** (= demonstrate, allow to be seen, indicate, appear) ●Her face **showed** her feelings. ●Can you **show** me the place on this map? ●I was **shown** the correct way to do it. ●The Spring has come; green leaves are **showing** at last. ●Let me **show** you your seat/where to sit. ●Please **show** me how to change the record.
noun
A (= theatrical performance, exhibition) ●Have you seen the **show** in the Town Hall?
B (= outward display, meaningless ceremony) ●I put on a **show** of interest but really I was bored. ●Of course it was all done for **show** but I thought it was splendid.
❖ *in compounds* ●**show**-business (theatre, acting etc) ●**show**-room (place for exhibiting trade goods)
❖ *in idioms* ●Look at all this waste! It [just] **goes to show** we buy too much. (proves the point) informal ●You work hard all day and what have you got **to show for** all your work? (as reward) informal ●She **showed me** [a]**round** her new house with great pride. ●We know you're a good driver but stop **showing off**! (trying to win admiration) ●You don't notice it till the sun shines on it; then it **shows up**. (becomes noticeable)

shut

verb irregular, **shut, shut** (≠ open, = close) ●Please **shut** the gate or the dog will get out. ●It won't **shut** properly. ●Have/Are the shops **shut** yet?
❖ *in idioms* ●I wish he would **shut up**. (be quiet, stop talking) informal ●All French businesses **shut down** for the summer holidays. (close completely)

sick

adjective
A (≠ well, = ill, diseased, unhealthy) ●My husband is **sick**; he's not coming to work today.
B (= [wanting to] vomit) ●I felt **sick** after I had eaten the meat and I had to go away and be **sick**.
C + *of* (= tired, full of dislike [for]) ●He was **sick** of routine, waiting for buses, being poor.
noun (= sick people) not *the ill ●The **sick** need special help.

sicken
verb (= nauseate, cause strong dislike) ●The pictures of the dying people **sickened** me.
sickening
adjective (= very unpleasant) ●The whole film, dealing with blood and cruelty, was **sickening**.
sickness
noun (= disease, illness) ●Some were absent owing to **sickness**.

side
noun (= lateral surface, position, aspect) ●Which **side** of the road is it on? ●Let's have a look at the other **side** of the paper. Also figuratively — the other **side** of a question. ●Whose **side** are you on?
adjective (= at, from, to the side) ●Go in by the **side** door. ●The medicine has unfortunate **side** effects. (additional, subsidiary)
inside/outside
See **in/out**.
aside
adverb
A (= to one side, out of the way) ●We stepped **aside** to let them go past.
B + *from* (= apart from) ●There are many other costs, **aside** from rent and heat.
sideways
adverb/adjective (= with one side forward) ●If it won't go through the door, turn it **sideways**. ●He gave me a **sideways** look.
❖ **in compounds** ●three-**sided** (eg triangular) ●**side**light (unimportant but interesting information) ●**side** street (unimportant/back street) ●**side**track (distract from main line [of thought])
❖ **in idioms** ●He was attacked **from all sides** (by different people, everywhere) ●He makes a little money **on the side** by working in the evening. (extra, often dishonestly) ●It's a nice room but a bit **on the small side** for me. (rather small) ●Will you **put this to one side** for me? (keep for use later) ●I prefer not to **take sides** [with either of them] when they quarrel. (be on one side, support one of them) ●She looks very small **by the side of** her brother. (compared with) ●Let's **look on the bright side**. (be optimistic)

sign /saɪn/
noun (= mark, notice, gesture, symbol with meaning, indication, signal) ●Addition is shown by the 'plus' **sign**: +. ●Does that **sign** say 'No Smoking'? ●He made a **sign** with his hand and we knew he wanted us to follow him. ●Dark clouds are usually a **sign** of rain. ●There is no **sign** of trouble.
verb (= write name to show identity, agreement) ●I forgot to **sign** the cheque.
signal
noun
A (= sign with intention, eg warning, informing, commanding) ●That red flag is a **signal** of danger. ●Look out for traffic **signals**. (lights)
B (= sound/image sent by waves) ●The TV **signal** is not strong in this area.
verb (= make a signal/sign) ●She **signalled** that she was going to turn left.
signify
verb (= have meaning, importance) ●This mark (@) **signifies** a price per item. ●His agreement doesn't **signify**; we'll do it anyway.
significant
adjective (= meaningful, with importance) ●**Significant** changes in technology are transforming education.
❖ **in compounds** ●**sign**post (road sign directing to a place) ●**sign** language (system for speaking to the deaf etc)
❖ **in idioms** ●He decided to **sign on**; he starts work today (join a workforce) ●He gave her a ring **as a sign of** his love. (to signify)

simple
adjective
A (≠ complicated, ≠ difficult, = easy [to understand]) ●His plan was very **simple**; he intended to kill

since

me and take my money.
B (≠ complicated, = basic)
• Bacteria are **simple** forms of life.
• She wore a **simple** dress with no ornament.
C (= natural, credulous) • She's only a **simple** child; she may be **simple** enough to believe your lies but I shan't.

simply
adverb
A (= plainly, clearly, naturally) • Can you explain it **simply**?
B (= just, only) • Can you **simply** show us and not try to explain it?

simplify
verb (= make plainer, easier, less detailed) • This book is a **simplified** dictionary.
❖ *in compounds* • **simple**-minded (weak in the head, foolish)
• **simple**-hearted (honest, trustful)

since
adverb with perfect tenses
(= subsequently, between then and now) • She left 5 years ago. We've never seen her **since**. • He was hurt in an accident and has been unable to walk ever **since**.
preposition
A (= from then till now) • The town has changed **since** 1950. • I have been waiting **since** two o'clock.
B (= from then till then) • He had lived there **since** his marriage and then, when his wife died, he left.
• He has lived here **since** he left that house/**since** became a widower/**since** that time. • It's a long time − ten years − **since** she died. (She died ten years ago. She has been dead for [not *since] ten years.)
+ *-ing* • **Since** leaving their old home, he has become interested in new things.
conjunction
A (= after past time when, during the period after, from then on)
• It's been ages **since** I've felt/I felt so happy. • I've disliked him [ever] **since** I met him in 1980.
B usually beginning a sentence, can be used with non-perfect tenses (= as, because, seeing) • **Since** you won't help me. I'll ask someone else. • **Since** he didn't understand, I explained it again more simply.
See also **as, because, for, from**.

singular
1 Some words have no plural form although they seem to be plural in meaning. See *non-countable*.
2 Quantities and amounts, which are in plural form are often considered as single items. • Ten miles **is** too far to walk. • Twenty dollars **was** too much to pay. • He stayed **another** two days.
3 When two things become one thing in our minds we treat *it* as singular. • Steak and chips **is** fairly cheap.
4 Some nouns can be either singular or plural, depending on circumstances. • The committee **has** agreed to the plan. • The committee **have** disagreed and split into different groups.
See also NON-COUNTABLE, NOUN, PLURALS.

sit
verb irregular, **sat, sat** (= be seated, eg in a chair, on a bench)
• Careful! Don't **sit** on the cat!
• I **sat** in the waiting room for an hour. • **Sit** the baby on the floor.
• [Please/Do] **sit** down.

seat
noun
A (= anything one can sit on)
• That box is not a very comfortable **seat**. • Please take a **seat**.
B (= place in theatre, car, etc)
• Can you get a **seat** for that play?
verb (= [cause to] sit, provide seats for) • They **seated** themselves round the table. • We were **seated** at the back. • They can **seat** 40 people in the large dining-room.
❖ *in idioms* • When the work is done you can **sit back** and enjoy the results. (rest, relax) • He sat [for] the exam but he failed. (took, did

162

the exam) •He **sat in for** me when I was ill. (took my place, stood in) •She's not here; she's **baby-sitting** for someone. (looking after a baby while the parents are out) •With people offering him good jobs, no responsibilities, and no hurry, he's **sitting pretty**. (in a good, fortunate position)

size
noun countable (=degree of bigness or smallness) •What **size** is this blouse? Is it a medium **size**? •It's the wrong **size**; two **sizes** too small.
non-countable •It is a place of some **size**. (quite big)
❖ *in compounds (verb)* •large-**sized** envelope •good-**sized** tomato •egg-**sized** lump of butter.
❖ *in idioms* •That's **about the size of it**. (a fair description of the situation) •He tried to **size me up**. (form an opinion of me, work out what I was like) informal

sleep
noun non-countable (=natural unconsciousness) •I didn't get much **sleep** last night: the baby kept me awake.
verb irregular, **slept, slept** (=rest in sleep, be asleep) •He **slept** for an hour after lunch.

asleep
adjective predicative only (=not awake) •'Are you **asleep**?' 'I was fast **asleep** until you asked me!'

sleepy
adjective
A (=tired, ready to sleep) •I'm going to bed; I feel **sleepy**.
B (=quiet, slow-moving) •He lives in a **sleepy** little village.

sleeper
noun
A (=a person sleeping — in a particular way) •He's a heavy **sleeper**; he won't wake up even if we make a noise.
B (=part of a train with accommodation for sleeping) •It's a very comfortable journey if you book a **sleeper**.
❖ *in compounds* •**sleeping**-bag

(usually warm bag for sleeping in when camping etc) •**sleeping** pill (tablet which helps you sleep)
❖ *in idioms* •I can't **get to sleep** when his radio is playing. (succeed in sleeping, usually negatives and questions) •I wish that baby would **go to sleep**! (fall asleep) •She's **losing sleep over** the problem. (not sleeping because of worrying about it) •The dog was very sick so the vet **put it to sleep**. (killed it mercifully) •I can't decide now; I'll **sleep on it**. (take time — a night — to think about it)

slight /slaɪt/
adjective (≠ great, = weak, inconsiderable) •It's a very **slight** fault; you can hardly see it. •I notice a **slight** smell of gas, do you?

slightly
adverb (=a bit, rather) •He was only **slightly** late. •He could change it very **slightly** but not as much as you suggest.
❖ *in idioms* •There is **not the slightest chance** that he will win. (there isn't any chance) •'Do you mind if I smoke?' '**Not in the slightest**.' (not at all)

slow
adjective (≠ quick, = taking a long time, inactive, unintelligent) •Only the **slow** trains stop at that little station. •He is a **slow** but steady worker. •He was too **slow** to realise what I meant.
adverb replacing **slowly** especially in these expressions •Please go/drive **slow**. •How **slow** it goes!
verb (=make, become slower) •The train **slowed** [down/up] as it came near the station.
❖ *in idioms* •It was a joke but she was too **slow off the mark/slow on the uptake** to see it. (slow to understand, see the point) •You're working too hard; you'll be ill if you don't **slow down**. (relax, take life easier)

small
adjective (≠ large, = little) **smaller, smallest** •I'd like a **small** drink,

SO

please. •He's a **small** farmer. (his farm is small)
Used for physical size only, not usually to express feeling about it; compare 'A **small** boy took it.' 'Poor little boy!' not *poor small boy, *silly small man
❖ *in compounds* •**small**-minded (mean-spirited, selfish) •**small** change (coins of little value) •**small** talk (light conversation, chat)
❖ *in idioms* •**I felt very small** when I realised how foolish I had been. (ashamed, humble) •**Small wonder** you get fat if you eat biscuits all day! (It's not surprising)

so

conjunction (= with the result that, with the purpose that, therefore) •It was late, **so** we had to hurry. •We hurried **so** [that] we didn't miss the bus. •I was told to do it, **so** I did it.

adverb
A (= in this way, in such a way, in the way already mentioned) •He is an adult and must be **so** treated. •The story is **so** told that you get a wrong impression. •You may think it accurate but it is not **so**. •'Is he trustworthy?' 'I believe/hope/think/imagine/expect/guess **so**.' Compare 'I think/fear not.'
B in expressions of agreement •'I like this place.' '**So do I**.' •'I'm leaving now.' '**So am I**.' •'I saw it on TV.' '**So did I**.' •'We were disappointed.' '**So were we**.' •'We have bought one.' '**So have we**.' •'I can swim.' '**So can I**.' Compare 'I don't like it.' 'Neither/Nor do I.'
C in expressions of surprised agreement •'You're wearing odd socks!' 'Oh! **So I am**!' •'You've left the keys inside.' 'Oh, dear, **so I have**.'
D for emphasis (= very) •Thank you **so** much! You have been **so** kind! I feel **so** very grateful!

so . . . that
+ *adjective* •He is **so** stupid that he can't boil an egg. Compare 'He's such a fool that'
+ *adverb* •She speaks **so** softly that

I can't hear what she says.
+ *many/much* •He has **so** much [that] he can easily afford to give us some of it. (such a lot) •They have **so** many [that] they can't even count them. (such a lot)

not so . . . as
(= not as . . . as) •He is **not so** rich **as** you think. •You're **not so/as** tall **as** me; you're a bit shorter than me.

so that
conjunction (= in order that) •I am saving money **so that** I can buy a new car. •I put it in the bank **so that** I shan't spend it on anything else. •He put it in the bank **so that** he should not be tempted to spend it.
conjunction (= with the result that) •He fell in the water, **so that** all his clothes got wet.

so as to
(= in order to) •He works hard **so as to** save money. •She wears gloves **so as** not **to** make her hands dirty.

❖ *in idioms* •'Psychologists say it's true' '**So what?**' (Why is that important? Why believe them?) informal •This **so-called** 'easy system' is very hard. (wrongly-named) •'Is it true?' 'My mother says **so**.' (says it is true) •**Even so**, I'd like to see for myself. (All the same, Nevertheless) •She says the bus goes at ten o'clock. **If so**, we've missed it. (If that is true, In that case) •He packed his shoes and socks and hats **and so on**. (and other things of this kind, etc) •It only costs a pound **or so**. (or a bit more, about £1) •You can borrow it **so/as long as** you take care of it. (if, provided that) •I started saving last week. **So far**, I've saved £5. (up to now) •**So/As far as I know**, he'll be here tomorrow. (To the best of my knowledge) •'You can speak to him now if you like.' 'Oh, good — **so much the better**.' (even better than the original idea) •This lorry driver is the king of the road, **so to speak**. (in a manner of speaking) • 'He has a lot of experience.' 'Yes, so I understand.' (I have already been told) • This problem is a real so-and-so. (substitute for a stronger word) • Imagine so-and-so needs money: he can do three things . . . (Mr X, a person in an example) • 'How are you feeling?' 'So-so.' (not well) • She is very tidy. Everything is arranged just so. (exactly, neatly) See also as, such, CAUSE, COMPARISON, CONJUNCTIONS.

some
  adjective/pronoun determiner used with plural and non-countable nouns, usually in positive statements
  A (= a quantity [of], a number [of]) • There's some bread in the cupboard and some biscuits in the tin.
  If we are not concerned with quantity we do not use the word some. 'Bakers sell bread.'
  If we wish to encourage the answer *yes* to a question, we can use some instead of the usual *any*. • 'Will you have some soup? It's delicious; let me give you some'. 'No, thanks, I have some already.'
  + *of* (before other determiners) • Some of this stuff is beautiful. • I sent cards to some of my friends. • Can I see some more of your photographs? (Compare 'none of this stuff/none of my friends/no more of them')
  B (= not others, not all, not enough) • Some people think it's a good idea. • He has some power, but he can't change things all by himself.
  C (= an unknown, often suggesting scorn) • He married some silly little girl. • There's sure to be some way of solving the problem. • Let's meet some time. (one day, not specified)
sometimes
  adverb (= occasionally, from time to time) Sometimes, the teacher makes a mistake.
something, somebody, someone
  pronouns (= a thing, a person)

• There's **somebody** at the door.
• He's got **something** in his hand. Compare 'There isn't anybody here.' 'I haven't got anything in my hand.' • 'I don't like this. Have you got **something** else?' (encouraging the answer 'yes')
somehow
  adverb (= in some way) We found it all very difficult but we managed **somehow**.
somewhat
  adverb (= rather) formal • It was **somewhat** more expensive than I had realised.
somewhere
  adverb (= in/at/to some place) • 'I left my pen **somewhere**.' • 'It's not here; it must be **somewhere** else.'
❖ *in idioms* • We waited **for some time**. (quite a long time) • He said he had a meeting **or something**. (I'm not exactly sure) • I hope we **see something of you** when you come to this country. (meet occasionally) • Perhaps there is **something in what he says**. (truth or value) • Your bag **is something like** mine. (slightly resembles) • Now we're **getting somewhere**. (making progress)
See also **any, no, none**.

soon
  adverb
  A (= in a short time, before long) • It will **soon** be time for coffee.
  B (= quickly) • Please reply as **soon** as possible.
sooner
  adverb
  A (= more quickly) • The train came **sooner** than we expected.
  B (= rather) • I'd **sooner** die than marry that man.
as soon [as]
  A (= when, immediately) • **As soon as** he saw her, he fell in love.
  B (= as willingly [as]) • She said she'd **as soon** die [as marry him].
❖ *in idioms* • 'When do you want it done?' 'Well **the sooner the better**.' (as soon as possible) • **Sooner or later**, she'll agree to marry him. (in the end) • I think he's getting better

sorry

but we must not **speak too soon**. (accept something as a fact before it is certain) •**No sooner had I gone** outside than the phone rang. (As soon as I went outside, the phone rang.) formal
See also **prefer, rather**.

sorry
adjective (≠ glad) •I'm **sorry** [that] you're not feeling well. •I'm **sorry** about your bad luck. •I feel **sorry**/am **sorry** for you because you are ill.
interjection
A to apologise for something done, not to ask permission. •**Sorry**! I stepped on your foot.
B to ask for a repetition •**Sorry**? I didn't quite hear what you said.

sorrow
noun (= [cause of] unhappiness) •His son's death was a great **sorrow** to him.
See also **excuse**.

sort
noun (= kind, type) •There are several different **sorts** of jam; which **sort** do you want? •All **sorts** of people use the library, not only students. •'What's a rose?' 'It's a **sort** of flower.'
verb (= put in order, arrange in groups) •**Sorting** all the washing into piles takes only a few minutes. •Please **sort** out the papers you want to keep and throw the rest away. •What a mess! Let's try to **sort** it out. (put it right, put matters straight)

sort of
adverb (= rather, in some way) informal •He said it was **sort of** funny. •It tastes like a banana, **sort of**, but not exactly.

sound
adjective (= in good condition, strong, based on good reasoning) •His heart is **sound**. •Fruit for freezing must be **sound**. •He uses **sound** arguments to support his opinions.
noun (= what can be heard, noise) •Does **sound** travel faster under water? •I heard a **sound** from the next room.

verb
A (= make a sound [with]) •**Sound** your horn when you come to the corner, to warn other drivers.
B (= seem, when heard) •That **sounds** like a good idea. •It **sounds** as if there will be trouble.

space
noun
A (= area/volume with nothing in it) •There must be a **space** to put my books. •Leave a **space** after that line.
non-countable •There's some **space** left at the back.
B (= what surrounds things, what is outside the earth's atmosphere) •Don't just stare into **space**; help me! •Astronauts explore **space**.
❖ *in compounds* •**space**-ship/craft (vehicle used in space) •**space**-suit (garment with air supply for use in space)

spare
adjective (= not in regular use, kept for possible need) •Where is the **spare** wheel for this car? •Can I sleep in your **spare** room? •There are **spare** light-bulbs/supplies in the store-cupboard. •I don't have much **spare** time nowadays.
verb
A (= give, afford to give) •Please **spare** a little money for these poor children. •Can you **spare** [me] a few moments of your time?
B (= be merciful to) •Please don't kill me! **Spare** me!
❖ *in idioms* •There was enough to drink and **to spare**. (some was left over, extra) •I will **spare you the details**. (mercifully not bore/upset you with them)

speak [to]
verb irregular, **spoke, spoken** (= say things, talk) •Children usually learn to **speak** before they are three. •Please would you **speak** more slowly? •I should like to **speak** to the manager. •Do you/Can you **speak** Japanese? •Is English **spoken** in your country? •He **spoke** about the need for co-operation.

stand [up]

speaker
noun
A (= person who speaks a language/makes speeches) ●He is a good **speaker** of German. ●Did the **speaker** keep the audience interested?
B (= part of sound apparatus, loudspeaker) ●Pop groups have very large **speakers**.

speech
noun
A (= power of speaking) Some words are used in **speech** but not in writing.
B (= formal talk to a group) ●Politicians are used to making **speeches**.
❖ **in idioms** ●They quarrelled and now they **don't speak to each other**; they're **not on speaking terms**. (ignore each other) ●**Generally speaking**, I agree with you. (In general, For the most part) ●He is the driving force, **so to speak/in a manner of speaking**, the power behind the throne. (as one might say) ●Forgive me if I **speak my mind**. (say what I really think) ●Who will **speak for** these defenceless people? (represent, support them) ●The facts **speak for themselves**. (make an effective argument without explanation) ●**Speaking for myself**, I disagree. (personally) ●Do **speak up**! I can't hear you. (Talk louder) ●It's a nice enough little house, **nothing to speak of**. (not special)

special /ˈspeʃəl/
adjective (≠ ordinary, = of a particular kind) ●Bring all your friends; it's a **special** occasion. ●We just chatted about this and that; nothing **special**.

specially
adverb
A (= for one particular purpose) ●His shoes are **specially** made for him.
B (= particularly, noticeably) ●He's not **specially** tall; just average height.

specialise [in]
verb (= limit your business, study, etc to particular things) ●He grows other flowers but he **specialises** in roses.

specialist [in]
noun (= expert) ●He is a **specialist** in plant diseases.

especial/especially
adjective/adverb same as **special/specially** (= above all) formal ●I was pleased with everyone's work, **especially** Sophie's.

spend
verb irregular, **spent, spent** (= pay out, use money, time etc) ●He **spends** a lot of money on the car. ●Does he **spend** any on his wife? ●Where will you **spend** your holidays? ●She **spent** an hour painting her nails.

spite
noun (= unreasonable dislike, desire to hurt) ●I don't think it was an accident, I think he broke my vase out of/from **spite**.

in spite of/despite
preposition (= opposing, defying) ●They played cricket **in spite of** the rain/**despite** the bad weather. (although it was raining)

spot
noun (= little area, dot, mark, particular place, pimple) ●That tie — the one with black **spots** — is made of silk. ●There is a **spot** of ink on your dress. ●I know a nice **spot** for a picnic. ●Young people often get **spots** on their faces.
verb
A (= notice) ●Can you **spot** your friend in this crowd?
B (= mark with spots) ●I can if he's wearing his **spotted** hat.

spotless
adjective (= perfectly clean) ●Her kitchen floor is always **spotless**.
❖ **in idioms** ●Could I have **a spot** of tea? (drop) informal ●When I saw her stealing, I asked her to leave, **on the spot**. (there and then) ●I found myself **in a spot [of bother]**. (a difficult situation/position/fight)

stand [up]
verb irregular, **stood, stood**
A (= be/put in an upright position,

167

start

not fall or move) ●Will everyone please **stand** [up] and sing hymn number 101. ●There were no seats on the bus so we had to **stand**. ●He **stood** the pot of flowers beside her bed. ●I shall not change my mind; I shall **stand** firm.
B (=be in a position, relative to others) ●He wants to know where he **stands**; is he in an advantageous position or not?
C often +-*ing* (=bear, tolerate) ●He can't **stand** crowds or waiting for buses. ●He's really irritating; I don't know how you **stand** it.
noun (=defensive position, official place, exhibition stall etc) ●The defending forces made a **stand** outside the town but were defeated. ●The leader took his **stand** in front of his team. ●Buy some fruit from one of those **stands** by the roadside.
❖ *in idioms* ●Sophie **stands a good chance of** getting the prize. (is likely to get it) ●You must **stand on your own [two] feet**. (be independent). ●Let me **stand you a drink**. (pay for one) ●An attack was expected; the army was **on standby**. (ready to be called into action) ●'VIP' **stands for** 'very important person'. (represents, by initial letters) ●My political party **stands for** social equality. (supports) ●If one teacher is away, another will **stand in** [**for him/her**]. (do his job) ●Your friend **stands out** from the crowd in his spotted hat. (is easy to see) ●Sophie is not an **outstanding** driver. (especially good, noticeable) ●From the **standpoint** of a baby, mothers are chiefly food and comfort suppliers. (point of view, way of seeing things) ●School furniture must **stand up to** very rough treatment. (stay good in spite of) ●She looks weak but she can **stand up for** herself. (defend)
See also **bear**.

start
verb
A (=begin, commence) ●We can **start** [off] early [for London] and **start** back here at four o'clock. ●Who **started** this fight? ●It **started** raining, so we came in. ●Shall we **start** with soup or fruit-juice?
B (=set in motion, cause to begin work) ●I couldn't **start** the car this morning. ●What you say has **started** me thinking. ●Don't **start** him talking about the army; he'll go on talking all night.
noun
A (=beginning of action in time or place) ●The runners waited at the **start** for the race to begin. ●I've never trusted him from the **start**.
B (=a sudden movement) ●I woke with a **start**: it was all a dream.
C (=advantage in time) ●The police will never catch him; he has six hours' **start**.
❖ *in idioms* ●She can't marry him; **for a start/to start with**, she's too young. (in the first place, firstly) ●Do you want to **start something**? (make trouble, start a fight) informal ●That idea was **a non-starter**. (one with no chance of success)
See also **begin**.

stative verbs
These are verbs referring not to events but to states. They are not used in progressive tenses. We can say ●**I am finding out** but not *I'm knowing*, because *know* is a stative verb. We can say ●**She is smelling the rose** to mean she is using her nose to detect its scent, but not *The rose is smelling nice*.
For a list of similar verbs, see PRESENT (present simple, [d])
For more details see CEG 4.27.

stay
verb
A (≠leave, =remain) ●Why don't you **stay** for dinner? ●**Stay** in your seat until the plane stops. ●We had to **stay** indoors because the weather was so bad. ●It looks lovely now but it won't **stay** clean for long.

stick

B (= live temporarily as a guest *with* a person, *at* a place, *for* a time) ●My mother is coming to **stay** for a few days. ●She's **staying** with us, not at the hotel.
noun (= period of a visit) ●She's just had a short **stay** in hospital.
❖ *in idioms* ●Is this music a passing fashion or is it **here to stay**? (permanently accepted) ●I comb my hair, but it won't **stay put**. (remain tidy, in position) informal ●We **stayed on/behind** after the others had gone. (didn't go at the expected time)

steal /sti:l/
verb irregular, **stole, stolen**
A + *object (thing)* [+ *from* + *owner/place*] (= take someone else's property unlawfully) ●He **stole** £2 from my pocket. Compare 'He robbed me of £2.' ●If you **steal** from shops, you are a thief and you will be charged with theft.
B (= move secretly, quietly) ●They **stole** out of the house at night.

stealthy
adjective (= furtive, trying not to be seen) ●She was having a **stealthy** look at my private diary.

step
noun (= pace, movement/sound of foot walking, stage in a series, place to put feet on stairs, ladder etc) ●The baby can walk only a few **steps**. ●I was woken by [foot] **steps** outside. ●The first **step** in the development of a new business is finding some money.
Usually, we speak of *stairs* inside a building and **steps** outside: ●They were photographed on the **steps** of the church.
verb (= move feet, walk, tread) ●He **stepped** confidently onto the stage. Then he **stepped** on a banana skin and fell on his face.

step-
prefix (= related through one [re-married] parent) ●**step**-mother ●**step**-brother ●**step**-child.
❖ *in idioms* ●Soldiers have to march **in step**. (in time, with all left feet moving at once) ●He is **out of step** with the others/with modern ideas. (not in harmony with) ●We must **keep step with** modern developments. (move forward as they do) ●Don't rush; do it **step by step**. (little by little, in stages) ●Has he **taken any steps** to improve the situation? (acted, taken action) ●The path is rough, so **watch your step**! (Be careful how you go — also figuratively, take care, be on your guard) ●Will the owner of ticket number 301 **step forward**? (come to the front, show himself)

stick
noun (= thin piece [of wood, chalk]) ●We need some **sticks** to light the fire. ●He must be blind; he has a white **stick**.
verb irregular, **stuck, stuck**
A (= adhere, fix with glue etc, become/stay fixed in position) ●Have you **stuck** a stamp on that letter? ●It won't **stick** properly. ●I can't open the door; it's **stuck**. ●They were good friends and they **stuck** together through all their troubles.
B (= pierce, put [through] push) ●You can tell if it's cooked by **sticking** a fork into it. ●He **stuck** a pen in my hand and ordered me to write.
C (= stand, bear) ●He came home because he couldn't **stick** the life abroad. informal

sticky
adjective
A (= adhesive, like glue) ●His face is **sticky** from eating jam.
B (= difficult) ●The exam was a bit **stickier** than he expected. informal
C (= unhelpful) ●Her father was quite **sticky** when I said we wanted to get married. informal
❖ *in idioms* ●I'm afraid you've **got the wrong end of the stick**. (misunderstood) ●When he said I had not been much help, it really **stuck in my throat**. (was very hard to accept) ●You'll finish the job if you **stick at it**. (keep working) ●Will you **stick by** me if I am

169

attacked? (continue to support)
●His ears **stick out** like wings.
(project) ●It **sticks out a mile** that she doesn't like him. (is very easy to see) ●The rain nearly made us give up but we **stuck to** our plan. (didn't change it) ●**I'm stuck**; can you help me with this? (I can't solve this problem) ●She seemed a bit **stuck-up**. (proud, feeling superior) informal ●If people attack you, you must **stick up for yourself**. (defend yourself)

still
adjective (= not moving) ●Keep **still** while I take your photograph.
adverb
A mid-position (= [even] up to now/then, ≠ not yet) ●He was **still** working hard when I left. (He hadn't/hasn't finished yet. Compare 'He was already working hard when I arrived.') ●Have some coffee; it's **still** quite hot.
B (= even so, nevertheless) ●I know it's not easy for you to arrive at the right time but you must **still** make an effort.
C (= even) + *more/less/comparative* ●I know you work quite hard but you'll have to work **still** harder/harder **still**.
D sentence adverb (= however) ●There's no coffee. **Still**, there's plenty of tea.
E (= besides, yet) ●I haven't finished; there's **still** another job to do.
See also **already, besides, even, yet**.

stop
verb (≠ go, = cease, prevent [moving], end) ●If you see a red light, **stop** [the car]. ●When the music **stopped**, the children stopped dancing. ●'Why did you **stop**?' 'I **stopped** to look at the map.'
[+ *object*] + *-ing* ●I **stopped** smoking last week. ●I **stopped** him smoking in the kitchen. ●I saw him smoking and I **stopped** him. ●You can't **stop** me saying what I think.
noun (= act of stopping, halt) ●We made several **stops** to buy things.
❖ *in compounds* ●bus **stop** (place where they stop) ●full **stop** (period, punctuation mark [.]) ●**stop**-cock (main tap controlling water supply)
❖ *in idioms* ●He will **stop at nothing** to get his own way. (do anything) ●We must **put a stop to** this nonsense. (bring it to an end) ●It's a long journey; we must **stop over** in Miami. (make a short stay) AmE ●If you can, please **stop by**. (visit me briefly) AmE

straight /streɪt/
adjective
A (≠ curved, = level, upright) ●Her hair is **straight**, not curly. ●Tell me when this picture is **straight**.
B (= in order) ●I'll put the room **straight**, after the party.
C (= honest, truthful) ●Are you being **straight** with me?
adverb
A (= in a straight line) ●Go **straight** down the road and you'll see it **straight** ahead.
B (= directly) ●If it happens again, go **straight** to the police.

straighten
verb (= make straight) ●The old road was **straightened** and widened. ●It's very confusing; let's **straighten** it out and make sense of it.

straight away
adverb (= immediately) ●Please ask the doctor to come **straight away**; it's urgent.

straight-forward
adjective (= honest, simply expressed) ●He was quite **straightforward** about it; he said he didn't like me. ●We need nice **straightforward** instructions that anyone can understand.
❖ *in idioms* ●Can I **set you straight** about that? (give you the facts, correct what you said) ●I couldn't **keep a straight face**. (I couldn't look serious; I had to smile) ●It was a **straight fight**. (between two opponents, not several)

strange /streɪndʒ/
adjective (= odd, surprising, unfamiliar) ●I heard a **strange** noise outside. ●It's **strange** that we

didn't hear it too. •He was alone in a **strange** town. •This job is still **strange** to me.

strangely
adverb (= oddly, in an unfamiliar way, surprisingly) •She was **strangely** dressed in fur boots and a tennis outfit. •**Strangely** [enough], no one noticed her.

stranger
noun (= unfamiliar person, person from another place) •A **stranger** came into the village shop and asked the way to the church. •You can be a **stranger**, but not a foreigner, in your own country.

subjunctive
The subjunctive mood, used in many languages to express doubts or wishes, has almost disappeared from English as a separate form, though its function remains. The following sentences illustrate its use •I wish I **were** 25 again! •If I **were** you, I'd leave home. •We suggested he **prepare** at once. •God **forbid** that any harm **come** to her!

The word *should* is often inserted before the form that looks like an infinitive •We suggested [that] he **should** prepare . . .

The words *may* and *might* also carry the meaning of a more formal subjunctive •**May** God forbid that any harm should come to her!

The subjunctive has the same form as the past tense in expressions such as •I wish I **knew**. •It's time we **left**. •If only they **understood**! and •Suppose somebody **saw** us. The verb *be* in these expressions often keeps its old forms *I were/he were* but this is no longer a rule •He wishes he **were** richer. •It's time he **was** here. •Suppose I **were/was** followed! The past subjunctive has the same form as the past perfect •If only I **had known** yesterday what I know today!
See also **may, might, should, wish,** CONDITION.
For more details see CEG 4.28.

subordinate
Subordinate clauses are parts of sentences which cannot stand alone. The clause **which cannot stand alone** is subordinate. It only makes sense when it is attached to the rest of the sentence.
For details of subordination, see CLAUSES.
For more details see CEG 11.5.

such
pronoun determiner (= so good/bad/unusual etc a thing) •Father Christmas? There's no **such** person.
+ *that* •It is a wonderful sight; **such** that it will never be forgotten. (one that is so wonderful that) •He stole from his own grandmother; **such** was his character.
+ *as* •They brought fruit, **such** as bananas, oranges, grapes and plums.
predeterminer •He's **such** a fool! •He's **such** a silly man! •They are **such** experts, **such** clever men! Compare 'He's/They're so foolish, so clever'. •Why do you speak to **such** people/**such** a person?
+ *that* •It was **such** a difficult exam that only five people passed. (so difficult that)
+ *as* •He doesn't need **such** a big glass as that. •You won't see him in **such** a place as a disco.
not such a
+ *noun* expressing comparison •I'm **not such a** fool as you think. (I'm cleverer) •It's **not such a** long way as you said. (It's nearer)
For more details see CEG 3.36.

sudden
adjective (= quick/unexpected) •His **sudden** death was a great shock. •We nearly fell off because of a **sudden** turn in the road.
suddenly
adverb (= unexpectedly, without warning) •The electricity failed and **suddenly** it was quite dark.
❖ *idiom* •**All of a sudden**, the lights went off. (suddenly).

suffix

suffix
Suffixes are parts of words, joined on at the end. Some can be used very freely to make new words. The suffixes most worth knowing are:

-**able** (able to be . . . -ed) • read**able** • drink**able** • wash**able** • unknow**able** • believ**able**

-**ation** (act/process of) • limit**ation** • re-organis**ation** • preserv**ation** • estim**ation**

-**er** (person who does . . .) • garden**er** • paint**er** • teach**er** • writ**er**; (thing which does . . .) • tin-open**er** • floor-clean**er** • coat hang**er** • knock**er**

-**ish** (rather [like]) • girl**ish** • yellow**ish**, • lat**ish** • dark**ish** • larg**ish** • clever**ish**

-**ism** (belief in) • modern**ism** • real**ism** • ideal**ism** • conservat**ism** • social**ism** • national**ism**

-**ist** (user of) • violin**ist** • cycl**ist** • organ**ist**

-**less** (without) • fear**less** • brain**less** • use**less** • child**less** • home**less** • point**less**

-**ly** (making adverbs) • cruel**ly** • heavi**ly** • open**ly** • simp**ly** • sympathetical**ly** • amusing**ly**

-**ness** (making nouns) • sweet**ness** • lazi**ness** • kind**ness** • forgetful**ness** • dirti**ness**

-**y** (making adjectives) • milk**y** • ic**y** • snow**y** • wooll**y** • nutt**y** • butter**y** • oil**y** • gass**y**

Use a dictionary to check the meanings of words ending with these suffixes: there are many alternative senses.

suggest /sə'dʒest/
verb (= cause to come to mind, put forward [an idea]) • What does this blood-stained knife **suggest**? Murder!
+ *-ing* • May I **suggest** waiting a moment before we decide?
+ *that* + [*should*] + *subjunctive* • I **suggest** that we [should] ask all the guests where they were at the time.

suggestion
noun (= proposal, idea, slight sign) • Your **suggestion** is very sensible. • There must be no **suggestion** of force. • I detect a **suggestion** of fear in her expression.

suggestive
adjective (= which brings ideas to the mind, often 'bad' thoughts) • He wanted to show me **suggestive** pictures!

suit /su:t/
verb (= satisfy, be convenient, look right with/on, be good for) • Which day would **suit** you best to meet? • His style of writing doesn't **suit** the subject. • I like your dress; it really **suits** you. • All this lying in bed doesn't **suit** him — he needs exercise.

noun
A (= set of matching clothes, jacket and trousers or skirt/clothes for a particular purpose) • 'You'd better wear a **suit** and tie for that meeting.' 'I didn't intend to wear a swim-**suit**!'
B (= one of four kinds of cards) • Hearts, diamonds, spades and clubs are the four **suits** in card-games.

suitable
adjective • A bathing-suit is not **suitable** for going shopping in.
❖ *in idioms* • You can **suit yourself**. (do what you like, if you want to be different) • **Nothing could suit me better.** (That's perfect, extremely convenient)

superlative
The superlative forms of short adjectives and adverbs end in **-est**. Long ones use **most** • quick**est** • dri**est** • hard**est** • fast**est** • light**est** • **most** complicated • **most** exciting • **most** beautifully • **most** cleverly. Note that adjectives using *-er*, *-est* are not necessarily matched by adverbs that do the same: sweet — sweet**est** — **most** sweetly. The rule about this is not always clear, but never use both; *most reddest is wrong, while both • red**dest** and • **most** red are possible.

sure

The opposite or negative idea is expressed by **least** •the **least** expensive (cheapest).
The article *the* is normally used with superlatives because they are 'definite': •**the** biggest apples •**the** most important question. However, this does not apply to adverbs: •We moved fast but he moved **fastest**. •The one who works [**the**] **hardest** gets the prize.
Most is sometimes used like *very:* •You are **most** helpful. (no article should be used)
See also COMPARISON, MORE, MOST

suppose
  verb
  A (= consider to be likely/true, expect) •What do you **suppose** will happen now? •People used to **suppose** that the world was flat. •Try that new restaurant; it's **supposed** to be very good.
  In expressions of agreement •'We must go soon.' 'Yes, I **suppose** so.' •'It doesn't matter much.' 'No, I **suppose** not.'
  B (= assume, as in an argument) •Let's **suppose** that plants respond to sound waves; does that mean they hear? •This line is **supposed** to be straight.
  conjunction
  A (= why not?) •**Suppose** we have a talk about it?
  B beginning sentence (= if) •**Suppose** the money's gone, what can we do?
supposing [that]
  conjunction (= if) •'**Supposing** we are/were/should be caught, what would happen to us?' •We'd be fined, **supposing** [that] we had any money.'
be supposed to
  verb (= ought, be presumed to) •This door **is supposed to** be kept open. •You're not **supposed to** shut it. It's not **supposed to** be shut. •'I can't understand your picture; what **is** this square thing **supposed to** be?' 'It's **supposed to**

be a house but I can't draw very well.'
supposition
  noun (= what is supposed, guess) •This evidence is based on **supposition**, not facts.
sure /ʃʊə*/
  adjective (= certain [to happen], effective) •'Are you **sure** this is the right house?' 'Yes, I'm **sure** of it.' •If I clean the windows, it's **sure** to rain. •Aspirin is a **sure** remedy for headache. •I'm **sure** you'll feel better soon. ('I strongly hope', but not as confident as 'I'm certain you'll be better soon')
  adverb (= certainly, yes, I agree) informal, mostly AmE •'Will you help me?' '**Sure**, I'll help you.'
surely [not]
  adverb
  A (= asking for confirmation, expressing surprise, reluctance to believe) •**Surely** that's your mother over there, isn't it? •You haven't forgotten me, **surely**? •**Surely** that's not the right price? •You're **surely** not going to church wearing that dress? (I can't believe you really intend to); compare 'You're certainly not going to church wearing that dress.' (I forbid it — go and change)
  B (= certainly, safely) •Slowly but **surely** they climbed up.
unsure
  adjective (= lacking confidence) •I feel very **unsure** about accepting such an important job.
ensure
  verb (= make certain, check) •Please **ensure** that this letter is posted today.
assure
  verb (= tell, almost promise) •I **assure** you it will be in the post before ten o'clock.
insurance
  noun (= paying money so that you will receive money if something happens/does not happen) •It is to my **insurance** company.
insure
  verb (= protect by paying insurance

173

surprise

money) ●I have to **insure** this car before I can drive it.

reassure
verb (=comfort by telling) ●Let me **reassure** you; when the letter is posted, you can legally drive the car.

❖ *in idioms* ●**Make sure** you post/of posting/to post it. (Don't forget, be certain to) ●Did you **make sure of** the address? (check that it's correct) ●He's very **sure of himself**, not at all nervous. (self-confident, self-assured) ●We agreed to meet at eight o'clock and at eight o'clock, **sure enough,** he arrived. (just as expected).
See also **certain**.

surprise /sə'praɪz/
noun (=[feeling caused by] unexpected event) ●His sudden arrival was a **surprise**. ●He showed no **surprise** at the news.
verb (=cause suprise) ●Your news does not **surprise** me. ●It does not **surprise** me that this has happened. ●Perhaps we should be **surprised** it hasn't happened before.

surprising
adjective (=causing surprise, unusual) ●The results of the experiment are **surprising**. ●A **surprising** number of people came. ●It's **surprising** [that] you haven't met.

❖ *in idioms* The sudden change of plan **took us by surprise.** (made us confused) ●**To my surprise** [I found] there was some money in my bank account. (surprisingly) ●'Will they succeed?' '**I'd be surprised.**' (I don't think so)

T

take /teɪk/
verb irregular, **took, taken**
A (≠ put, = remove [+from], gain [a hold of]) ●You can **take** the parcel when you have paid for it. ●**Take** this knife and cut some bread. ●You can **take** your ring and never speak to me again!
B (≠ bring, carry [away from here]) ●Who will **take** me to the station?

●When I visit my grandmother, I usually **take** [her] a little present. ●**Take** your umbrella [with you]; it looks like rain.
C (=have room for, bear) ●This lift **takes** only six people. ●I can't **take** much more of her bad behaviour. ●This suitcase is expensive but it will **take** a lot of hard treatment.
D (=accept, use) ●Please **take** my advice/seat/bicycle. ●You should **take** the opportunity/chance. ●He refuses to **take** his medicine/responsibility/the consequences.

takings
noun plural (=money taken by a shop) ●A thief broke in and went off with all the **takings**.

❖ *in compounds* ●**take**-away (shop selling cooked food to eat elsewhere — AmE 'carryout') ●**intake** (number of items taken in) ●**overtake** (pass another vehicle etc) ●**take**over (control of a company by buying shares in it)

❖ *in idioms* ●**How long will this take** [to do]? (How much time is required for it?) ●You agree, **I take it?** (I suppose, assume) ●She **took me for his daughter!** (thought I was, but I'm not) ●**What do you take me for?** (Do you think I'm a fool?) informal ●He was **very taken with/by** her. (attracted to) ●She has a comfortable life and she **takes** her comfort **for granted.** (assumes it is permanent/natural/deserved) ●He **took it for granted that** I would agree. (supposed without asking) ●**Take it from me,** this is a good thing to buy. (Believe me, trust my advice) ●Don't hurry! **Take your time!** (There's no need to rush) ●When his wife died, he **took to** staying at home. (started the habit) ●I have tried cooking it your way but I didn't really **take to it.** (like, feel happy with it) ●When did the meeting **take place?** (happen) ●**Don't take any notice!** (Ignore it) ●You have **taken a lot of trouble** to get this right. (worked hard) ●He is very good at **taking** people off. (mimicry, imitating them) •I was slightly **taken aback** when she asked me why I looked so funny. (surprised, embarrassed) •He **takes after** his father: he hates work. (resembles [a parent or grandparent]) •What is left when you **take away** 25 from 100? (subtract — answer 75) •I didn't mean to call you a liar; I **take it back**. (withdraw the remark) •Please **take down** these figures. (write) •This dress is too loose; can you **take it in**? (make it tighter, smaller) •His story almost **took me in**. (deceived me, made me believe it) informal •It's hard to realise what's happened; I can't **take it in**. (absorb, understand) •What time does the plane actually **take off**? (leave the ground) •It's the sort of job you'd do well. Will you **take it on**? (undertake it, say you will do it) •He was **taken on** by a large firm as a clerk. (employed, given a job) •We don't have to stay at home; let me **take you out** to a restaurant. (be the host on a visit to a restaurant, theatre or similar entertainment) •I've done enough of this; will you **take over** for a while? (do the job instead of me) •He **took up** parasailing when he was 62. (started doing it [of sports, hobbies]) •All my time is **taken up with** domestic matters. (used up, filled) •She is **so taken up with** her new friend that she won't think of anything else. (interested in)

talk
verb usually intransitive (=speak, use words) •Animals can communicate but they can't really **talk**. •Let's **talk** seriously about your future. •He **talked** to us about his experiences.
noun
A non-countable (=way of talking) •Do you understand baby-**talk**?
B countable (=period of talking, [formal] speech) •I had a little **talk** with him about it. •The teacher gave us a long **talk** on our future responsibilities.

talker
noun (=person who talks [a lot]) •What a **talker** she is! •He's a poor/good **talker**.

talkative
adjective (=vocal, inclined to talk) •He's not very **talkative**; he never has much to say.

❖ *in idioms* •I always feel he is **talking down to** me. (speaking as if I were inferior) •He tried to **talk me into** buying his old car. (persuade me to buy) •He wants to marry Sophie. We must **talk him out of it**. (persuade him not to) •They must **talk it over with** their parents before they decide. (discuss seriously)
See also **say, speak, tell**.

tall
adjective (≠ short) mostly used of people and upright objects •My brother is a few centimetres **taller** than I am/me. •Could you climb that very **tall** tree? •It's 20 metres **tall**.

❖ *in idioms* •He likes telling **tall stories** but he doesn't expect you to believe them. (incredible, unlikely accounts) •300 before tomorrow? It's **a tall order** but I'll do my best. (difficult thing to do, a challenge)
See also **high, long**.

taste
verb
A intransitive, stative, not used in progressive (=have a flavour) •This coffee **tastes** good, but it never **tastes** as good as it smells. •Does the medicine **taste** bitter?
B transitive, dynamic (=test, experience the flavour) •He is **tasting** the cheese before he buys it. •When you have a cold, you can't **taste** food very well.
noun
A (=one of the senses) •**Taste** is closely related to smell.
B (=[sensation produced by] flavour) •Do you like the **taste** of garlic? •This cream has a slightly sour **taste**.
C (=ability to choose, judgement, sense of beauty, appropriateness in art, manners, clothes etc, personal

175

liking) •His remarks were true but offensive, and therefore in bad **taste**. •**Taste** changes from generation to generation. •She has expensive **tastes**; she likes to wear diamonds. •I hope the food is to your **taste**.

tasteless
adjective
A (= without flavour) •These vegetables are overcooked and **tasteless**.
B (= without sensitivity) •She wears **tasteless**, cheap, showy clothes.

distasteful
adjective (= unpleasant to do) •Cleaning the bathroom is a **distasteful** but necessary job.

tasty
adjective (= with a strong flavour) •This cheese is very **tasty**; you won't need very much.

tasteful
adjective (= carefully chosen, showing good taste) •He wore a **tasteful** grey silk tie with a very faint stripe.

tear
noun
A /tɪə*/ (= drop of salty liquid from the eye) •A **tear** ran down her cheek as she spoke. •I was almost in **tears** when I heard her story.
B /teə*/ (= a hole caused by tearing) •I can't wear this shirt; there's a **tear** in the sleeve.
verb /teə*/ irregular, **tore, torn** (= pull apart roughly, remove by force, move at speed) •He **tore** a sheet into pieces to make a rope and escape through the window. •The children eagerly **tore** the paper off their presents. •The police car **tore** through the town, flashing its lights. figurative •I was **torn** between my love for my family and my loyalty to a friend. figurative.

torn
adjective (= ripped, ragged) •Her old **torn** dress was all she had to wear.

tell
verb irregular, **told, told**
A (= inform) •Don't you know? Let me **tell** you.
+ *person object* [+ *about* + *something*] •He won't **tell** me about his childhood.
+ *person* + *thing* •We'll **tell** everyone the good news.
+ *thing* + *to* + *person* •Don't **tell** the secret to your sister. •Do you always **tell** the truth? •The light **tells** you whether it's on or off.
B (= recognise, understand by seeing etc) •The twins are so much alike that I can't **tell** one from the other/**tell** which is which/**tell** them apart. •'He's dead.' 'How can you **tell**?'
+ *whether/if* •You can **tell** whether it's ready by putting a fork in.
C + *person* + *to* + *infinitive* (= order, direct) •She **told** me to wait here. •I was **told** to get in touch with you. •Do as you're **told** and don't argue. •If I **tell** you to do it, do it.
❖ *in idioms* •There are 55 people employed here, **all told**. (altogether, if you count everybody) •There's **no telling** when he'll come back. (It's impossible to know) •He **told me off** because I was late. (spoke angrily, critically, to me) •I'd rather not **tell tales** about my friends. (give away their secrets, talk about their affairs)

temper
noun (= [angry] mood) •'Why is he in such a **temper**? He was in a very good **temper** a few minutes ago.' •'He's been reading a letter and it made him lose his **temper**.'

tense
Verbs take different forms according to tense (time) and aspect (showing relationship to a present point in time). The names of the different forms are called 'tenses' even when they refer also to aspect. The names and uses of all the four present tenses are listed under the

entry **present:** *present simple, present progressive, present perfect simple and present perfect progressive* Similarly, the four past tenses *(past simple, past progressive, past perfect simple* and *past perfect progressive)* are listed under **past**. In addition, we talk about future tenses, but English refers to the future without a 'pure' future tense. The names *future tense* and *conditional tense* are used for structures using the modal verbs *shall, will, should* and *would* which are related to other ideas besides the future.

See **will, would,** CONDITION, FUTURE.

Here are some useful general rules about English tenses. They all have exceptions but they are chosen for their general usefulness:
1 When the main idea or main verb of a sentence is future, the subordinate verb is *present tense* ●He'll come when/if he's ready. ●I'll go where I **like** and say what I **want** to wear. ●He's going to ring as soon as he **has** finished the job. ●We're leaving tomorrow, if you **don't** mind. ●Anyone who **comes** late will have to wait outside. ●When I **know** the answer, I'll tell you.
2 When we are reporting things said or thought we use the natural tense for the situation ●It seemed to me/I thought/I said to myself that I **was** making progress. ('I am making progress,' I said to myself — a thought remembered later.)
3 Passive forms must correspond with active ones. Use the same tense of the verb *be* + *past participle* ●They have eaten it./It **has been** eaten. ●Someone saw him./He **was seen**. ●Did they pay you?/Were you **paid**? ●Will anyone use it?/**Will** it **be** used?

Passive progressives are rare, except in the present — keep the sentence active or find another expression ●We had been repairing it for a week./It **had been** undergo**ing** repairs.
4 The past subjunctive looks exactly like the past (except the verb *to be* — *I were, he were*) so conditional clauses depending on conditional main verbs use past tenses ●He would come if he **were** ready. ●If we **didn't have** water, we'd die. ●We thought that we should be killed unless we **escaped**.

Similarly, the past perfect is used in clauses dependent on past conditionals ●He'd have come if he'**d been** ready. ●If we **hadn't had** water, we should have died. ●We should have been killed unless we **had escaped**.

See also CONDITION, FUTURE, PAST, PERFECT, PRESENT, PROGRESSIVE. For more details see CEG 5.

than /ðæn/, /ðən/
conjunction introducing comparisons
comparative + *than* + *noun*
●Oranges are bigger **than** tangerines.
comparative + *than* + *pronoun subject* ●I can run faster **than** you [can run].
comparative + *than* + *clause*
●I can walk faster **than** you can run.
comparative + *than* + *-ing*
●'What's worse **than** finding an insect in an apple?' 'Finding half an insect.'
rather + *accepted choice* + *than* + *rejected choice* ●I'd rather stay here **than** go out. ●We'd rather buy ice creams **than** oranges.
preposition (= in comparison with)
comparative + *than* + *pronoun object* ●You can run faster **than** I can/**than** me.
comparative + *than* + *noun equivalent* ●He left the house later **than** [the] usual [time].
❖ *in idioms* ●He leaves before eight o'clock, **more often than not**. (usually) ●He is **nothing more than** a thief. (simply)
See also COMPARISON.

thank

thank /θæŋk/
  verb (= express gratitude) •Sophie **thanked** him for his kind offer of help, but rejected it.

thanks
  noun (= words expressing gratitude) •[I'd like to say] **thanks** for helping me.

thankful
  adjective (= very grateful) •They were **thankful** to escape from that terrible place.

thank you
  interjection (= I'm grateful to you) •'Would you like some more tea?' '**Thank** you.' (implies 'Yes, please.') 'No, **thank** you.' ('I'm grateful but I don't want any more.') •**Thank** you for the lovely present you sent me.

❖ *in idioms* •You **have** [**only**] **yourself to thank** for the difficulty you're in. (You must blame yourself for it; it's your own fault) •**Thank goodness/God/heaven** he's safe! (What a relief!) •It was **thanks to** his laziness that we were all late. (because of)

that /ðæt/
  adjective demonstrative, determiner; plural **those**
  A pointing to something away from the speaker (= over there, ≠ this) •If I sit in this chair, you can sit in **that** one.
  B referring to something specified •**That** dress you're wearing is very pretty. •Can you remember **that** man we met here?
  pronoun demonstrative; plural **those** •**That**'s father's chair; you can't sit in **that**. •Where did you buy **that**? In one of **those** little shops? •'Who's **that**? Is it the same man?' '**That**'s not very likely; he went to Rome.' •Do you believe **that**?
  adverb (= so, to such a degree) informal •Yes, I like it but I don't want to steal it — I don't want it **that** much.!
  conjunction /ðət/ subordinate, introducing clauses but often omitted

1 in indirect speech
(a) statements •He said [**that**] he didn't like her. She replied **that** his opinion did not interest her.
(b) commands/suggestions (+ *should*) •He ordered **that** the gates should be closed. (the gates to be closed) •Do you recommend **that** I should go now? •I didn't insist [**that**] he should pay cash. •May I suggest **that** you [**should**] take an umbrella? •I propose **that** they [should] stay here.
2 after adjectives expressing personal reactions, importance, urgency, often in sentences beginning with *It* •I'm sorry [**that**] you're ill. •She was anxious [**that**] you should come. •It's necessary [**that**] they [should] go now. •It's funny **that** he hasn't telephoned.
3 after verbs of knowing and thinking; used more than the alternative infinitive •'Do you consider [**that**] he is the best?/Do you consider him to be the best?' 'I understand **that** he is well-qualified, but I feel **that** he needs more experience.'
See also SUBJUNCTIVE.

relative pronoun
1 used as subject of defining relative clause, replacing *who* or *which* especially when both people and things are referred to •The passengers and the suitcases **that** were still waiting had to be transferred to another plane.
2 used as object of defining relative clause but often omitted (= contact clause) •The man [**that**] I met/spoke to/gave the money to asked me out to dinner. •The jacket [**that**] you lent me is too big.

so that
  conjunction (= in order that) expressing purpose and sometimes result. See **so**.

so ... that
  adverbial (= to the degree that) See **so**.

❖ *in idioms* •He started shouting and **at that point** I decided to leave. (then) •**So that's it!** (Now I understand.) ●He fell over and **after that** he didn't move. (when he was lying on the ground) ●Does he often behave **like that?** (in such a way) ●It seems to be a chronic problem, **that is** [**to say**], it happens regularly. (in other words) ●He obviously needs a doctor; and **that's that.** (that settles the matter, it is all there is to be said) ●**In that case** I'll make an appointment for him. (If the situation is as you say) See also RELATIVE.

the
  article definite, determiner, can be used with all nouns, singular, plural and non-countable.
  Used:
  1 when it is clear who or what is meant ●A taxi came along and **the** driver (of the taxi) opened **the** door (of the taxi) and we asked him to take us to **the** hotel (not any hotel, our hotel).
  2 when only one person/thing exists ●**The** sun shines down on **the** earth and provides heat and light.
  3 to emphasise importance or special quality of noun following ●This is **the** cowboy-film!
  4 with adjectives used as nouns ●**The** English/**The** rich/**The** young have some very strange habits.
  Not used:
  1 with abstract nouns used in a general sense ●Heat and light are important to us. (But 'The sun's heat varies from place to place.')
  2 with names of materials ●This shirt is made of cotton. (But 'The cotton from India is very cheap.')
  3 with names of times after *at, by, on* ●Come back on Monday.
  4 with names of meals after *at, by, on, during, for* and *have* ●Can we have breakfast early?
  5 in some common phrases ●Go by car. ●Stay in bed. ●Go to school. ●He is at work. ●Travel by air. ●He went to prison.
  adverb (showing proportional change) + *two comparatives* ●**The** harder you work, **the** more you earn. ●**The** more exercise you take,

the fitter you will be.
See also **a/an, some,** ARTICLES.

their /ðeə*/
  adjective possessive, determiner, 3rd person plural ●Where have they put **their** coats?
theirs
  pronoun possessive, 3rd person plural (=belonging to them) ●'Whose clothes are these?' 'Not ours; they must be **theirs**.'
then
  adverb
  A (=at that time, next) ●In 2050, if you're still alive **then,** it will all be very different. ●Cook the bacon first, **then** the eggs.
  B (=in that case) ●He has no ticket. He can't come in, **then.**
  C (=as a result, therefore) ●If a=4 and b=3, **then** a+b=7.
  ❖ *in idioms* ●I see him **now and then.** (sometimes, not very often) ●He paid cash, **there and then.** (immediately, on the spot) ●**Now then,** let's get to business. (opening remark, calling attention)

there /ðeə*/
  adverb
  A (=to, at, in that place, ≠here) ●Don't go over **there**; stay here. ●I like the Zoo. Have you ever been **there?**
  B drawing attention
  + *verb* + *noun* ●**There** goes Sophie in her new car.
  + *pronoun* + *verb* ●**There** she goes, driving too fast as usual.
  C substituting for/introducing a real subject at the beginning of a clause, usually + *be* ●**There** were a lot of people waiting. (A lot of people were waiting) ●Has **there** been an accident? ●I don't want **there** to be any confusion.
  interjection expressing satisfaction, sympathy etc ●Perhaps this key will open it. **There!** It's open. ●**There!** Have you hurt yourself?
therefore
  adverb (=for that reason, so) ●I wasn't there. **Therefore,** I didn't see.
  ❖ *in idioms* ●If you keep trying you'll **get there.** (succeed, reach

179

these/those

your goal) •It costs $200 **there and back**. (journeys in both directions) •**There you are**; exactly what you asked for! (when offering something or with the meaning — I told you so)

these/those /ðiːz/ /ðəʊz/
adjectives/pronouns demonstrative, plural of **this/that** •'Are **these** [green shoes] yours?' 'No, **those** [red ones over there] are mine.'

they/them /ðeɪ/ /ðem/, /ðəm/
pronouns
A 3rd person plural subject/object, people or things •When will your parents arrive? Are **they** coming tomorrow? Are you meeting **them**? •'Have a peppermint?' 'No thanks; I don't like **them**. **They**'re too strong.'
B (= people in general, unspecified) •**They** say a broken mirror brings bad luck.
C to replace *he* or *she*, informally •Everyone knows what **they** must do.
Notice short forms •**they'll** /ðeɪl/ (they will) •**they'd** /ðeɪd/ (they had/they would) •**they've** /ðeɪv/ (they have)

themselves
pronoun reflexive, 3rd person plural •We can't serve all those people; they must help **themselves** to food.
Also emphatic •They built the house **themselves**. (not someone else's work)
❖ *idiom* •The children are working **by themselves** today. (without help, alone)

thing /θɪŋ/
noun (= any [nameless] object, entity, matter) •What's that funny **thing** in your hand? •Time is a very interesting **thing** to talk about. •**Things** aren't always what they seem.
❖ *in idioms* •We must telephone **first thing** in the morning. (as early as possible) •You ask why it's so expensive. **For one thing**, the work is done by hand. (one reason, possibly out of several) •It's a

good thing to do your exercises before breakfast. (sensible) •It's **a good thing** someone cooks your breakfast for you. (lucky) •**The thing I want to know** is . . . (What I want to know is)

think /θɪŋk/
verb irregular, **thought, thought**
A (= use the mind) •Wait a minute! I'm **thinking** [about it].
B [+ *that*] transitive (= consider, believe) •He **thought** [that] I was serious. •'Who do you **think** will win?' 'I **think** I shall.' •What do you **think** of my new hat? •I don't **think much of** her taste in hats. (have a low opinion of)
noun (= period of thinking) informal •I'll have to have a **think** about it.

thought
noun non-countable
A (= act of thinking, consideration, intention) •He remained deep in **thought**. •You must have some **thought** for the future. •Is there any **thought** of making improvements?
B countable (= something thought, idea, opinion) •Why don't you tell him your **thoughts** about it?

thoughtful
adjective
A (= expressing thought) •She had a very **thoughtful** look; at last she spoke.
B (= considerate, careful) •It was very **thoughtful** of him to leave some milk in the fridge for us.
❖ *in idioms* •I was just **thinking aloud**. (saying what came into my mind, not making a formal statement) •I didn't **think twice**. I said yes. (hesitate) •I'd **think better of** him if he worked harder. (have a higher opinion of) •I almost bought that hat, then I **thought better of it/had second thoughts**. (changed my mind) •He **thinks nothing of** walking ten miles to work. (considers it normal) •When he asked her to marry him she had to **think it over**. (consider carefully) •When you plan a long journey it's

throw

best to **think it out/through**. (plan the details) ●What crazy idea will he **think up** next? (invent)

this /ðɪs/
adjective demonstrative, determiner; plural **these**
A pointing to something near the speaker (=here, ≠ that) ●**This** coffee we're drinking is nicer than that awful coffee we had yesterday.
B referring to something specified ●My mother has a horrible dog. **This** dog is so horrible that no-one likes it.
C (=a certain) informal ●There was **this** woman on the bus . . .
pronoun demonstrative; plural **these** ●Use that towel. Don't use **this**; it's dirty. ●'**This** is my brother.' 'How do you do?' ●**This** is Mr Carter's secretary speaking.
adverb (=to such a degree, so) informal ●The fish was about **this** long.
❖ *in idioms* ●We must stop for a moment **at this point**. (now, here) ●Look, hold it **like this!** (the way I'm holding it) ●We were just chatting about **this, that and the other**. (various things) ●I can tell you **this much**, he's gone abroad. (only this — I can't say where etc)

though
See **although**.

through /θru:/
preposition
A (=in at one side and out at the other, by way of, by means of, as a result of) ●Which pipe does the water go **through**? ●He lost his key and had to get in **through** the window. ●It was **through** his help that she got the job.
B (=from beginning to end, over a large area of, between, among) ●We went on driving **through** the night. ●Our journey took us **through** forests, and **through** countries we didn't know. ●Look **through** these photographs and choose the best.
adverb (=in at one side and out at the other all the way, to the end, to success) ●The door was shut; we couldn't go **through**. ●You needn't change trains; this one goes **through** to Paris. ●Have you read this document right **through**? ●I didn't enjoy the exam but I got **through**.
adjective
A (=direct, going from end to end) ●**Through** trains don't stop here.
B (=finished, no longer friends) ●Wait a minute. I'm nearly **through**. ●If she behaves like that, we're **through**.

throughout
preposition/adverb (=during every part of) ●He'll be unconscious **throughout** [the operation].
❖ *in idioms* ●Open Wednesday **through/thru Saturday**. (AmE, from the beginning of Wednesday to the end of Saturday, inclusive) ●My shoes are **wet through**. (thoroughly, completely wet) ●**No through road**. (Road sign — no exit at the other end) ●Operator, can you **put me through** to this number? (make a telephone connection) ●**Are you through?** (BrE Are you connected to the other speaker? AmE Have you finished speaking? etc) ●I'm **through with** waiting; I'm going home. (I'm not waiting any more) informal
See also **breakthrough, cut through, fall through, get through, go through, let through, look through, pull through, put through, see through, think through, wash through, wear through**.

throw /θrəʊ/
verb irregular, **threw, thrown** (=send through the air, move with force) ●**Throw** the ball to another player. But compare ●**Throw** a stone at someone. (intending to hurt) ●I was **thrown** backwards by the explosion. ●If you don't behave, I'll **throw** you out. ●Would you **throw** me that cloth?
noun (=throwing) ●That was a good **throw**; right on target.
❖ *in idioms* ●Don't **throw** that paper

tie

away; I can use it. (dispose of, put in the rubbish bin) •Can you **throw some light on** this mystery? (explain, illuminate) figurative •He had a good job but he **threw it up**. (gave up, stopped doing it) •This food is horrible; it makes me want to **throw up**. (vomit, be sick) slang

tie
noun
A AmE **neck-tie** •You must wear a **tie** in that restaurant.
B (= connection, bond) •He has family **ties** which keep him here.
verb (= fasten with string etc, using knots) •I'm **tying** the dog to the fence so that he can't run away.

❖ *in idioms* •The contract **tied him down** to a short period in which to repay the loan. (forced him to accept the condition) •Do these facts **tie in with** your theory? (correspond, fit) •His money is **tied up** in his business. (invested, not available for use) •I can't come on Monday, I'm **tied up**.(busy)

tight /taɪt/
adjective (≠ loose, = firmly fixed, fitting closely) •I can't open this box; the lid's so **tight**. •These **tight** shoes are really hurting my feet.

❖ *adverb* (≠ loosely) •Hold me **tight**, don't let me go!

tightly
adverb more commonly used than **tight** •The case was **tightly** packed with £5 notes.

tighten
verb (= [cause to] become tight) •His hand **tightened** on his gun.

tights
noun plural (= like [pair of] stockings joined as one garment, worn by women) •The dancers wore elegant gold **tights**.

❖ *in compounds* •**tight**-fisted (mean, ungenerous with money) •**tight**rope (wire stretched tightly, for acrobats to walk on, showing their skill) •water-**tight**/air**tight** (sealed so that air, water, etc cannot get in or out)

❖ *in idioms* •Having no gun, he was in **a tight corner**. (a difficult/ dangerous situation) •Just **sit tight**

and say nothing. (don't move/don't reveal your opinion)

till
preposition/conjunction (= until, up to the time when) **Until** is slightly more formal and is preferred at the beginning of long clauses •We stayed awake **till** 2 am/**till** Monday. •Wait **till** I call you. •Don't get off the bus **till** you get to the station. •I didn't recognise the place **until** I saw a few houses that were there when I was young. •They promised to be faithful **till**/to death.

time
noun
A non-countable (= what is measured in hours, years etc) •We cannot stop **time** moving on.
B countable (= period or point) •We must leave the glue to get hard for a **time**. •What's the **time** now?
It's time + past [subjunctive] with present meaning •**It's time** we went home now. (time for us to go) •**Isn't it time** you were in bed?
C (= experience connected with period) •Did you have a good **time** at the party? •He has had a hard **time** recently.
D (= time worked, pay received) •He gets paid **time** and a half if he works on Sunday mornings, but he usually only works part-**time**.
verb (= record a speed, arrange something to happen at a certain time) •You ran a mile in 5 minutes; I **timed** you. •The speeches were **timed** for after lunch.

timing
noun (= control over speed, tempo etc) •His voice is fine but his **timing** poor.

times
preposition (= multiplied by, ×) •Three **times** four is twelve. (3 × 4 = 12) •Three **times** as many people live there now.

❖ *in compounds* •**time**-limit (period within which something must be done) •**time**-saving (reducing time spent — a washing-machine is

time-saving) •**time**-table (plan with times of classes, buses, events)
❖ *in idioms* •He arrived **in good time/ahead of time/before time**. (early) •He's **ahead of his time**. (too modern for most people) •Come in **one at a time**. (one by one) •He can do three jobs **at a time**. (at once) •They all came **at the same time**. (together) •He's silly. **At the same time**, I like him. (All the same, Yet) •He's living here only **for the time being**. (temporarily) •**I have no time for** people who behave like that. (dislike) •If we get a taxi, we'll be there **in no time**. (very quickly) •I'd like to see that TV programme but I shan't be home **in time**. (early enough) •He's certainly **taking his time**. (not hurrying, going rather slowly) •**Spend your time** sensibly. (Don't waste time) •What can you do to pass the **time** when you're waiting for a plane? •I'm afraid he's a bit **behind the times**. (old-fashioned) •**At times** he feels very ill. (sometimes) •**How many times must I tell you?** (I have told you many times already) •Using this new machine, you can do the work **in half the time**.
Notice **once, twice, three times, four times** etc.

tired
adjective
A (= needing rest, fatigued) •I'm so **tired**, I could sleep standing up.
B + *of* (= bored, irritated) •I'm **tired** of hearing her complaints.
tire
verb (= [cause to] become tired) •She never **tires** of talking about her holiday in Morocco.
tiresome
adjective (= irritating/boring) •Her conversation is rather **tiresome**.
tiring
adjective (= hard, exhausting) •I found working in a restaurant very **tiring**.
to /tuː/, /tʊ/, /tə/
preposition
A (= [in a direction] towards, as far as, facing, ≠ from) •Is this the road **to** Cambridge? •Are you going **to** the station? •I'm on the way **to** London. •He turned the wheel **to** the left. •How do you get **to** the sea from here? •It's ten kilometres **to** the beach. •Throw the ball **to** me. (not *at me, unless you intend to hurt) •He stayed from Friday **to** Monday.
+ *object* + *to* + *person* •Give the money **to** me. (Give me the money.) •You can say anything **to** him. •Explain it all **to** your mother. •Don't lend the car **to** Sophie.
B marking the infinitive
Sometimes the infinitive of a verb is used with **to**, sometimes without. See INFINITIVE for lists of verbs followed by infinitive with **to** and other uses.

towards
preposition
A (= in the direction of, not necessarily reaching) •Was he going **towards** the station or the sea?
B (= just before) •We left **towards** evening.
C (= for partly paying/fulfilling) •He offered me £5 **towards** my expenses.
❖ *in idioms* •It **doesn't matter to him**. (He doesn't mind) •[I drink] **to your health**. (a toast) •They won the match; **6 games to 3**. (compared with) •Is the coffee **to your liking?** (Is it as you like it?) •**To our surprise**, it cost us nothing. (Surprisingly) •**Thanks to you**, we're safe. (Because of you) Usually after certain verbs •What happened **to** your car? •It used **to** look so smart! •Don't listen **to** him! •Who does this jacket belong **to**? •It seems **to** me you're wrong. •Do you agree **to** pay?
See also **according to, as to, at, close to, due to, from, near** [**to**], **next to, owing to, see to, take to, till**, PREPOSITIONS.

today /təˈdeɪ/
noun (= this present day/time)

together

●**Today**'s his birthday. ●People of **today** don't wear armour.
adverb
A (= during/on the present day) ●Shall we do the shopping **today** or tomorrow?
B (= nowadays) ●At one time we needed candles; **today** we all have electric light.

together
adverb
A (= in company, in one place, group) ●The children play **together** in the garden.
B (= to make a join) ●Tie these strings **together**.
C (= at the same time) ●All my problems seem to come **together**.
D (= near each other) ●Do you think these two colours look right **together**?
❖ *in idioms* ●I soon **put two and two together**. (worked out what the answer was) ●We must **get together** soon and have a talk. (meet) ●We can't do this job if we don't **pull together**. (co-operate)

too /tu:/
adverb
A not at the beginning of a sentence (= as well, also) ●I love chocolate. Sophie loves it, **too**, so don't eat it all. ●He speaks French. Yes, and German, **too**. ●He can swim. She can, **too**. (compare 'He can't swim. She can't, either.')
B (= excessively, more than enough) ●You eat [far] **too** much; you'll get fat. ●This dress is [much] **too** small for you [to wear].
+ *adjective* + *to* + *infinitive* ●The suitcase is **too** small to hold all your clothes.
+ *adjective* + *a/an* + *noun* + *to* + *infinitive* ●It's **too** small a case to hold them all.
not + *too* + *adjective/adverb* often for understatement ●The weather's not **too** bad. (It's quite good.) ●This work is not **too** well done. (It's rather badly done.)
NB The strength of an expression with **too** can be varied by using **much, rather, a bit, a little, a lot** and **far** but not *fairly, *quite or *very. ●This coffee's rather **too** hot to drink. ●It's also a little/a bit **too** strong. ●I was much/a lot/ far **too** tired to work. ●Perhaps you try to do **too much** (*pronoun*) ●You worry **too much** (*adverb*) ●There's much **too much** sugar in this coffee. (*adjective*)
See also **also, either, much**.

touch /tʌtʃ/
verb
A (= [be in] contact) ●If the wires are **touching**, the bomb will explode. ●Don't **touch** the switch!
B (= affect) ●I was [very] **touched** by your kind letter.
noun
A non-countable (= sense of feeling) ●He can't see; he finds his way by **touch**.
B (= contact, slight amount, skill) ●The horse responds to a **touch** on the reins; only a **touch** is needed. ●Riders, like artists, develop a delicate **touch**.

touchy
adjective (= easily irritated, difficult to handle) ●Don't mention money; he's a bit **touchy** about it today. In fact our finances are a rather **touchy** problem.
❖ *in idioms* ●We must **keep in touch**; I'd be sorry to **lose touch with** you. (maintain contact/fail to communicate with) ●He didn't say much about it; he just **touched on** it. (mentioned it briefly) ●He's a bit **out of touch with** modern life. (unaware of new developments etc)

---

transitive
(of verbs, taking an object or needing an object to make complete sense) eg *hit, enjoy, test, hate, demand*. Many verbs can be used either with or without an object, others, like *give* need two objects ('ditransitive'). Most people learn how these verbs are used by seeing/hearing examples — as in this book, but for detailed information, use a large dictionary.

See also INTRANSITIVE.
For more details see CEG 7.3.

travel
verb (= move, go from place to place) ●He doesn't like **travelling**; he prefers to stay at home. ●Light **travels** faster than sound.
noun non-countable (= travelling in general) ●**Travel** is much easier than it used to be.
See also **journey, trip**.

treat
verb
A (= deal with, consider) ●He **treats** his dog like a child. ●She **treats** my complaints as jokes. ●If you **treat** this leather carefully, it will last for years.
B (= try to cure, medically etc) ●Doctors usually **treat** this disease with powerful drugs.
C (= buy someone something in friendliness) ●I'll **treat** you [to a drink/to the theatre].
D (= apply a process, in order to change) ●Has this milk been **treated** with heat or chemicals, or is it natural?
noun (= a pleasant, often unexpected, experience) ●Going to the Zoo was a great **treat** for the children.

treatment
noun (= method of treating, materials used) ●Exercise and drugs are both used in the **treatment** recommended by the doctor. ●The **treatment** of the subject in this book is very detailed.

trip
verb (= [cause to] fall because of catching foot, and [figuratively] make a mistake) ●He **tripped** over a stone and fell in the river. ●I think you are trying to **trip** me up with your difficult questions.
noun (= journey, often with a purpose) ●He is away on a business **trip** this week. ●A day-**trip** to the sea costs only £5. ●It's a long **trip** to make in one day.

trouble /'trʌbəl/
verb (= [cause to] be worried, inconvenienced, disturb) ●She is **troubled** by the pains in her stomach. ●I'm sorry to **trouble** you, but could you please move your car; I can't get out. ●Other people's problems don't **trouble** him at all.
noun
A (= difficulty, worry, inconvenience) ●'Did you have **trouble** finding the place?' 'That was the least of my **troubles**; I seem to be in **trouble** with the police for driving too fast.' ●Could I stay here tonight, if it's not too much **trouble** [for you]?
B (= disorder, fault, illness) ●There has been **trouble** in Ireland for many years. The **trouble** is that they can't agree on a system of government.
❖ *in idioms* ●He's **taken a lot of trouble** to help me. (tried very hard) ●If you go in there, you're **asking for trouble.** (causing yourself danger) ●He **got her into trouble.** (caused her to be punished)

true
adjective (≠ false, = factual, real, faithful) ●Is it **true** that you're leaving? ●It shows **true** courage to suffer without complaining. ●He thinks his wife is **true** to him.

truly
adverb (= exactly, sincerely, really) ●A spider is not **truly** an insect. ●He was **truly** sorry for his mistake. ●Yours **truly** (Yours sincerely) before signature on informal but not personal letter

truth
noun (= what is true, ≠ lies) ●You should always tell the **truth**.

truthful
adjective (= honest) ●This is a **truthful** account of what happened.

trust
verb (= believe in, depend on, have faith in) ●Don't **trust** him; he's dishonest. ●This timetable is out of date and not to be **trusted**. ●He **trusts** to luck; he doesn't **trust** in God or doctors. ●I **trust** you to lock the house properly.

185

try

noun
A (=firm belief, faith, solemn responsibility) •A child's **trust** in his parents' love is very important, so parents are in a position of great **trust**.
B (=[group with] control of money etc) •Her father's money is held in **trust** for her until she is 21.

trustworthy
adjective (=reliable) •He knows our secret; he is completely **trustworthy** and will not tell anyone.

trustee
noun (=person[s] appointed to control business affairs etc) •The **trustees** of the company are very careful and refuse to take risks.

❖ *in idioms* •I didn't check what he said; I **took it on trust**. (accepted it as true) •**I trust you** and your wife **are** well? (hope, assume) •I shouldn't **trust Sophie with** my car. (let her use it)

try /traɪ/
verb, **tried, tried**
A (=test, by experiment) •Have you **tried** this shampoo? It's nice.
+ *-ing* •I've **tried** washing my hair in that but it was not a success.
B (=attempt, make an effort) •Can't you open the bottle? Let me **try**.
+ *to* + *infinitive* •I **try** to understand but it's so complicated. I'll just have to **try** [even] harder.
+ *and* + *infinitive,* informal •**Try and** understand, please. (to understand)
C (=put on trial, in a law court) •He was **tried** for murder and found guilty.
noun (=attempt) •It was a good **try** but it didn't succeed.

trying
adjective (=annoying, causing pain) •Long illnesses are very **trying** for both the patient and the family.

❖ *in idioms* •She enjoys going to shops and **trying on** expensive clothes. (putting them on to see the effect, fit etc) •It seems a good idea but we shan't know till we **try it out**. (put it into practice)

turn

verb (=[cause to] revolve, move round, change position/direction/colour etc) •The wheel **turns** 60 times per minute. •The flowers **turn** to face the sun. •**Turn** the chops over and cook the other side. •You have to **turn** right at the lights. •Your hair will **turn** green if you use this shampoo. •The witch **turned** the prince into a frog.

noun
A (=turning movement, revolution) •Give the wheel a half-**turn,** that's all.
B (=change of direction) •There's a sharp **turn** in the road here.
C (=appointment, place in an order) •You came after me; it's my **turn** first.
D (=attack of illness) •She had a nasty **turn** this morning. informal

turning
noun (=corner, place where side road joins) •It's past the next **turning.**

❖ *in compounds* •**turn**table (place to put record on record-player) •**turn**stile (special gate for one person at a time) •over**turn** (upset, destroy)

❖ *in idioms* •We take it in **turns** to drive/**take turns at** driving. (one after the other) •The meat was cooked **to a turn**. (perfectly) •That radio's very loud. **Turn it down.** (reduce the volume) •He asked her to marry him but she **turned him down**. (said no) •It's late; time to **turn in**. (go to bed) informal •**Turn off** the lights/fire/radio/gas before you go. (stop, switch off) •You must **turn off** the main road when you reach this village. (leave it) •**Turn on** the light, radio (etc). (Switch on) •A large crowd **turned out** to greet the President. (gathered, came out) •The policeman told me to **turn out my pockets**. (empty them, show contents) •He did an experiment which didn't **turn out** as he expected. (produce the result) ●He **turned his business over** to his son. (gave him control of it) ●She felt very lonely and she had no one to **turn to.** (ask for help) ●'I can't find my glasses.' 'Don't worry; they'll **turn up.**' (appear, be found)

twice /twaɪs/
adverb predeterminer (=two times) ●Take the medicine **twice** a day. ●I've already seen that film; I don't want to see it **twice.** ●She works **twice** as hard as you for half the pay.
❖ *in idioms* ●I've met him **once or twice.** (not often) ●He didn't **think twice** when I offered him a job. (hesitate)

U

un-
prefix used freely with adjectives, adverbs and verbs (=negative) ●un**aware** ●un**fortunately** ●un**tied** ●un**cooked.**
Other negative prefixes: *non-, in-, im-, il-.*

uncountable
See **non-countable.**

under
preposition
A (≠ over, =in a lower place than, below) ●The cat is hiding **under** the bed.
B (=less than) ●I bought it for **under** £1. ●No children **under** 12 allowed in.
C (=in obedience to) ●**Under** the regulations, young children can't see this film. ●His staff like working **under** him.
adverb (=in/to a lower place) ●He said, 'I can't swim' and then went **under.**
underneath
preposition/adverb (=[so as to go] under [something], beneath) ●I found the money hidden **underneath** [a pile of papers].
❖ *in compounds* ●**under**-carriage (wheels etc on aircraft) ●**under**-current (hidden flow of water, or figuratively, feelings hidden) ●**under**-ground (tube, subway or sometimes unofficial, eg **under**ground newspapers) ●**under**wear/**under**clothes (worn next to body) ●**under**growth (bushes, plants etc less tall than trees around them) ●**under**line (mark for special attention, emphasise) ●**under**taker (funeral director)
❖ *in idioms* ●**Under these conditions/present circumstances** it is impossible to work. (As things are) ●I **was under the impression** [that] you were his wife. (thought mistakenly) ●Everything is **under control.** (controlled) ●Look it up. It **comes under** 'T' for transport. (is recorded, filed in that section)
See also **below, beneath.**

understand
verb irregular, **understood, understood,** not used in progressive (=comprehend, know the meaning or nature of, have been told) ●Did he **understand** [the problem]? ●My wife doesn't **understand** me. ●I **understand** [from your letter] that you are hoping to borrow some money.

understanding
adjective (=sympathetic) ●I explained my mistake and she was very **understanding** about it.
noun
A (=comprehension) ●This theory is beyond my **understanding.**
B (=agreement, private arrangement) ●We have come to an **understanding** about the way the money is paid.

unless
conjunction (=if . . . not, except if) not used for imaginary events ●You'll be late **unless** you hurry. ●I shouldn't say this **unless** I was certain about it.
See also **if.**

until
See **till.**

up
adverb often adverbial particle

forming phrasal verbs, completing the sense of verbs of motion, sometimes with a figurative sense (≠ down, = in a superior position, completing an action successfully) •His temperature has gone **up**. (increased) •Isn't that lazy girl **up** yet? (out of bed) •He broke it **up** into little pieces. •Tie this parcel **up** tightly. •It's expensive, when you add **up** all the costs.
adjective (= raised, at a higher level, ended) •Is the flag **up**? •The temperature's **up** again. •Your time is **up**. Stop now.
preposition (= to, in a higher position, along, against the current) •The cat climbed **up** a tree. •It's still **up** the tree. •Sophie lives **up** the street. •We started swimming **up** the river.
upper
adjective (= higher, ≠ lower) •The laboratories are on the **upper** floor.
upward[s]
adverb (= up, increasing, getting higher) •The balloons floated gently **upwards**.
upon
preposition same as **on**, more formal
upright
adjective/adverb (= straight up, honest) •The centre post must stand **upright**. •I don't tell lies; I'm an **upright** man.
❖ *in compounds* •**up**hill (eg path, difficult because rising) •**up**bringing (early training, home life) •**up**keep ([cost of] maintaining) •**up**set ([cause] worry, disturbance)
❖ *in idioms* •**Speak up!** I can't hear you. (speak louder) •He walks **up and down** the room. (backwards and forwards, to and fro) •**What's up?** (What's happening?) •**What's up with** Sophie? (What's the matter with her?) •**What is she up to?** (What is she doing? — I suspect it's something wrong) •He'll soon be **up and about**. (walking again after an illness) •He wants to start playing tennis again, but he's not

up to it. (strong enough) •I can't decide; **it's up to you**. (you must decide) •**Up to now**, nothing's happened. (so far) •Is this information **up-to-date?** (recent) •They blew **up** the bridge with dynamite. (destroyed with explosives) •If I **do the washing-up**, will you **do the drying-up?** (wash and dry dishes) •He **rang me up** at two o'clock in the morning. (telephoned) •His strong opponent soon **got the upper hand**. (control, victory)
See also **bring up, catch up [with], come up, cover up, cut up, do up, get up, give up, grow up, keep up [with], make up, mix up, save up, shut up, take up, tie up.**

us /ʌs/, /əs/
pronoun 1st person plural, object •They won't hurt **us**; they know we're friendly. •We can both sit here; there's room for both of **us**/**us** both. •Let **us**. (plural imperative, usually shortened to *let's*) •**Let's** show them how fast we can run.

use /juːz/
verb (= employ, put to use, finish [up]) •Have you ever **used** a sewing-machine? •We've **used** [up] all the film. •Can you **use** this box again? •What is this thing **used** for?
noun /juːs/ (= using, being used, purpose, advantage) •Children must learn about the safe **use** of electricity. •This machine is not in **use** at the moment. •What **use** does this thing have? •What's the **use** of worrying?

used to
+ *infinitive* (= formerly, once, did something) •He **used to** write to me often but now he seldom does. •You **used** not to smoke/You didn't **use to** smoke; why have you started smoking? •'Do you smoke?' 'No, I **used to**.'
For more details see CEG 4.26.
be used to
+ *object*/+ *-ing* (= be accustomed to) •'I'm **used to** noise; it doesn't

keep me awake.' ●'Are you **used to** sleeping in a very quiet room?' ●Don't speak to her so roughly; she's not **used to** such unpleasant behaviour.
useful
adjective (= helpful, effective) ●This knife with a tin-opener on it is very **useful** when you're camping.
useless
adjective (= of no use, incompetent) ●This bent knife is **useless**; throw it away. ●He's **useless** in the kitchen; he can't even boil water.
used
adjective (= second-hand, not new) ●You can buy a good **used** car quite cheaply.
user
noun (= person, organisation which uses something, not *employer) ●The biggest **user** of coal is industry.

❖ **in idioms** ●It's **no use** crying. (Crying will do no good) ●I've **got no use for** people like you. (don't like such people) ●You can't work here; this room is **in use**. (already being used) ●He **makes use of** every opportunity, which is good, but he also **makes use of** his friends, which is not so good. (exploits, takes advantage of)

usual /'juːʒʊəl/
adjective attributive after *the*, but more often predicative (= customary) ●'Is it **usual** to give a taxi-driver a tip?' 'Yes, the **usual** tip is about 10%.' ●She came late, as **usual**.
usually
adverb all positions (= often, generally) ●He **usually** leaves before eight o'clock.
unusual/unusually
adjective/adverb (= not usual(ly)) ●That's an **unusual** necklace you're wearing; the pearls are **unusually** large. (particularly, very)

V

vary /'veərɪ/
verb (= [cause to] be different) ●He has a routine which never **varies**.
various
adjective (= of different kinds, several) ●His house is painted in **various** colours. ●**Various** people have asked me about it.
varied
adjective (= changing, not staying the same) ●He's had a **varied** life, working at different jobs in different places.
variable
adjective (= changeable, not steady) ●The wind is **variable** today. (not predictably from the same direction.)
variety
noun
A (= assortment) ●We have a **variety** of rings to choose from.
B (= sort, type) ●Some **varieties** of orange taste better than others.
variation
noun (= [the result of] varying) ●His voice is boring to listen to because there is no **variation** in tone. ●She cooks simple food but sometimes with a few clever **variations** of her own.
invariably
adverb (= always, without exception) ●If I don't take a raincoat, it rains, **invariably**.

verb
Verbs, the most important class of words in a language, are sometimes explained as 'doing words'. In English, a verb may consist of one or several words, each expressing such concepts as negation (*not*), modality (*would, can* etc), tense (*was, is,* etc), aspect (*-ing, have*), passive (*be + -ed*). In spoken English these words or markers are often reduced to very small sounds. ●Wouldn't [1] they've [2] been surprised if you'd [3] done it?

very

This is a negative question, with the main verb [1, 2] passive, conditional perfect and the subordinate verb [3] past perfect, marked by 'd, (= had). For explanations of the various ways of forming and using verbs, see also ASPECT, AUXILIARY VERBS, CONTRACTIONS, NEGATIVE, PASSIVE, QUESTIONS, TENSE.
For more details see CEG 8.9.

very /'verɪ/
adverb
Used to intensify adjectives and adverbs ●She's a **very** careful student but she works **very** quickly. Used to intensify comparatives or past participles, only if they have really become adjectives ●He is **very** tired/pleased/excited/surprised/disappointed/well-known/contented. But 'He is *much* loved/admired/hated/written about/commented on/discussed/remembered.'

Comparatives can be intensified with **very much** ●She is **very much** cleverer/sillier/nicer/nastier/more good-looking/more sensitive than her sister.

Even superlatives can be intensified ●This is the **very** best quality/the **very** last ticket/the **very** latest model. But **very** cannot be used with **most**, so we say 'She's quite/easily/absolutely the most idiotic student I've met.'
adjective used for emphasis (often = actual) ●This is the **very** bed he died in. ●That's the **very** thing I was looking for.

❖ **in idioms** ●He's **not very** enthusiastic. (rather unenthusiastic) used for understatement ●'Is the coffee hot?' '**Not very.**' (only slightly, not actually cold) ●At last she had her **very own** room. (not shared) ●'Do it again please.' 'Oh, **very well.**' (All right, if I must) expresses unwillingness ●Working hard is **all very well** but you need to relax sometimes. (good but)
For more details see CEG 8.9.

view /vju:/
noun
A (= ability to see/be seen, prospect) ●My **view** of the stage was not very good because I was right at the back. ●The hills were lost to **view** in clouds. ●Is there a pretty **view** from your window?
B (= opinion, idea) ●In my **view**, the law should be changed. ●What are your **views** on this subject?
verb (= look at, inspect, consider) ●If you are interested in buying the house you can **view** it tomorrow. ●She **views** this job only as a way of making a little extra money.
viewer
noun (= person who watches, especially TV). ●We apologise to **viewers** for the poor quality of that film.

❖ **in idioms** ●What do you have **in view** this evening? (planned) ●**In view of** Sophie's inexperience, we must forgive her for crashing the car. (Taking into consideration) ●All the pictures **on view** are for sale. (shown) ●He bought the flat **with a view to** sharing it with his friend. (intending to share it) ●From the child's **point of view**, bed-time is unnecessary. (viewpoint, way of considering)

visit
verb (= go to see/spend time in) ●The family usually **visits** us at Christmas. ●Have you ever **visited** Turkey? ●We're **visiting** the art galleries tomorrow.
noun (= act, time of visiting) ●He is making/paying/going on a **visit** to New York soon. ●I had a **visit** from the doctor today.
visitor
noun (= person who visits)
●**Visitors** must leave the hospital at the end of visiting hours.

W

wait [for]
verb
A (= stay somewhere until something happens/someone

want [to]

comes) •How long must we **wait**? •I've been **waiting** for the bus for an hour and a half. •'There's a parcel **waiting** for you.' 'Never mind the parcel; it can **wait**.' •As he isn't here, I'll sit and **wait** for him. Compare 'He isn't here yet, but we expect him to come soon.' (think he will)
B (= attend to, act as a servant) •Waiters and shop-assistants are paid to **wait** on customers.
noun (= period of waiting) •It seemed a long **wait**.
await
verb (= wait for, be ready for) formal •We **await** your reply. •A warm welcome **awaits** you in sunny Bali.
❖ *in compounds* •**waiting** list (eg for returned tickets) •**waiting**-room (for doctors' patients etc)
❖ *in idioms* •She hates making decisions; she always says **'Wait and see'**. (let things happen) •Hurry up! Don't **keep me waiting**. (make me wait for you) •The murderer was **lying in wait** for her. (hiding, ready to attack) •I shall be late, so **don't wait up** for me. (Go to bed if you want to, before I come in). •Don't push; you have to **wait your turn**. (be patient till the time comes for you) See also **expect**.
wake [up]
verb irregular, woke, woken, but also sometimes waked, waked (= stop sleeping) •The baby **wakes up** at five o'clock in the morning usually, but today she **woke** at four o'clock. •Her crying **woke** us all up. •Are you tired? Here's some coffee to **wake** you up.
noun (= track behind car or boat etc) •I'll go first; you follow in my **wake**.
waken
verb (= [cause to] wake) formal •The town was **wakened** by enemy gunfire.
awaken
verb usually intransitive (= [cause to] wake) formal •He **awoke** early in the morning, to the sound of birdsong.
awake
adjective (≠ asleep, = conscious) •I was [wide] **awake** and ready for breakfast.
verb irregular, awoke, awoken usually intransitive (= wake up) formal •My companions had **awoken** before dawn.
wakeful
adjective (= not sleeping) •We have a **wakeful** baby so we often have **wakeful** nights.
walk
verb (= go on foot, but not run) •The last bus had gone, so we **walked** here.
noun (= process of walking, a period of walking for pleasure) •You can recognise him by his **walk**. •Let's go for a **walk** on the hills.
❖ *in idioms* •He's very clever; he **walked off with** the prize, (won it easily) and **walked into** a good job. (obtained it easily) •The union leaders disagreed and **walked out** [of the meeting]. (left, to show their disapproval) •She's very domineering; she **walks all over** her husband! (treats badly, dominates)
want [to] /wɒnt/
verb
A not progressive (= have a desire for/to) •He's hungry; he **wants** some food. •He likes it here; he **wants** to stay. •Good. I **want** him to stay. I don't **want** him to go. In fact, I **want** him kept/to be kept here. •'Do you **want** coffee/to play tennis?' ('Would you like?' if said in a friendly way, but it is more an enquiry than an offer) answers 'Yes, please/Yes, I'd like to.'
B +-*ing* (= need) •My hair **wants** cutting. •People who hurt children **want** putting in prison.
noun (= need, lack) •The plants died from **want** of water. •These people have always lived in **want**. •The garden is in **want** of attention.

wanting
preposition (= without) ●This cheque is **wanting** a signature.
unwanted
adjective (= not required, unpopular) ●**Unwanted** food can be thrown away. ●He felt **unwanted** because no one spoke to him.
-wards
suffix (= in the direction of) making adverbs ●up**wards** ●down**wards** ●out**wards** ●in**wards** ●back**wards** ●for**wards** ●home**wards** ●heaven**wards**
warm /wɔ:m/
adjective (= pleasantly heated, heated enough, giving a feeling of comfort) ●Come and get **warm** by the fire. ●You need **warm** clothes for climbing mountains. ●Wool is **warmer** than cotton. ●He gave them **warm** thanks for their help.
verb (= make warm) ●The water is slowly **warmed** by the sun.
warmth
noun (= state of being warm) ●The **warmth** of the room made him sleepy.
❖ *in compounds* ●**warm**-hearted (friendly) ●**warm**-up (preparation time, eg physical exercise)
❖ *in idioms* ●Can we **warm up** these left-over vegetables? (re-heat) ●This party needs **warming up**; let's have some music. (to be more exciting) ●I didn't like him at first but now I'm **warming to** him. (beginning to like)
warn
verb (= tell about something bad which may happen, how to prevent it) ●We **warned** him of the danger but he would not listen. We **warned** him not to swim near the rocks. ●I wish you had **warned** me [that] you might be late; then I would not have worried.
warning
noun
A (= act of warning) ●The volcano erupted without any **warning**.
B (= something that warns, notification) ●His death must be a **warning** to others who think of swimming near those rocks. ●You must send a **warning** if you intend to take legal action.
was /wɒz/, /wəz/
verb part of the verb *to be,* past tense, after *I, he, she, it;* negative, **was** not/**wasn't**.
See also **be**.
wash /wɒʃ/
verb (= clean [with liquid], flow) ●Do you **wash** the dog with soap and water? ●Don't forget to **wash** behind your ears. Compare 'I'm going to **wash**.' (get myself clean) ●I'm going to do the **washing**. (wash clothes, towels etc) ●The Atlantic **washes** around the rocky coastline, sometimes **washing** oil onto the shore, sometimes **washing** away small pieces of the land.
noun
A (= action of washing) ●Give the car/your face a good **wash**.
B (= laundry, clothes in process of washing) ●I can't wear my new shirt; it's in the **wash**.
washable
adjective (= that can be washed without damage) ●You must have this jacket dry-cleaned; it's not **washable**.
❖ *in compounds* ●**wash**-room (usually lavatory in a public building) ●**wash**-basin (fixed bowl for washing hands, face) ●**wash**-out (failure) ●**washing** machine (for washing clothes) ●dish**washer** (machine or person for washing dishes)
❖ *in idioms* ●I'm going to **wash up**/do the **washing up** (wash the dishes, saucepans etc) ●I **wash my hands of** you and your crazy scheme! (take no responsibility for) informal ●Never mind! It will all **come out in the wash**. (be all right in the end) informal ●This dirty mark will never **wash out**. (go away with washing) ●I'm going to bed early; I'm **washed out**. (very tired) informal
waste
noun
A (= failure to use completely or

well) ●What a **waste** —wearing your best clothes for gardening!
B (=unwanted material) ●Poisonous **waste** sometimes gets into rivers and kills the fish.
verb (=use wrongly, not use fully) ●He **wastes** his time and money on having fun instead of working. ●Turn the lights off; don't **waste** electricity.
adjective
A (=useless, discarded, damaged) ●Throw **waste** paper in the bin, unless you have some use for it.
B (=unproductive, deserted) ●He leaves his car on a bit of **waste** land.

wasteful
adjective (=extravagant, inclined to waste) ●He's rather **wasteful**; one of his **wasteful** habits is leaving the hot water tap running.

watch /wɒtʃ/
verb
A (=look at, for some time) ●I was **watching** television when all the lights went out. ●Let's sit outside and **watch** the sun set[ting]. ●Nobody's **watching** us, so give me the money.
B (=take care, guard, be on the look-out) ●Will you **watch** the baby for five minutes while I go to the shop? ●**Watch** what you're doing with that knife — you might easily cut yourself.

noun
A (=act of watching) ●He promised to keep **watch** all night but he went to sleep. ●We're on the **watch** for a good bargain.
B (=small clock, usually worn on wrist) ●My **watch** has stopped; what's the time?

watchful
adjective (=observant, careful to notice) ●The teacher was **watchful** enough to spot any signs of trouble in the class.

❖ *in idioms* ●**Watch out!** You nearly knocked me over. (a warning of danger or simply 'Be careful') ●Your new teacher is very strict, so **watch your step**. (behave properly,

don't do anything silly) informal ●He doesn't like work; he's always **watching the clock**. (waiting for work to end)

water /ˈwɔːtə*/
noun non-countable (=most common liquid) ●Could I have a glass of **water**, please? ●Help! Someone's fallen in the **water**.
verb (=supply water to) ●Don't forget to **water** the horses. ●The plants need to be **watered** daily.

❖ *in compounds* ●**water**fall (eg Niagara) ●**water**front (part of town near water, especially in ports) ●**water**mark (in paper, marks showing high and low sea levels) ●**water**proof (impermeable, eg raincoat) ●**water**shed (high land between rivers, point when things must change) ●under**water** (below the water's surface)

❖ *in idioms* ●He doesn't make much money but he **keeps his head above water**. (out of difficulty) ●If you discuss philosophy with him, you will soon be **in deep water**. (complexity, difficulty) ●If my mother finds out, I'll be **in hot water**. (trouble, danger of punishment) ●He spends money **like water**. (freely, as if there was an endless supply) informal ●This account **does not hold water**. (is not true or reasonable) informal ●His early speeches were very extreme but recently they have been **watered down**. (weakened, diluted, made easier to accept)

way
noun
A (=route, the [right] road) ●I don't know the **way** to the station.
B (=distance) ●It's a long **way** from here.
C (=method) ●'What's the right **way** to clean/of cleaning leather?' 'Do it [in] this **way**.'
D (=manner) ●He smiled in an encouraging **way**. (encouragingly)
adverb
A +*preposition* +*adverbs* (=far) informal/AmE ●My calculations were **way** out. (inaccurate)

193

B after a place-noun (=near) informal •He lives out Hampstead **way**.
❖ **in idioms** •I'm afraid he had an accident and he's **in a bad way**. (badly hurt, very ill) •We **made our way** through the crowd to the door. (progressed, with some difficulty) •Please **make way** for the fire engine to get to the fire. (clear a path) •'Do you like the picture?' 'Yes, **in a way**, but I don't understand it.' (with some reservations) •Your mother telephoned, **by the way**. (I mention it in passing)/**By the way**, your mother telephoned. (I forgot to say so before) •She's determined to **get her own way** (do what she wants to do); she won't **give way** to anyone else. (yield) •He **went out of his way** to help me. (took special trouble) •You can stay or go, but you **can't have it both ways**. (you have to choose) •Your car is **in the way** (causing an obstruction); please get it **out of the way**. •We visited some very **out-of-the-way** places. (obscure, little-known) •I'm not rich but I can **pay my way**. (not owe money to others) •He's quite sensible, though he has some **funny ways**. (strange habits, customs)

we
pronoun 1st person plural, subject (=you and I/others and I/you and others and I) •Shall **we** sit here, Sophie? •**We'd** like you to come to the meeting. **We're** [all] in favour of peace. •**We'll** meet again next week, when **we've** finished the preparations.
See also **us**, CONTRACTIONS.

weak
adjective (≠strong, =feeble, diluted) •He has to wear very thick glasses because his eyes are so **weak**. •Do you like your coffee **weak?**

weaken
verb
A (=make weak) •The illness has **weakened** his heart.
B (=become less determined) •I'm trying to eat less but I often **weaken** and eat chocolate.

weakness
noun
A (=being weak) •The **weakness** in the argument is this.
B (=strong liking for something [bad]) •Chocolate is my **weakness**, but you have a **weakness** for cream, which is worse.

wear /weə*/
verb irregular, **wore, worn**
A (=have on the body/face) •I've **worn** this same dress to about ten parties. •She never **wears** jewellery or make-up.
B (=use up by rubbing, being in use) •The steps are **worn** [away/down] by the feet of many visitors.
noun
A (=wearing) •After only a year's **wear**, I threw it away.
B (=deterioration from use) •My old car is showing signs of **wear**.
C (=type of clothing) •Men's evening **wear** is on the first floor, holiday **wear** in the basement.

wearing
adjective (=tiring) •Doing a job and looking after a family is very **wearing**.
❖ **in compounds** •hard-**wearing** (durable) •**worn**-out (tired) •out**worn** (old-fashioned) •foot**wear** (shoes etc) •under**wear** (clothes worn next to the body)
❖ **in idioms** •You will **wear the batteries out** if you leave the radio on. (use them up) •After I'd taken an aspirin the pain began to **wear off**. (become less)

week
noun (=period of 7 days, or sometimes the working week, not including the week-end) •He works a 40-hour **week**. •I work hard during the **week** but on Sundays I relax.

weekly
adjective/noun (=[something] happening once a week) •When does she do the **weekly** shopping? •He takes a daily paper and two

weeklies. (magazines, newspapers)
❖ *in idioms* ●He'll be here **a week today/today week.** (in a week's time exactly)

weigh /weɪ/
verb
A (=discover, have the weight [heaviness] of) ●She's very fat; I bet she **weighs** 100kg. ●Have you **weighed** these potatoes? How much/What do they **weigh**?
B (=influence) ●My opinion doesn't **weigh** with him; he won't take any notice of what I say.
weight
noun (=heaviness) ●You'll lose **weight** if you don't eat. ●The **weight** of the coffee is shown on the packet.
❖ *in compounds* ●under**weight** (too light) ●over**weight** (too heavy) ●heavy**weight** (person of more than usual physical strength or importance)
❖ *in idioms* ●I was **weighed down with** heavy shopping/misery. (burdened) ●You must **weigh** [**up**] **the advantages and disadvantages** before you decide. (balance them against each other) ●He doesn't **pull his weight**; it isn't fair. (work as hard as the others)

welcome
verb (=greet [a visitor], receive [with pleasure]) ●Visitors are **welcomed** with flowers. ●I **welcome** your suggestion.
noun (=greeting on arrival) ●The President was given a splendid **welcome** by crowds of children.
interjection (=I/we greet you) ●**Welcome** home! ●**Welcome** to New York!
adjective
A (=acceptable, wanted) ●Hot drinks were very **welcome** after our long, cold walk.
B +*to* +*infinitive* (=allowed, free) ●You are **welcome** to borrow any of my books.
C +*to* +*noun/pronoun* (=free to take, because not wanted) ●It's a horrible place; you're **welcome** to it.

well
noun (=source of underground water) ●The village water comes from a **well**.
adverb **better, best**
A (=in a good, right way, thoroughly) ●He speaks the language badly but he reads it **well**. With practice, he'll speak **better**. ●Salad vegetables must be very **well** washed. ●Do you know him/his work **well**? ●Put this food **well** out of the way of the cat.
B (=justly, suitably) You may **well** look ashamed of yourself! ●I can't very **well** ask for money when I know he is in debt himself.
C (=with favour) ●He is **well**-thought of/spoken of by his fellow-workers.
adjective **better, best** (=healthy, satisfactory) ●I'm not feeling **well**; in fact I'm un**well** — where's the bathroom? ●We've found the money after all; all's **well** — you can stop worrying about it.
interjection (=expressing surprise, doubt, acceptance, or as a signal that a new subject is coming) intonation is very important in showing meaning ●**Well!** Look at that amazing sight! ●**Well**, . . . I'm not sure I can afford it. ●**Well**, OK. Let's go now. ●**Well**, the next thing that happened was. . .
❖ *in compounds* ●**well**-advised (sensible) ●**well**-connected (socially — knowing or related to important people) ●**well**-informed (knowing a lot) ●**well**-known (famous) ●**well**-meaning (with good intentions) ●**well**-off (rich, lucky) ●**well**-worn (overused)
❖ *in idioms* ●You have to pay for food **as well as** accommodation. (besides, in addition to) ●There may be travel expenses, **as well**. (too, also) ●'I've broken that green glass.' '**Just as well**; it was a horrible thing.' (no harm is done) ●She never listens; you **might/may just as well** talk to the wall. (it would have the same result) ●'Have you finished?' '**Pretty**

well.' (almost) •**Well done!** You've done [very] well. (Congratulations! — produced a good result) •**You'd do well to** put a lock on the door. (You would be wise) •Company directors **do themselves very well** at lunch time. (give themselves good food, comfort) •The patient is **doing well.** (progressing satisfactorily) •It's **all very well** saying kind words but what about some help? (good but not good enough) See also **good.**

were /wɜː*/, /wə*/
verb part of verb *to be,* past tense, after *you, we, they;* also used in 1st and 3rd persons in correct, formal English as a subjunctive •If I **were** you, I'd ask the doctor. •I wish he **were** here now.
See also **be.**

what /wɒt/
pronoun determiner, used in questions (= which [thing or person] from an unknown number/amount) •**What's** his name/the time/the news? •**What** are they doing? •**What** does it mean? •**What** can be done about it? •Tell me **what** you're going to do. •**What** [did you say]? •**What?** I don't believe it! •**What** is he? **What's** his job? Teaching?
pronoun (= the thing/a thing that) •Please believe **what** he tells you. •You can wear/say/think **what** you like. •**What** you do with your money is your own business. •Do you understand **what** I mean?
predeterminer (= how surprisingly good or bad!) •**What** a shame! •**What** an opportunity! •**What** rubbish!
+ *adjective* •**What** a ridiculous hat! •**What** beautiful legs! •**What** a silly old fool he is!
❖ *in idioms* •This cupboard's full of paints and brushes **and what not/and what have you.** (and other things) informal •We'll keep **what few** things are useful. (the few which) •'He's going to Japan.' '**What for?**' (Why?) •'She isn't wearing shoes.' '**So what?**'/'**What** of it?' (It isn't important, is it?) •**What's this switch for?** (What is its purpose?) •**What if** I push it? (What will happen?) •**What's their new house like?** (Describe it) •**What's it like,** living by yourself? •She says we could use her car, **and what's more,** she'll pay for the petrol. (and more important:) •He's very experienced; he knows **what's what.** (the important things) •He's a good scholar, I know, but has he got **what it takes** to put it into practice? (the necessary qualities) •**What the hell/devil** (etc) are they doing to my car? (to express anger, surprise) •**What/How about** [going out for] a drink? (I suggest; do you agree?) •**What about** money? (You have forgotten/haven't dealt with the subject of) •Don't worry; **what's his name/what d'you call him** will pay. (someone we know, whose name I can't remember)
See also **whatever, which.**

whatever
pronoun/adjective determiner
A (= any [thing] at all that) •He is grateful for **whatever** [help] he gets.
B (= no matter what) •**Whatever** the officer tells you to do, you must do it.
C in negatives and questions (= at all) •I have no interest **whatever** in cricket.
D (= anything else like that) informal •You can add a little cheese, tomato or **whatever** to the basic mixture.
E (= what?) but showing surprise •**Whatever** does he mean?
Compare 'What on earth . . .?'
See also **however, whenever, whoever** etc.

when
conjunction
A (= at the time at which) •I'll call you **when** breakfast is ready. NB not *will be ready •She was only a little girl **when** I first knew her. •He always knows **when** I'm unhappy.
B (= while) Compare •You were

out **when** we were discussing it. and ● You went out **when** we started discussing it.
C (=if) ●**When** you don't like someone, it's hard to be sympathetic.
D (=considering that, since, as) ●It's impossible to explain **when** you don't even listen. ●How can you remember that, **when** you're only 20 years old?
E after a comma (=and then) ●The doors will open at seven o'clock, **when** the play will begin. ●I had hardly opened the door, **when** they recognised me and stopped me.
pronoun (=what time?) ●'He's been a friend of hers for some time.' 'Oh, since **when**?'
See also **hardly, than, whenever**.

whenever
conjunction
A (=at any time at all) ●You can have breakfast **whenever** you like.
B (=every time) ●**Whenever** I'm unhappy, he cheers me up.
adverb
A (=at any [such] time) informal ●We send cards at Christmas, birthdays, holidays or **whenever**.
B (=when?) but showing surprise ●**Whenever** did you manage to prepare all this food?

where
adverb used in questions (=in/to what place) ●**Where** is Sophie going?
pronoun (=what place) ●**Where** does this come from?
conjunction/relative adverb (=in/at/to/on which, referring to place) ●Put it [on the shelf] **where** you found it. ●She's going home, **where** she can rest. ●[The place] **where** we were before was nicer.

whereabouts
adverb (=where, in a roughly defined area) ●She lives in London but I don't know **whereabouts**.

whereas /weər'æz/
conjunction connecting opposites (=but) formal ●She's very lively, **whereas** he's always half asleep./

Whereas he's rather lazy, she's quite energetic.

wherever
conjunction (=at/to all places, anywhere [that]) ●The dog follows me **wherever** I go. ●Sit down **wherever** you like.
adverb
A (=anywhere at all, any such place) ●He leaves things in the kitchen, on the floor, under the bed or **wherever**.
B (=where?) but showing surprise ●**Wherever** did you find this very unusual picture?

whether /'weðə*/
conjunction
A (=if ... or not) ●He asked Sophie **whether** she could drive. ●I'm not sure **whether** he was joking.
+ *infinitive* ●I wondered **whether** to phone you. (if I should phone you)
preposition + whether ●It depends on **whether** he likes you [or not].
B (=no matter if ... or) ●He's agreed to pay me, **whether** he likes me or hates me.
C (=no one knows if it is ... or ...) ●**Whether** by good luck or by hard work, he succeeded and became a rich man. ●**Whether** or not she's good-looking, she's certainly a good cook.

which
pronoun/adjective determiner, used in questions when choosing (a thing or person from a known number) Compare with: *What?/Who?*
●**Which** [of these photographs] are yours? ●**Which** of your girl-friends is this? ●She asked me **which** I liked best but I don't know **which** is **which**!
relative pronoun
A (=being the one[s] that) in defining clauses; more formal than *that*, used for things, not people ●In the letter **which** came last week, he mentioned a problem. The letter **which** I sent in reply offered a solution. ●What was the problem to **which** you were referring? (Compare in ordinary

197

whichever

speech 'the letter that came', 'the letter I sent,' 'the problem you were referring to')
B (=and/because etc, offering extra information in parenthesis, between commas, sometimes brackets) in non-defining clauses, for things ● Your letter, **which** arrived last week, is very interesting. The problem of money, **which** has not yet been solved, is clearly very important. Our business account, **which** payments are made to,/to **which** payments are made, could be used. ● There are two possibilities, one of **which** is very attractive.
See also COMMAS, RELATIVE.
For more details see CEG 3.33.

whichever
pronoun/adjective determiner
A (=any one [of a known number of possibilities]) ● Here are three pencils; take **whichever** [one] you like.
B (=no matter which) ● **Whichever** method you use, the result is much the same.

while /waɪl/
noun (=period of time) ● We had to wait a little **while** for him. ● I haven't seen him for a long **while**.
conjunction (also **whilst**)
A (=during the time that) ● We looked at magazines **while** we were waiting. ● The postman came **while** I was out.
B at beginning of sentence (=although) ● **While** I understand your point of view, I do not share it.
C (=whereas) ● You look at the children as a parent, **while** I see them as a teacher.

who /huː/, /hʊ/
pronoun used in questions (=what person/people?) ● **Who** will help me finish the job? ● **Who** were you talking to on the phone? ● 'I'm going out.' '**Who** with?'
relative pronoun
A (=being that one [person]/those ones) in defining clauses; more usual than *that*, used for people, not things ● People **who** help me will get a drink. ● The man **who** I was speaking to asked me out to dinner. (Compare 'whom I was speaking to/to whom I was speaking,' both preferred by many English speakers but not used universally. The most natural expression in ordinary conversation is 'the man I was speaking to')
B (=and/because etc, offering extra information, between commas) in non-defining clauses; for people as subject, and sometimes as object ● My mother, **who** loves shopping, knows all the nicest shops. ● My aunt, **who** I don't like much, is rich.
See also **whom** (used after prepositions), RELATIVE.

whoever
pronoun
A (=anybody that) ● Bring **whoever** you like to the party.
B (=no matter who) ● You can't come in, **whoever** you are.
C (=who?) but showing surprise ● **Whoever** would phone me at three in the morning?

whole /həʊl/
adjective usually attributive with article, singular (=entire, complete) ● He ate the/a **whole** chicken. ● Are you telling the **whole** truth? ● You can easily spend a **whole** day there.
noun (=complete thing, sum of all parts) ● Look at the subject as a **whole** before you examine the details.
wholly
adverb (=completely) ● He was not **wholly** convinced.
❖ *in compounds* ● **whole**-hearted (fully sincere, enthusiastic)
● **whole**sale (sold in large quantities, usually for re-sale, ≠ retail)
● **whole**some (healthy, clean)
❖ *in idioms* ● On the **whole**, it works well. (generally) ● She tells him terrible lies and he swallows them **whole**. (believes completely)

whom
pronoun going out of use in ordinary conversation; used in

careful speech and writing
1 in questions and as relative referring to person object ●'I shall leave today.' 'With **whom**?' ●**Whom** did he meet at the theatre?
2 in defining clauses: formal ●The gentleman **whom** she encountered addressed her with courtesy. ●The person from **whom** the message came/**whom** the message came from did not say his name.
3 in non-defining clauses ●The President, **whom** we had expected earlier, arrived at four o'clock
4 always after prepositions ●The President, for **whom** we all have great admiration, agreed to come. See also **that, who,** RELATIVE.

whose /huːz/
pronoun/adjective determiner, used in questions (= of or belonging to whom?) ●**Whose** coat is this? She wants to know **whose** it is.
relative pronoun
A (= of whom, sometimes of which) in defining clauses ●The student **whose** work is best will get the prize. ●I'd like a room **whose** windows look out over the sea. (with windows which)
B (= of whom, sometimes of which) in non-defining clauses ●Sophie, **whose** work is awful, will certainly not get a prize. ●This play, **whose** fame is world-wide, is very funny. (which is world-famous)
NB Do not confuse **whose** with **who's** (= who is/who has) See also **of**.

why /waɪ/
adverb/conjunction used in questions and as a relative (= for what reason?/the reason that) ●'**Why** did you get angry? I asked you **why** you got angry. **Why** don't you answer me?' '**Why** should I?' (often = I needn't) ●I can't understand **why** he was so late. (don't know)
+ *not* + *infinitive* ●**Why** not ask him? (you should ask him) ●He was late. Is that **why** you were angry? ●I'm not sure [of the reason] **why** she's leaving. ●She must be unhappy; **why** else would she leave?

wide /waɪd/
adjective (= broad, ≠ narrow) ●Are **wide** ties fashionable again? ●The **widest** part of the river is near the sea; it is nearly a mile **wide**. ●He has a **wide** knowledge of his subject.
adverb (= to make a wide opening etc) ●The door/Her eyes/His arms opened **wide**.

widely
adverb (= over a large area, by many people, to a large degree) ●The villages are **widely** separated. ●It is not **widely** known that he is ill. ●Our opinions differed **widely**.

widen
verb (= grow, make wider) ●The road was **widened** to allow lorries to use it.

width /wɪdθ/
noun (= size from side to side) ●The **width** of the table is about a metre. ●We must use the full **width** of the cloth.

❖ *in compounds* ●**wide**-eyed (with an innocent or surprised expression) ●**wide**spread (very common, often found) ●**wide**-awake (fully conscious, aware) Notice that *broad* is used for more abstract expressions generally; *broad-minded, broadly speaking* etc. See also **broad, narrow**.

will
verb modal auxiliary; negative **will not/won't**, used to form future tenses. In 1st person questions and negatives, often replaced by *shall*. Contracted to **'ll**. ●They **will** be here tomorrow, **won't** they? I hope you **will** be able to meet them. (But notice the possible ambiguity of '**Will** you meet them?' either 'Please do; I invite you/ask you to meet them' or 'Is it your plan/intention . . ./**Will** you be meeting them?') ●I shall not see him. (simple future, no comment on feelings)/I **will** not see him. (I refuse)

win

It sounds slightly unnatural to older English speakers to say 'I will be 29 tomorrow' because it suggests there is a possible choice. They say, 'I shall be 29 tomorrow'. In modern English, the word **will** is used more and more, but it sometimes has its non-future meaning (= to be willing) and this can cause confusion because we do not use future tenses in subordinate clauses when the main verb refers to the future. Compare 'We'll all be cold if you open the window.' (ordinary conditional sentence) and 'We'll all be glad if you will (= are willing to) open the window.' This meaning is very clear in question-tags after imperatives with the intention of suggesting 'if you are willing' •Sit down here, **will** you? •Don't forget to telephone, **will** you? •Bring that book, **won't** you? •Shut up a minute, **will** you?

Future tenses using **will**:
Future simple •He **will** work.
Future progressive •He **will** be working.
Future perfect •He **will** have worked.
Future perfect progressive •He **will** have been working.
All these tenses are occasionally used with the sense 'I assume . . .' •You **will** be the new student. (I assume you are the new student) •You **will** have already met the other students[?] (I assume you have)
noun
A singular (= determination, intention) •You need a strong **will** to work hard on your own. •He married her against his father's **will**.
B (= testament, written instructions left by someone who dies) •His father left him nothing in his **will**.

willing
adjective (= ready, agreeable to a proposal) •I'll do the washing up if you're **willing** to help me.

willingly
adverb (= with pleasure, without resistance) •'Will you help me?' '**Willingly**.' (certainly)
See also FUTURE, **shall**, **would**.
For more details see CEG 6.5.

win
verb irregular, **won, won** (= be first, best, take [a reward]) •He entered the competition and he **won** [it]. He **won** the prize. He **won** the race. but 'He beat all the other competitors/defeated his enemies/earned money by doing a job.'
noun (= victory, success, usually in sport) •Our team has had three **wins** this season.

winning
adjective (= attractive, charming) •Her **winning** smile delighted him.

winnings
noun (= money won) •He won his bet and spent his **winnings** on a new car.

winner
noun (= person/animal that wins) •The **winner** gets a gold medal.

wind /wɪnd/
noun (= moving air) •The **wind** blew the little boat off course.

wind /waɪnd/
verb irregular, **wound, wound** (= twist, turn round and round) •The cable is **wound** on a large drum. •Please **wind** down the window of the car. •The little paths **wind** between the trees.
❖ *in idioms* •Let's **wind up** the evening with a dance/a song. (bring to an end) •After all the excitement, she needed a few moments to **unwind/wind down**. (grow calm again)

wise
adjective (= with good sense, judgement; ≠ foolish) •If you are **wise**, you will not listen to such foolish advice. •It was **wise** of you to keep a little money in case of difficulty. (You were wise to) •That was a **wise** decision.

wisdom
noun (= being wise) •He showed great **wisdom** when he spoke of the reasons for his decision.

-wise
suffix (= in connection with) informal •Money**wise**, he has no problem; health**wise**, he must be careful.

wish
verb
A (= want [something impossible at the time])
+ *subjunctive* •He **wishes** he were taller/was taller. •I **wish** you were here now. •I **wish** you had been here yesterday. •I **wish** you didn't dislike me so much. •I **wish** I hadn't said those terrible things about her. •Do you ever **wish** you were somebody else?
+ *conditional* •I **wish** you would visit me.
B + *to* + *infinitive* (= want, in polite requests etc) •I **wish** to speak to the manager. •You may speak to him if you **wish** [to].
+ *object (person or thing)* + *to* + *infinitive* •I **wish** you to leave at once. •The manager **wishes** the damage to be paid for.
C + *person* + *thing* (= hope someone has something) •We **wished** him a happy birthday.
•**Wish** me luck for my exam.
noun (= desire, feeling of wanting) •She has always had a great **wish** to travel round the world. Now her **wish** has come true. •His **wish** to be alone/His **wish** for peace explains his refusal to work in a crowded office.

with
preposition
A (≠ without, = accompanied by, near, having, by means of) •I'm going to have lunch **with** my sister. •You can put your books **with** mine. •Who's that man **with** all those teeth? •He opened the door **with** a special key. •The bottle must then be filled **with** water. (It will be full of water.)
B (= in favour of, in the same direction as, at the same time as) •In this case, I'm **with** the workers against the management. •It's always easier to swim **with** the stream. •Your playing has improved **with** more practice.

withdraw
verb
See **draw**.

within
preposition (= inside) •It will be ready **within** an hour.

❖ *in idioms* •Are you **with me**? (Do you understand?) •It has **nothing to do with** me. (It is not connected with me, not my business) •**Up with** the workers! **Down with** the government! (We are [not] in favour of) •Stop **fighting with each other**. (against) but •He is **fighting with us** against our enemies. (by our side) •**What's the matter/wrong/up/the trouble with** him? (in his case, character etc) •He has **fallen out with** everybody. (quarrelled) •Don't go so fast; I can't **keep up with** you. (go as fast as) •This furniture is not **in keeping with** the style of the room. (appropriate for) •Have you been/kept **in touch with** your old school friends? (in communication) •He's very friendly; he **gets on** [**well**] **with** everybody. (has friendly relations) •I **could do with** a long cold drink after all that hard work. (I'd like) •He was **mixed up with/in with** some men who are now in prison. (connected, friendly, with bad people)
See also **agree** [**with**], **alternate** [**with**], **bear** [**with**], **begin with**, **bring** [**with**], **catch up** [**with**], **deal with**, **faced** [**with**], **go with**, **get on with**, **go on with**, **have it out with**, **meet** [**with**], **mix** [**with**], **provide** [**with**], **put up with**, **reason** [**with**], **share** [**with**], **stay** [**with**].

without
preposition (≠ with, = not having, lacking) •Do you take your coffee with sugar or **without**? •I felt very lonely **without** my friends.
+ *-ing* •Can you look at him **without** laughing? •You can't make an omelette **without** breaking eggs. •I tried to go **without** him noticing. •**Without** actually seeing

201

wonder

it, it's hard to understand the attraction.
❖ *in idioms* ●When you're camping you have to **do without** luxuries. (manage, cope, carry on, not having them) ●If there isn't any coffee, we must simply **go without**. (manage, etc) ●You must bring the money, **without fail**. (definitely, certainly) ●We tried to open it, **without success**. (but we couldn't, unsuccessfully) ●He left **without a word**. (saying nothing) ●**It goes without saying** that we'll come to your wedding. (Of course, it is understood)

wonder /ˈwʌndə*/
verb
A (=ask oneself, express a wish to know, sometimes silently) ●'Is this her house?' 'I **wonder**; it doesn't seem the same as I remembered it.' +*indirect question* ●I **wonder** if it's true. ●He **wondered** if it was true. ●We were **wondering** how you made this tea.
B +*at* (=be surprised, want to know why) ●I **wonder** at you; how can you be so rude? ●We were all **wondering** at your rudeness. ●If he's tired after 14 hours work, it's not to be **wondered** at.
But ●The visitors admired the pictures on the walls: they thought them **wonderful**.
noun (=feeling of surprise, admiration or what causes it) ●We gazed at the brilliant sunset in/with **wonder**. ●Scientists constantly astonish us with new **wonders**.
❖ *in idioms* ●**It's no wonder** he's tired; he's been working for 14 hours. (not surprising) ●**It's a wonder** he doesn't fall asleep. (surprising) ●**I wonder if** you could help me. (Please help me) a polite formula ●A little garlic in your cooking **works/does wonders**. (transforms it, makes a great improvement)

word /wɜ:d/
noun (=spoken or written bit of language representing an idea) ●There are many **words** in English that are difficult to spell. ●Can you remember the **words** of this song?
❖ *in idioms* ●Can I **have a word**/**a few words** with you? (a short conversation) ●I **gave you my word** and I **kept my word**. (promised, kept my promise) ●He was not very interesting; **in other words**/**in a word**, boring. (that is to say/in short) ●'Did he offer you the job?' 'Not **in so many words**, but he made me understand I could have it.' (explicitly, in plain language) ●When he said he'd pay, I **took him at his word** and ordered the best. (believed and acted on what he said) ●**Take my word for it**, you are making a mistake. (believe me) ●She **repeated his speech word for word**. (verbatim, exactly) ●Idioms cannot be **translated word for word**. (one word at a time)

work /wɜ:k/
noun non-countable (=activity with purpose, nature of job, place, materials, product of job) ●I must go; I have a lot of **work** to do. ●He found **work** as a waiter, but the **work** of a small restaurant did not interest him. Now he's out of **work**. ●What time do you go to **work**? ●I have admired your **work** for a long time.
verb (=act purposefully, use effort, be/make effective) ●I have never **worked** in a factory. ●She **worked** hard to make this garden. ●This medicine doesn't **work**; I still feel very ill. ●Can you **work** this machine?
NB ●Machines **work** well. ●People **work** hard.
❖ *in compounds* ●**work**-force (whole group of people who work in [an] industry) ●**working**-man (one who works with his hands) ●**workman** ([semi-] skilled tradesman, craftsman) ●**workmanlike** (well-organised, practical)
❖ *in idioms* ●Now, let's **get to**/**set to**/**go to work on** this problem. (start working on it) ●I **had my work cut out to** finish the job in an

202

hour. (It was difficult for me) •I can't **work out** why it costs so much. (calculate, decide by thinking) •Eight hours a day at £4 an hour **works out at** £32 a day. (comes to [a total]) •I hope all your **plans work out** as you expect. (result, develop) •She got very **worked up** when I told her the bad news. (excited, moved, upset)
See also **job**.

world /wɜːld/
noun
A (= the earth) •English is used all over the **world**.
B (= the/a universe) •We know only our own **world** with the Sun at the centre but there are many other **worlds**, too.
C (= people generally) •The whole **world** knows his name.
D (= particular group of people) •I know little of the musical **world**. •The Western **world** can learn from the East.
❖ *in compounds* •**world** war (involving many nations) •**world** power (nation with great influence) •**world**-wide (all over the world)
❖ *in idioms* •A part-time job can be **the best of both worlds** — some money and some free time. (offering advantages of two kinds without the need for a choice) •Where/What/How **in the world** . . .? (expressing surprise; wherever/whatever/however) •I sometimes get cross with Sophie but I really **think the world of her**. (care very much about) •I would not hurt her **for the world**. (for any reason, certainly not) •Their way of life is **worlds apart**. (completely different)

worry /ˈwʌri/
verb (= [cause to] be anxious, worried) •You look unhappy; is something **worrying** you? •You **worry** too much; try to relax.
noun (= [cause of] feeling of anxiety) •Money — or the lack of it — is a constant **worry** for most of us. •Her face is lined with years of **worry**.

worse /wɜːs/
adjective/adverb comparative (of **bad, badly,** ≠ better) •His room is dark and dirty and mine is [even] **worse**. •I can't sing well, but he sings **worse** than I do. •**Worse** still, he sings in public. •Don't try to change it; you'll only make it **worse**. •If this headache gets any **worse**, I'll take some aspirin.
❖ *in idioms* •I was tired and hungry and **to make matters worse**, I'd lost my key. (on top of those problems) •Business **went from bad to worse** and he finally sold the shop. (deteriorated) •You'll **be none the worse for** a little exercise. (it will not harm you) •His health seemed to improve but then there was **a change for the worse**. (a bad change)
See also **better**.

worst /wɜːst/
adjective/adverb superlative (of **bad, badly,** ≠ best) •This is the **worst** storm I've seen. •Who suffered **worst**? •She's the sweetest but the **worst**-dressed woman I know.
❖ *in idioms* •Everything's gone wrong and **the worst of it is** it's my fault. (the nastiest thing about it) •**If the worst comes to the worst**, we can sleep on the floor. (if necessary, because things turn out very badly) •We can make only a small profit at best; **at worst**, we lose several hundred dollars. (the most extreme possibility)
See also **best**.

worth /wɜːθ/
preposition (= of the value of, deserving) •Is this ring **worth** a lot of money? •I don't know how much it's **worth**. •I like it but I don't think it's **worth** £300. •A beautiful garden is **worth** all the trouble it takes. •I work very hard at my garden, but is the result **worth** my while?
+ *-ing* •The service is slow but the food is **worth** waiting for. •Is this book **worth** reading? •These shoes are worn out; they're not **worth**

would

mending. •'Is life **worth** living?' 'That depends upon the liver.' *noun* (= value) •I'd like ten pounds' **worth** of petrol/apples (etc), please. •No one recognised his true **worth** until he was dead.

worthless
adjective (= valueless, useless) •He doesn't know anything about it, so his ideas are practically **worthless**.

worthwhile
adjective (= worth doing, knowing, seeing etc) •He wants to do a **worthwhile** job, not just earn enough money to live. •Was [the trip to see] that castle **worthwhile**?

worthy /ˈwɜːðɪ/
adjective (= deserving) + *of* •Your project is **worthy** of our support.
+ *passive infinitive* •He was **worthy** to be made a minister.
❖ *in idioms* •My advice, **for what it's worth** is 'Take the money'. (I admit it is not necessarily very valuable) •He'll do it **if you make it worth his while**. (pay him enough)

would
verb modal auxiliary; negative **would not/wouldn't**
1 corresponding to *will* in indirect speech, and as main verb in conditional sentences, possible for all persons but *should* is more often used in the 1st person when there is a need to avoid the idea of willingness. •He said it **would** be there soon. ('It will be here soon.') •You **would** be pleased if he liked it./You **would** have been pleased if he'd liked it. (You will be pleased if he likes your work)
2 corresponding to *will* but more polite/tentative because it implies a condition (often = if you agreed) •Perhaps you **would** open the window? •**Would** you wait a moment? •He **wouldn't** expect to be paid.
3 often added to requests to make them more polite •Just wait here, **would** you? •**Would** you mind if I smoked? (more hesitant than 'Do you mind if I smoke?')
4 to express 'future in the past' •I looked at the room which **would** be my home for the following three years.
5 first person only, to express willingness/unwillingness •He asked me to marry him and I said I **would**. •I said I **wouldn't** marry him. In other persons the idea of willingness is not necessarily present or absent •He **wouldn't** go to school. (could be refused or meaning 7 below)
6 with *rather* •**Would** you rather go by car or train? (Which would you prefer?) •He **would** rather not travel at all.
NB The contracted form **'d** can cause confusion: •I'd = I should, I **would**, I had.
7 meaning 'used to' — slightly literary •When I was a child, we **would** walk many miles without complaining. •He **wouldn't** go to school during harvest-time. (he regularly didn't)
8 with stress, **would** implies criticism •I told him to leave it alone but he <u>would</u> interfere. (insisted on interfering) •Well, he **would** . (It's not surprising; he's an interfering sort of person)
See also **shall, should, will,** CONDITION, FUTURE.

write /raɪt/
verb irregular, **wrote, written** (= put words on paper, etc) •Please **write** to me when you're away. •I'll **write** you a long letter. •I'll **write** to you. (AmE •I'll **write** you.) •Don't trust your memory; **write** it down. •Have you **written** all those details in your notebook?
❖ *in idioms* •After the accident, Sophie's car was a **write-off**. (a complete ruin, impossible to repair) •This critic gives that film a very good **write-up**. (review) •You must have the agreement **in writing**. (written)

wrong /rɒŋ/
adjective (≠ right, = incorrect, evil, unsuitable) •This answer is **wrong**;

2+2=4, not 5. •You've put this book on the **wrong** shelf. •It is quite **wrong** to take money without asking. •But this is the **wrong** time to ask him for money!
adverb (=wrongly, usually after *go* and *get* [something]) •We're not in the right road; where did I go **wrong**? •I hope I didn't get your name **wrong**, Mr Prysylski? Have I spelt it **wrong**?
noun non-countable (=evil) •Animals do not distinguish between right and **wrong**. (good and evil actions)
verb (=be unfair to) •You **wrong** him when you say he never tries, because he does sometimes try.
wrongly
adverb (=incorrectly) especially before past participles, and in parenthesis •The letter was **wrongly** addressed. •He believed, **wrongly**, that it was for him.
Wrong and **wrongly** are more or less the same in other cases.
❖ in idioms •He was right and you were **in the wrong**. (mistaken, it was your fault) •I was caught **on the wrong foot**. (unprepared) •Don't **get on the wrong side of her**; she can be very spiteful. (out of her favour) •**What's wrong with** the tea? ('Why are you complaining about it?' usually implies that nothing is wrong — the tea is fine)

Y

yes
adverb
A (=positive reply, ≠no) •'Do you think English is difficult?' '**Yes**.' •'Isn't it a lovely day?' '**Yes**, it is.'
B in answer to a call •'Sophie!' '**Yes**, mother?'
C to encourage a speaker to go on •**Yes**, what then?

yet
adverb
A in negatives and questions, with present and perfect tenses (=now, up to this/that moment, so far) •We needn't go **yet**. •We haven't finished supper **yet**. •They had not **yet** drunk their coffee when they were told to leave. •Nobody has arrived/is here **yet**. •'Has she decided what to do **yet**?' 'No, she's still undecided; she hasn't **yet** made her mind up.'
B (=even, still) •Yesterday you looked beautiful; today you look **yet** more beautiful.
conjunction (=but [even so]) •He was very tired, **yet** he went on working. •What he said was surprising, **yet** true.

you
pronoun
A 2nd person, singular, plural, subject and object •If **you** help me, I'll help **you**.
It is sometimes necessary to show that the plural meaning is intended •**You** must all follow me. •I shall ask **you** young people to help.
B (=anybody, one, a person) less formal than *one* •**You** never know what the weather will be. (Nobody knows) •**You** have to get there early to get a seat. (One has to)
Short forms: •**You're** right. •**You've** already finished? •**You'd** be glad if she agreed. •**You'll** be late if you don't hurry.
See also **your, yours**, CONTRACTIONS.

young /jʌŋ/
adjective (≠old, =in an early stage of life) used with people, animals or figuratively of things. The normal word for things is *new* •The child is too **young** to be left alone. •I have two **younger** brothers and one **younger** sister. •It's a **young** country with **young** ideas.
noun (=young animals) •Most animals will fight to protect their **young**.

youth /juːθ/
noun
A non-countable (=early life, time of being young) •The old men were remembering their **youth**.
B countable (=young man) •A

205

your

group of **youths** had gathered outside the cinema.
C (= young people seen as a group) •Unemployment is wasting the talent of the country's **youth**.

youthful
adjective (= young-looking, young-seeming) •She's not young but she has a **youthful** skin.

your /jɔː*/, /jə*/
adjective possessive, determiner, 2nd person singular, plural
A (= belonging to you) •**Your** hair looks nice. •Where's **your** mother? •This is **your** letter, not mine.
B (= one's) •They always ask **your** name when you go in.

yours /jɔːz/
pronoun possessive, 2nd person singular, plural
A (= thing[s] belonging to you) •Is this letter **yours**? •Sophie is a friend of **yours**, isn't she? •Some of my work is all right, but all of **yours** is perfect.
B (= at the end of a letter)
•**Yours**,
            Sophie
(for personal but not intimate letters) •**Yours** sincerely (for people you have met or spoken to — letters beginning *Dear Mr/Mrs/Miss*) •**Yours** faithfully/**Yours** truly (for people you have not met or spoken to — letters beginning *Dear Sir/Madam*)

yourself
pronoun reflexive, 2nd person singular, plural, **yourselves** •Take care of **yourself**! •I can't do your work for you; you must do it **yourself**. •I hope you all enjoyed **yourselves** last night.
❖ *in idioms* •You **don't seem quite yourself** today. (the way you usually are) •You needn't come; **please yourself**. (do what you like; often suggests irritation) •Shall I help you, or can you do it **by yourself**? (alone)

Z

zero [0] /ˈzɪərəʊ/
noun (= name of the sign, nought) Used more in AmE than BrE but everywhere in scientific contexts •The temperature was 5 below **zero**. (−5°C)
Telephone numbers eg •3041 = three-oh-four-one/three-zero-four-one/three-nought-four-one.

Index of Related Words

colouring

A

a bit see **bit**
a lot see **a lot of**
ability see **able**
abroad see **broad**
accidental see **accident**
accidentally see **accident**
accommodating see **accommodate**
accommodation see **accommodate**
account for see **account**
accused see **accuse**
across see **cross**
action see **act**
active see **act**
activity see **act**
actually see **act**
adjoining see **join**
admirable see **admire**
admiration see **admire**
admirer see **admire**
admission see **admit**
admittance see **admit**
advice see **advise**
advisable see **advise**
adviser see **advise**
advisor see **advise**
affection see **affect**
affectionate see **affect**
affectionately see **affect**
afterwards see **after**
agreeable see **agree**
agreement see **agree**
alight see **light**
alike see **like**
alive see **live**
all ready see **already**
allowable see **allow**
allowance see **allow**
alone see **lonely**
aloud see **loud**
alternately see **alternate**
alternative see **alternate**
alternatively see **alternate**
anger see **angry**
anxiety see **anxious**
apparent see **appear**
apparently see **appear**
appearance see **appear**
argument see **argue**
arise see **rise**
arrangement see **arrange**
arrival see **arrive**
as if see **as**
as soon [as] see **soon**
as though see **as**
as. . .as see **as**
ashamed [of] see **shame**
aside see **side**
asleep see **sleep**
assure see **sure**
await see **wait** [**for**]
awake see **wake** [**up**]
awaken see **wake** [**up**]

B

backwards see **back**
badly see **bad**
barely see **bare**
bathe see **bath**
bathroom see **bath**
be supposed to see **suppose**
because of see **because**
been see **be**
beginner see **begin**
beginning see **begin**
-behaved see **behave**
behaviour see **behave**
being see **be**
belief see **believe**
belongings see **belong**
boring see **bore**
born see **bear**
both. . .and see **both**
breadth see **broad**
breakdown see **break**
breath see **breathe**
broaden see **broad**
broadly see **broad**
busily see **busy**
business-like see **business**

C

careful see **care**
careless see **care**
certainly see **certain**
choice see **choose**
cleaner see **clean**
cleaning see **clean**
closely see **close**
colloquialism see **colloquial**
colloquially see **colloquial**
coloured see **colour**
colourful see **colour**
colouring see **colour**

colourless

colourless see **colour**
comforting see **comfortable**
commonly see **common**
commonplace see **common**
comparable see **compare**
comparative see **compare**
comparatively see **compare**
comparison see **compare**
consideration see **consider**
considering see **consider**
consul see **council**
content[ed] see **content**
continual see **continue**
continually see **continue**
continuous see **continue**
continuously see **continue**
counsel see **council**
crossroads see **cross**

D

deadly see **dead**
dealer see **deal**
death see **dead**
decision see **decide**
deeply see **deep**
dependent see **depend** [on]
depth see **deep**
difference see **different**
difficulty see **difficult**
direction see **direct**
directly see **direct**
disability see **able**
disabled see **able**
disagree see **agree**
disagreeable see **agree**
disagreement see **agree**
disappear see **appear**
disappointment see **disappoint**
discolour see **colour**
discover see **cover**
disinterested see **interest**
dislike see **like**
disorder see **order**
disorderly see **order**
disquiet see **quiet**
distance see **distant**
distasteful see **taste**
doubtful see **doubt**
dress up see **dress**
due to see **due**

E

each other see **each**
ease see **easy**
easily see **easy**
effective see **effect**
effectively see **effect**
efficient see **effect**
either. . .or see **or**
enable see **able**
enjoyable see **enjoy**
enjoyment see **enjoy**
enlarge see **large**
enquiry see **enquire**
ensure see **sure**
especial see **special**
especially see **special**
essence see **essential**
essentially see **essential**
even if see **even**
-ever see **ever**
every- see **every**
everyday see **day**
everywhere see **every**
except for see **except**
excepting see **except**
exception see **except**
exceptional see **except**
exceptionally see **except**
explanation see **explain**

F

fairly see **fair**
fasten see **fast**
fastener see **fast**
feel as if see **feel**
feel as though see **feel**
feel like see **feel**
feeling see **feel**
final see **finish**
finely see **fine**
flight see **fly**
following see **follow**
foolish see **fool**
forgiveness see **forgive**
forgiving see **forgive**
formal see **form**
former see **form**
-free see **free**
freely see **free**
friendly see **friend**
friendship see **friend**

lover

frighten see **fright**
frightful see **fright**
funny see **fun**
furnish see **furniture**

G

generalise see **general**
generally see **general**
gladly see **glad**
going to see **go**
gratitude see **grateful**
greatly see **great**
growth see **grow**

H

had [= 'd] rather [than] see **rather**
had better see **better**
handy see **hand**
happily see **happy**
harmful see **harm**
harmless see **harm**
hearing see **hear**
height see **high**
helpful see **help**
helping see **help**
helpless see **help**
highly see **high**
homely see **home**
hopefully see **hope**
hopeless see **hope**

I

idealism see **ideal**
idealist see **ideal**
ideally see **ideal**
ignorant see **ignore**
immediate see **immediately**
impartial see **part**
impatience see **patient**
impersonal see **person**
impersonally see **person**
improvement see **improve**
in the meantime see **mean**
inactivity see **act**
inadvisable see **advise**
incomparable see **compare**
independent see **depend** [on]
indirect see **direct**
indoor see **in**
indoors see **in**
inner see **in**

inside see **in**
inside see **side**
insurance see **sure**
insure see **sure**
intention see **intend**
intentional see **intend**
interested see **interest**
interesting see **interest**
into see **in**
invariably see **vary**
invitation see **invite**
inwardly see **in**

J

joint see **join**
jumpy see **jump**

K

-keeper see **keep**
keeping see **keep**
killer see **kill**
kindly see **kind**
knowledge see **know**
knowledgeable see **know**

L

largely see **large**
lastly see **last**
lately see **late**
latest see **late**
laughter see **laugh**
leader see **lead**
leaning see **lean**
learner see **learn**
learning see **learn**
length see **long**
liar see **lie**
life see **live**
lighten see **light**
lightly see **light**
-like see **like**
likelihood see **likely**
liking see **like**
lively see **live**
living see **live**
lone see **lonely**
loosen see **loose**
loss see **lose**
lots see **a lot of**
loudly see **loud**
lover see **love**

211

lower

lower see **low**
lowly see **low**
luckily see **luck**
lucky see **luck**

M

mainly see **main**
mains see **main**
manageable see **manage**
management see **manage**
manager see **manage**
marriage see **marry**
married see **marry**
maybe see **may**
meaning see **mean**
meaningful see **mean**
meanwhile see **mean**
meeting see **meet**
memory see **remember**
-most see **most**
mostly see **most**
movement see **move**
moving see **move**

N

natural see **nature**
naturally see **nature**
nearby see **near**
nearly see **near**
necessarily see **necessary**
nerves see **nerve**
nervous see **nerve**
nevertheless see **never**
next to see **next**
no one see **no**
nobody see **no**
not so. . .as see **so**
not such a see **such**
nothing see **no**
now [that] see **now**
nowadays see **now**
nowhere see **no**
numberless see **number**
numerous see **number**

O

occasional see **occasion**
occasionally see **occasion**
oddly see **odd**
odds see **odd**
offence see **offend**

offender see **offend**
offensive see **offend**
one another see **another**
ones see **one**
onto see **on**
opening see **open**
openly see **open**
or else see **else**
orderly see **order**
other than see **other**
otherwise see **other**
out of see **out**
outfit see **fit**
outline see **line**
outright see **out**
outside see **out**
outside see **side**
outsider see **out**
outward see **out**
outwardly see **out**
outwards see **out**
overdo see **do**
overhear see **hear**
owing to see **owe**
owner see **own**

P

pained see **pain**
painful see **pain**
painless see **pain**
pains see **pain**
painstaking see **pain**
pair [off] see **pair**
partial see **part**
particularly see **particular**
particulars see **particular**
partly see **part**
patience see **patient**
patiently see **patient**
payment see **pay**
perfection see **perfect**
permissible see **permit**
permission see **permit**
permissive see **permit**
personal see **person**
personality see **person**
personally see **person**
personnel see **person**
persuasion see **persuade**
persuasive see **persuade**
pick up see **pick**
pick-up see **pick**
pleasant see **please**

pleased [with] [to] see **please**
pleasing see **please**
pleasure see **please**
possibility see **possible**
possibly see **possible**
post- see **post**
practicable see **practice**
practical see **practice**
practically see **practice**
practise see **practice**
preferable [to] see **prefer** [to]
preferably see **prefer** [to]
preference [for] see **prefer** [to]
pretence see **pretend**
pretentious see **pretend**
pride see **proud**
promising see **promise**
-proof see **prove**
proof see **prove**
properly see **proper**
proven see **prove**
provided [that] see **provide**
providing [that] see **provide**
provision see **provide**
provisional see **provide**
provisionally see **provide**
purposeful see **purpose**
purposefully see **purpose**
purposely see **purpose**

Q

quickly see **quick**
quieten [down] see **quiet**

R

rarely see **rare**
rarity see **rare**
rather than see **rather**
realise see **real**
realism see **real**
reality see **real**
realize see **real**
really see **real**
reasonable see **reason**
reasonably see **reason**
reassure see **sure**
reckoning see **reckon**
recognisable see **recognise**
recognition see **recognise**
refusal see **refuse**
regarding see **regard**
regardless of see **regard**

regretfully see **regret**
regrets see **regret**
regrettably see **regret**
reminder see **remind** [of]
rightly see **right**
risky see **risk** [of]
robber see **rob**
robbery see **rob**

S

safely see **safe**
safety see **safe**
sale see **sell**
satisfaction see **satisfy**
satisfactory see **satisfy**
satisfied [with] see **satisfy**
satisfying see **satisfy**
savings see **save**
saying see **say**
scarcely see **scarce**
seat see **sit**
secondary see **second**
seeing [that] see **see**
-self see **self**
self- see **self**
selfish see **self**
selfless see **self**
seller see **sell**
sensation see **sense**
sensational see **sense**
senseless see **sense**
sensible see **sense**
sensitive see **sense**
sensual see **sense**
sensuous see **sense**
settlement see **settle**
shame see **ashamed**
shameful see **ashamed**
shameful see **shame**
shamefully see **shame**
shapely see **shape**
sharpen see **sharp**
sharply see **sharp**
shorten see **short**
shortly see **short**
shorts see **short**
sicken see **sick**
sickening see **sick**
sickness see **sick**
sideways see **side**
sight see **see**
signal see **sign**
significant see **sign**

signify

signify see **sign**
similar see **same**
similarly see **same**
simplify see **simple**
simply see **simple**
sleeper see **sleep**
sleepy see **sleep**
slightly see **slight**
so as see **as**
so as to see **so**
so that see **so**
so that see **that**
so . . . as see **as**
so . . . that see **so**
so . . . that see **that**
some one see **some**
somebody see **some**
somehow see **some**
something see **some**
sometimes see **some**
somewhat see **some**
somewhere see **some**
sooner see **soon**
sorrow see **sorry**
sort of see **sort**
speaker see **speak** [to]
specialise [in] see **special**
specialist [in] see **special**
specially see **special**
speech see **speak** [to]
spotless see **spot**
step- see **step**
sticky see **stick**
straight away see **straight**
straight-forward see **straight**
straighten see **straight**
strangely see **strange**
stranger see **strange**
such as see **as**
suddenly see **sudden**
suggestion see **suggest**
suggestive see **suggest**
suitable see **suit**
supposing [that] see **suppose**
supposition see **suppose**
surely [not] see **sure**
surprising see **surprise**

T

takings see **take**
talkative see **talk**
talker see **talk**
tasteful see **taste**
tasteless see **taste**

tasty see **taste**
thank you see **thank**
thankful see **thank**
thanks see **thank**
the one/the ones see **one**
the people see **people**
the same as see **as**
themselves see **they**
therefore see **there**
though see **although**
thought see **think**
thoughtful see **think**
throughout see **through**
tighten see **tight**
tightly see **tight**
tights see **tight**
times see **time**
timing see **time**
tire see **tired**
tiresome see **tired**
tiring see **tired**
torn see **tear**
touchy see **touch**
towards see **to**
treatment see **treat**
truly see **true**
trustee see **trust**
trustworthy see **trust**
truth see **true**
truthful see **true**
trying see **try**
turning see **turn**

U

unable see **able**
unavailable see **available**
uncertain see **certain**
uncommon see **common**
uncover see **cover**
underneath see **under**
understanding see **understand**
undo see **do**
undress see **dress**
uneasy see **easy**
unexpected see **expect**
unexpectedly see **expect**
unfasten see **fast**
unfriendly see **friend**
unhappily see **happy**
unkind see **kind**
unlike see **like**
unlikely see **likely**
unreasonable see **reason**

unselfish see **self**
unsure see **sure**
unusual see **usual**
unusually see **usual**
unwanted see **want** [**to**]
upbringing see **bring**
upon see **up**
upper see **up**
upright see **up**
upward see **up**
used see **use**
useful see **use**
useless see **use**
user see **use**
usually see **usual**

V

variable see **vary**
variation see **vary**
varied see **vary**
variety see **vary**
various see **vary**
viewer see **view**
visitor see **visit**

W

wakeful see **wake** [**up**]
waken see **wake** [**up**]
wanting see **want** [**to**]
warmth see **warm**
warning see **warn**
washable see **wash**
wasteful see **waste**
watchful see **watch**
weaken see **weak**
weakness see **weak**
wearing see **wear**
weekly see **week**
weight see **weigh**
whereabouts see **where**
whether. . .or [not] see **or**
wholly see **whole**
widely see **wide**
widen see **wide**
width see **wide**
willing see **will**
willingly see **will**
wind see **wind**
winner see **win**
winning see **win**
winnings see **win**
wisdom see **wise**
-wise see **wise**
withdraw see **draw**
withdraw see **with**
within see **with**
worthless see **worth**
worthwhile see **worth**
worthy see **worth**
would [= 'd] rather [than] see **rather**
wrongly see **wrong**

Y

youth see **young**
youthful see **young**

KWANG TOONG BOOK DEPARTMENT STORE
WESTERN-LANGUAGE BOOK
60. CHUNG KING S. RD., SEC. 1. TAIPEI.
TEL:(02) 3110581-3
29. CHIEN KUO SAN RD., KAOHSIUNG
TEL:(07) 2216008